GW01086914

LAW AND LITERATURE

Law and Literature presents an authoritative, fresh and accessible new overview of the many ways in which law and literature interact. Written by a team of international experts, it provides a multifocused history of literary studies' critical interest in ideas of law and justice. It examines the effects of law on writers and their work, ranging from classical tragedy to comics, and from East Africa to Elizabethan England. Over twenty chapters, contributors reveal the evolving and polyvalent historical associations between law and literature, both past and present, and trace the intellectual genesis of the concept of law in literary studies, focusing on major developments in the history of the interdisciplinary project of law and literature, as well as the changing ideas of law, and the cultural contests in which it has figured. *Law and Literature* will appeal to graduates and scholars working on the intersection between law and literature and in key related areas such as literature and human rights.

KIERAN DOLIN is Associate Professor of English and Cultural Studies at the University of Western Australia. He is the author of *Fiction and the Law* (1999) and *A Critical Introduction to Law and Literature* (2007).

CAMBRIDGE CRITICAL CONCEPTS SERIES

Cambridge Critical Concepts focuses on the important ideas animating twentieth- and twenty-first-century literary studies. Each concept addressed in this series has had a profound impact on literary studies, as well as on other disciplines, and already has a substantial critical bibliography surrounding it. This new series captures the dynamic critical energies transmitted across twentieth-and twenty-first-century literary landscapes: the concepts critics bring to reading, interpretation, and criticism. By addressing the origins, development, and application of these ideas, the books collate and clarify how these particular concepts have developed, while also featuring fresh insights and establishing new lines of inquiry.

Cambridge Critical Concepts shifts the focus from period- or genre-based literary studies of a key term to the history and development of the terms themselves. Broad and detailed contributions cumulatively identify and investigate the various historical and cultural catalysts that made these critical concepts emerge as established twenty-first-century landmarks in the discipline. The level will be suitable for advanced undergraduates, graduates, and specialists, as well as to those teaching outside their own research areas, and will have cross-disciplinary relevance for subjects such as history and philosophy.

Published Titles

Time and Literature
Edited by THOMAS M. ALLEN
University of Ottawa

Law and Literature
Edited by KIERAN DOLIN
The University of Western Australia

Trauma and Literature
Edited by ROGER KURTZ
The College at Brockport, State University of New York

Forthcoming Titles

The Global South and Literature
Edited by RUSSELL WEST-PAVLOV
University of Tübingen

Food and Literature
Edited by GITANJALI SHAHANI
San Francisco State University

Animals and Literature
Edited by BRUCE BOEHRER, MOLLY HAND and BRIAN MASSUMI
Florida State University and University of Montreal

Orientalism and Literature
Edited by GEOFFREY NASH
University of Sunderland

Terrorism and Literature
Edited by PETER HERMAN
San Diego State University

Technology and Literature
Edited by ADAM HAMMOND
University of Toronto

Affect and Literature
Edited by ALEX HOUEN
University of Cambridge

Climate and Literature
Edited by ADELINE JOHNS
University of Surrey

Decadence and Literature
Edited by JANE DESMARAIS and DAVID WEIR
Goldsmith College and Hunter College

LAW AND LITERATURE

EDITED BY

KIERAN DOLIN

University of Western Australia

CAMBRIDGE
UNIVERSITY PRESS

University Printing House, Cambridge CB2 8BS, United Kingdom

One Liberty Plaza, 20th Floor, New York, NY 10006, USA

477 Williamstown Road, Port Melbourne, VIC 3207, Australia

314–321, 3rd Floor, Plot 3, Splendor Forum, Jasola District Centre, New Delhi – 110025, India

79 Anson Road, #06–04/06, Singapore 079906

Cambridge University Press is part of the University of Cambridge.

It furthers the University's mission by disseminating knowledge in the pursuit of education, learning, and research at the highest international levels of excellence.

www.cambridge.org
Information on this title: www.cambridge.org/9781108422819
DOI: 10.1017/9781108386005

First published 2018

Printed in the United States of America by Sheridan Books, Inc.

A catalogue record for this publication is available from the British Library.

Library of Congress Cataloging-in-Publication Data
NAMES: Dolin, Kieran, editor.
TITLE: Law and literature / edited by Kieran Dolin.
DESCRIPTION: New York : Cambridge University Press, 2017.
IDENTIFIERS: LCCN 2017035064 | ISBN 9781108422819 (hardback) |
ISBN 9781108435192 (paperback)
SUBJECTS: LCSH: Law and literature.
CLASSIFICATION: LCC K487.L7 L38 2017 | DDC 809/.933554–dc23
LC record available at https://lccn.loc.gov/2017035064

ISBN 978-1-108-42281-9 Hardback

Contents

Acknowledgments

Many people have helped in bringing this volume to fruition. I am especially grateful to Ray Ryan of Cambridge University Press for his support and belief in the project at key stages of its development. I must also thank Edgar Mendez and other staff at Cambridge University Press for their ready assistance with administrative and production matters. I also wish to record my appreciation of the work of all the contributors for their keen engagement in the aims of the volume. I particularly acknowledge Peter Leman, Mark Fortier, and Diana Shahinyan for stepping into their roles late in the writing period, and Klaus Stierstorfer for timely and sage advice. Many colleagues and friends at the University of Western Australia have taken an encouraging interest in or made suggestions toward the progress of this collection, particularly Ned Curthoys, Tony Hughes-d'Aeth, Judy Johnston (now in Wollongong), Andrew Lynch, Alexandra Ludewig, Jani McCutcheon, Philip Mead, and Bob White. I am very grateful to Steven de Haer for his indispensable assistance with the bibliography and the preparation of the manuscript. My deepest thanks go to my family, whose support and love have been constant and sustaining.

Introduction

Kieran Dolin

Questions of law and justice have long engaged the literary imagination. In Sophocles' *Antigone* a tragic dilemma confronts the heroine: If she buries the body of her brother Polynices in accordance with divine law, she disobeys a proclamation of King Creon forbidding that very act. Two millennia later, Ariel Dorfman's *Death and the Maiden* explores the procedures for redressing human rights violations after the overthrow of a dictatorship, as a torture victim subjects her torturer to an impromptu trial. In an after-dinner speech to the Canadian Bar Association in 1970, Northrop Frye explained this preoccupation by saying that "all respect for the law is a product of the social imagination, and the social imagination is what literature directly addresses."[1] The vocabularies and methods of literary studies have changed since Frye spoke, but interest in the social functions of the imagination, and the ideological effects of literary works, has only grown. The practices of both law and literature converge around such fundamental issues as language and interpretation, the formation of subjectivity, and the connection of narrative and authority. The intersection of social ideology and *poesis* or linguistic creation became the focus of sustained interdisciplinary study through a dedicated law and literature movement in the 1980s. That movement has ramified, encountering new influences and taking new forms, but its key insight remains, as Ravit Reichman affirmed in 2009, that "the texts of law and literature jointly contribute to what legal scholar Robert Cover called a *nomos* or normative universe."[2] The range and significance of this dialogue with legal history and philosophy makes law a vital element in contemporary critical discourse.

[1] Northrop Frye, "Literature and the law," *Law Society of Upper Canada Gazette*, 4 (1970), 70–7.

[2] Ravit Reichman, *The Affective Life of Law* (Stanford: Stanford University Press, 2009), p. 5. Cover's concept of *nomos* is explained by Cathrine O. Frank in Chapter 3 of this volume.

Introducing his 1961 anthology of legal prose, *The Law as Literature*, Louis Blom-Cooper wrote of "the harmony of law and literature."[3] That view depended on a traditional understanding of literature and culture as "the best that has been thought and said in the world," and on an acceptance of the justice of the legal system; it offered a celebratory account of law and literature.[4] Blom-Cooper's anthology and others like it remind us that legal writing and oratory are forms of rhetoric, compositions that seek to move their audiences toward particular understandings of events. They are exercises in a specifically *legal* imagination, articulating ideals and circumstances in ways that recall literary texts. Among the examples selected are Gandhi's speech to the court in his 1922 trial for sedition and Albert Camus' *Reflections on the Guillotine*. In the same year as Blom-Cooper's anthology, Robert Bolt's celebrated play about the trial of Thomas More, *A Man for All Seasons*, was published, and the much-publicized trial regarding the publication of D. H. Lawrence's *Lady Chatterley's Lover* saw a more oppositional relationship between law and literature take shape. In this context, literary texts potentially transgress the boundaries of traditional morality and law. As is well known, a parade of distinguished literary critics gave evidence on behalf of the publisher, Penguin Books, testifying to the "literary merit" of Lawrence's novel, and helping the defense to success.[5] Adding to the sense of an altered understanding of law in society was H. L. A. Hart's new work on jurisprudence, *The Concept of Law*. A number of general points may be drawn from this snapshot of cultural history, the first, and most obvious, being that literature as a field of writing is shaped by censorship laws and other legal regimes. As Nancy Paxton shows in Chapter 20 of this volume, such laws may function in constructive ways as well as setting limits to expression. Second, and more broadly, when viewed in the context of legal history, literary study may be seen as part of "the complex history of freedoms," as James Simpson puts it.[6] Third, the relationship between law and literature is a close but shifting one, always significant, but ever open to revision from new social forces. Law, then, is one of the key *interrelations* of literature.[7]

[3] Louis Blom-Cooper, *The Law as Literature* (London: Bodley Head, 1961), p. xiii.

[4] Matthew Arnold, *Culture and Anarchy* [1869]. (New Haven: Yale University Press, 1994), p. 5.

[5] See C. H. Rolph (ed.), *The Trial of Lady Chatterley* (Harmondsworth: Penguin, 1961) for the transcript of the trial.

[6] James Simpson, *Reform and Cultural Revolution*. The Oxford English Literary History, vol. 2: 1350–1547 (Oxford: Oxford University Press, 2002), p. 1.

[7] See Richard H. Weisberg and Jean-Pierre Barricelli, "Literature and law" in Joseph Gibaldi and Jean-Pierre Barricelli (eds.), *Interrelations of Literature* (New York: Modern Languages Association, 1982), pp. 150–75.

These events from a year chosen among many possible candidates are indicative of "the intricate and multivalent historical interactions" between literature and law.[8] This volume, through its twenty newly commissioned essays, attempts to reveal something of the range and intensity of those valencies. Part I offers an account of the *origins* of the interdisciplinary project of law and literature, and of how key theoretical shifts, especially poststructuralism, narrative theory, and historicist studies, reshaped the literary-critical study of law. Many of the concepts and arguments discussed in this foundational section of the volume are taken up independently in the later chapters. In the second and largest part of the book, Part II, a survey of the historical *development* of legal and literary intersections is presented in a series of chapters devoted to major phases of literary history, from the classical era to the present. Each of these chapters offers a broad conspectus supplemented by a reading of key texts, or takes a particular trial or idea as representative of larger legal-cultural formations. The risks of periodization are more than usually present in this context, with the ancient and medieval worlds represented by a chapter each, with some periods denominated by century and others by reign or cultural movement, in all of which the particular but representative conflicts and confluences must be tracked in two cultural domains. The collection ends by focusing in Part III on a number of *applications* of the dialogue between literary and legal studies that have practical effects in the contemporary system of law and the institution of literature. Accordingly, it includes chapters on such topics as laws that bear upon authorship and the freedom of representation, the cultural afterlives of trials, and narratives that enlarge the recognition of rights and civil wrongs by the courts.

The latter provide ready answers to the question of contemporary relevance, which is commonly raised in respect of humanities research by university administrators, governments, and others for whom the social utility of knowledge is equated with scientific advances. In this context it is worth noting a controversial review of law and literature as an interdisciplinary field by Julie Stone Peters. Peters argued that the field's practitioners, whether based in literary studies or law, tended to construct illusory images of the other discipline in order to remedy felt limits in their own: "literature's wounded sense of its insignificance, its inability to achieve some ever-imagined but ever-receding praxis; law's guilty sense of its

[8] Gregg D. Crane, *Race, Citizenship and Law in American Literature* (New York: Cambridge University Press, 2002), p. 10.

collaborationism, its tainted complicity with the state apparatus."[9] This strong critique led her to advocate for a broader interdisciplinary field of law, culture, and the humanities; however, her survey had omitted any consideration of historical studies of the changing relations between law and literature at different periods. It prompted robust defences of the law and literature project from Richard Weisberg, Peter Brooks, and Christine L. Krueger, among others. Krueger articulated a feminist account of gender advocacy in the literature and law of Victorian England that explicitly linked her historicist research to ongoing emancipatory movements in modern society, and that emphasis on "praxis" informs her account of historicist approaches to law and literature in Chapter 4.[10] Critics working on law and literature scholarship will frequently draw out their implications for the present, sometimes explicitly, at other times leaving them to be inferred by readers.[11] As this collection of essays adopts a broadly historicist approach to its subject, I suspect most of its contributors would subscribe in one form or other to a sense that the study of the past formations of law and literature will inform our understanding of present issues. Further, such studies may well be informed by the critic's interests, even as he or she attempts to elucidate the different beliefs, values, and intentions of the society being studied.

One benefit of the historical scope of a volume like this is that it affords what Robin Wharton calls in Chapter 18 "a long view" of the history of technologies of communication. Specifically, it enables readers to see the changing interfaces of law, language and society in oral, scribal, print, and digital cultures. This book therefore adopts a broad definition of literature that includes texts in the form of traditional songs from East Africa, forensic oratory, medieval homilies, judicial opinions, long-form television drama, and comics. In doing so, it attempts to encompass some ancient, postcolonial, or non-Western perspectives on law and justice as well as concepts from Europe and America.[12] Equally, just as it has seemed

[9] Julie Stone Peters, "Law, literature and the vanishing real: on the future of an interdisciplinary illusion" in Austin Sarat, Cathrine O. Frank and Matthew Anderson (eds.), *Teaching Law and Literature* (New York: Modern Languages Association, 2011), p. 78.

[10] Christine L. Krueger, *Reading for the Law: British Literary History and Gender Advocacy* (Charlottesville: University of Virginia Press, 2010).

[11] See for example Robert A. Ferguson, *Law and Letters in American Culture* (Massachusetts: Harvard University Press, 1984), pp. 9–10 and Brook Thomas, *Civic Myths: A Law-and-Literature Approach to Citizenship* (Chapel Hill: University of North Carolina Press, 2007), p. xi.

[12] For an internationalist sampling of contemporary law and literature writing, see special focus in the *World Literature Today* 86:6 (Nov–Dec 2012).

essential to address both popular and elite cultural forms of past eras, so also it has seemed important in this volume to explore the effects of visual as well as print narrative media in the dissemination of concepts of law in contemporary culture.

Contributors to this volume are drawn from universities in several nations, including Australia, Canada, Denmark, England, Germany, Ireland, and the United States, and this relative diversity allows for a degree of variation in their critical methods and voices. An editorial recognition that "the field of law and literature research ... has become increasingly differentiated" – as Klaus Stierstorfer, the author of Chapter 1, put it in a review article on the field – seemed an important counterpoint to the volume's overall commitment to a historical account of legal-literary relations.[13] Consequently, different approaches to the relationship between literature and the history of legal and social ideas will be found in the various chapters: For example, Ioannis Ziogas reads the iconology of the body in the trial of Phryne through contemporary theories of sovereignty; Mark Fortier draws on intellectual history to produce a complex history of equity in early modern literature; Cheryl Nixon offers a feminist historical account of eighteenth-century fiction and the law of family; and Stephanie Jones brings poststructuralist and postcolonial concerns to the analysis of an East African case from the 1920s. This methodological pluralism aids in the discernment of those "constellations" of literary discourse and legal forms that help us to understand the past and shed light on current configurations of *nomos* in our own or other societies.[14] Indeed, Benjamin speaks of the historian's work as "grasp[ing] the constellation which his own era has formed with a definite earlier one." Brook Thomas concludes his *Cross-Examinations of Law and Literature* by invoking these words.[15] Such knowledge may assist in addressing the discrepancy "between reality and vision" in our normative worlds, and therefore Benjamin's description serves as an appropriate final note on which to introduce this collection.

[13] Klaus Stierstorfer, "Law and (which?) literature: new directions in post-theory?" *Law and Humanities*, 5 (2011), 41–51.

[14] Here I draw on Walter Benjamin's idea of cultural constellations, with acknowledgements to the anonymous reader for Cambridge University Press who suggested this term. See David Cerniglia, "Constellation" in Michael Ryan (ed.), *The Encyclopedia of Literary and Cultural Theory* (Maldon: Wiley-Blackwell, 2011), www.literatureencyclopedia.com/subscriber/tocnode.html?id=g9781405183123_chunk_g97814051831235_ss1-6.

[15] Brook Thomas, *Cross-Examinations of Law and Literature* (Cambridge: Cambridge University Press, 1987), p. 254.

PART I

Origins

CHAPTER 1

The Revival of Legal Humanism

Klaus Stierstorfer

The chapter title rightly implies that the connection between law and "the humanities" is not a recent invention. It is prominent in classical antiquity, most notably in Aristotle,[1] and intimately tied in with the Western origins of rhetoric;[2] it can be traced in Hebrew cultural history, where the central, closely allied corpora of the *halachah* and the *haggada* could be translated as "law" and "literature" respectively, as P. G. Monateri points out;[3] and wherever an inclusive definition of "literature," following the Latin meaning of *litteratura* as "use of letters, writing, system of letters . . . writings, scholarship,"[4] has been applied, law texts of all kinds would automatically fall within the wider purview of literary or textual scholarship. Thus, when the first complete narrative history of English literature appeared in 1836, Blackstone's *Commentaries on the Laws of England* or Jeremy Bentham's writings on law were, as a matter of course, presented in their respective periods under the category of "Miscellaneous Writers," and hence as part and parcel of that literary history, just as with major works in historical scholarship or in science (such as Newton's *Principia*).[5] The historical depth, but also the conceptual as well as quantitative scope of this tradition, especially in the connection between literature and the law, has been

1 See for instance Kathy Eden, *Poetic and Legal Fiction in the Aristotelian Tradition* (Princeton: Princeton University Press, 2014).

2 Michael Gagarin, "Rhetoric and law in Ancient Greece" in Michael MacDonald (ed.), *The Oxford Handbook of Rhetorical Studies* (Oxford: Oxford University Press, 2014). See www.oxfordhandbooks.com/view/10.1093/oxfordhb/9780199731596.001.0001/oxfordhb-9780199731596-e-002 (accessed October 7, 2016).

3 Pier Giuseppe Monateri, "Diaspora, the West and the law" in D. Carpi and K. Stierstorfer (eds.), *Diaspora, Law and Literature* (Berlin and Boston: De Gruyter, 2016), pp. 7–22, 13.

4 "literature, n." *OED Online*, esp. "etymology" and meanings 1, 2, 4, and 5. See www.oed.com/view/Entry/109080?redirectedFrom=literature#eid (accessed October 7, 2016).

5 Robert Chambers, *History of the English Language and Literature* (Edinburgh: William and Robert Chambers/London: Orr and Smith, 1836), pp. 185f, 263f.

impressively documented in recent bibliographies.[6] Moreover, myth-like founding figures and events have also emerged. In the German tradition, there is Jakob Grimm's famous assertion that law and literature had "risen from the same bed,"[7] and the fact that the first meeting of *Germanisten*, which memorably took place in 1846 in Frankfurt, was convened by a law professor and emphasized in its denomination not its object of study in a body of texts in the German vernacular, but an orientation toward Germanic as opposed to Roman law.[8] Further instances can be traced in the past where legal scholars or practitioners, such as C. K. Davis or James Fitzjames Stephen in Britain or John H. Wigmore and, most notably, Benjamin N. Cardozo in the United States, had literary leanings and hence frequently figure in a pre-history to the developments described in the following.[9]

For all this long and chequered relationship throughout the course of Western cultural history, however, the renewed emphasis on the necessity of exchange between law and the humanities with the aim of "rehumanizing" the law is recent. The revival of legal humanism is now regularly identified with a particular moment in American academia in the 1970s: the rise of what has come to be labeled as the "law and literature movement." Although the developments in that particular phase of legal scholarship are steeped in a long tradition of humanist approaches to the law, their specific impact was incisive and had a long-lasting influence on what has since been done in the rich and blossoming interdisciplinary scholarship between law and the humanities worldwide.

Two main lines of explanation, which are not mutually exclusive, have been established to answer the question about the causes for the renewed interest in the humanities in the American law schools at that point in recent history. First, and perhaps less intriguingly, it is seen as a consequence of the academic job market in the United States. Student numbers in the humanities had risen exponentially in the 1960s, with a consequent surge in the numbers of doctorates and hence aspiring new academics

[6] Christine A. Corcos, *An International Guide to Law and Literature Studies* (Buffalo and New York: William S. Hein & Co, 2000); Thomas Sprecher, *Literature und Recht. Eine Bibliographie für Leser* (Frankfurt: Vittorio Klostermann, 2011).

[7] Jakob Grimm, "Von der Poesie im Recht," *Zeitschrift für die geschichtliche Rechtswissenschaft*, 2(1) (1816), 25–99. §2: "Dasz recht und poesie miteinander aus einem bette aufgestanden waren, hält nicht schwer zu glauben."

[8] See Klaus Röther, *Die Germanistenverbände und ihre Tagungen: Ein Beitrag zur germanistischen Organisations- und Wissenschaftsgeschichte* (Köln: Pahl-Rugenstein, 1980), pp. 15–16.

[9] Apart from the bibliographies listed in n. 6, see Richard Posner, *Law and Literature: A Misunderstood Relation* (Massachusetts and London: Harvard University Press, 1988), p. 12 (and footnotes 24 and 25).

in the humanities far beyond the needs generated by the expansion of the studentship. When the rise in student enrolment numbers flattened out in the early 1970s, the job market quickly became tense, a development exacerbated by significant budget cuts in the humanities in the late 1970s.[10] Hence, graduates from the humanities had to seek employment elsewhere. Looking back from 1985, Martha Minow described the impact of these developments on the law departments:

> [T]he job market for Ph.D.'s [sic] constricted dramatically in the last 15 years. Bluntly put, people who in the past would join academic departments instead went to law school and joined law faculties. These people brought with them questions and methods of inquiry common in nonlegal disciplines, and subjected law to scrutiny.[11]

This view may reflect aspects of the academic job market at the time, even if it is currently still more a claim than an insight drawn from sustained analysis and research. As an explanation for the reorientation of legal studies toward the humanities it carries, however, a potentially pejorative undercurrent. It presents the humanist revival in law as an accidental contingency of market developments, and, moreover, carries the implication that the inspiration for the revival was itself less inspired than it was driven by dire (economic) necessities and spearheaded by academics who could not find employment in their field of choice, and hence did not constitute their discipline's elite who, even under constrained circumstances, would get the few tenured positions on offer in their own fields.

The second line of explanation understands the revival of legal humanism as a reaction precisely against such approaches of reducing social and cultural developments to market forces, as notably seen in the work that is usually labeled "law and economics." A movement that has evolved into a widely established constituent in American law departments and in the curricula of legal training,[12] the modern origins of law and economics are generally identified in the early 1960s. By most accounts, the credit for this

[10] The funding levels for the National Endowment Fund for the Humanities can here be taken as an indicator. See www.humanitiesindicators.org/content/indicatordoc.aspx?i=75 (accessed October 8, 2016).

[11] Martha Minow, "Law turning outward," *Telos*, 73 (1987), 91. See also Richard Posner, "Law and literature: a relation reargued," *Virginia Law Review*, 72 (1986), 1353; Harold Suretsky, "Search for a theory: an annotated bibliography of writings in the relation of law to literature and the humanities," *Rutgers Law Review*, 32 (1979), 727–39; and Jeanne Gaakeer, "Close encounters of the 'third' kind" in D. Carpi and K. Stierstorfer (eds.), *Diaspora, Law and Literature* (Berlin and Boston: De Gruyter, 2016), p. 66 (footnote 87).

[12] See, for a standard textbook, Robert Cooter and Thomas Ulen, *Law and Economics* (Boston: Pearson Education, 1986; 6th edn., 2012), and Richard Posner's classic *Economic Analysis of the Law* (New York: Wolters Kluwer Law and Business, 1970; 9th edn., 2014).

initial impetus is shared on the one hand by Ronald Coase at the University of Chicago, and specifically his 1960 article "Problem of Social Cost," and on the other by Guido Calabresi at Yale and his work on tort law from 1960 onwards, as presented in particular in his seminal article "Some Thoughts on Risk Distribution and the Law of Torts."[13] As Cooter and Ulen explain, law had of course had some traditional overlap with economics long before in areas such as "antitrust law, regulated industries, tax, and some special topics like determining monetary damages";[14] however, the new movement brought economic expertise to fields of legal concern not usually associated with economic considerations, "such as property, contracts, torts, criminal law and procedure, and constitutional law,"[15] which now, it was claimed, benefited from the strengths of economic reasoning: "Economics has mathematically precise theories (price theory and game theory) and empirically sound methods (statistics and econometrics) for analyzing the effects of the implicit prices that laws attach to behavior."[16]

Richard Posner, another of the galleon figures of law and economics, neatly summarizes the scholarly attractiveness of this approach:[17]

> To me the most interesting aspect of the law and economics movement has been its aspiration to place the study of law on a scientific basis, with coherent theory, precise hypotheses deduced from the theory, and empirical tests of the hypotheses ... Economics is the most advanced of the social sciences, and the legal system contains many parallels to and overlaps with the systems that economists have studied successfully.

Such eulogy of law and economics is strongly reminiscent of the "two cultures" debate popularized in C. P. Snow's Rede Lecture in 1959. It is contemporary with the beginning of the law and economics movement, whose agenda clearly tries to establish law on the side of the sciences, not the humanities.

[13] Ronald Coase, "The problem of social cost," *Journal of Law and Economics*, 3 (1960), 1–44; Guido Calabresi, "Some thoughts on risk distribution and the law of torts," *Yale Law Journal*, 70(4) (1961), 499–553. For a survey, see, for instance, Martin Gelter and Kristoffel Grechenig, "History of law and economics," *Preprints of the Max Planck Institute for Research on Collective Goods* (2014–15); Francesco Parisi and Charles K. Rowley (eds.), *The Origins of Law and Economics: Essays by the Founding Fathers* (Northampton and Massachusetts: Edward Elgar Publishing, 2005).

[14] Cooter and Ulen, *Law and Economics*, p. 1.

[15] Cooter and Ulen, *Law and Economics*, p. 1.

[16] Cooter and Ulen, *Law and Economics*, p. 3.

[17] Richard Posner, "Foreword" in M. Faure and R. van den Bergh (eds.), *Essays in Law and Economics: Corporations, Accident Prevention and Compensation for Losses* (Antwerpen: MAKLU, 1989), pp. 5–6, 5. The quotation has achieved emblematic status through its use as an epigraph in Cooter and Ulen, *Law and Economics*, p. 1.

Movements trigger counter-movements: What happened in some American law departments in the 1970s can be understood in these terms. The discipline that was brought in as a counterweight to economics was literary studies. The law and literature movement, which gathered momentum from the 1970s onwards, clearly set out to give weight to the humanities in legal scholarship, in opposition to a more science-based approach as brought in by the economists. And movements need protagonists. Although the law and literature movement has several foundational figures to look up or back to, the opening shot is widely credited to James Boyd White in his textbook *The Legal Imagination*, first published in 1973.

In the 1985 preface to the abridged version of this book, White succinctly sums up the position he takes in it: "For me law is an art, a way of making something new out of existing materials – an art of speaking and writing. And ... this book accordingly addresses its law student reader 'as an artist'."[18]

With this, White turns against "certain kinds of dehumanizing modern institutions and practices"[19] to be found on the law and economics side. White had studied classics for his BA at Amherst College, then went on to Harvard for graduate studies in English literature, and only then moved to Harvard Law School for his LLB. As his MA in English was completed in 1961, his move into law certainly predates the suspicion of being motivated by the statistics of flagging job markets in the humanities during the 1970s, and his distinguished career as, at the same time, Hart Wright Professor of Law, Professor of English Language and Literature, and Adjunct Professor of Classical Studies at the University of Michigan amply testifies to his multidisciplinary talents.[20] The linkage between English literature and the law had been a surprising and enlightening experience in his early career, as he writes: "When I went to law school after doing graduate work in English literature, I found a continuity in my work that I had not expected."[21]

White takes his departure from the view that the legal profession is very much bound to language in general, and to a specific, professional

[18] James Boyd White, *The Legal Imagination: Abridged Edition* (Chicago: University of Chicago Press, [1973] 1985), p. xiv.

[19] White, *The Legal Imagination*, p. xiv.

[20] For James Boyd White's biographical details, see his personal homepage at www-personal.umich.edu/~jbwhite/.

[21] James Boyd White, *When Words Lose Their Meaning* (Chicago: University of Chicago Press, 1984), pp. xi–xii.

language in particular. He thus positions himself in between what he calls the "natural law tradition" on the one hand, which he sees as "positivistic and rule-focused," and what has come to be called "critical law theory" on the other, where he sees law reduced "to policy choices and class interests." For him, law is, as he puts it, "what I call a language, by which I do not mean just a set of terms and locutions, but habits of mind and expectations – what might also be called a culture."[22] He further elaborates:

> The law makes a world. And the law in another sense, as the profession we teach and learn and practice, is a kind of cultural competence: an art of reading the special literature of the law and an art of speaking and writing – of making compositions of one's own – in this language. It is a branch of rhetoric.[23]

In his discourse analysis *avant la lettre*, White identifies law as a way of world-making which discursively establishes what can be said and seen and what is excluded, silenced, or overlooked. His argument rests on rhetoric which he trims with a legal focus: "As the object of art is beauty and of philosophy truth, the object of rhetoric is justice: the constitution of a social world."[24] He further defines rhetoric as "the study of the ways in which character and community – and motive, value, reason, social structure, everything, in short, that makes a culture – are defined and made real in performances of language." Hence law for him becomes "an art essentially literary and rhetorical in nature, a way of establishing meaning and constituting community in language."[25] Here is also the link to poetry: "Indeed, in its hunger to connect the general with the particular, in its metaphorical movements, and in its constant and forced recognition of the limits of language, the law seemed to me a kind of poetry."[26]

By instilling such language awareness in his law students and training them to be in "control over a language by taking a position outside it," they will be able "to recognize, more than the language in other hands would be made to say, more than it seems to want to say." This is the lesson to be learnt from the literary author who "speaks two ways at once: using a language and at the same time recognizing what it leaves out. He is defined less by the language he uses than by the relationship with it . . . less by his material than by his art."[27]

The focus on literature in this rehumanizing project of the emerging law and literature movement against the dehumanizing forces of "the market"

[22] White, *The Legal Imagination*, pp. 12f. [23] White, *The Legal Imagination*, p. xiii.
[24] White, *When Words*, p. xi. [25] White, *When Words*, p. xi. [26] White, *When Words*, p. xxiv.
[27] White, *The Legal Imagination*, p. 71.

is in keeping with a traditional conception of literature in its modern sense as it became established in the nineteenth century. In its classical foundations of the *literae humaniores* in the traditional universities, literature was promoted as a solid basis of general knowledge about what it means to be human beyond what theological arguments might have to say. In its vernacular traditions, literature had risen to a primary inspiration of national identity. It was widely perceived as a platform of moral instruction and orientation, gradually even replacing religion, which was losing its unifying focus given that, as in Britain, the nation was becoming (again) more inclusive toward its various denominations and sectarian creeds. The underlying concept of literature's function as a social and political corrective and a moral institution here goes back to Matthew Arnold's specification of culture, notably in *Culture and Anarchy* (1869), and reaches the law and literature movement through Lionel Trilling's view of literature and literary criticism as a critique of liberalism. In his milestone publication *The Liberal Imagination* (1950),[28] Trilling writes: "To the carrying out of the job of criticizing liberal imagination, literature has unique relevance, not merely because so much of modern literature has explicitly directed itself toward politics, but more importantly because literature is the human activity that takes the fullest and most precise account of variousness, possibility, complexity, and difficulty."[29]

Although James Boyd White is justly seen as one of the founding figures of the law and literature movement, his understanding and use of literature appears diffuse, in parts contradictory, and oscillates through his works. There is his wider use of the term "literature," which includes legal texts. This he needs for his agenda to project lawyers and judges as (literary) interpreters, critics, writers, and, indeed, artists. When he speaks about "the special literature of the law"[30] or writes about Shakespeare and other "non-legal literature,"[31] it is clear that legal texts form a subgroup within the wider literary domain. This inclusive use of the term clashes, however, with his references to Modernist approaches to literature in particular, such

[28] The historical line of influence from Arnold through Trilling to the Law and Literature Movement was succinctly described and analyzed by Robert Weisberg in "The law-literature enterprise," *Yale Journal of Law and the Humanities*, 1 (1988–9), 7. The connection is also revisited and further explained, without any reference to Weisberg, in Austin Sarat, Matthew Anderson, and Cathrine O. Frank, "Introduction: on the origins and prospects of the humanistic study of law," in A. Sarat, M. Anderson, and C. O. Frank (eds.), *Law and the Humanities: An Introduction* (Cambridge: Cambridge University Press, 2010), pp. 5–6.

[29] Lionel Trilling, "Preface" in *The Liberal Imagination: Essays on Literature and Society* (New York: New York Review of Books, 1950), p. xxi.

[30] White, *The Legal Imagination*, p. xiii.

[31] White, *The Legal Imagination*, p. 40.

as that of Henry James, E. M. Forster, and Joseph Conrad, who have a very specific and distinctive concept of a capitalized "Literature" and its epistemic, narrative, and social or cultural uses. At the same time, his references to literary texts can be described either as eclectic or panoramic, as they cover the classics, British and American literary history, and a number of other European samples, not to speak of pertinent works of criticism from the Renaissance to his own present.

At least three distinct, though connected, uses of such references to "Literature" emerge. First, other disciplinary idioms, "languages," or "literatures" such as the poet's, the critic's, or the historian's are presented in their specificity to create a foil for a clearer perception of the hallmarks of legal discourse. Second, such comparison may yield insight into a neighboring disciplinary "language," such as the novelist's or poet's, but may not be directly applicable to legal "language." Thus, metaphor, irony, and ambiguity are described as literary devices to "control language," which White considers "likely to be of little use to us as lawyers." Still, these literary strategies are instructive for lawyers in an indirect way, as they show how "the writer asserts control over a language by taking a position outside it"[32] – a feat White recommends to lawyers, too, even if they must achieve it by different means from those followed by literary authors. The third use of referring to literary history and literary criticism is White's suggestion that in certain instances, there can be direct application of literary devices and critical insight. T. S. Eliot's "Tradition and the Individual Talent" (1921) is perhaps the most revealing instance, even if White somehow fails to develop it to its full potential. He quotes Eliot on the "whole of literature" having "a simultaneous existence" and asks his student reader to transfer this to the "common law judge," but does not fully exploit the dynamics of Eliot's historical model here.[33] Another example is the differentiation between flat and round characters, as developed by E. M. Forster in *Aspects of the Novel* (1927). White comes back to this time and again in encouraging (future) lawyers and judges to strive for the round character type in their assessments, and not accept mere caricature.[34] In other words, lawyers and judges are warned against taking a reductive view of the people they have to deal with professionally by limiting them to "objects" in a legal discourse, but encouraged to contextualize and understand their wider personalities and circumstances.

[32] White, *The Legal Imagination*, p. 71. [33] White, *The Legal Imagination*, p. 228.
[34] White, *The Legal Imagination*, p. 117 and *passim*.

This is as far as White took it at the time (and in several publications afterwards). Much of the criticism leveled against his approach ever since accuses him of a tendentious, moralizing view of literature, underpinning a political agenda, as Richard Posner comments: "He [White] mines literature for support for his political views."[35] While White's turn to literature and rhetoric was unmistakably in direct opposition to the conservative bias in law and economics, Posner's criticism must be seen as reductive of White's achievements, with his multiple and divergent uses of literature and rhetoric. Nevertheless, the political profile in the positions around the law and literature movement in America was becoming much more pronounced. Such deepening political entrenchment coincided with a cognate, second characteristic in the further development of the law and literature movement: During the 1970s and throughout the 1980s, literary criticism and theory hugely expanded both in the number of schools and approaches that emerged and in the emphasis and often the acerbity with which these developments were propounded or opposed, resulting in what is frequently referred to as the "theory wars," which lasted well into the 1990s: a profusion of – often mutually exclusive and regularly vituperative – theories and methodologies in literary scholarship. Structuralist and poststructuralist, (neo-)Marxist, feminist, gender, queer, new historicist, psychoanalytical, postcolonial, and other theories, with their resultant methodologies, had begun to inundate many literature departments across Western academia, providing scholars in law and literature with a bewildering wealth of new material and inspiration.

Both aspects – the political emphasis and the widening of theoretical and methodological horizons – are clearly marked in what Sarat, Anderson, and Frank identify with some justice as the second part of the "genesis of the field" of "law and the humanities": the 1988 founding of what they point out was "the first scholarly journal devoted exclusively to the field," the *Yale Journal of Law and the Humanities* (YJLH). In his introduction to the journal's first issue, "The Challenge Ahead," Owen M. Fiss, Stirling Professor at Yale Law School, did not mince his words: He saw "part of the impetus" of the new journal as "political – a desire to escape from the conservative political thrust of Law and Economics" and that school's "willingness ... to see the market ... as the preeminent mechanism for ordering social relations." Alongside some other new launches at Yale at the time, Fiss characterizes the journal as "part of the progressive and

[35] Richard Posner, *Law and Literature* (Massachusetts and London: Harvard University Press, 3rd edn., 2009), p. 470.

liberal revival now taking place at Yale and perhaps at other law schools," emphasizing that "the interdisciplinary study of the law is not the property of the right."[36] Fiss set the agenda to "combat the instrumentalism and scientism of Law and Economics and to restore an appropriate place for value judgements in the study of law," even if he warned at the same time not to "cojoin law with other disciplines such as literature, history, philosophy, psychiatry, which make inquiry into values central"[37] – a warning duly slighted by practically all contributors to the journal's first issue and ever since.

In fact, the most substantial contribution to the first issue of YJLH primed its focus directly on law and literature. In the expansive opening article, "The Law-Literature Enterprise," Robert Weisberg critically presented much of what had happened in the field so far and began to differentiate, assess, and order the various approaches he identified. He subdivided the law and literature "enterprise" into two main categories, "law in literature" and "law as literature." In his definition, the former "comprises works of fiction and drama (rarely lyric poetry) which deal with legal issues as express content," which then can be used "to educate lawyers – to deabstract and 'humanize' them."[38] The second, "more elusive part" he calls "law as literature," which in turn is split into two "sub-parts." Of these, one focuses on "legal writing in terms of style and rhetoric," with classical rhetoric as "the common denominator between literature and legal writing," as James Boyd White had elaborated. The other "sub-part" of law as literature takes its cue from the concept of interpretation. Here, as Weisberg sees it, "[l]awyers associate their difficulty in construing legal prose with the more prestigious difficulty in construing literature," and they thus "extend the forms of literary criticism to allegedly non-literary works."[39] It is Weisberg's great achievement to have traced and critically followed up these "forms of literary criticism" as they continued to evolve and, together with Guyora Binder, to have collected them in their magnum opus in the field, *Literary Criticisms of Law*, published in 2000. In this *summa*-like book, Binder and Weisberg expand, update, and systematize what Weisberg had started in his earlier article, offering now a comprehensive run-through of a large part of important approaches as they emerged and were discernible within the field of literary studies (interpretive, hermeneutic,

[36] Owen Fiss, "The challenge ahead," *Yale Journal of Law and the Humanities*, 2 (1988–9), v.
[37] Fiss, "The challenge ahead," vi. [38] Weisberg, "The law-literature enterprise," 17.
[39] Weisberg, "The law-literature enterprise," 42.

narrative, rhetorical, deconstructive, cultural) and evaluating them in their functionality as criticisms of law.[40]

In all, Robert Weisberg's take on law and literature, although generally sympathetic and encouraging, showed an apprehensiveness and hesitancy, especially in the area he designated as "law in literature," which other proponents of law and literature did not share. He was directly taken up on this in a "Response," printed in the same issue of the journal, by his namesake Richard H. Weisberg. The latter takes umbrage at Robert Weisberg's intimations that lawyers must be considered outright "doltish"[41] if the need is felt that they read literary works and learn from them qualifications that a commonsensical approach to their handicraft would already have endowed them with anyway, and that law in literature studies are therefore stating the obvious at best and harbor no further benefits for the legal expert. Against this, Richard H. Weisberg avers: "Where, as in so many modern novels, law itself is a pervasive, overt theme, the literary linkage of irrationality to legal discourse becomes a unique source of learning for lawyers." He goes on to provide a knowledgeable list of examples before concluding: "We must teach and think about these texts because, here and now, they are the best medium to instruct ourselves and our students about what we do."[42]

The claims Richard H. Weisberg here put forward had been eloquently substantiated in his earlier monograph, *The Failure of the Word*, of 1984.[43] There he took his departure from Nietzsche's concept of *ressentiment*, applied it to readings of the legal subjects treated in Dostoevsky, Flaubert, Camus, and Melville, and showed how the type of hollow wordiness in law and lawyers portrayed there must be seen as conniving with the worst side of Nazi thought and the ensuing atrocities. Naturally, Weisberg's argument has come in for extensive criticism,[44] but whatever the truth of his claim here, the book remains a showpiece of how philosophical, literary, and legal readings of literary texts can be brought together into a sophisticated and challenging argument of impressive reach and explanatory purchase.

[40] Guyora Binder and Robert Weisberg, *Literary Criticisms of Law* (Princeton: Princeton University Press, 2000).

[41] Weisberg, "The law-literature enterprise," 18.

[42] Richard H. Weisberg, "Family feud: a response to Robert Weisberg on law and literature," *Yale Journal of Law and the Humanities*, 1 (1988–9), 72.

[43] Richard H. Weisberg, *The Failure of the Word: The Protagonist as Lawyer in Modern Fiction* (New Haven and London: Yale University Press, 1984).

[44] See Richard Posner, "From Billy Budd to Buchenwald (reviewing Weisberg, Richard H., *The Failure of the Word: The Protagonist as Lawyer in Modern Fiction* (1984))," *Yale Law Journal*, 96 (1987), 1173–89.

Richard H. Weisberg continued this line of thought in *Poethics*, his 1992 monograph, where he tried to (re-)unite, in the eponymous neologism and in the book's argument, poetics and ethics – or, as he puts it, "to match ethics and aesthetics in legal rhetoric."[45] Again, his literary interpretations are set "to urge upon poethical readers justice through language and not articulateness shorn of ethics."[46] Here, the kind of literature and the kind of "poethical" readings he offers are to help the legal practitioner to steer clear of the Scylla of the "universe of cost-benefit analysis" to be found in legal economics on the one hand, and the Charybdis of "postmodern thought, at an extreme of nihilism"[47] and the "disastrous hermeticism of poststructural literary criticism"[48] on the other. The "greater ethical awareness" he expects from "stories about law" in his conclusion has a strong aesthetic component: "No bad judicial opinion can be 'well written'. No seemingly just opinion will endure unless its discursive form matches its quest for fairness. 'Objective' treatment of corrupt legal materials is itself corrupt, however seemingly benign."[49]

In this statement about a quasi-classical *kalokagathia* in legal texts Weisberg is an exponent of the radical alignment between law and poetics or aesthetics, which others even within the field of law and literature would not take quite as far. Critical voices against the basic tenets of law and literature scholars were, however, also coming from outside of the movement. First of all, as could be expected, opposition was mounted by adherents of law and economics, law and literature's main *bête noir*, and here most notably from one of its figureheads, Richard A. Posner, Judge (later Chief Judge) at the United States Court of Appeals for the Seventh Circuit in Chicago and Senior Lecturer at the Law School of the University of Chicago. The first edition of Posner's now classic grand reckoning with law and literature appeared in the same year as the first issue of YJLH, 1988, and was republished in 1998 and in a third, again much revised and expanded, edition in 2009.[50] Posner is by no means unsympathetic to the law and literature venture, expressing "a warm though qualified enthusiasm" for it and granting that it could "provide a valuable supplementary perspective" but could neither "illuminate the Holocaust

[45] Richard H. Weisberg, *Poethics and Other Strategies of Law and Literature* (New York: Columbia University Press, 1992), p. 40.

[46] Weisberg, *Poethics*, p. 41. [47] Weisberg, *Poethics*, p. 5. [48] Weisberg, *Poethics*, p. xii.

[49] Weisberg, *Poethics*, pp. 251–2.

[50] Richard Posner, *Law and Literature: A Misunderstood Relation* (Massachusetts and London: Harvard University Press, 1988; 2nd edn., 1998, 3rd edn., 2009). The subtitle was dropped from the second edition onwards.

[as Richard Weisberg argued] nor debunk the economic approach to law [as practically everyone writing in the field at the time was arguing]."[51] He contends:

> I do not think the field will expose the roots of fascism, overthrow conventional understandings – if there are any – of such classics as *Hamlet* and *Billy Budd*, humanize law, reveal the deepest flaws of capitalism, socialism, or Christianity, solve the age-old problem of objectivity in law, or bring on (or forestall) the universal reign of text scepticism.[52]

In the third edition of his book, Posner adds a whole chapter entitled "But Can Literature Humanize Law?" There he takes James Boyd White and Martha Nussbaum to task for being reductive in their "moral readings of works of literature,"[53] only to conclude with a quotation from John Fisher: "The humanities do not humanize."[54] While Posner has a place for literature in society in its own right, he curtly states that law and literature was "a misconception about how the study of literature can improve the law . . . by humanizing lawyers. It cannot do that."[55]

Another line of criticism against the law and literature approach was aimed at its focus on interpretation. Thus, Robin West turned against what she saw as "interpretivism," emphasizing: "Despite a superficial resemblance to literary interpretation, adjudication is *not* primarily an interpretive act . . . Adjudication is *in form* interpretive, but in substance it is an exercise of power in a way which truly interpretive acts, such as literary interpretation, are not."[56]

She therefore points to the "need then to understand our laws not only as 'texts' that embody our traditions and our cultural ideals, but also as interactive instruments of violence, violation, compassion or respect."[57] West here contributed to a wider argument against an all too textualist or "interpretivist" approach to the law, a scepticism which has shaped the field of research in critical law theory. As will be further explored in the following chapter, this runs roughly parallel to the law and literature engagement, with some overlap, but also with the major difference of a stronger focus on power, gender, and politics, which

[51] Posner, *Law and Literature* (1st edn.), p. 353.
[52] Posner, *Law and Literature* (1st edn.), p. 356.
[53] Posner, *Law and Literature* (3rd edn.), p. 472.
[54] Posner, *Law and Literature* (3rd edn.), p. 493.
[55] Posner, *Law and Literature* (3rd edn.), p. 3.
[56] Robin West, "Adjudication is not interpretation: some reservations about the law-as-literature movement," *Tennessee Law Review*, 54 (1987), 207. Italics in the original.
[57] Robin West, "Communities, texts, and law: reflections on the Law and Literature Movement," *Yale Journal of Law and the Humanities*, 1 (1988–9), 155. A similar point was made by Robert Cover in "Violence and the word," *Yale Law Journal*, 95 (1986), 1601–29.

looks beside and beyond the hermeneutic, interpretative, and textualist perspectives in the law and literature field.

Such widening of the scope in the efforts to "humanize" the law can also be traced as a development from within the law and literature movement. Again, Robert Weisberg is a good lead on this. Writing about the "interpretation debate" in his YJLH article of 1988, he first of all discussed the attempts at delimiting the impending threat of uncontrollable indeterminacy in interpretation by referring to Ronald Dworkin's simile of legal interpretation as a "chain novel,"[58] where each new participant in the production of the fictional text is free to add to their liking, but at the same time tied to the text written so far. He also brought in Stanley Fish's reduction of interpretive determinacy to the consensus of the respective interpretive community,[59] but then criticized the entire debate so far: "The interpretation debate . . . never reaches the anthropological view that both law and literature are part of the formal archaeology of a culture."[60] Weisberg here does not sidestep textuality for something besides or beyond it, but introduces the concept of culture as the wider field which encompasses both law and literature, which are part of it and which – arguably – might also accommodate the concerns in the foreground of critical legal theory. A decade later, he specifies this point in his book with Guyora Binder and, as the upshot of their analysis of all the various "literary criticisms of the law," eventually champions "a cultural criticism of the law" in the final chapter:

> We can "read" and criticize law as part of the making of a culture . . . The enterprise we propose would place legal critique roughly within the emergent interdisciplinary movement of cultural studies. This movement has blurred the boundaries between the humanities and the social sciences by viewing the phenomena studied by political scientists, sociologists, economists, and historians as social "texts" available for interpretation and criticism.[61]

Weisberg here joined the broader development within the humanities which is frequently summed up as the "cultural turn"[62] and which appeared in literary scholarship under the labels of new historicism and cultural

[58] Ronald Dworkin, "Law as interpretation," *Texas Law Review*, 60 (1982), 527–50, 527.
[59] See Stanley Fish, "Interpretation and the pluralist vision," *Texas Law Review*, 60 (1982), 495–505.
[60] Weisberg, "The law-literature enterprise," 46.
[61] Weisberg, *Literary Criticisms of the Law*, p. 463.
[62] For example, Doris Bachmann-Medick, *Cultural Turns: Neuorientierungen in den Kulturwissenschaften* (Hamburg: Rowohlt, 2006) and its English translation, *Cultural Turns: New Orientations in the Study of Culture* (Berlin and Boston: De Gruyter, 2016).

materialism.[63] Just as White or Weisberg has connected law and literature within the wider frame of language, rhetoric, or textuality, this approach sees law and literature as set in the wider sphere of a culture and being contingent on it. This approach opens the interdisciplinary angle and implicates the social sciences in any attempt to humanize the law, thus widening the scope of approaches, strategies, and concepts beyond the strictly literary ones.

The cultural studies approach to the law has, arguably, remained the most lasting heritage of the law and literature movement worldwide. Certainly, the impact which the American law and literature movement had in similar fields of scholarly interest in Europe has headed in that direction, even if much differentiation is necessary and needs to be spelled out at least in the form of a sketchy, concluding outlook. First, while the American movement had mainly originated from law departments, with only a few, though notable, exceptions such as the work carried out by Brook Thomas at UCI, the picture is much more diverse in Europe. Wherever law and literature considerations have been taken up here, the impetus came, more often than not, from literature departments, again with highly noteworthy exceptions.[64] This is, in fact, an interesting parallel to the development in law and economics, where in the United States the impetus came from legal scholars, while the European reception was driven by their counterparts in economics and literary studies respectively.[65] And it was precisely in the wake of the cultural turn as advocated by Robert Weisberg that the discussion between the humanities and legal studies became more urgently – and perhaps logically – localized. As law is increasingly understood in its cultural contingency, cultural specifics will gain in weight: The European culture, with its very diverse legal traditions – in particular the profound difference between the case law focus predominant in the United States and England as against the civil

[63] For example, Hans Bertens, *Literary Theory: The Basics* (London and New York: Taylor and Francis, 2008), pp. 135–53.

[64] The work of Jeanne Gaakeer, a judge and law professor working in the tradition of James Boyd White, is unique in many ways. See Jeanne Gaakeer, *Hope Springs Eternal: An Introduction to the Work of James Boyd White* (Amsterdam: Amsterdam University Press, 1998), and many further publications. The two Italian law and literature associations are both (co-)chaired by legal scholars: Daniela Carpi (literary studies) and Pier Giuseppe Monateri (legal studies) for the Associazione Italiana di Diritto e Letteratura (AIDEL), and Carla Faralli with M. Paola Mittica (both legal studies) for the Italian Society for Law and Literature (ISLL). Each have numerous publications in the field to their name.

[65] Gelter and Grechenig, "History of law and economics," p. 1: "In continental Europe, law & economics was re-imported as a discipline within economics, driven by economists interested in legal issues rather than by legal scholars."

law tradition widely prevalent in continental Europe – provides a very different cultural context from the American hotbed which bred the law and literature movement. Importantly, this includes the political context as well: Whereas law and literature has always been primarily perceived as a left-leaning undertaking in the wider American perception and practice, such political pigeon-holing is hardly relevant in the European scenario. In a much discussed article, Greta Olson even goes so far as to identify shortcomings and "moments of blindness" in European law and literature scholarship caused by modeling itself too narrowly on the American movement's precedent, and therefore encourages:

> I would call to my European colleagues to remember that the Law and Literature movement arose in its most recent manifestation out of a frustration with legal training, interpretation, and practice in America ... Copying the forms of this scholarship by adopting an adversarial scenario ... will only lead us into imitative scholarship. Rather, the peculiarities of our own legal systems have to be kept in mind.[66]

Applying a cultural studies approach to humanizing the law thus specifies that the agenda be adapted to more localized scenarios, and not only in America or Europe, but in other parts of the world and in far-off cultures as well. At the same time, it broadens the conceptual reach in a further, inter- or even transdisciplinary move, where not only can critical legal studies and the social sciences be brought in, but even economics as the erstwhile antagonist might no longer appear so adversarial – as Gelter and Grechenig observe in their genealogy starting from a common origin, to which the law and literature movement could comfortably be added: 'The void left by the abandonment of formalism was filled with innovative jurisprudential movements in the second half of the 20th century, including the legal process school, critical legal studies, and not least law and economics.'[67]

Clearly, the cultural study of the law remains state of the art in the various efforts to humanize the law today, with much more promising work to be done. Nevertheless, the teleology in Binder and Weisberg's book may also be misleading, as it monodirectionally shows studying law *in* literature as passé and reduces adaptations in law *as* literature to milestones on the road to cultural criticisms of the law. There is still much to be gained from analyzing what happens to law when it becomes an

[66] Greta Olson, "De-Americanizing law-and-literature narratives: opening up the story," *Law & Literature*, 22(2) (2010), 361.

[67] Gelter and Grechenig, "History of law and economics," p. 3.

object of literature, and vice versa. And the push to re-interpret literary texts and theorize their uses continues to produce new insight and methodologies which should at least be tested in other fields, including legal studies.[68] Humanizing the law remains a challenge across many disciplines, facing the continued need for abstract regulation on the one hand and for accommodating actual human situations which are diverse and heterogeneous on the other. Legal standardizations of such situations are ineluctable but come at a cost which has to be accounted for and shared as equally as possible.

[68] For some suggestions, see Klaus Stierstorfer, "Law and (which?) literature: new directions in post-theory?" *Law and Humanities*, 5(1) (2011), 41–51.

CHAPTER 2

Law Meets Critical Theory

Peter Leman

> I have been suggesting that the encounter of deconstruction and the law may be interesting and productive, but it seems nearly preordained – they seem in some sense made for each other.
>
> Jonathan Culler (1988)

Coincident with the emergence of law and literature as a recognizable intellectual project in the 1970s and 1980s was the thing/event/context we call "critical theory." Continental theories of language, in particular, as articulated by the so-called "poststructuralists," found their way into Anglo-American academies, and in time, few disciplines in the humanities and social sciences were unaffected by the encounter. We speak now of the era of "high theory" when names like Derrida, Foucault, Lacan, Deleuze, Barthes, Kristeva, and others were on everyone's lips, though not always in the mode of application or praise: the antifoundationalism of post-structuralist theory was inherently unsettling, and many saw its methods as unavoidably amoral and even nihilistic.[1] Thus, the personified action described in this chapter's title was not always comfortable or agreeable. Law, like so many other disciplines, also met critical theory, and some celebrated the encounter, seeing it as the beginning of a new era in our understanding of the politics of jurisprudence and the indeterminacy of legal meaning, while others saw critical theory as a threat to legal justice itself. In this chapter, I will examine both points of view and how they relate to a key phase in the emergence and development of law and literature as a distinct field, but before doing so, I want to point out another meaning in this chapter's title.

"Law meets critical theory" refers, of course, to the historical encounter between the discipline of law and those theories or epistemological methods

[1] See Owen Fiss, "Objectivity and interpretation" in S. Levinson and S. Mailloux (eds.), *Interpreting Law and Literature: A Hermeneutic Reader* (Illinois: Northwestern University Press, 1988), pp. 229–49.

that fall under the broad designation "critical theory."[2] However, "meet" also means "to fulfill or satisfy." This sense might be seen as antithetical to the first: We speak of initial meetings, which imply a prior separateness or unfamiliarity between two entities, but to meet in the sense of *fulfill* suggests a mutual need or a prior abstract familiarity, even if unconscious, that achieves satisfaction or completeness when two entities come together. It is easiest and relatively unproblematic to understand critical theory's impact on law, generally, and law and literature, specifically, as consistent with the first sense of "meeting": Given how dramatically theories of deconstruction, for example, troubled the generally accepted foundationalist assumptions about legal meaning, one would be justified in seeing law and critical theory as separate and unfamiliar – indeed, even as *unlikely* – bedfellows who met for the first time in the 1980s. However, is there any sense in which law and critical theory satisfy one another? Is there any sense in which they fulfill – or fulfilled, for a time at least – something missing or desired in the other? I wish to suggest that despite the intense criticisms of poststructuralism and critical theory that came from some corners – or, perhaps, centers? – of the law, there is also a way of seeing the meeting, in both senses, as natural. As Jonathan Culler wrote in 1988, law's encounter with deconstruction, in particular, "seems nearly preordained – they seem in some sense made for each other."[3]

How is this so? What was it about the intersection between law and critical theory in the late twentieth century that seemed "preordained"? To

[2] A brief word on this: unfortunately, "critical theory" is not a particularly precise term, so the boundaries I draw around it here will be somewhat artificial and dictated by 1) the form of this chapter (i.e., length limitations), and 2) the figures and theories most relevant to the theoretical turn, if we can call it that, in law and literature studies. In the broad sense, "critical theory" has been treated as more or less equivalent to literary theory and philosophy throughout history (such that Hazard Adams could title his widely taught literary theory anthology, first published in 1971, *Critical Theory since Plato*), and in the narrow sense, "Critical Theory" (in caps) refers to the Frankfurt School, the early twentieth-century group of Marxist social critics and philosophers in Germany including Max Horkheimer, Theodor Adorno, Walter Benjamin, and Herbert Marcuse, among others. With the arrival of the French poststructuralists in the 1960s and 70s, however, the term was extended to theorists such as Jacques Derrida, Michel Foucault, Roland Barthes, Jacques Lacan, Jean Baudrillard, et al., and even today, critical theory loosely encompasses a range of thinkers who continue to work in and respond to the Frankfurt and/or French poststructuralist traditions, including Jürgen Habermas, Alain Badiou, Judith Butler, Gayatri Spivak, Giorgio Agamben, Slavoj Žižek, and many others. Because the poststructuralists were most central to law's encounter with critical theory in the 1980s and 90s, my focus will generally be on them. Derrida was, of course, the most influential of these thinkers and continues to play an important role, but more recent law and humanities scholarship engaging with critical theory on some level has also turned to Benjamin, Arendt, Agamben, and others. See, for example, the works listed in n. 11 of this chapter.

[3] Jonathan Culler, "Deconstruction and the law" in J. Culler (ed.), *Deconstruction: Critical Concepts in Literary and Cultural Studies* (London and New York: Routledge, 2003), vol. 2, p. 182.

answer this, we might look first to thematic preoccupations: Critical theory was not a manifestly legal or juridical enterprise (or set of enterprises, as critical theory, we should remember, was hardly homogenous or singular), but many of the most prominent thinkers directly addressed legal questions at different points in time. Most obvious and influential, of course, is Derrida's essay "Force of Law: The 'Mystical Foundation of Authority'" (1992), which is itself a response to Walter Benjamin's analysis of law and justice in "Critique of Violence" (1921). Derrida examines law or legal philosophy in a number of other works, including "Declarations of Independence" (1976), "The Law of Genre" (1980), "The Laws of Reflection: Nelson Mandela, in Admiration" (1987), and "Before the Law" (1992), among others. In a very different framework, Michel Foucault revealed a critical interest in juridical institutions in his highly influential *Discipline and Punish* (1975). And Jürgen Habermas's *Between Facts and Norms* (1992) is part of a larger project throughout his career of investigating the relationship between law and politics. Many other examples abound – the point is, of course, that critical theory's wide-ranging attentions to human history and experience, to language and institutions, inevitably settled here and there on issues of equal concern to legal scholars. In other words, prior to any official encounter or act of "applying" one to the other, law and critical theory orbited a similar set of problems or thematic loci. Because of this, therefore, their eventual encounter might have appeared, as Culler says, "preordained."

However, "preordained" is quite a strong term – perhaps *too* strong – and an overlapping thematic accumulation may not be enough to justify it. We might, then, consider looking a bit deeper, historically and etymologically. In 1991, Brook Thomas published a "state of the field" essay titled "Reflections on the Law and Literature Revival."[4] Like "preordained," "revival" gestures toward a prior connection or promise of connection which has returned or come to fruition in the present (this may account, partly, for the religious connotations).[5] As Thomas explains, law and literature were much more intimately connected in the eighteenth-century United States, but later separated as each discipline developed its

[4] Brook Thomas, "Reflections on the law and literature revival," *Critical Inquiry*, 17(3) (1991), 510–39.

[5] Thomas also explains that, for him, "revival" "calls attention to the quasi-religious nature [law and literature] has for those continuing to grant literary classics representative status" (514). I discuss the question of representation – what Thomas and others call the "crisis of representation" – as it affected law and literature in greater detail later in the chapter.

own technologies of professionalization.[6] The law and literature movement, then, could be, and often is, seen as a revival of that prior relationship. Similarly, we might see the meeting between law and critical theory as a reunion or revival of sorts, though the connection is, historically speaking, a bit deeper. In thinking about the timeliness of critical theory in "dark times," Wendy Brown traces the origins of the word "critique" to the Greek term *krisis*. Referring generally to a deliberative, reason-driven process, *krisis*, for the ancient Greeks, "focused on . . . evaluating and eventually judging evidence, reasons, or reasoning."[7] Brown's suggestion is that the DNA of modern critique as embodied in critical theory owes something to the ancient practices of *krisis* (from which we also get the term "crisis," or a turning point). Brown also points out that *krisis* became particularly important in Greek law: *krisis* "was a jurisprudential term identified with the art of making distinctions, an art considered essential to judging and rectifying an alleged disorder in or of the democracy."[8] Thus, Brown continues, "the project of critique is to set the times right again by discerning and repairing a tear in justice through practices that are themselves exemplary of the justice that has been rent."[9] If such is still the project of critique, Derrida's enigmatic declaration that "Deconstruction is justice" might begin to make sense.[10]

My point, of course, is not to equate law and critical theory – or even critical theory and justice, as Derrida does (if that is even what he does) – but to suggest that the natural – or the "preordained," if we accept Culler's hyperbole – nature of their meeting in the late twentieth century might be traced to a common point (among many points) of origin, or a common conceptual inheritance that values deliberation, judgment, weighing evidence, and making (or breaking down) distinctions of different kinds. Both law and critical theory value, address, and generate turning points, conceptually and otherwise. If we accept this story, and perhaps we do not, it enables us to consider the possibility that law's meeting with critical theory was not accidental or entirely new, but a kind of reunion in which each met or fulfilled something in the other at a crucial historical moment.

6 Robert A. Ferguson examines this early connection and later separation in *Law and Letters in American Culture* (Massachusetts: Harvard University Press, 1984).

7 Wendy Brown, *Edgework: Critical Essays on Knowledge and Politics* (Princeton: Princeton University Press, 2005), p. 5.

8 Brown, *Edgework*, p. 5.

9 Brown, *Edgework*, p. 6.

10 Jacques Derrida, "Force of law: the 'mystical foundation of authority'" in D. Cornell, D. Carlson, and M. Rosenfeld (eds.), *Deconstruction and the Possibility of Justice* (London and New York: Routledge, 1992), p. 15.

The fact that critical theory continues to prove influential in law and literature studies suggests that the meeting persists, though whether or not law fulfills critical theory, or vice versa, is certainly an open-ended question.[11] In the remainder of this chapter, I examine the emergence of law's relationship with critical theory in more detail before highlighting a few examples of scholars who have found the fruits of that relationship to be productive in advancing our understanding of law and literature. I cannot, of course, provide a comprehensive overview, but I hope at the very least to gesture toward a few influential moments and studies that illustrate the complexities and consequences of the crisis, or turning point, that was law's meeting with critical theory.

Meeting Places: Law Schools and English Departments

There are two separate spaces in which the law and critical theory encounter first occurred: law schools and English departments. When assessing the impact of the encounter, it is necessary to take both into account. To understand how and why critical theory emerged in conversation with law on these two fronts, however, we first need to look back a few decades to recall briefly the consequences of the early twentieth-century shift from legal formalism to legal realism. This shift is perhaps most famously captured in Oliver Wendell Holmes Jr.'s *The Common Law* (1881), in which he states, "The life of the law has not been logic: it has been experience."[12] Responding to a trend in nineteenth-century American law that sought to identify fundamental moral or ethical "axioms" from which one could deduce rules to apply to particular cases, Holmes instead emphasized the concrete historical, social, and even personal (e.g., a judge's prejudices) relations of the law. Holmes ultimately paved the way for the emergence of theories of jurisprudence and adjudication that turned from the application of abstract rules toward a more pragmatic approach that took into account social realities and public policy. What was called "legal realism" came to dominate American legal institutions, just as classical legal thought had in previous decades, and, over time, legal realism and its

[11] For recent studies that incorporate or draw upon critical theory – broadly conceived – in studying law and literature, see, among others: Ravit Reichman, *The Affective Life of Law: Legal Modernism and the Literary Imagination* (Stanford: Stanford University Press, 2009); James Martel, *The One and Only Law: Walter Benjamin and the Second Commandment* (Ann Arbor: University of Michigan Press, 2014); Awol Allo (ed.), *The Courtroom as Space of Resistance: Reflections on the Legacy of the Rivonia Trial* (Burlington: Ashgate, 2015).

[12] Oliver Wendell Holmes, *The Common Law* (Massachusetts: Belknap Press, 2009 [1881]), p. 3.

alliance with the social sciences developed into more specific alliances such as "law and society" and "law and economics." The latter, for our purposes, is particularly important. Emerging in the 1970s and centered at the University of Chicago, law and economics scholars shared with legal realists a belief that law should be based on "social realities."[13] Legal economists maintained that "the public interest is best served by minimizing the social costs of a policy, costs that can be measured by mathematically based economic formulas that determine the maximization of wealth."[14] The law and economics movement has had a staggering influence: writing in 1993, Anthony Kronman, former Dean of Yale Law School, described it as "the intellectual movement that has had the greatest influence on American academic law in the past quarter-century."[15]

We begin to sense here the emergence of a need that would invite or otherwise precede the encounter between law and critical theory: the emphasis on economic costs led legal economists to "[dismiss] values in determining social costs," and some saw this as having a reductive and even dehumanizing effect on the law.[16] Law and economics has been as divisive as it has been influential, and it thereby inspired "rival academic movement[s]."[17] In three of these rival movements, we first witness the encounter(s) with critical theory: critical legal studies (CLS), critical race theory (CRT), and law and literature. The first two, of course, appeared primarily in law schools. On that front, the scholars who identified with the CLS movement shaped a new approach to law that was critical of both classical legal thought and law and economics. CLS was highly interdisciplinary – a trait shared with law and economics – and drew heavily on the work of critical theorists who had begun to exert a profound influence on a range of academic disciplines. In asserting that law is inherently political, that rules do not compel outcomes, and that legal education and practice contribute to alienated subjectivities, CLS scholars drew on various theories, including those of the Frankfurt School, deconstruction, structuralism and poststructuralism, psychoanalysis, and hermeneutics.[18] Among these many points of contact, it is, perhaps, safe to say that deconstruction exerted

13 Thomas, "Reflections," 512. 14 Thomas, "Reflections," 512.

15 Anthony Kronman, *The Lost Lawyer: Failing Ideals of the Legal Profession* (Massachusetts: Belknap Press, 1993), p. 166. For the early history of the law and economics movement, see Chapter 1 of the present volume.

16 Thomas, "Reflections," 512.

17 Gary Minda, "The law and economics and critical legal studies movements in American law" in N. Mercuro (ed.), *Law and Economics* (Dordrecht: Springer Netherlands, 1989), p. 88.

18 Robert L. Hayman, Nancy Levit, and Richard Delgado (eds.), *Jurisprudence Classical and Contemporary: From Natural Law to Postmodernism* (Minnesota: West Group, 2002), p. 404.

the strongest influence, or, at the very least, provoked the strongest responses. Whereas scholars such as J. M. Balkin, Roberto Unger, and Drucilla Cornell drew on deconstructive methods to critique legal ideology,[19] others such as Owen Fiss, Patricia Williams, and Catherine MacKinnon worried that deconstruction and poststructuralism would undermine rights protections and, when allowed to influence legal decision making, ultimately be incapable "of sustaining or generating a public morality."[20]

Patricia Williams' critique of CLS contributed to the larger project of CRT. Like CLS, CRT recognized the law as deeply political and presented a challenge to certain ideas in law and economics, but unlike CLS, CRT scholars focused their attention on questions of racial justice and racial hierarchies in the law. Williams asserted, for example, that in its critique of rights discourse, CLS "ignored the degree to which rights-assertion and the benefits of rights have helped blacks, other minorities, and the poor."[21] Taking this a step further, Kimberlé Crenshaw, in challenging "both the New Left and New Right critiques of the Civil Rights Movement," argued that the "single-minded effort to deconstruct liberal legal ideology" in CLS failed to recognize that for blacks and other minorities, coercion "explains much more about racial domination than does ideologically induced consent."[22] This is not to say that CRT scholars rejected critical theory as such – in fact, in another piece, Williams writes about her own racial consciousness, noting that she has spent her life "recovering from the

[19] See: Jack M. Balkin, "Deconstructive practice and legal theory," *Yale Law Journal*, 96 (1987); Jack M. Balkin, "Tradition, betrayal, and the politics of deconstruction," *Cardozo Law Review* 11 (1990) 1613–30; and Drucilla Cornell, "Violence of the masquerade: law dressed up as justice" in J. Culler (ed.), *Deconstruction: Critical Concepts in Literary and Cultural Studies* (London and New York: Routledge, 2003), vol. 2, pp. 194–210. Cornell asserts, for example, that "Deconstruction is understood to rip away law's pretension to be other than politics" (p. 194). Roberto Unger, regarded as one of the leading figures of CLS, does not explicitly invoke deconstruction, but according to Jonathan Culler, "one can identify both themes and strategies of argument [in the work of CLS scholars like Unger] that seem comparable to those of deconstruction" (Culler, "Deconstruction and the law," p. 183). See, for example, *The Critical Legal Studies Movement* (Massachusetts: Harvard University Press, 1986), in which he uses the terms "critique" and "construction" to describe his challenge to legal objectivism and formalism, on the one hand, and his effort to go beyond negative critique to construct viable alternatives on the other.

[20] Owen Fiss, "The death of the law?" *Cornell Law Review*, 72(1) (1986), 15. See also: Patricia J. Williams, "Alchemical notes: reconstructing ideals from deconstructed rights" in R. L. Hayman, N. Levit, and R. Delgado (eds.), *Jurisprudence Classical and Contemporary: From Natural Law to Postmodernism* (Minnesota: West Group, 2002), pp. 417–21; Catherine MacKinnon, "Points against postmodernism," *Chicago-Kent Law Review*, 75(3) (2000), 687–712.

[21] Williams, "Alchemical notes," 417.

[22] Kimberlé Williams Crenshaw, "Race, reform, and retrenchment: transformation and legitimation in antidiscrimination law," *Harvard Law Review*, 101(7) (1988), 1334, 1357.

degradation of being divided against myself, within myself."[23] Though she does not mention specific theoretical influences, this idea resonates strongly with the work of postcolonial critical theorists such as Edward Said, Franz Fanon, and Homi Bhabha.[24] Later in the same article, Williams describes developing an "ambivalent, multivalent way of seeing" that she recognizes as being "at the heart of critical theory, feminist theory, and the so-called minority critique."[25] Thus, as both object of critique and means of framing certain kinds of questions, critical theory spread further into legal debates and discourses through CRT.

One of the key questions raised by CRT scholars in their criticisms of CLS had to do with representation and representativeness: i.e., to what extent does CLS or the law, generally, represent the interests and perspectives of minorities? The crisis beneath this question found expression outside the law, of course, and its appearance here directs us to the other space of encounter between law and critical theory: CLS and CRT were two points through which critical theory began to exert an influence on legal thinking through law schools, but its influence was also felt through the English departments toward which humanistically inclined legal scholars turned and where, they found, critical theory had already caused a bit of a stir. Derrida's 1966 lecture "Structure, Sign, and Play in the Discourse of the Human Sciences," delivered at Johns Hopkins University, marked the arrival of poststructuralism in American academies, and literary theory thereby entered a new phase. Indeed, as Brook Thomas wrote a couple of decades into this phase,

> [T]he humanities are experiencing what can be called a crisis of representation. In its extreme form this crisis results from questions raised about the very possibility of representation. Full representation, various post-structuralists proclaim, is structurally and rhetorically impossible. Instead, any attempt at representation inevitably involves misrepresentation. In its less extreme form the crisis involves questions about the representative status of humanistic works themselves.[26]

In responding to the scientism and abstractions of law and economics and CLS, legal scholars such as James Boyd White and Owen Fiss turned to

[23] Patricia J. Williams, "The obliging shell: an informal essay on formal equal opportunity," *Michigan Law Review*, 87(8) (1989), 2140.

[24] See: Edward Said, *Orientalism* (New York: Pantheon, 1978); Franz Fanon, *Black Skins, White Masks* (New York: Grove Press, 1967 [1952]) and *The Wretched of the Earth* (1961). New York: Grove Press, 2004 [1961]; Homi Bhabha, *The Location of Culture* (London and New York: Routledge, 1994).

[25] Williams, "The obliging shell," 2151.

[26] Thomas, "Reflections," 512–13.

the humanities in order to "restore to legal studies a proper place for the question of values" (as outlined in the previous chapter).[27] The irony of this turn was that in seeking to counter the political conservatism of law and economics, Fiss and others unwittingly aligned themselves with cultural conservatives who shared their assumption that "great" works of literature contained and expressed universal human values. As Thomas indicates, however, many in the humanities, due largely to the challenges presented by poststructuralism, had begun to question such values and whether or not literature can be representative of anything beyond the historically specific and contingent values of particular authors and the cultural/social contexts in which they wrote.

Fiss and others were unsettled by this crisis – critical theory's influence on CLS was one of the things they had hoped to escape or at least counter by turning to the humanities, but the humanities themselves were well into a new era of theory-dominated discourse. Fiss famously characterized these theories as a "new nihilism" that threatened legal interpretation by recasting the interpretive act as a choice among "any number of possible meanings," ultimately rendering objectivity impossible.[28] What Fiss saw as nihilism, however, others, such as Sanford Levinson, saw as an opportunity to recognize, make sense of, "and make do with the fractured and fragmented discourse available to us," whether in law or literature.[29] The encounter with critical theory in the developing discourses of law and literature did not spell the end of the movement, in other words, but it did mark a point of departure, with some maintaining the view that literature and the humanities are expressive of essential human values and others seeing in poststructuralism and other critical theories modes of thought that could facilitate necessary challenges to the hegemonic discourses of the law. As Thomas writes, "Work in law and literature varies according to how seriously it takes this crisis of representation and representativeness."[30] Accordingly, the remainder of this chapter will discuss a few examples of those who have welcomed this crisis as a critical and theoretical opportunity, with particular attention to deconstruction and psychoanalysis. In identifying these examples, however, I recognize the clear complication that I may be implicitly assigning representativeness to texts that are themselves engaged with or a product of the crisis of representation.

[27] Owen Fiss, "The challenge ahead," *Yale Journal of Law & the Humanities*, 1 (1988), x.

[28] Fiss, "Objectivity and interpretation," pp. 230–1.

[29] Sanford Levinson, "Law as literature" in S. Levinson and S. Mailloux (eds.), *Interpreting Law and Literature: A Hermeneutic Reader* (Illinois: Northwestern University Press, 1988), p. 173.

[30] Thomas, "Reflections," 513.

Whether or not these studies are, in fact, representative of larger or dominant trends, I will leave to the reader to determine. At the very least, they reveal some of the ways in which the encounter between law and critical theory changed the way we talk about the connection(s) between law and literature.

Interpreting the Legal Text: Law, Literature, Deconstruction

Separately, for both law and literature, interpretation is a core disciplinary craft: whether one is interpreting the Constitution or a Toni Morrison novel, the ability to read closely and derive significant meaning from a text is essential to successful legal and literary practice. Theories of what interpretation is, how to do it, and how a text generates meaning vary widely, of course, but it was perhaps inevitable – preordained? – that the two fields would intersect at this point of commonality. And it was at this point that critical theory, particularly deconstruction, began to shape scholarly conversations, as some in the law looked to literature in fashioning different responses to law and economics and CLS. The range of works exploring deconstruction and legal interpretation is wide, of course, but the basic tenor of these conversations is well illustrated by two influential essay collections: *Interpreting Law and Literature: A Hermeneutic Reader* (1988), edited by Sanford Levinson and Steven Mailloux, and *Deconstruction and the Possibility of Justice* (1992), edited by Drucilla Cornell, Michel Rosenfeld, and David Gray Carlson. The first collection is not solely about hermeneutics and the latter is not solely about deconstruction, but at that point of overlap they jointly exerted a compelling influence on theoretically informed approaches to questions of interpretation in law and literature.

Levinson and Mailloux's collection offered a selection of texts "designed to represent the especially rich interaction . . . between legal and literary hermeneutics" over the preceding decade.[31] Most of the essays, in one way or another, are oriented by the longstanding debate between originalist and non-originalist modes of constitutional interpretation. With essays from prominent legal scholars and/or practitioners, such as Justice William Brennan Jr., and literary scholars, including E. D. Hirsch Jr. and Walter Benn Michaels, the volume offers varied perspectives on the interpreter/text relationship, authorial intentionality, context, plain meaning, and more.

[31] Sanford Levinson and Steven Mailloux, "Preface" in S. Levinson and S. Mailloux (eds.), *Interpreting Law and Literature: A Hermeneutic Reader* (Illinois: Northwestern University Press, 1988), p. xii.

Only a handful of the twenty-four essays address poststructuralist theory explicitly: e.g., Michael Hancher's "Dead Letters: Wills and Poems" (discussing Roland Barthes and the legal implications of the "death of the author"); Clare Dalton's well-known "An Essay in the Deconstruction of Contract Doctrine" (in which she deconstructs the "doctrinal dichotomies" of contract law[32]); and David Couzens Hoy's "Interpreting the Law: Hermeneutical and Poststructuralists Perspectives" (comparing Habermas and Gadamer with Derrida on questions of interpretation). As significant as these contributions are, what is particularly fascinating about the collection is the extent to which Derrida and deconstruction seem present, though not always visible, in nearly every contribution. On the one hand, this is an effect of a recurring anxiety – sometimes explicit (as in Fiss's "Objectivity and Interpretation"), more often implicit – about the extent to which certain contemporary theories might lead to radical subjectivity and indeterminacy in legal interpretation. On the other, Derrida's presence/absence is an effect of Levinson and Mailloux's suggestion that the collection itself is a product of deconstruction, even if individual contributions are wary of its theories: Noting in their Preface that deconstruction is "one of the most influential contemporary approaches to literary analysis," they emphasize that one of the goals of deconstruction is to reveal the "repressed elements within a discourse" and thereby disrupt disciplinary claims to "unity, self-sufficiency, and determinacy."[33] Inasmuch as law sought to repress and exclude the literary in asserting claims of determinacy with increasing professional rigor in the eighteenth and nineteenth centuries, its return as represented and enacted by the anthology itself is thus a product – even, perhaps, an act – of deconstruction.

The other collection – *Deconstruction and the Possibility of Justice* – is, obviously, very much a product of and engagement with deconstruction on questions of law and justice. Beginning with Derrida's famed "Force of Law: The 'Mystical Foundation of Authority'," the collection devotes a substantial section specifically to "Deconstruction and Legal Interpretation." As in the previous volume, the authors here recognize that the "practice of legal interpretation is mired in a deep and persistent crisis."[34]

32 Clare Dalton, "An Essay in the deconstruction of contract doctrine" in S. Levinson and S. Mailloux (eds.), *Interpreting Law and Literature: A Hermeneutic Reader* (Illinois: Northwestern University Press, 1988), p. 286.

33 Levinson and Mailloux, "Preface," pp. x–xi.

34 Michel Rosenfeld, "Deconstruction and legal interpretation: conflict, indeterminacy and the temptations of the new legal formalism" in D. Cornell, D. Carlson, and M. Rosenfeld (eds.), *Deconstruction and the Possibility of Justice* (London and New York: Routledge, 1992), p. 152.

We might also call this a crisis of foundationalism, or a pervasive uncertainty about "the availability of objective criteria" for assigning stable meaning to legal texts.[35] While some blame poststructuralist theories for reinforcing or even causing this indeterminacy, the authors in this volume see value in deconstruction's ability to address and work with/within such indeterminacy without resorting to either a false promise of fixity or complete arbitrariness in hermeneutic practice. In "The Idolatry of Rules," for example, Arthur Jacobson distinguishes between dynamic and static systems of jurisprudence, suggesting that the former, which would include the law of Moses, the "jurisprudence of right" (found in Hobbes and Hegel), and the common law, resist the tendency toward rule-idolatry – i.e., treating rules as though already complete and fully formed – found in static systems such as positivism and naturalism.[36] Through a poststructuralist reading of the play among writing, rewriting, and erasure in Moses' law-creating collaboration with Elohim and Yaweh in the Old Testament, Jacobson demonstrates how the crisis of interpretation is a product of rule-idolatry, of our desire to have fully formed rules that guide action and interpretation. Because rules are always in the process of being created, however, dynamic jurisprudences instead value the struggle with creation: "Rules rule only when persons struggle at every moment with them, use them in deeds to create a record."[37] Dynamic jurisprudences, thus, "treat law as the expression of a personality rather than an instrument of order."[38] Like the other authors in the volume, Jacobson offers a model of interpretation that may not necessarily resolve the crisis, but which recognizes that our desire for resolution, for completeness and fixity, is part of the problem.

The crisis of interpretation is only one of the many crises to which deconstruction has responded, or with which deconstruction has become entangled, in law and literature scholarship. In the many years since those represented here, scholars have continued to explore, with varying degrees of directness, deconstruction's relevance to questions of law and justice. Wai Chee Dimock's 1996 *Residues of Justice*, for example, examines the figure of "commensurability" in our theories of justice, arguing that despite the popular ideal, justice actually possesses a "nonfoundational character" whose language "abstracts as much as it translates and omits as much as it

[35] Rosenfeld, "Deconstruction and legal interpretation," p. 152.

[36] Arthur J. Jacobson, "The idolatry of rules: writing law according to Moses, with reference to other jurisprudences" in D. Cornell, D. Carlson, and M. Rosenfeld (eds.), *Deconstruction and the Possibility of Justice* (London and New York: Routledge, 1992), p. 131.

[37] Jacobson, "The idolatry of rules," p. 135.

[38] Jacobson, "The idolatry of rules," p. 130.

abstracts."[39] Justice tries to "resolve its conflicts into a commensurate order," but it inevitably fails in the face of the "stubborn densities of human experience," leaving behind troubling residues that cannot be fully resolved.[40] More recently, in *Persons and Things* (2008), Barbara Johnson explores the blurry boundaries between persons and things (in law, literature, life), recognizing that deconstruction has often "gravitated to the inanimate" and might, therefore, offer a productive framework for thinking about and working through questions of materiality and different forms of legal personhood.[41] There are, of course, many more examples, but hopefully those which I have briefly summarized here suggest at least some of the ways in which law's meeting with deconstruction, in particular, has generated an unusual, and unusually provocative, series of conversations in both legal scholarship and the humanities. Deconstruction, of course, is not the only critical theory circulating within law and literature conversations, nor is it an isolated theory – as in CLS scholarship, deconstruction often overlaps or works in tandem with Marxist, feminist, critical race, and psychoanalytic theories. To illustrate one of the other directions the meeting between law and critical theory has opened up, therefore, I will devote the final section of this chapter to law and psychoanalysis.

Investigating the Legal Unconscious: Law, Literature, Psychoanalysis

As a literary/critical theory, psychoanalysis is generally traced back to Freud and then through the work of the Frankfurt School, where it provided useful models for new forms of social critique in conjunction with Marxism and existentialist philosophy; in addition, psychoanalysis later became identified with the French poststructuralists due, in particular, to Jacques Lacan, although Derrida also ventures into the territory of the unconscious in texts like *Resistances of Psychoanalysis* (1998) and *The Work of Mourning* (2001). (In Peter Fitzpatrick's work, particularly *Modernism and the Grounds of Law* [2001], we find an engaging synthesis of Derridean deconstruction and post-Freudian psychoanalysis.) Derrida is not the sole or even primary touchstone in scholarship connecting law and psychoanalysis, however. At a more general level, the most recurrent theme in such scholarship, or perhaps the most recurrent claim, is that psychoanalysis

[39] Wai Chee Dimock, *Residues of Justice: Literature, Law, Philosophy* (California: University of California Press, 1996), p. 5.
[40] Dimock, *Residues of Justice*, p. 5.
[41] Barbara Johnson, *Persons and Things* (Massachusetts: Harvard University Press, 2008), p. 4.

provides a model for thinking about the legal unconscious: the secrets, the traumas, the untold stories, the forms of disorder that lurk just beneath the surface of law's self-presentation of order and orderliness. Robert A. Ferguson suggests, for example, that the "surface narrative of a courtroom transcript" might be compared to "the consciousness of the individual," and the legal unconscious, therefore, would consist of those stories the law excludes and represses.[42] Psychoanalysis is, thus, on the one hand a kind of allegoresis wherein theories of the mind become symbolic of the visible and invisible structures of the law (sharing, with deconstruction, an interest in the law's exclusions and repressions); on the other, it provides a method of directly addressing mental states and representations of mental states in law and literature. Psychoanalysis has thus enabled us to think about confession, blame, guilt, intent, insanity, melancholy, repression, and trauma in new ways in relationship to legal and literary texts.

Peter Goodrich's *Oedipus Lex: Psychoanalysis, History, and Law* (1995), for example, illustrates how psychoanalysis enables us to find and recuperate what the law has lost or otherwise seeks to hide. Focusing on the persistent association between melancholy and law in the Reformation and Renaissance, Goodrich suggests that because melancholy is understood as the symptom of an unconscious "lost love-object," it is the primary goal of "a jurisprudence of melancholia to reconstruct the lost objects of legal life."[43] Such objects can be both individual (i.e., "youth, vigor, manners, emotions" for those who study law) and institutional (i.e., the "authentic sources" and "native common law" that existed prior to the imposition of written law).[44] This negative loss, however, "inevitably has a positive representation," and Goodrich speculates that we might see the "positive imagery of law, the dreams of order, science, reason, and justice" as "simply the melancholic lawyer's projection to cover the lack of reason, system, and justice" in the law.[45] Beneath the ordered surface of the law, in other words, we might find forms of disorder indicative of the ongoing losses perpetuated by or otherwise experienced within the law. By "thinking historically of psychoanalytic jurisprudence," Goodrich addresses contemporary issues (similar to those of CLS) through an analysis, ultimately, of the law's repression of images and women – in doing so, Goodrich identifies "an unconscious or repressed tradition within the legal institution"

[42] Robert A. Ferguson, "Untold stories in the law" in P. Brooks and P. Gewirtz (eds.), *Law's Stories: Narrative and Rhetoric in the Law* (New Haven and London: Yale University Press, 1996), p. 89.

[43] Peter Goodrich, *Oedipus Lex: Psychoanalysis, History, Law* (Berkeley: University of California Press, 1995), p. 7.

[44] Goodrich, *Oedipus Lex*, p. 7. [45] Goodrich, *Oedipus Lex*, pp. 7–8.

that poses a threat by virtue of its indeterminacy and, thereby, holds the promise of a "critical jurisprudence [that] can offer some elements of political radicalism."[46]

Whereas Goodrich is interested in how psychoanalysis can help uncover repressed traditions within the law, a number of other scholars have turned their attention to the traumas both hidden and perpetuated by the law. In *The Juridical Unconscious: Trials and Traumas in the Twentieth Century* (2002), for example, Shoshana Felman identifies a connection between the courtroom and traumatic events that "hitherto had remained hidden or legally unreadable."[47] The readability of this link, she argues, emerged in the twentieth century due to the unique confluence of three key factors: First, the development of psychoanalysis as a distinct field of study and practice, bringing with it an understanding of both individual (private) and collective (public) forms of trauma; second, "the unprecedented number of disastrous events on a mass scale," including both world wars, that traumatized millions; and last, "the unprecedented and repeated" effort to use the law as a way of coping and coming to terms with these large-scale traumas.[48] Psychoanalysis, in short, enabled us to recognize trauma, and the law was called upon to resolve and heal it. However, in doing this work, the law was confronted with "processes that are unavailable to consciousness" and, consequently, struggled to make them legible within its framework.[49] In tracing these intersections and slippages between the traumatic and the juridical, Felman focuses on two "trials of the century": the 1961 trial of Nazi leader Adolf Eichmann and the 1995 trial of O. J. Simpson. Though obviously very different, the two trials, Felman argues, both "dramatized or triggered an emblematic crisis in the law" – i.e., in both, we witness interruptions that mark a shift between a need to address small-scale private traumas and an overwhelming imperative to deal with large-scale collective trauma.[50] In analyzing how the law struggled through these processes, Felman turns to literature and what she calls "literary justice," or the capacity of literature to "[encapsulate] not closure but precisely what in a given legal case refuses to be closed and cannot be closed."[51] Literature, thus, helps make visible and legible what the law either excludes or fails to comprehend and contain.

[46] Goodrich, *Oedipus Lex*, pp. 13, 15.

[47] Shoshana Felman, *The Juridical Unconscious: Trials and Traumas in the Twentieth Century* (Massachusetts: Harvard University Press, 2002), p. 2.

[48] Felman, *The Juridical Unconscious*, p. 2.

[49] Felman, *The Juridical Unconscious*, p. 4.

[50] Felman, *The Juridical Unconscious*. p. 4.

[51] Felman, *The Juridical Unconscious*. p. 8.

As with deconstruction and hermeneutics, the scholarship on psychoanalysis is extensive and wide-ranging – there is much more that has been done, and I openly acknowledge the irony of my inevitable exclusions and unintentional repressions. I hope, however, that these examples are suggestive of the kinds of questions raised in the encounter between law and psychoanalysis, or, we might say, between law and its own unconscious. And although Fiss feared the "death of the law," the law is at least alive, if not alive and well, and the directions, opportunities, questions, paths to the hidden and unknown opened up by the meeting between law and critical theory, generally, have yet to be exhausted. Perhaps, though the initial meeting is long past, there are still needs in both critical theory and law that can be met by the other.

CHAPTER 3

Narrative and Law

Cathrine O. Frank

Law and literature both are deeply invested in representation – of facts, of events, and of persons – and perhaps the most significant historical tension between the disciplines has been in their respective conventions of representation, or more particularly in the story that emerges out of their narrative rules, techniques, and objectives. This chapter begins with a brief history of the narrative turn in law and literature that distinguishes it from other "literary" approaches to law and highlights a series of symposia and publications focused on the concept of legal storytelling. To exemplify the difference between official "legal" stories that can be told and heard at law and those that become audible in other literary fields, I turn to the forgotten history of George Edalji, the Staffordshire solicitor who served three years for horse-ripping before Arthur Conan Doyle took up his cause. Doyle's intervention might suffice to interest a literary scholar, but it is Julian Barnes's 2005 novel *Arthur and George* that best illustrates the interplay of competing legal, literary, fictional, and nonfictional stories and their impact on both individual character and national culture, rendered starker by the historical nature of Barnes's fiction and the implied story it tells of the real present.

The final section of the chapter returns to the aims of narrative jurisprudence and recent work on the "resurgence of character" in narratives of national and cultural identity that illustrate the legal force of cultural narratives, the cultural force of legal narratives, and the necessity of counternarrative in an age of renewed essentialism.

Law, Literature, and Narrative Jurisprudence

As a movement, law and literature has been criticized for lacking a coherent set of principles and for practicing a nominal interdisciplinarity that brings the two fields together largely to confirm their respective identities. If this is so, law and literature is nonetheless a self-reflective movement that, in its forty-year history, has often stopped to survey and assess the implications of the work progressing under its rubric.[1] While no two histories of the movement are precisely the same, "narrative" looms large in all: traceable throughout as a general attention to stories about law, linked with rhetoric as a mode of argument in law, taken as the linguistic object of interpretation, or identified as a discrete strand of jurisprudence that calls attention to "'outsider' narratives," which fall outside frames of legal recognition or are interpolated into master narratives that misrecognize or misrepresent the subject's particular experience.[2] I begin by connecting a disposition toward narrative generally with the particular narratives advocated among theorists of "outsider jurisprudence."[3]

In his 1983 essay "Nomos and Narrative," legal scholar Robert Cover observed that narrative is foundational to all normative activity and grounds every aspect of the *nomos* or "normative world." "History and literature cannot escape their location in a normative universe," he writes, "nor can prescription, even when embodied in a legal text, escape its origin and its end in experience, in the narratives that are the trajectories plotted upon material reality by our imaginations."[4] With references to history, literature, and law, the passage captures the power of aesthetic and cultural forms both to give meaning to experience and to entail "prescription" such that culture acquires a force like law. At the same time, it insists that legal texts are inseparable from "experience." Rules derive from, are directed toward, and act upon experience (their "origin" and "end"), which constitutes a "material reality" upon which the "imagination" constructs or "plots" a future course of action. Sounds like fiction.

Cover contends that the work of world-creating (and -maintaining) is always a social action. Each community locates its principles and stories, often in a central text, and commits to living out its implications. If legal

[1] See, for example: Michael Freeman and Andrew D. Lewis (eds.), *Law and Literature: Current Legal Issues* (Oxford: Oxford University Press, 1999), vol. 2; Guyora Binder and Robert Weisberg (eds.), *Literary Criticisms of Law* (Princeton: Princeton University Press, 2000); Austin Sarat, Cathrine O. Frank, and Matthew Anderson (eds.), *Teaching Law and Literature* (New York: MLA, 2011).

[2] Peter Brooks, "Narrative transactions: does the law need a narratology?" *Yale Journal of Law and Humanities*, 18(1) (2006), 1.

[3] Mari Matsuda, "Public response to racist speech: considering the victim's story," *Michigan Law Review*, 87 (1989), 2320. Quoted in Kim Lane Scheppele, "Foreword: telling stories," *Michigan Law Review*, 87 (1989), 2084. See also Robin West, *Narrative, Authority, and Law* (Ann Arbor: University of Michigan Press, 1993), p. 424. West includes law and literature, critical legal studies, feminist legal theory, and critical race theory.

[4] Robert Cover, "Nomos and narrative" in M. Minow, M. Ryan, and A. Sarat (eds.), *Narrative, Violence and the Law: The Essays of Robert Cover* (Ann Arbor: University of Michigan Press, 1993), p. 96.

institutions, legal interpretations, or law enforcement seem especially directed toward making and maintaining social worlds, Cover reminds readers that the *nomos* is a world out of which law emerges and with which law is in a sense identical. Both are described as a "system of tension": *nomos* "between reality and vision," and law "linking a concept of reality to an imagined alternative."[5] And as a process, both *nomos* and law are essentially aspirational, poised between the real and ideal and weighing the former by the latter. In this system, narrative supplies the "normative significance"; it makes the meaning that shapes understanding and inspires the commitment to live out that meaning: "To inhabit a *nomos* is to know how to *live* in it."[6] Imagine then, as Kim Lane Scheppele asked readers to do, the impact of being excluded from the creation, interpretation, or reconfiguration of the dominant narrative: "How are people to think about the law when their stories, the ones they have lived and believed, are rejected by courts, only to be replaced by other versions with different legal results?"[7]

Cover's and Scheppele's observations make visible two sets of tensions which also mark an historical junction in scholarship in narrative and law. First there is the gap between the real and the ideal that narrative seeks to mediate, but there is also variation within the "concept of reality" and even within the ideal that a community takes as its starting place and which outsider narratives are poised to remediate. This point informs Robin West's early critique of the centrality of textual interpretation in the creation of communities and her call for a more inclusive "interactive community" that would recognize "those whom the community's texts exclude, violate, or objectify."[8] Linking the "narrative voice and law-and-literature movement" in their promise to restore those experiences to public consciousness, West shows that both draw from a humanistic belief that literature's capacity to mobilize different perspectives and engage readers in others' experiences promotes empathy.[9]

Nevertheless, West also shows where narrative jurisprudence parts ways with law and literature insofar as the stories need not be literary. Richard Delgado's depiction of a hypothetical faculty search, for example, illustrated the structural conditions, power relations, differing experiences, and narrative accounts of a demographically changing profession which, as

[5] Cover, "Nomos," p. 101. [6] Cover, "Nomos," p. 97. [7] Scheppele, "Foreword," 2080.

[8] Robin West, "Communities, texts, law: reflections on the law and literature movement," *Yale Journal of Law and Humanities*, 1 (1988), pp. 131, 154, 145.

[9] West, "Communities," 155.

Scheppele explained, required both practical reforms and new scholarly methodologies. "Counterstorytelling," in Delgado's parlance, offered "psychic self-preservation" to the individual, enhanced "group solidarity," disrupted the complacency borne of the dominant group's familiar and successful storytelling, and promised to break down "intellectual apartheid."[10]

In the early 1990s, then, "narrative and law" might denote the application of insights gleaned from poststructural literary theory to interpretation of legal texts, a turn to literature for its empathic potential and critical commentary on law, or an increasing emphasis on the potential for stories told *within* the legal community to articulate alternative experiences of wrongs – and all were associated with the legal academy.[11] In *Law's Stories: Narrative and Rhetoric in the Law* (1996), Paul Gewirtz and Peter Brooks drew attention to the "form, structure, and rhetoric" of legal argument and cautioned that "storytelling in law is narrative within a culture of argument" that directs the affective and descriptive elements of storytelling toward drawing the "coercive force of the state" to one's side.[12] What then, asks Gewirtz, wins a legal decision-maker's acceptance, especially when that story comes from an avowed outsider who by definition encounters barriers of unfamiliarity, skepticism, or discomfort in his listeners?[13] Ten years later, Peter Brooks asked again: "why doesn't the law pay more attention to narratives, to narrative analysis and even narrative theory?"[14] "Does the Law Need a Narratology?" – a set of tools that would enable it to 'talk narrative talk' and reconnect in an explicit, formal way with the rhetorical roots of "argumentation through narrative?"[15] Most recently, Robin Wharton and Derek Miller have pointed "New Directions in Law and Narrative" (2015) and called for "narratives of the law that constrain and define the possibilities of legal practice."[16] One such example, Andrew Bricker argues, is the archetypal form of the legal opinion, which by exhibiting specific conventions in a historically consistent manner shows itself to be an opinion and activates

10 Richard Delgado, "Storytelling for oppositionists and others: a plea for narrative," *Michigan Law Review*, 87 (1989), 2437–8, 2440.

11 Literary and cultural studies approaches to narrative and law, absent the specific moniker "law and literature," comprise a longer list. See Christine L. Krueger's chapter in this volume.

12 Paul Gewirtz, "Narrative and rhetoric in the law" in P. Brooks and P. Gewirtz (eds.), *Law's Stories: Narrative and Rhetoric in the Law* (Yale: Yale University Press, 1996), pp. 4–5.

13 Gewirtz, "Narrative and rhetoric," p. 6.

14 Brooks, "Narrative transactions," 3.

15 Brooks, "Narrative transactions," 2, 21.

16 Robin Wharton and Derek Miller, "New directions in law and narrative." *Law, Culture, and the Humanities* (2016), 4. DOI: 10.1177/1743872116652865.

the genre's legitimating authority.[17] By contrast, "historically transitory" acts of legal storytelling – for example, those connected to rules covering witness competency or witness testimony and victim impact statements – demonstrate the ubiquity of narrative but also make it appear merely "incidental" to law.[18]

Paul Gewirtz's question about the way narratives gain traction with their intended audience, however, suggests that historicizing those acts of narration is critical to understanding their effects. The tension here between the archetypal and the ephemeral parallels the competing demands of coherence (the validated narrative of events) and particularity (the individual's experience) that trouble narrative jurisprudence. In the next section I turn to the public record of George Edalji's prosecution, to explore his "self-believed story" (to borrow Erving Goffman's term) and consider the structural and historical conditions that prevented it from being heard and endorsed at law.[19]

"A kind of squalid Dreyfus case": George Edalji, Arthur Conan Doyle, and the Court of Public Appeal

In 1906, when George Edalji was convicted of mutilating a pony and terrorizing his neighborhood, Great Britain had no court of criminal appeal. From 1848, questions of law arising from civil cases could be referred to the Court for Crown Cases Reserved, but these questions did not pertain to facts established in the original trial and were not mooted by the defendant. Only in 1907, and partly through the influence of Edalji's case, did defendants gain a right of appeal to a new court.[20] Appeals were certainly made, however. In this section, I survey Edalji's story as it was plotted at law, and the alternative story as it was debated in government and in the press. What were the stock stories that informed the investigation into Edalji and his trial? How did his outsider story counter them, and how, in the absence of formal mechanisms of appeal, did his partial success nevertheless depend on the advocacy of strong insiders in a way that left his own story still unheard?

George Edalji was sentenced to seven years' hard labor for slashing a horse and for masterminding a campaign of harassment – a strange pastime

[17] Andrew Bricker, "Is narrative essential to the law? Precedent, case law, and judicial emplotment," *Law, Culture, and the Humanities* (2015), 11. DOI: 10.1177/1743872115627413.

[18] Bricker, "Is narrative essential," 2–3.

[19] Quoted in Scheppele, "Foreword," 2079.

[20] J. H. Baker, *An Introduction to English Legal History*, 4th edn. (London: Butterworths, 2002), p. 139.

for the bookish solicitor and author of *Railway Law for the "Man in the Train"* whose father was vicar of Great Wyrley. However, such anomalies were cited by prosecution and defense alike, and especially by Edalji's most famous advocate, as evidence in their favor.

Accounts of the prehistory of the trial and of subsequent measures to overturn the conviction point first to Edalji's ethnicity. George's father, Bombay-born Shapurji Edalji, had converted to Christianity and trained in England as an Anglican clergyman.[21] Following his marriage to Charlotte Stoneham, Charlotte's uncle gave him the living of St. Mark's. No official, public account pointed to the Rev. Edalji's ethnicity as having impaired his reputation in the community, and none cited George's Anglo-Indian heritage as being directly at issue.[22] However, the letters that began to plague the Edaljis, from 1888 to 1889 and again from 1892 to 1895, routinely employed variations on their "blackness."[23] Certainly, racial prejudice dominates Conan Doyle's explanation of the reasons for targeting George. In a community of farmers and miners such as Great Wyrley, George's education and gentlemanly status were also poised to rankle British attitudes about class. Add ethnic difference and prominent social position to the effect of extreme myopia on his expression and, in Conan Doyle's view, George must have "seem[ed] a very queer man to the eyes of an English village, and therefore to be associated with any queer event."[24]

Further queering George, the prosecutor Mr. Disturnal referred to the "extraordinary arrangement" by which George and his father had slept in the same bedroom for more than seventeen years.[25] Speculation about the reason ran the gamut from Mrs. Edalji's leftover habit of nursing George's sister, to the Rev. and Mrs. Edalji's passionless marriage, to the possibility of child sexual abuse. Clearly incommensurate, the reasons put forward nevertheless exacerbated George's difference and predisposed belief in his guilt. During the three-day trial, more than one witness was reported to have said he "was not a right sort,"[26] and Chairman of the Sessions Reginald Hardy ventured that "the offense had been committed

[21] Michael Risinger, "Boxes in boxes: Julian Barnes, Conan Doyle, Sherlock Holmes and the Edalji case," *International Commentary on Evidence*, 4(2) (2006), 3–4.
[22] Risinger, "Boxes in boxes," 34–5.
[23] Risinger, "Boxes in boxes," 36; note 164 on p. 40. Risinger relies on Gordon Weaver's *Conan Doyle and the Parson's Son* (Cambridge: Vanguard Press, 2006) and Stephen Hines and Steven Womack's *The True Crime Files of Sir Arthur Conan Doyle* (New York: Berkeley Prime Crime, 2001).
[24] Arthur Conan Doyle, "The strange case of George Edalji," *New York Times*, February 2, 1907.
[25] "The Great Wyrley outrages," *Mercury* (Litchfield), October 30, 1903.
[26] "The Great Wyrley outrages," *Mercury* (Litchfield), October 23, 1903.

by some person possessed of a peculiar twist in the brain"; he found it "impossible to arrive at any motive."[27]

The verdict did find a disposition, however, in Edalji's Oriental character, and reinserted the "very queer man" into a stock story that could explain his behavior. The jury recommended mercy because of Edalji's "personal position"; however, Hardy weighed the "disgrace inflicted on the neighbourhood" more heavily and passed a sentence of seven years' penal servitude.[28] *The Mercury* devotes a full section to Edalji's demeanor, which shows how the verdict transforms him from a composed professional into an "Oriental-type." A "slight pallor" came over his face when he first heard the sentence, but then he "seemed to become darker, almost black"; his light suit "emphasized the black face and the staring, wide-opened gleaming eyes"; he "passed into a hypnotic trance" and at last "sighed ... and visibly relaxed into resignation. It was the Oriental's acceptance of fate."[29] Here George's physical transformation is keyed to his new (or rediscovered) character, not merely as a criminal, but as an Oriental whose criminality is un-English.

Yet "character" in the nineteenth century was not to be altered by a single event, and the report suggests rather that it is Edalji's English mask that drains away with the verdict. Finally, *The Mercury* reveals the operative stock story. Picking up where the prosecution left off, it discloses information which had not been introduced at trial – that Edalji had been connected with the "gross" and "coarse" series of anonymous letters – and asks readers to interpret this new information in an old way. Playing up its own objectivity (the revelation about the letters becomes "permissible" only once the conviction is reached), it positions readers to draw on what the discourses of a racialized criminology suggested to have been known all along. George's appearance is claimed to be patently criminal: "Those who closely studied this extraordinary criminal in the dock would have no doubt that he is a degenerate of the worst type" and, further, he is said to have "gained for himself the reputation of being a lover of mystery – another Oriental trait." If George Edalji relaxed into resignation, *The Mercury*'s use of stock stories about "the subtle Eastern mind" made it possible for readers to relax as well by attributing all the anomalies of the Wyrley outrages – starting with the mixed marriage of a Parsee convert and his prestigious position as vicar – to a recognizable type.

Efforts to secure Edalji's release began almost immediately following the conviction, but it was not until May 1907, following the report of a

[27] "Outrages," October 30. [28] "Outrages," October 30. [29] "Outrages," October 30.

Committee of Inquiry, that Home Secretary Herbert Gladstone recommended a free pardon. Space allows only two observations on the process of review and the committee's findings. One is that the committee lamented the absence of a trial report that would have clarified the jury's position, particularly regarding the so-called Greatorex letters of 1903. Drawing on press coverage instead, their report routinely refers to what they "take to be" the jury's conclusion, what the jury "must be taken to have held," or "the finding at which we think the jury arrived" about Edalji's authorship.[30] Recourse to "the best newspaper reports" was part of the usual practice of review, but the committee's near-total reliance on it here not only heightens the legal significance of cultural narratives but also shows how they actually effected Edalji's pardon.[31] A second observation concerns the procedure of returning the committee's assessment to the chairman of the sessions, the judge, and even the investigating police for commentary, which drew special criticism from Conan Doyle.[32] Indeed, it is no wonder that he took his version of Edalji's case directly to the papers, since they had standing within existing practices of review and yet remained outside the potential corruptions of officialdom.

This is not to suggest, of course, that government intervention was inherently flawed or that public opinion was foolproof, however much Conan Doyle pandered to his readers' self-complacency. In his peroration, Conan Doyle praises an unerring, rational-minded public in an effort to create conscientious readers freed from the self-interest of government insiders (in effect, creating a new group to claim solidarity with the outsider Edalji). At the same time, he regrets pitting a public tribunal against the Home Office because the implied criticism might undermine public confidence and "weaken the power of the forces that make for law and order."[33] Yet as a representative body, the House *was* the public and, in the matter of appeals, the only conduit between it, the Home Secretary, and the Crown. Before Conan Doyle concerned himself in the case, the exposé journal *Truth*, edited by Liberal MP Henry Labouchère, had been active in its support of Edalji. In a July 1907 address, F. E. Smith

[30] Arthur Wilson, John Lloyd Wharton, and Albert de Rutzen, "Papers relating to the case of George Edalji" in House of Commons Papers, Great Britain, Parliament. Vol. 67. Cd. 3503 (1907) (London: Eyre and Spottiswoode, 1907), pp. 5, 403.

[31] See: Sir Kenelm Digby, "Note to the Home Office in dealing with criminal petitions," a memorandum on the procedure of the Home Office and the Home Secretary written in regard to the Adolf Beck case. Digby's memo was included as an Appendix to Wilson, Wharton, and Rutzen in "Papers relating to the case of George Edalji," pp. 7–9.

[32] Digby, "Note to the Home Office," 7.

[33] Arthur Conan Doyle, "The strange case of George Edalji," *New York Times*, February 3, 1907.

(Member for Liverpool) mentions the 10,000 signatories who petitioned the Home Secretary to review the case and calls for a new public inquiry.[34] We have seen one of the ways in which the newspapers framed Edalji's story; how did this story look to Conan Doyle?

"The Strange Case of George Edalji" first appeared in the *Daily Telegraph* on January 11 and 12, 1907, with the *New York Times* running a similar spread on February 2 and 3. The opening paragraph of the first instalment in the *Times* proclaims that one look at George sufficed to show both why he was suspected and why he must have been innocent of the crimes. As noted, Conan Doyle makes much of George's physical appearance: the "vacant bulge-eyed staring appearance" that came of his extreme myopia and his dark skin signal the otherness on which the author grounds his defense.[35] While Conan Doyle ends by buttering up his readers, he starts by abjuring "preconceived theory" in favor of an impartial study of the evidence on both sides. If the investigation was neutral, it nevertheless led to his current partisanship. Begging to "tell the strange story from the beginning," he "hope[s] that the effect of my narrative will be to raise such a wave of feeling in this country as will make some public reconsideration of the case inevitable."

And let it be said that Conan Doyle's account is curious in its own right, too. The narrative maintains that differences of race and class influenced the case from the beginning: "Is it not perfectly clear, looking at his strange swarthy face and bulging eyes, that it is not the village ruffian, but rather the unfortunate village scapegoat, who stands before you?" Yet Conan Doyle's criticism of Home Office protocols in the second instalment deploys the same discriminatory tropes used in the *Mercury* reportage. This is no rhetorical lapse: Doyle reverses the relationship between outward appearance and true Englishness. George is visibly othered but thoroughly English, while the face of "British justice" hides "oriental despotism."[36] To illustrate this pattern of behavior more clearly, Doyle cites the recent Adolf Beck case but turns to a yet "more classic example, for in all its details this seems to me to form a kind of squalid Dreyfus case." The outsider targeted, the professional reputation maligned, a campaign for redress led by another literary light, and questions of forgery all support the analogy, but Conan Doyle turns reluctantly to the worst point of comparison: "that in the one case you have a clique

[34] House of Commons Debate, Great Britain, July 18, 1907. Vol 178. cc 994–1017. See also: House of Commons Debate, Great Britain, June 10, 1907. Vol 175. cc 1079–80.

[35] Doyle, "Strange case," February 2.

[36] Doyle, "Strange case," February 3.

of French officials going from excess to excess in order to cover an initial mistake, and that in the other you have the Staffordshire police acting in the way I have described." Conan Doyle's narrative marshals the outrage of a liberal, English lover of justice and defender of the weak, but even here it is possible to see a stock story of honor and chivalry fighting corruption at work. The tale was effective, and by May of that year Edalji had his pardon. But why? How did this outsider's story manage to gain public support and to reach decision-makers within government?

First, the comparison to Dreyfus resonated with Edalji's other supporters. The *New York Times* proclaimed: "Conan Doyle Solves a New Dreyfus Case."[37] F. E. Smith "recalled a time when we involved ourselves in our own virtue and talked of the secret dossier in France."[38] So, one reason it worked is that it was already familiar. Conan Doyle took a story that should have reflected the superiority of British institutions, especially the common law, and used it to indict the corrupt officials who were harming it. Second, Doyle's tone is both chivalric and regretful. He doesn't want to impugn the government, but his belief in law and order require him to demand a public inquiry. The third reason combines the story's familiarity with Conan Doyle's ethos: This is a story of Britain's historical relationship with France, a story of Britain's imperial identity, *and* a true detective story written by the creator of Britain's most famous consulting detective. "The Strange Case of George Edalji" appealed because, as the *New York Times* reported, it "reads like a new adventure of Sherlock Holmes . . . which, being an accurate statement of an actual case loudly calling for rectification, is doubly thrilling."[39] Nevertheless, one has to wonder whether this version came appreciably nearer the story Edalji himself would have told. Sometimes quoted in other reports, he wrote few accounts, the most notable of which appeared in the sporting magazine *Umpire* – a marginal paper for a marginal figure when compared to the high-profile advocacy of Conan Doyle and an international press.[40]

Thus far I have presented Edalji's story as it appeared in the press, in official public debate, and in the literary nonfiction of Doyle's true-crime narrative. I turn now to its further retelling in Julian Barnes's novel

[37] "Conan Doyle solves a new Dreyfus case," *New York Times*, February 2, 1907.
[38] Great Britain, HC Deb 18 July 1907 vol .178 cc. 994–1017.
[39] "Conan Doyle solves," February 2.
[40] Bernard O'Donnell, *Cavalcade of Justice* (New York: MacMillan, 1952). Repeated in Roy Glashan, *The Case of Mr. George Edalji*, Project Gutenberg Australia, July 2012, http://gutenberg.net.au/ebooks12/1202671h.html#pt3

Arthur & George (2005).[41] As an alternative form of legal storytelling, the novel's exploration of Englishness, its structural emphasis on beginnings and endings, and its alternating narrative point of view imaginatively voice George Edalji's story. Providing the outlet that scholars of narrative jurisprudence advocated for in the 1990s as well as the attention to legal emplotment called for by more recent scholars, Barnes's novel reinserts Edalji's case – and others like it – into public consciousness.

"Three-quarters of justice": Plot, Character, and the Self-Believed Story in *Arthur & George*

Julian Barnes described the development of *Arthur & George* in a 2006 interview with Xesús Fraga. Originally planning a short piece, he opted for the novel format instead and considered placing "a contemporary story of racial prejudice" alongside historical fiction.[42] The idea was abandoned, however, on the thinking that only a poor reader would miss the connections. Barnes positions good readers, then, to see the parallels by emphasizing two themes in Doyle's narrative of the case – the importance of race and the comparison to Dreyfus – and by playing with the causal chain of its narrative structure and the perspective through which it is told.

Part three of the novel, "Ending with a Beginning," reimagines Arthur's first meeting with George and emphasizes Doyle's suppositions about race in the 1907 articles. Whether due to teasing by officemates or ridicule on the train, George's racial difference draws commentary throughout the novel, yet his thoughts reveal a persistent conviction of his own Englishness alongside resistance to his father's observation that "others may not always entirely agree" (52).[43] In this first conversation with Arthur, George is surprised to hear that Arthur concurs with his father. Denying that "race prejudice has anything to do with my case" (264), George explains: "I was brought up as an Englishman." Through the omniscient point of view, Arthur is shown to understand this rational approach but also to dismiss the conclusion George draws from it: "It is not his fault if he is unable to see what others can" (267). Instead, Arthur suggests that both he and George are "unofficial Englishmen" (268). Glimmerings of George's self-believed story and the question of his insider/outsider status emerge from

[41] Julian Barnes, *Arthur & George* (London: Jonathan Cape, 2005).

[42] Julian Barnes, "Interview by Xesús Fraga, 10 July 2006" in V. Guignery and R. Roberts (eds.), *Conversations with Julian Barnes* (Jackson: University of Mississippi Press, 2009), pp. 134–47, 135.

[43] Parenthetical page numbers refer to the Vintage edition of Julian Barnes' novel *Arthur & George*.

this exchange. George recognizes that he was made an outsider – convicted and struck from the Roll of Solicitors – by official acts, and can only be reinstated by the same. Thus, he enlists Arthur's help because he "appeared to be part of official England." However, this reclassification has no bearing, as yet, on George's self-understanding. If George misses the irony in Arthur's comment, it nevertheless causes him to reconsider his own position:

> How is he less than a full Englishman? He is one by birth, by citizenship, by education, by religion, by profession. Does Sir Arthur mean that when they took away his freedom and struck him off the Rolls, they also struck him off the Roll of Englishmen? If so, he has no other land. He cannot go back two generations. (268)

Here George confronts the incompatibility of his self-believed story with the official story suggested by the verdict and even with the more sympathetic view of Arthur, who, the narrative voice reveals, harbors still different interpretations he means to exploit.

Arthur's strategy for effecting an official revision is to embarrass the government by "mak[ing] the Edalji Case into as big a stir as they did with Dreyfus over there in France" (299). Following publication of the *Daily Telegraph* articles, George and Arthur meet again and the scene is repeated, this time from George's revisionary perspective. For George, the articles "made him feel like several overlapping people at the same time: a victim seeking redress; a solicitor facing the highest tribunal in the country; and a character in a novel" (366). And of course Barnes's "George," Conan Doyle's "George as Dreyfus," and the historical George Edalji have been all those things. In this sense, Barnes's metafictional layering of stories offers yet another variation on what was already a multiform construction of Edalji's character. The Dreyfus analogy remains particularly telling, however. Barnes comments on the lack of historical attention to Edalji's case, but also on an English response that even at the time was comparatively weaker than French reaction to Dreyfus. Considering the prominence of the comparison, however, Barnes suggests that Edalji's defenders might have known their own efforts were equally as likely as the original trial to end in uncertainty and partial justice.[44] The novel amplifies this point in George's assessment of Arthur's case against Royden Sharp.

Barnes delineates Arthur's increasing frustration with George's skepticism and lack of gratitude for the story that inculpates Sharp. George, like Dreyfus,

[44] Barnes, "Interview with Xesús Fraga," 146.

disappoints by not being "up to the mystique of his own affair" (372). George is similarly dissatisfied with the interview because Sir Arthur's case (with its reliance on circumstantial evidence, contamination of material evidence, and identification of the letter-writer with the horse-ripper) is too much like the Staffordshire Constabulary's case against him (374). George's comparison thus reminds readers that "strong representations" of evidence are interested narratives designed to prosecute or defend. [45] Was justice achieved the first time that Edalji went to court? In the press or the Home Office? In Barnes's novel? "You don't really know who the bad guy was in the end."[46]

Perhaps for that reason, the novel is preoccupied with beginnings and endings. Arthur asks: "How can you make sense of the beginning if you don't know what the ending is?" (239). Animating everything from questions of spiritualism to his methods of fictional narrative and the construction of legal argument, this question dominates Barnes's development of Arthur's worldview. It informs the novel's four-part structure as well, the titles of which – "Beginnings," "Beginning with an Ending," "Ending with a Beginning," "Endings" – are all variants of the theme. Applied to narratives of justice, the predicament becomes clear: We need an ending to make sense of the beginning, but we don't know what the ending is. What we have are prospective, provisional endings that emphasize the way those conclusions are reached. For proponents of legal storytelling, this premium is especially high when story elements are adapted to "standard narrative sequences" whose meaning is predetermined.[47] By juxtaposing several stock stories yet undercutting their narrative sequence, their beginnings and ends, *Arthur & George* destabilizes the power of any one of them to show "what really happened" (336).

Barnes has been criticized for departing from the historical record and thus breaking a tacit compact with the reader.[48] But the value of even realist fiction does not lie in its adherence to common-law rules of evidence, whose exclusionary nature contributes to the silencing of stories. Recalling that the creation of a *nomos* is a collective, aspirational activity in which the present is evaluated in reference to an alternative vision of what may or ought to be, one may conclude that fiction does its best work *because* it has greater latitude. Robert A. Ferguson is instructive on this point.

[45] Alexander Welsh, *Strong Representations: Narrative and Circumstantial Evidence in England* (Baltimore: Johns Hopkins University Press, 1992).

[46] Barnes, "Interview with Xesús Fraga," p. 146.

[47] Brooks, "Narrative transactions," 26.

[48] Risinger, "Boxes in boxes," 4, 31.

Describing a "continuum of publication" through which a trial comes to inhabit public consciousness, he suggests that fiction is the final and perhaps most effective way of working through its meaning.[49] What then does fiction's latitude teach about history, evidence, and legal storytelling? As Lisa Rodensky argued for the nineteenth-century novel, narrative omniscience makes states of mind available to the reader in distinction to the limited access of legal counsel and expert witnesses.[50] Thus, Barnes' recourse to a third-person narrator in *Arthur & George* gives readers an innocent, victimized "George." Michael Risinger suggests that this foreknowledge voids the narrative of its "evidentiary interest."[51] On the contrary, readers have access to George's self-believed story. Read with the aims of narrative jurisprudence in mind, Barnes' depiction of George's hapless innocence puts into relief the ways that features of his story can be emplotted, how evidentiary elements from handwriting and hairs to character and culture could be organized into different narratives. The result is not a relativistic allowance for all perspectives, however: Trials end in decisions, and appeals "judge the frameworks in which the verdict was reached."[52] Rather, the stakes are high because only some self-believed stories are "officially approved, accepted, transformed into *fact*," while others are "officially distrusted, rejected, found to be untrue, or perhaps not heard at all."[53]

Conclusion

Robin West discusses the "moral value" of rights talk and storytelling as modes of dispute resolution and observes that stories are told in order to attribute or deflect responsibility, while rights talk prevails when the goal is to make responsibility appear irrelevant.[54] The legal stories told for and against George Edalji coincided with questions of responsibility, and although much of my discussion has focused on the emplotment of narrative elements, the idea of character – the central figure whose story motivates that plotting – has never been far behind. As George tells Arthur, "I want my name back again" (261) – a name he surrendered to

[49] Robert A. Ferguson, "Untold stories in the law" in P. Brooks and P. Gewirtz (eds.), *Law's Stories: Narrative and Rhetoric in the Law* (Yale: Yale University Press, 1996), p. 84. "A story wrongly refused by the law will return in a republic of laws as cultural narrative and, often enough, as renewed legal event. The law does not get beyond what it has not worked through" (p. 97).

[50] Lisa Rodensky, *The Crime in Mind* (Oxford: Oxford University Press, 2003).

[51] Risinger, "Boxes in boxes," 32.

[52] Peter Brooks, "Narrative transactions," 21.

[53] Scheppele, "Foreword," 2080.

[54] West, *Narrative, Authority, and Law*, pp. 257, 426.

"the court's right to decide a prisoner's name" because, as his solicitor explained, "What you call mispronouncing, I would call ... making you more English" (148).

Nicola Lacey's work on responsibility attribution, although not connected with legal storytelling per se, is especially important in this regard because it emphasizes the allocation (versus the discovery) of responsibility and links it to a resurgence of "character essentialism" in both criminal law philosophy and crime prevention.[55] Comparing a contemporary "crisis of security" to the late nineteenth century, Lacey observes a similar response in the "construction of criminal classifications": "Just as the late nineteenth-century classifications reflected prevailing anxieties and contemporary scientific theories and technologies, so today's categories – the anti-social youth, the sex offender, the migrant, and, above all, the terrorist – are appropriate symbols of otherness relative to contemporary anxieties and technologies."[56]

In Chief Constable Capt. Anson's assessment of the case, George ticks all these boxes.[57] In his interview with Fraga, Barnes comments on the novel's putative connection to the 9/11 attacks: "'I've had *Arthur & George* put to me as being in part post-9/11 because it deals with how people with the wrong skin colour are always suspected. And I said, 'Well, I'm sorry, but I never thought of it. I didn't think it for a moment'."[58] What he did appear to think of, however, was a set of themes that are transhistorical, even as their particular expression is historically contingent. In the early twentieth century, Arthur Conan Doyle saw racial prejudice at the root of a white constabulary's investigation of an Anglo-Indian British citizen. In the early twenty-first century, Julian Barnes considered, then abandoned, setting a contemporary mirror against Edalji's story. If only poor readers could miss the theme's relevance, as he suggested, then good readers can surely see its parallels in modern racism, Islamophobia, and distrust of asylum seekers and immigrants.

[55] Nicola Lacey, "The resurgence of character: responsibility in the context of criminalization" in R. A. Duff and S. Green (eds.), *Philosophical Foundations of Criminal Law* (Oxford: Oxford University Press, 2011), pp. 156, 160.

[56] Lacey, "Resurgence," 173. Lacey's notes provide several examples of contemporary cases relating to detention of suspected terrorists (note 37 on p. 164) and past "reprehensible but non-criminal conduct" (note 41 on p. 166), for example.

[57] Anson makes miscegenation and atavism the source of all George's troubles but quickly moves to physical unattractiveness combined with sexual repression as further explanations of his behavior (p. 341).

[58] Barnes, "Interview with Xesús Fraga," p. 144.

I have focused discussion of the relationship between narrative and law on their world-creating potential and on the stories that help to maintain the normative world. In concluding, I gesture toward the implications of this pairing by thinking of the call for outsiders' stories in the context of both the continuous and the aspirational goals of the *nomos*. That is, by comparing individuated, real experiences to a collective ideal, outsider narratives promise to reframe, or in some cases to authenticate, that vision by making it more inclusive. At the same time, the aspirational nature of the *nomos* suggests that narrators must consent to seeing that visionary ideal in a sense remain only partially realized so that it can always offer an alternative to real life. What then should various legal actors do with the stories they tell and hear? Barnes doesn't say, but his attention in the many cases of George Edalji to the various narrators' motives and assumptions – as well as the historical and contextual pressures framing the ways their arguments could be heard, understood, and acted upon – offers a compelling experiment in the ineluctable "imposition of narrative form on life."[59] Perhaps he would agree with Peter Brooks that "the best we can hope for is a more critical awareness of the storied nature of our thinking, as well as the material presented to our thought."

[59] Brooks, "Narrative transactions," 26.

CHAPTER 4

Law and Literature and History

Christine L. Krueger

Thinking historically about law and literature has become a common, if not obligatory, scholarly practice. Yet historicism was largely absent from the founding of the interdiscipline. For the influential "law and literature movement" in particular, New Critical and neo-Aristotelian paradigms seemed better suited to promoting literature as a humanizing corrective to legal reasoning that they believed to be rule-bound, unempathetic, and unjust. If putting law and literature into conversation required some deft disciplinary negotiations, that was nothing compared to the demands of synthesizing both with history. This chapter tells a story of how this came about: what developments urged historicism on law and literature, what practical, methodological and ideological challenges were overcome, what benefits have accrued from this new multidisciplinary practice, and what problems it presents. In effect, this chapter historicizes how an interdisciplinary practice became a multidisciplinary one.

I begin with the methodological and ideological challenges that complicated the development of law, literature, and history as a multidisciplinary practice, and the imperatives that compelled their synthesis. Two forces that influenced both law and literature likewise transformed the discipline of history: New Historicism and the theorization of historical traumas, principally in Holocaust studies. New Historicism may be the more obvious influence, though not an uncomplicated one. The impact that Holocaust studies has had on transitional justice movements constitutes an equally potent – and even competing – influence on what history means for law and literature. Therefore, no account of the multidiscipline can ignore how justice (law), witness testimony (narrative/literature), and memory (history) have been intertwined in transitional justice processes, most notably South Africa's Truth and Reconciliation Commission.

The second part of the chapter focuses on examples of scholarship that fostered multidisciplinary practices. These texts might engage not only law, literature, and history, but also political theory, psychoanalytic theory, and feminist theory. I look first at the significance of the Holocaust in the work of Richard H. Weisberg, a founder of the law and literature movement. I suggest that Weisberg's insistence that law and literature address the Holocaust necessarily entails historicism. Weisberg's *Failure of the Word* (1984), *Vichy Law and the Holocaust in France* (1996), and 1999 essay reflecting on twenty years of law and literature bookend the other examples I discuss: Barbara Shapiro's *"Beyond Reasonable Doubt" and "Probable Cause": Historical Perspectives on the Anglo-American Law of Evidence* (1991); Alexander Welsh's *Strong Representations: Narrative and Circumstantial Evidence in England* (1992); and Carole Pateman's *The Sexual Contract* (1988). Each historicizes Anglo-American law both synchronically and diachronically, tracing the evolution of epistemological, social, and political issues over the long arc from the early modern period to modernity, attentive to particular historical conditions and drawing evidence from canonical and non-canonical works. The chapter concludes with a discussion of South Africa's Truth and Reconciliation process, drawing on work by various scholars, including Pumla Godobo-Madikizela, a member of the TRC.

My discussion is confined to the English common law tradition, which is likely to be of greatest significance to readers of this volume. Nevertheless, as I will conclude, current uses of law, literature, and history urge us to be more international, as well as interdisciplinary.

Disciplinary Barriers

Literary and legal theorists have resisted historicism for reasons unique to their disciplines and approaches. It might seem obvious that a legal system based on precedents would be historically self-conscious. Instead, the very legitimacy of common law depended upon the fiction that each new legal decision reiterated the truth of prior decisions, albeit in new circumstances. To admit that law evolved over many decisions and revisions of precedent would be to demystify the law's transcendent authority and locate legal power in judges.

Historical jurisprudence first emerged as an influential force in Sir Henry Maine's *Ancient Law* (1861), and later in such works as James Fitzjames Stephen's *History of the Criminal Law of England* (1883) and *The History of English Law Before the Time of Edward I* by Frederic William Maitland and Sir Frederick Pollock (1895). While we may think of historicism as a critical tool to expose entrenched power and denaturalize oppressive social relations, Victorian positivists, notably John Austin, construed historical jurisprudence as reactionary, reasserting tradition against scientific efforts at improving law.

As A. V. Dicey put it in 1905, "Historical research . . . tends to quench the confident enthusiasm necessary for carrying out even the most well approved and the most beneficial among democratic innovations."[1] Historicism, then, was resisted by both traditional common law thinkers and positivist legal reformers.

Nevertheless, in the decades preceding the law and literature movement, historians produced such magisterial works as William S. Holdsworth's thirteen-volume *History of English Law* (1903–66).[2] These may have become indispensable guides for current law and literature scholarship, but they did not necessarily intervene in legal thinking. And while legal theorists may have ignored law *as* history, historians devoted much attention to law and literature *in* history. For example, laws governing censorship attracted the attention of social, political, and literary historians.[3] Copyright law was also addressed as a matter of both legal and literary history. Well before postmodern theories of the author, Benjamin Kaplan, in *An Unhurried View of Copyright* (1967), mooted the idea that conceptions of authorship arose from copyright law.[4] But the domain of law and literature was drawn to exclude a host of robust scholarly relationships with history.

Perhaps the most telling omission of historical literary criticism from the founding of the law and literature movement may be Ian Watt's *Rise of the Novel* (1957).[5] Among the preeminent works of literary criticism in the twentieth century, Watt's study argued that realist fiction succeeded in a

[1] A. V. Dicey, *Lectures on the Relation between Law and Public Opinion in England* (London: Macmillan, 1962 [1905]), p. 461.

[2] See also Leon Radzinowicz, *History of English Criminal Law and Its Administration from 1750*, 3 vols. (London: Macmillan, 1948–1968); J. H. Baker, *An Introduction to English Legal History* (London: Butterworths, 1971); John Beattie, *Crime and the Courts in England, 1660–1800* (Princeton: Princeton University Press, 1986).

[3] In such studies as Charles Gillet's *Burned Books: Neglected Chapters in British History and Literature* (New York: Columbia University Press, 1932); F. S. Siebert's *Freedom of the Press in England, 1476–1776* (Urbana: University of Illinois Press, 1952); Donald Thomas's *A Long Time Burning: The History of Literary Censorship in England* (New York: Praeger Publishers, 1969) and Leona Rostenberg's *The Minority Press and the English Crown: A Study in Repression, 1558–1625* (Nieuwkoop: B. De Graaf, 1971).

[4] In *Copyright in Historical Perspective*, Lyman Ray Patterson, a lawyer, produced what remains a definitive and comprehensive account of how copyright shaped British literature from the Anglo-Saxon period to the nineteenth century. See Lyman Ray Patterson, *Copyright in Historical Perspective* (Nashville: Vanderbilt University Press, 1968).

[5] Ian Watt, *The Rise of the Novel: Studies in Defoe, Richardson and Fielding* (Berkeley: University of California Press, 1957).

new literary marketplace by addressing readers as jurors, presenting them with evidence through plot and character, and asking them to render judgment based on the facts put before them. Though early advocates of the literary imagination in legal reasoning relied heavily on novels for their evidence, it was not Watt's historicized account of the genre that underlay their arguments. Historicism challenged claims for literature as the instantiation of stable meanings and transhistorical values. The significance of *Rise of the Novel* for law and literature would eventually be recognized in Welsh's *Strong Representations.*

New Criticism, which banished historical scholarship from literary interpretation, was favored by early law and literature advocates. Robert Weisberg and Guyora Binder locate New Criticism at the head of a line of practices, from reader-response through structuralism to hermeneutics, which connected law and literature via their formal features.[6] New Criticism endowed the aesthetic qualities of literary forms with ethical and philosophical significance. But it would not survive challenges from postmodernism and cultural criticism.

New Historicism, which brought postmodern theories to the interpretation of history, inspired literary critics to historicize law and literature topics. Michel Foucault's *Madness and Civilization: A History of Insanity in the Age of Reason* (1964) and *Discipline and Punish: The Birth of the Prison* (1975) influenced scholarship on the legal persecution of deviance and provided the Panopticon as a compelling metaphor for the rise of a surveillance state. Early examples of New Historicist literary critics' engagement with legal themes include D. A. Miller's *The Novel and the Police* (1986), John B. Bender's *Imagining the Penitentiary: Fiction and the Architecture of the Mind in Eighteenth-Century England* (1987), and Marie–Christine Leps's *Apprehending the Criminal: The Production of Deviance in Nineteenth-Century Discourses* (1992). What is more, some traditional topics in the history of literature and law were revisited under the auspices of New Historicism. Citing global threats to freedom of speech in 1984, Annabel Patterson, in *Censorship and Interpretation: The Conditions of Writing and Reading in Early Modern England*, revisited early modern censorship in terms of poststructuralist theories of the lyric.[7] Mark Rose, in *Authors and Owners: The Invention of Copyright* (1993),

[6] Robert Weisberg and Guyora Binder (eds.), *Literary Criticisms of Law* (Princeton: Princeton University Press, 2000), pp. 115–25.

[7] Annabel Patterson, *Censorship and Interpretation: The Conditions of Writing and Reading in Early Modern* (Madison: University of Wisconsin Press, 1984), pp. 124–25.

credited Roland Barthes and Foucault with having "stimulated" reconsiderations of the legal constructions of authorship.[8]

Still, while New Historicism brought literary critics into the field of law and literature, it often complicated exchanges with both historians and lawyers. New Historicism debunked literature as a repository of transcendent values. Of what use could this version of literature be to legal thinkers who looked to literature to provide ethical meaning for legal decision-making? Conversely, New Historicist literary critics often failed to do justice to legal history. Viewing history through the lens of Foucault or Lacan tended to reveal the same pictures of power and repression, of disciplinary discourses and the "law of the father," regardless of historical period or nation. Historians influenced by postmodernism might connect with literary criticism attentive to the material conditions of literary production. How New Historicist literary critics represented legal history, however, could strain credulity. And those literary scholars who undertook to refine New Historicist accounts of legal history encountered considerable practical and methodological obstacles. Legal documents were not preserved and organized in such a way as to facilitate historical – much less literary – research. Beyond the problem of access, interpretation of legal documents required expertise in case law, trial procedures, and legal terminology. It would be some time before literary critics succeeded in bringing to historical legal documents the interpretive tools of literary analysis.

Of course, these disciplinary negotiations were taking place in larger historical contexts, which conjoined law, literature, and history. The Holocaust raised devastating anxieties about representation – aesthetic, legal, and historical. Theodor Adorno's declaration in 1951 that "writing poetry after Auschwitz is barbaric" crystallized how literature and the aesthetic could not escape the traumatic history of injustice. The Nuremberg trials had presented an unprecedented spectacle of legal procedure as some remedy for crimes against humanity. They also focused attention on the forensic probity of testimony and documentary evidence of genocide. Documentary records of these and other war crimes trials strained conventional historical explanations and invited psychoanalytic and anthropological interpretations. Hannah Arendt's *Eichmann in Jerusalem: A Report on the Banality of Evil* (1963) is likely the best-known and most controversial example of debates over the meaning of justice in war crimes trials.

[8] Mark Rose, *Authors and Owners: The Invention of Copyright* (Massachusetts: Harvard University Press, 1993), p. 1.

Holocaust testimony, it was determined, required new disciplinary collaborations, and projects commenced to collect videotaped interviews of survivors. These efforts could confer historical, psychological, and ethical meaning on testimony, operating not from traditional legal conceptions of evidence, but rather from literary and psychoanalytic principles. For example, the Video Archive of Holocaust Survivors' Testimonies at Yale (now the Fortunoff Video Archive) was founded in the early 1980s by Laurel Fox Vlock, Geoffrey H. Hartman, and Dori Laub, MD. Fox Vlock was a documentary film maker and reporter. Hartman was a leading exponent of deconstruction and influential critic of Romantic poetry and Laub is a psychiatrist. This multidisciplinary endeavor would preserve a historical record of Holocaust survivors, informed by an understanding of testimony that differed fundamentally from its status in legal contexts. In *Testimony: Crises of Witnessing in Literature, Psychoanalysis and History*, Laub and his coauthor, the literary theorist Shoshana Felman, describe the listeners (interviewers of survivors) in these terms: "They have to learn . . . how to bond with the narrator in a common struggle to release the testimony which, in spite of inhibitions on both sides, will allow the telling of the trauma to proceed and to reach its testimonial resolution."[9] This archive, along with other Holocaust archives around the world, established a paradigm for documenting genocide through first-person narratives. The archives also had a profound effect on how history should be done.

This is evident in the "Historians' Debate" of 1986–9 in Germany. The prospect of Germany's integration into the West after reunification posed the question: How would Germany's national identity continue to be defined by the Holocaust? As Dominick La Capra notes, the debate raised two broader questions: "whether one could neatly separate between arenas or spheres in modern life (the professional and the public spheres, for example) and whether one could define history in purely professional, objective, third-person terms under the aegis of a structurally differentiated or even autonomized paradigm of research."[10] The historian Ernst Nolte asserted that Germany should no longer be identified with Hitler's "Final Solution"; significantly, the leading rebuttal came from the political philosopher Jürgen Habermas.[11]

9 Shoshana Felman and Dory Laub (eds.), *Testimony: Crises of Witnessing in Literature, Psychoanalysis and History* (London: Taylor and Francis, 1992), p. xvii.

10 Dominick La Capra, *History and Memory after Auschwitz* (Ithaca: Cornell University Press, 1998), p. 67.

11 For a discussion of the "Historians' Debate" in Holocaust studies, see La Capra, *History and Memory*, pp. 49–68.

Habermas, Adorno, and Arendt were among the philosophers and political theorists who called on historians to transform their methodologies to address the Holocaust and historical trauma. La Capra, Hartman, and Felman were among the literary critics who exerted similar pressure. The common theme was that not only understanding, but also justice, required more capacious and multidisciplinary methods of interpretation. Their claims had implications for law, as well. Richard Weisberg's influential contributions to our interdiscipline reveal how the legacy of the Holocaust engaged law and literature with history, in a manner distinct from New Historicism.

Lest Law and Literature Forget: Richard H. Weisberg and History

In his groundbreaking books *The Failure of the Word: The Protagonist as Lawyer in Modern Fiction* (1984) and *Poethics: And Other Strategies of Law and Literature* (1996), Weisberg had objected to postmodern theories for their axiomatic indeterminism. Frequently he turned to Holocaust history to demonstrate that not merely theory but also justice was at stake. For example, citing Stanley Fish's *Is There a Text in This Class?*, Weisberg writes that "[Fish's] powerful endorsement of the view that professional norms cannot exist apart from the practices of the community allegedly bound by those norms must eventually run up against holocaustic barriers."[12] For Weisberg,

> the lesson of Vichy [France] is that professional communities *cannot* accept theories denying the objective existence of texts. They must resist such theories, yet fight to understand what is meant by textuality as something apart from any reader or group of readers, and then substantively learn to evaluate the motives and subjective biases from which all texts are generated ... [Vichy lawyers'] zeal in interpreting [Nazi] legislation, unconstrained by traditional (textual) French notions of egalitarianism and personal freedom, exemplifies the risks to professional communities of theories privileging situation over standards.[13]

Weisberg declared in *Vichy Law and the Holocaust in France* (1996) that "Selective forgetfulness has no place in the post-Holocaust world."[14] Drawing upon archives of historical legal documents, historical scholarship, and postmodern theories, Weisberg aimed to debunk the prevailing

[12] Richard H. Weisberg, *Vichy Law and the Holocaust in France* (London and New York: Routledge, 1996), p. 173.

[13] Weisberg, *Vichy Law*, p. 175.

[14] Weisberg, *Vichy Law*, p. 3.

myth that all French were part of the resistance. And he brought to bear the very aims for legal education that he had been espousing through the law and literature movement. In speculating on why the French legal profession collaborated in Nazi terror, he notes habits shared by lawyers of the United States, United Kingdom, Canada, and Australia, *viz.*, "*an ingrained approach to the reading of legal texts*" [original italics] that enabled a select group of "others" to be excluded from legal protection. "Unless legal education changes – in part because it has learned from these events – liberal constitutional cultures must turn to the other side of the coin, and they must constantly insist on *less flexible* readings of the legal system's egalitarian stories."[15] Weisberg thereby added a historical perspective to the requirements for a legal education that contributes to justice.

In "Literature's Twenty-Year Crossing into the Domain of Law: Continuing Trespass or Right by Adverse Possession?" Weisberg defended his approach to law and literature in historicist terms. His rebuttal of postmodernist anti-foundationalism concluded,

> postmodernists have only grudgingly perceived that post-war strategies of language have perhaps been wrongly geared as a response to the referential and idealist "simplicity" of Hitler's rhetoric, geared in fact to avoid at all costs all referential language, all clarity of speech, all quests for meaning and even law. Now, with new work revealing that the Holocaust emerged at least as much from complex, creative and even deconstructive strategies of oppressive speech . . . law and literature has eschewed any unambiguous alliance with an antifoundational program.[16]

Putting his project of law and literature into a historical context, Weisberg asserts, "The events of this tragic century have more than fulfilled the prophetic signs emerging from Melville, Dostoevsky, and Kafka – that the West was ready for a cataclysm, and that the innocent of the world would suffer horribly during the death throes of the dominant culture."[17] This is one form of historicist thinking – looking at literature of the past for explanations of the present and ethical principles for law's future. "Our goal, so far unreached," Weisberg concludes, "is justice."

Weisberg represents a major line of thought about history in the field of law and literature. Significantly, though they share ethical concerns, this strand stands apart theoretically from LaCapra's and Felman's approaches

[15] Weisberg, *Vichy Law*, p. 4.
[16] Richard H. Weisberg, "Literature's twenty-year crossing into the domain of law: continuing trespass or right by adverse possession?" in Michael Freeman and Andrew Lewis (eds.), *Current Legal Issues: Literature and Law* (Oxford: Oxford University Press, 1999), vol. 2, pp. 55–56.
[17] Weisberg, "Literature's twenty-year crossing," p. 60.

to historical trauma. Weisberg may share more with Habermas, who similarly reads the past to discern new social formations for attaining justice in the present. Trauma studies may share methodologies with New Historicism, but the latter neither confines itself to examples of historical trauma nor brings the same ethical commitments to its subject matter. New Historicists may take up law and literature topics with skepticism about power and the disciplining effects of discourses, but often their work makes no presentist claims about history. Increasingly, they draw upon the materials of traditional empiricist historical scholarship of law and literature. As I suggested at the outset, then, a host of ethical and methodological commitments have arisen since the founding of the law and literature movement that have brought historians, legal scholars, literary critics, and others into conversation to practice multidisciplinary methods of interpretation. Significantly, multidisciplinary scholarship, such as that of Shapiro, Welsh, and Pateman, contributes a more robust defense of Weisberg's aims for law and literature.

A History of Truth across the Disciplines: Barbara Shapiro's *"Beyond Reasonable Doubt" and "Probable Cause": Historical Perspectives on the Anglo-American Law of Evidence*

Barbara Shapiro's multidisciplinary explorations of the history of truth in the early modern period represent a key development for historical approaches to literature and law. In *Probability and Certainty in Seventeenth-Century England: A Study of the Relationships between Natural Science, Religion, History, Law, and Literature* (1983) she demonstrated that law did not constitute an autonomous institution and body of doctrine, but functioned dynamically within a network of discourses in evolving ideas of truth and belief. How legal doctrine and criminal procedure could reveal the workings of that dynamic was the subject of *"Beyond Reasonable Doubt" and "Probable Cause": Historical Perspectives on the Anglo-American Law of Evidence* (1991).

Nothing is more fundamental to legal decision-making than the interconnection between epistemology and justice, or, more baldly, the true and the good. Investigating this relationship as discursively constructed and historically contingent required a reconceptualization of legal decision-making and methodological innovation. To demonstrate how law interacted with – and shaped – the transformation of dominant ideas of what was *probably* true, Shapiro translated across disciplines, examining texts from law, religion, and philosophy from 1500 to 1800. That is, she proceeded synchronically and diachronically. Though Shapiro covers an extensive span of time – actually reaching back to the Middle Ages and suggesting implications for contemporary law – she resists applying a master narrative. She reads with attention to differences among discourses at particular points in history as well as how they change across time.

Moreover, Shapiro draws attention to the problems posed by legal history. "Law is a particularly challenging branch of intellectual history," she reflects, "because, at least in the common-law world, the actors being observed have a particular interest in disguising what the historian seeks to discover."[18] The processes of legal decision-making, she notes, are largely unrecorded. "What we can know about the history of this aspect of the law of evidence is very limited because of the black box of the jury, and of the magistrate, for that matter . . . Almost no historical or even contemporary record exists of what actually goes on in the minds of the actors in the criminal justice system." What judges do say "typically reduces itself to such talismanic formulas as 'beyond reasonable doubt' and 'probable cause.'"[19]

In the absence of direct evidence, then, she models how a multidisciplinary approach reveals "the way in which religious and philosophical notions concerning the nature of truth and the appropriate methods of attaining it affect legal concepts of evidence and proof."[20] From dense and often undigested guides to magistrates and jurors, among other sources, Shapiro identifies developing pressures on conceptions of jury trials and jurors' duties, leading to the juror becoming an evaluator of fact. This new function demanded reliable epistemological guidelines and Shapiro argues that, while legal doctrine was influenced by standards of proof in other disciplines, legal conceptions of probability and certainty exerted a major influence beyond law.

Formalism Has a History: Alexander Welsh's *Strong Representations* (1992)

Strong Representations: Narrative and Circumstantial Evidence in England historicized formalist analysis in the interdiscipline of law and literature. Welsh had addressed Victorian law and literature in *George Eliot and Blackmail* (1985) and *From Copyright to Copperfield: The Identity*

[18] Barbara Shapiro. *"Beyond Reasonable Doubt" and "Probable Cause": Historical Perspectives on the Anglo-American Law of Evidence* (Berkeley: University of California Press, 1991), p. 249.

[19] Shapiro, "Beyond reasonable doubt," p. xii.

[20] Shapiro, "Beyond reasonable doubt," p. xii.

of Dickens (1987). His influential 1990 article, "Burke and Bentham on the Narrative Potential of Circumstantial Evidence," marked a move into the study of probability and its representational forms.[21] *Strong Representations* would take up where Shapiro's *Beyond Reasonable Doubt* left off. Welsh focused on the period 1700–1900, but like Shapiro, he saw the need for new, multidisciplinary investigation into the long arc of epistemological and ethical transformations from the early modern period into modernity. And, like Shapiro, Welsh considered law to be a key force in this dynamic – not an autonomous category of discourse and practice, but one jostling alongside not only literature but theology and science, as well. "The history of narratives founded on circumstantial evidence is multifarious," Welsh wrote, "and neither lawyers nor novelists nor psychologists would have pushed the evidence so far, or forged so many chains, were it not for important precedents in science and natural religion."[22]

The principal differences between Welsh and Shapiro are suggested by his title. For Welsh, evidence and belief arise from multidisciplinary dynamics, but they are constituted through "representations." He investigates the formal narrative qualities of probative circumstantial evidence across disciplines – how they are mutually constitutive and how they evolve over time. For the period he studies, he takes "strong representations" to mean those that

> [O]penly distrust direct testimony, insist on submitting witnesses to the test of corroborating circumstances, and claim to know many things without anyone's having seen them at all. They may be religious or legal or literary representations, as long as no devilish or miraculous interventions are admitted. They are very much of the Enlightenment, representations that mirror without mystery the Pauline evidence of things not seen.[23]

"To make a representation," he explains, "means to subordinate the facts to a conclusion that makes a difference one way or the other."[24] That is, representations of evidence employ narrative devices of selection, emphasis, order, point of view, etc., as a rhetorical strategy regardless of discipline or genre. Interestingly, he locates the origins of this insight connecting literary narrative strategies with the management of legal evidence in Ian Watt's *The Rise of the Novel.* "Watt's implicit comparison

21 Alexander Welsh. "Burke and Bentham on the narrative potential of circumstantial evidence," *New Literary History*, 21 (1989–90), 607–27.

22 Alexander Welsh, *Strong Representations: Narrative and Circumstantial Evidence in England* (Baltimore: Johns Hopkins University Press, 1992), p. 7.

23 Welsh, *Strong Representations*, p. 8.

24 Welsh, *Strong Representations*, p. 9.

between Defoe's or Richardson's realism and Fielding's," Welsh writes, "applies equally well to distinctions between direct and indirect evidence, or between evidentiary facts and facts arranged, in Burke's terms, 'narratively and historically.' In a given trial, each kind of evidence may have its virtues, as the nature of the case of personality of the witnesses will determine. The same is true of the novel."[25]

Welsh brings to his subject a literary historian's appreciation for the conditions of authorship and publication, as well. The explosion of print culture, in Welsh's argument, exerts its own influence on how evidence is evaluated and managed. He attributes the evolution of modern "adjectival law" to treatises on rules of evidence and published law reports, which burgeoned in the late eighteenth century. Such authoritative tomes as *Wigmore on Evidence* should be understood in part as ways of managing proliferating "legal" publications, such as trial accounts (including the Old Bailey Sessions Papers), sensational pamphlets, and legal digests.

Finally, Welsh reads a range of literary genres (fiction, poetry, criticism), as well as extensive professional and popular legal, theological, and scientific materials. This includes a historicized example of law *as* literature: a chapter on the epistemological import, historical contexts, and rhetorical devices of James Fitzjames Stephen's *Introduction to Evidence* (1872). Stephen, "whose authority in English criminal law" Welsh describes as being "as great as Fielding's in the novel," treats circumstantial evidence almost exclusively in murder cases, thereby betraying an anxiety about religious attitudes toward human life in the age of Lyell's geology, something he shares in common with Tennyson's *In Memoriam.*[26] Lyell, Welsh notes, was also a barrister. In sum, *Strong Representations* set a high bar for the multidisciplinary study of the history of evidence.

Telling a Difference Story: Carole Pateman's *The Sexual Contract* (1988)

The Sexual Contract is a leading example of how theories of difference were historicized – a critical element in historicizing law and literature. Difference as the principle by which inequities and subjugation are constituted was, of course, a central concern of much law and literature scholarship. Feminists and critical race theorists, for example, found in law and literature an opportunity to combat present-day legal oppression with literary liberation – at the same time critiquing the interdiscipline for its

[25] Welsh, *Strong Representations*, p. 63.

[26] Welsh, *Strong Representations*, pp. 152; 154–5.

resistance to difference. And though it would seem to have been an obvious point of engagement among law and literature practitioners from various disciplines, questions of difference were – and to some degree remain – confined within disciplinary and theoretical silos. Ahistorical conceptions of law, literature, and difference, though not the sole causes of these disconnects, were major contributors. Treating difference not as an ahistorical absolute but as a historically constructed system of social organization in significant ways enabled – perhaps demanded – multidisciplinary approaches. Significantly, one such breakthrough argument came from a political theorist. Carole Pateman approached law not as an autonomous institution or a transhistorical metaphor, but as one entity in a network of evolving social practices with unjust, ongoing, and remediable consequences.

Pateman historicized difference as a mechanism of political subordination with a sweeping, detailed, and vigorously argued history of social contract theory, demonstrating how it necessarily entailed sexual inequality. Drawing on feminist historians such as Gerda Lerner, Pateman demonstrated that patriarchy was neither a relic from long-gone kinship structures nor an abstraction of postmodern feminist theory; rather, it was an identifiable aspect of the writings of Locke, Rousseau, and other social contract theorists. From its origins in the seventeenth century, social contract theory depended upon an unacknowledged sexual contract – the marriage contract – with the result that women's inferior legal status became a constitutive feature of liberal democracy.

By demonstrating that gender subordination was inherent in the transition from status to contract, Pateman made a radical challenge to received histories of modern political structures since Maine's influential *Ancient Law*. Moreover, she argued that our failure to recognize how social contract theory historically obscured its dependence on the sexual contract prevented us from understanding how women were necessarily disadvantaged in contemporary liberal democracy. If "patriarchy" was no longer a historical dinosaur, relegated to the era of kinship politics, but was instead a vital part of an ongoing historical legacy, then its function in contemporary social and political relationships demanded attention. Pateman extends her own argument to the social and legal status of contemporary sex workers and surrogate mothers.

Pateman's argument may have gone to the heart of legal history, but it met resistance. Nor did law and literature respond immediately to feminist challenges. But in time, the history of difference – gender, race, sexuality – became a major focus of law and literature. Two years after *The Sexual Contract* was published, literary critic Carolyn Heilbrun and law professor Judith Resnik drew attention to the persistent resistance to feminism in the law and literature movement.[27] They argued that law and literature remained "indifferent to the rich infusion of feminist theory in literature departments and to the claims that feminist jurisprudence was making in law."[28] Their work sparked defensive responses, but also encouraged feminist scholars to address the history of women through literature and law. They were joined by critical race theorists similarly objecting to claims that law could be equitably administered if it failed to address racial difference. Many theories contributed to the press for a recognition of difference in law, and they often came from literary theory and appealed to literary texts as a corrective to the historical legacies of legal oppression.[29]

Pateman, Shapiro, Welsh, and Weisberg help us to recognize how lines of inquiry and methods of analysis integrated historical thinking into law and literature. For us, such key concepts as evidence, testimony, agency, and equity all have histories constructed across multiple disciplines. What requires our attention now is how our practices have fostered new legal and political processes that institutionalize historical narration as a response to atrocity and as a means to transition to just, democratic political structures from oppressive, violent, even genocidal, regimes. It may be hard to see what impact historicizing law and literature might have beyond the academy. But the theoretical underpinnings of our multidiscipline are largely those to which advocates of truth and reconciliation processes appeal. That law, literature, and history would become intertwined in transitional justice processes during the same period in which the interdiscipline of law and literature was coming to embrace historical approaches is no mere coincidence. If we engage in historical approaches to law and literature, then we should be aware of how the theories we employ are shaping justice in the present and future.

[27] Carolyn Heilbrun and Judith Resnik, "Convergences: law, literature and feminism," *Yale Law Journal*, 99 (1990), 1913.

[28] Judith Resnik, "Singular and aggregate voices: audiences and authority in law & literature and in law & feminism" in Michael Freeman and Andrew Lewis (eds.), *Current Legal Issues: Literature and Law* (Oxford: Oxford University Press, 1999), vol. 2, p. 688.

[29] See, for example, Susan Sage Heinzelman and Zipporah Wiseman (eds.), *Representing Women: Law, Literature and Feminism* (Durham: Duke University Press, 1994).

Witnessing History/Achieving Justice

Law and literature's engagement with history – and a web of other disciplines – has had profound practical consequences for how we have come to respond to atrocities since the Holocaust. As we have seen, the Holocaust radically challenged assumptions about justice, representation, aesthetics, and history. The urgent demands for justice and reconciliation posed by new acts of mass violence tax our ability to mount meaningful responses. Martha Minow has described contemporary responses to atrocities as:

> lurch[ing] among the rhetorics of law (punishment, compensation, deterrence): history (truth); theology (forgiveness); therapy (healing); art (commemoration and disturbance); and education (learning lessons). None is adequate and yet, by invoking any of these rhetorics, people wager that social responses can alter the emotional experiences of individuals and societies living after mass violence.[30]

Minow makes these remarks as editor of *Breaking the Cycles of Hatred: Memory, Law and Repair*, a collection of essays bringing together scholars from many fields with the hope that their shared insights might yield new practices that disrupt the narrative of violence, trauma, and revenge. Minow herself exemplifies this phenomenon. A leading legal theorist, she has been involved in many human rights projects, including the Independent International Commission on Kosovo and the UN High Commission on Refugees. Significantly, her thinking on post-atrocity justice and healing has been shaped by literary and philosophical theories of history. Responding to her own question – "After mass atrocity, what can and should be faced about the past?" – she cites conflicting answers from Jean Baudrillard, Milan Kundera, the philosopher Hermann Lubbe, and the journalist Tina Rosenberg, among others. How histories of violence are narrated conditions the likelihood of justice and peace in the future. "Living after genocide, mass atrocity, totalitarian terror," Minow writes, "makes remembering and forgetting not just about dealing with the past. The treatment of the past through remembering and forgetting crucially shapes the present and the future of individuals and entire societies."[31]

30 Martha Minow, *Breaking the Cycles of Hatred: Memory, Law and Repair* (Princeton: Princeton University Press, 2002), p. 27.

31 Martha Minow (ed.), *Between Vengeance and Forgiveness: Facing History after Genocide and Mass Violence* (Boston: Beacon Press, 1998), pp. 118–19.

In other words, these traumatic events necessarily conjoin law, literature, and history with real urgency.

Julie Stone Peters, a skeptic of law and literature, cites the interdiscipline as one key source of the testimonial practices that have been institutionalized in transitional justice movements. "What lies behind claims about the value of post-atrocity narrative," she argues,

> are a set of views influenced by ancient Christian traditions of confession and redemption and by modern psychoanalysis, but borrowed also from literary and narrative theory of the past quarter century. These views were promulgated most directly by what became known in the 1980s as the "law and literature movement," with its 1990s offshoot, the "legal storytelling movement" ... These movements entered into dialogue with less narrowly legal and more global sub-disciplines and theoretical movements: Holocaust studies, with its discussion of the nature and limits of the representation of atrocity and the paradoxes of memorial; feminist criticism and critical race theory, with their discussion of the liberatory force of counter-hegemonic narrative; Latin American "testimonio" and trauma studies, with their discussion of witness bearing and the curative power of truth.[32]

But even for this critic of law and literature in the domain of post-atrocity politics, more history – not less – is the answer. Having proffered this genealogy of "truth commissions and other testimonial venues," Peters urges us to "look at the intertwined histories of modern literature and modern rights, histories that are ... inextricably linked from the eighteenth century onward. Understanding these linked histories may help us not only to contextualize contemporary claims about the function of narrative in the representation of human rights abuses, but also to look critically at some of their strongest assumptions."[33]

South Africa's Truth and Reconciliation Commission (TRC) is the best-known example of how this process has led to what Claire Moon has termed the "reconciliation industry."[34] Mark Sanders's analysis of the report of South Africa's TRC succinctly illustrates how law, personal narratives, and history are linked. Whereas the Commission solicited, attended to, and recorded testimony from both victims and perpetrators of apartheid, in its five-volume written report "extracts from testimony are

[32] Julie Stone Peters, "Literature," the "rights of man," and narratives of atrocity: historical backgrounds to the culture of testimony," *Yale Journal of Law and the Humanities*, 17(2) (2003), 255–6.

[33] Peters, "Literature," 254, 256.

[34] Claire Moon, *Narrative Political Reconciliation: South Africa's Truth and Reconciliation Commission* (Maryland and London: Lexington Books, 2008), pp. 2–5.

illustrative, first-person attestations to the veracity of the historical narrative, written in the third person, that encloses them." Sanders reminds us that the report explicitly states that its purpose is not "to write the history of th[e] country." Nevertheless, he argues that "the cumulative effect is of a thorough historical reckoning, albeit one driven by an exposure and cataloguing of human rights violations so relentless that it leaves little space for anything *other* than a history of gross human rights violations."[35]

The TRC brings home to us the real-life impact of our scholarly theories and practices. This is made particularly vivid in the writing of Pumla Godobo-Madikizela. A theorist of transitional justice movements, she brings a complex multidisciplinary perspective to the matrix of identities she inhabits as a black South African woman, a professor of psychology, and a member of the TRC. In *A Human Being Died that Night: A South African Story of Forgiveness* (2003), Godobo-Madikizela reflects on her own subject positions and their competing responses to history. As a member of the TRC, she writes,

> My emotions were becoming increasingly confused, but only in the sense that they represented my multiple identities, the past, and the present: as a child, student and adult growing up under the apartheid regime; as a human being able to feel compassion for the suffering of others; as a member of the Truth and Reconciliation Commission expected to remain levelheaded in my thinking about the past.[36]

Both national and personal healing demand a robust theory of forgiveness, Godobo-Madikizela argues – a narrative that negotiates the ferociously difficult demands of historical trauma and future peace.

First, Godobo-Madikizela acknowledges that the TRC was "essentially a political project, the creation of a political compromise that played out in the public domain." There are limits to what the legal, political, and narrative structures of the TRC could contribute to transitional justice, bypassing the real social and psychological work of processing historical trauma. Godobo-Madikizela presents two options for dealing with historical trauma, both taken from Holocaust theorists – respectively, Hannah Arendt and Emanuel Levinas. She rejects Arendt's argument that the Holocaust transcends human ethics and politics and therefore lies outside

[35] Mark Sanders, *Ambiguities of Witnessing: Law and Literature in the Time of a Truth Commission* (Stanford: Stanford University Press, 2007), p. 151 and citing the South African *Truth Commission Report*, vol. 5, p. 257.

[36] Pumla Godobo-Madikizela, *A Human Being Died that Night: A South African Story of Forgiveness* (Boston: Mariner Books, 2003), pp. 33–4.

the domains of forgiveness or justice, remarking that "One of the problems with these views, which have come to represent conventional wisdom on the subject of forgiveness in some circles, is that they are no longer realistic in light of actual practice in post-conflict situations."[37] Instead, Godobo-Madikizela seeks to break the cycle of violence and turns to Levinas, as well as Julia Kristeva and Jacques Derrida, to theorize "restorative justice" and reconciliation. She poses the question: "is Levinas's ethics compatible with the political realm?"[38] Her answer begins with literature, specifically Julia Kristeva's analysis of *Crime and Punishment*, in which Kristeva counters "Arendt's conceptualization of the term [forgiveness], [and] contends that forgiveness is a means to initiate a new beginning."[39] Next she turns to Derrida's reflections on history and forgiveness. Derrida, she writes, "expands the boundaries of the forgivable beyond Hannah Arendt's ethical limits, revealing its complexity. Placing it in an historical context he resists giving the absolute 'final word' on what can or cannot be forgiven."[40]

What does this tell us about the state of law, literature, and history as a multidiscipline? First, it tells us that these three disciplines – and their practitioners – have been inextricably connected in current events. What was once a matter of overcoming academic silos, or methodological disputes, is now a practical reality with wide impact. Julie Stone Peters once opined that literary scholars were drawn to legal topics to compensate for their irrelevance in human affairs. As her own more recent work indicates, history has thrust literature into politics with a vengeance. Second, our practice takes place in a context that is not only more interdisciplinary, but also international. My focus here has been on the English common law tradition, which partly encompasses South Africa. But our multidiscipline will increasingly be compelled to be comparative and take into account distinctive traditions of law, literature, and history. Finally, that our most urgent agenda should be to historicize law and literature more fully, whatever our area of research. As I have argued elsewhere, such scholarship "demonstrates the historically contingent political impact of legal and literary texts for outsider advocacy." Historical approaches to law and literature, regardless of the particular subject matter, caution against claims that any discourse possesses reliably salutary qualities. What is demonstrated by the scholarship I have discussed here is that we live with the legacy of modernity, "inherited

[37] Godobo-Madikizela, *A Human*, p. 47.
[38] Godobo-Madikizela, *A Human*, p. 59.
[39] Godobo-Madikizela, *A Human*, p. 50.
[40] Godobo-Madikizela, *A Human*, p. 46.

conceptions of justice [that] have been imagined across a variety of discourses, literature and law each making distinctive contributions and offering salutary mutual critiques."[41]

Finally, historical approaches to law and literature should not merely dissolve differences among disciplinary methodologies. Rather, they should challenge us to become more deeply literate in an array of distinctive disciplines – law, literature, history, theology, philosophy, psychology, politics, economics, science – so that each enhances our critical understanding of the others. As practices of teaching and scholarship, historical approaches to law and literature contribute an informed, sympathetic critique to projects that wisely engage the full range of human discourses to advance the common good.

41 Christine L. Krueger, *Reading for the Law: British Literary History and Gender Advocacy* (Charlottesville: The University of Virginia Press, 2010), pp. 2, 13.

PART II

Development

CHAPTER 5

Law and Literature in the Ancient World: The Case of Phryne

Ioannis Ziogas

The Attic orator Hyperides (390–322 BCE) famously defended the courtesan Phryne in a trial of impiety. The story goes that when Hyperides felt that his rhetorical skills were failing him and his client was about to be convicted, he made a move that saved Phryne's life: He disrobed her, exposing her lovely breasts to the eyes of the stunned jurors who subsequently acquitted her.[1] While Hyperides' speech *In Defense of Phryne* was considered a masterpiece by Greek and Roman thinkers, it is the display of Phryne's breasts that decides the case, not the orator's eloquence. The case of Phryne gave rise to discussions about the nature of forensic oratory and became a stock argument against defining rhetoric as the art of persuasion exclusively through speech.[2] Quintilian, who gives Phryne the agency of revealing her body, says that "people believe that Phryne was acquitted not by Hyperides' speech, however admirable it was, but at the sight of her stunning body, which she bared by drawing aside her tunic."[3] In a fictional collection of letters between famous courtesans and their lovers, Alciphron (300 CE) challenges the ineffectuality of Hyperides' rhetoric through the words of the courtesan Bacchis.[4] In her letter to Phryne, Bacchis urges her not to believe people when they say that Hyperides would have lost the case had he not torn her robes to expose her breasts to the jurors. It was his pleading (*synegoria*), Bacchis adds, that made his timely gesture persuasive. The spectacle that made the jurors speechless would have been meaningless without Hyperides' address and his gesture is thus not a testament to the failure of words but part of his carefully calculated rhetoric.

Ancient critics are interested in analyzing the persuasive force of Phryne's body in the context of forensic oratory, a line of inquiry that I find

[1] The main sources of the story are Athenaeus, *The Learned Banqueters* 13.590d–e and Plutarch, *Lives of Ten Orators* 849d–e.
[2] See Craig Cooper, "Hyperides and the trial of Phryne," *Phoenix*, 49 (1995), 317–18.
[3] Quintilian, *Institutio Oratoria* 2.15.9.
[4] Alciphron, *Epistle* 4.4.

particularly intriguing, but which has been by and large abandoned in recent criticism in classics. Classical scholarship has mostly focused on the rather fruitless issue of the story's historicity; the fact that there was a trial of Phryne and that Hyperides defended her seems to be uncontroversial, but whether he exposed her breasts in order to win the case is disputed.[5] While I do not mean to dismiss scholarship that aims to tell historical facts from fictions, the case of Phryne is a good example for testing the methodologies of historical positivism in the field of legal narratives. The main difficulty in establishing the facts of the trial of Phryne consists in the fundamental interaction between courtroom proceedings and literary genres. Tragic performances, for instance, are obsessed with the issue of justice and are deeply influenced by legal procedures.[6] The word *agon* ("contest"), which can mean "action at law" or "trial," becomes an integral part of comic and tragic performances, which often include a debate (*agon*) between dramatic characters. The stage turns into a courtroom and the spectators play the role of jurors.

In the case of Phryne, Hyperides resembles a playwright who stages a tragedy, casting his client as the main heroine. In an anonymous rhetorical work, the author says that Hyperides "introduced Phryne dressed in a pitiable garb, beating her naked breast and tearing her tunic, and the jurors saw and acquitted her out of pity."[7] Following Hyperides' instructions, Phryne dons the costume of a tragic victim and performs in the courtroom, begging for her life.[8] By arousing pity, Phryne succeeds in winning over the judges, simultaneously acting as a defendant and a tragic heroine. The introduction of women lamenting in court was common practice in Athens and aimed at moving the judges to take pity on the defendant, but pity (*eleos*) was also the main emotion that a successful tragedy had to arouse in the spectators.[9] As we shall see below, the jurors' reaction to the revelation of Phryne's breasts is a combination of pity and fear toward

[5] See Cooper, "Hyperides and the trial of Phryne"; Esther Eidinow, *Envy, Poison, and Death: Women on Trial in Classical Athens* (Oxford: Oxford University Press, 2016), pp. 23–30.

[6] On interactions between acting on the tragic stage and the performance of litigants in the courtroom, see Craig Cooper, "Demosthenes, Actor on the Political and Forensic Stage" in C. Mackie (ed.), *Oral Performance and Its Context* (Leiden: Brill, 2004), pp. 145–61; Edith Hall, *The Theatrical Cast of Athens: Interactions between Ancient Greek Drama and Society* (Oxford: Oxford University Press, 2006), pp. 353–92. On litigants' conscious efforts to distinguish their forensic performance from that of tragic actors, see Edward Harris, "How to 'act' in an Athenian court: emotions and forensic performance" in S. Papaioannou, A. Serafim, and B. de Vela (eds.), *The Theatre of Justice: Aspects of Performance in Creco-Roman Oratory and Rhetoric* (Leiden: Brill, 2017), pp. 223–42.

[7] C. Walz, *Rhetores Graeci* (Stuttgart, 1832–6), 7.335.

[8] Cooper, "Hyperides and the trial of Phryne," 312–13.

[9] See Aristotle, *Poetics* 1149b21.

the divine, an emotive response that is key in Aristotle's definition of tragedy. The dramatic and rhetorical devices of tragic poets and forensic orators converge.[10]

Courtroom proceedings are a major influence on ancient drama, but the tragic genre in turn had a lasting impact on the dramatic aspect of public trials. The case of Phryne does not simply evoke tragic women in general, but brings to life the myths of Clytemnestra and Helen in particular. These "mythical" aspects of the trial of Phryne are not evidence that the story of her naked body is a fiction. Quite the contrary, they suggest the power of mythological narratives to define the proceedings and outcome of a trial. The exposure of Phryne's breasts for the sake of arousing pity is a foil for one of the most famous scenes from Aeschylus' *Libation Bearers*, in which, as Orestes readies his sword to kill his mother Clytemnestra, she bares her breast in an appeal to move him to pity and thus save her life:

> Stop, my son, and have respect, my child, for this breast, at which you many times drowsed while suckling the nourishing milk with your gums.[11]

Clytemnestra's display of her breast as evidence of maternity has a powerful effect on Orestes, who subsequently hesitates to kill his mother and asks his friend Pylades for advice. Pylades breaks his silence and reminds Orestes that Apollo's oracles and sworn pledges oblige him to kill Clytemnestra. Orestes' revenge turns into a miniature trial. Clytemnestra is the defendant who attempts to arouse pity by baring her breast, Pylades the prosecutor who claims that she should be sentenced to death according to divine law, and Orestes the judge who is finally convinced by Pylades. "I judge you the winner, you have advised me well" are Orestes' words to his friend. Pylades wins the case and Clytemnestra loses her life.[12]

Despite her maternal pose, there is latent eroticism in Clytemnestra's gesture, especially if we take into account that the baring of her breast evokes and contrasts with the way in which her sister Helen escaped from certain death at the hands of her husband Menelaus. After the sack of Troy, Menelaus takes his unfaithful wife back and is about to kill her but drops his sword at the sight of her lovely breast. This version of the myth is attested in Aristophanes' *Lysistrata* and Euripides' *Andromache*

[10] See Kostas Apostolakis, "Pitiable dramas on the podium of the Athenian law courts" in S. Papaioannou, A. Serafim, and B. de Vela (eds.), *The Theatre of Justice: Aspects of Performance in Creco-Roman Oratory and Rhetoric* (Leiden: Brill, 2017), pp. 133–56.

[11] Alan Sommerstein (trans.), *Aeschylus, Oresteia: Agamemnon, Libation-Bearers, Eumenides, Aeschylus* (Massachusetts: Harvard University Press, 2009), pp. 896–8.

[12] Sommerstein (trans.), *Aeschylus: Oresteia*, p. 903.

(both fifth century CE), but it should be older. The ancient scholia on the *Lysistrata* and the *Andromache* attribute this tradition to the lyric poet Ibycus and Lesches' *Little Iliad.*[13] Representations of this myth were also popular in the visual arts.[14] Both Euripides and Aristophanes stress the sex appeal of Helen's breasts, which literally disarm Menelaus. In *Lysistrata*, the eponymous heroine urges the women to arouse their husbands by wearing see-through robes, only to deny them sexual satisfaction. The Spartan Lampito then adds a mythological example from her hometown: "Like Menelaus! As soon as he peeked at bare Helen's melons, he threw his sword away, I reckon."[15] In Euripides' *Andromache*, Peleus berates Menelaus for his inability to punish his unfaithful wife: "And when you had taken Troy . . . you did not kill your wife when you had her in your power, but when you saw her breasts, you threw away your sword and kissed the traitorous bitch and fawned on her, proving no match, coward that you are, for Aphrodite's power."[16] The physical allure of Helen's body incapacitates Menelaus' judgment and saves her life.

This version of the myth is in play in the debate between Hecuba and Helen in Euripides' *The Trojan Women.*[17] As is often the case in Euripides, the stage turns into a courtroom in the dramatic culmination of the tragedy. Helen is the defendant, Hecuba the prosecutor, and Menelaus the judge. Helen's speech is in line with the tradition of the sophist Gorgias' defense of Helen in his *Encomium of Helen.*[18] Yet, despite Helen's powerful rhetoric, Hecuba successfully refutes her arguments and wins the case. But her forensic victory is not meant to last. Even though Menelaus appears convinced that Helen is guilty and convicts her to be stoned to death,[19] the Athenian audience knew that the myth of Helen, despite its flexibility and variety, would barely allow a version in which Menelaus

[13] See Malcolm Davies, *Epicorum Graecorum Fragmenta* (Göttingen: Vandenhoeck & Ruprecht, 1988), p. 58; Malcolm Davies, *Poetarum Melicorum Fragmenta I: Alcman, Stesichorus, Ibycus* (Oxford: Oxford University Press, 1991), p. 289.

[14] See Lilly Kahil, "Hélène" in *Lexicon Iconographicum Mythologiae Classicae* 4 (1988), pp. 538–50.

[15] Jeffrey Henderson (trans.), *Aristophanes. Birds. Lysistrata. Women at the Thesmophoria* (Massachusetts: Harvard University Press, 2000), pp. 155–6.

[16] David Kovacs (trans.), *Euripides: Children of Heracles. Hippolytus. Andromache. Hecuba Euripides* (Massachusetts: Harvard University Press, 1995), pp. 627–31.

[17] David Kovacs (trans.), *Euripides, Trojan Women. Iphigenia among the Taurians. Ion* (Massachusetts: Harvard University Press, 1999), pp. 903–1059.

[18] Helen's speech in the *Troades* presents a world ordered by the interacting forces of desire (*eros*), violence (*bia*), and persuasion (*peitho*), precisely Gorgias' triangulation on the forces at work on Helen in the *Encomium.* See Nancy Worman, "The body as argument: Helen in four Greek texts," *Classical Antiquity*, 16 (1997), 181.

[19] David Kovacs (trans.), *Euripides, Trojan Women. Iphigenia among the Taurians. Ion* (Massachusetts: Harvard University Press, 1999), pp. 1036–41.

sentences his wife to death and has her executed. Both the trial and the conviction of Helen in *The Trojan Women* suppress and evoke the mythological version of the story according to which Helen's stunning beauty saved her life, a version attested in Euripides' *Andromache.* When Hecuba warns Menelaus: "I approve your intention, Menelaus, to kill your wife. But avoid looking at her lest she capture you with desire,"[20] the audience is fully aware that the Greek hero will be incapable of resisting Helen's beauty. Rhetoric, however masterful, cannot acquit Helen, in contrast with her irresistible body, which saves her from certain death at the hands of her husband. As Nancy Worman argued, in *The Trojan Women* Helen's speech is anchored on the demonstrative force of her body, which she uses as a magnet in a charged visual field in order to attract and thus convince her angry husband.[21] Helen's strategy draws on Gorgias' *Encomium of Helen,* a key work for the interdependence of visual impact and verbal persuasion in the case of Helen.

The tension and interaction between artful rhetoric and irresistible beauty lie at the heart of Euripides' trial of Helen as well as ancient discussions about the trial of Phryne. Both cases put the female body up against *logos* ("speech" and "reason") and revolve around fundamental questions of justice: the balance between subjective emotions and objective judgment and the contrast between human and divine law. In *The Trojan Women,* Helen begs Menelaus by his knees to spare her life.[22] The combination of a powerful speech with an emotional appeal to pity anticipates the drama of Phryne. Hyperides' gesture of disrobing his client, which presents a highly sensual spectacle of supplication before the jurors, should thus be interpreted against the background of the judgment of Helen.[23] The courtesan's naked body is powerful because it represents the locus and corpus of signification; her nudity becomes meaningful thanks to the mythological intertexts that are inscribed in the act of her disrobing.[24] Phryne is the embodiment and reenactment of a compelling mythological precedent that has the power to cross the boundary between the stage and the courtroom, literature and law.

[20] Kovacs (trans.), *Euripides: Trojan Women,* pp. 890–1.

[21] Worman, "The body as argument," 187–95.

[22] Kovacs (trans.), *Euripides: Trojan Women,* pp. 1042–3.

[23] Eroticism and supplication coexist already in *Iliad* 1, in the scene of Thetis' supplication to Zeus. The audience of the *Iliad* knew that Zeus was in love with Thetis.

[24] For the body as the essential site in which meaning is construed, see Roland Barthes, *S/Z* (trans. R. Miller) (London: Cape, 1974), pp. 214–16 and Roland Barthes, *The Pleasure of the Text* (trans. R. Miller) (New York: Hill and Wang, 1975). On Helen's body as argument, see Worman, "The body as argument."

The exposed breast of Phryne in a masterfully directed performance seemingly satisfies the male jurors' desire for unmediated truth and simultaneously projects the illusory yet irresistible images of Helen's divine body. The jurors are drawn into a mythological narrative with a predetermined outcome and inevitably spare Phryne's life.

The passages from Euripides' *Andromache* and Aristophanes' *Lysistrata* discussed above reveal male anxieties about controlling female sexuality. Peleus brings up the myth of Menelaus' failure to punish Helen in order to challenge his masculinity. Aphrodite, the personification of erotic desire, renders Menelaus impotent and incapable of carrying out justice. Lampito's reference to the myth in *Lysistrata* is particularly successful. Just as Helen disarmed Menelaus by revealing her alluring breasts, the women in the play aim at putting an end to war by teasing their men during a sex strike. Myth thus becomes the paradigm for real action in the play. Aristophanes' comedy deals with male anxieties about the impossibility of controlling the elusive and potentially sovereign power of female sexuality.

This mysterious source of desire for the female body is ultimately traced in the sphere of the divine. This is a crucial aspect for understanding the judgment of Helen and the trial of Phryne. Menelaus' wife cannot be tried and put to death because her goddesslike figure sets her above human law. Hyperides' evocation of Helen's special status aims at establishing a similar state of exception for Phryne. The issue of Helen's guilt looms large already in the *Iliad*. In her public appearance in *Iliad* 3, her divine body is the catalyst to men's judgment. Helen appears on the walls of Troy in the midst of Trojan elders, King Priam's advisors, who are described as eloquent men of prudence.[25] Helen presents herself to a kind of High Court of Justice or Supreme Court comprising King Priam and a number of elderly judges. The words of the elders and Priam add to the sense that Helen is on trial. The elders' first words are "No blame,"[26] exonerating the Trojans and the Achaeans for fighting for her instead of Helen for causing the war; it seems that the effect of her dazzling beauty renders the issue of her guilt irrelevant. The elders judge the warriors, not Helen, yet the focus is on her divine body: "Surely there is no blame on Trojans and strong-greaved Achaeans if for long time they suffer hardship for a woman like this one. Terrible is the likeness of her face to immortal goddesses."[27]

[25] Homer, *Iliad* 3.146–53. [26] Homer, *Iliad*, 3.155.

[27] Richmond Lattimore (trans.), *The Iliad of Homer* (Chicago: Programmed Classics, 1951), 3.156–58 (modified).

Fear of the divine sublimates men's anxiety about female beauty. Helen's resemblance to a fearsome goddess can justify the folly of a destructive war. In his turn, Priam starts by saying that in his eyes Helen is not to blame, but the gods.[28] Responsibility is removed from Helen and transferred to the gods; the trial is over and Helen is acquitted. Priam then shifts the focus from the body of Helen to the bodies of the Achaean warriors who are ready to die for her. Helen turns from spectacle to spectator.

The divine nature of Helen's beauty renders any incriminating evidence void, and Hyperides relies on this mythological tradition. The public appearance of Helen in the midst of the Trojan elders, who have not a single word of blame against her once they catch sight of her, adds another intertextual layer to the revelation of Phryne's body. The orator stages a version of Helen's exoneration at the sight of her divine beauty. Like Helen, Phryne occupies a liminal space between earth and heaven. Her flesh, the very mark of her humanity, is evidence of her relation to the divine. The recognition of divinity through the revelation of the female body recalls another scene from *Iliad* 3: Aphrodite is disguised as an old woman, in order to urge Helen to join Paris in the bedroom. But Helen recognizes the goddess once she catches sight of her stunning neck, lovely breasts, and flashing eyes.[29] Similarly, the jurors acknowledge Phryne's divinity once they see her naked breasts. The evocation of heavenly beauty is important in a trial of impiety, the charge against Phryne. Phryne's goddesslike body is strong evidence against the accusation of disrespecting the gods, since it would be absurd to convict a divinely beautiful woman of "ungodliness" (*asebeia*).[30] Thus, Hyperides not only stages a version of the judgment of Helen but also appropriates the myth to serve the particular purposes of Phryne's trial.

Phryne's naked body is the screen upon which images of divine beauty are projected. Helen's encounter with Aphrodite in *Iliad* 3 highlights the close affinities between the heroine and the goddess. In the *Catalog of Women*, an archaic Greek epic attributed to Hesiod, Helen's unparalleled beauty is described with the unique phrase "she who had the beauty of golden Aphrodite,"[31] an epic formula that is indicative of the close connection between Helen and Aphrodite. This comparison stresses the heroine's divinity and is also relevant to the trial of Phryne. Like Helen, Phryne is Aphrodite's double. The very act of disrobing Phryne resembles

[28] Homer, *Iliad*, 3.163–5. [29] Homer, *Iliad* 3.385–98.

[30] On charges of *asebeia*, see Eidinow, *Envy, Poison, and Death*, pp. 48–52.

[31] *Catalog of Women*, fragment 196.5 M-W.

the unveiling of a statue of Aphrodite. Athenaeus attests that, even though she was rarely to be seen nude, once at a public festival Phryne took off her robe, let her hair loose, and entered the sea. At the sight of this spectacle, the sculptor Apelles was inspired to create "Aphrodite Rising from the Sea." Praxiteles, who was in love with her, also used her as the model for his Aphrodite of Knidos, another statue in which the goddess is represented nude.[32] Thus, the effect of Hyperides' gesture is that the jurors visualize artifacts depicting the goddess of love naked and, what is more, statues of Aphrodite for which Phryne was the model. Semenov is on the right track when he argues that the jurors' reaction is explained if we consider that they imagined themselves to be seeing the embodiment of Aphrodite.[33] This is already suggested by Athenaeus, who mentions the statues of Aphrodite for which Phryne was the model. According to Athenaeus, Phryne's disrobing and Hyperides' subsequent lament "caused the jurors to feel a superstitious fear of this priestess and temple-attendant of Aphrodite, and to give in to pity rather than put her to death."[34] The source of the jurors' fear of gods, dismissed as superstitious, is Phryne's religious devotion to the cult of Aphrodite. Hyperides' stratagem is successful because it relies on a number of compelling intertextual and intervisual allusions and illusions. His gesture projects mythological scenes from epics and tragedy as well as visual representations of the naked goddess of love. Phryne's naked body is covered with many layers of texts and images.

The evocation of the statue of a venerable goddess not only raises Phryne's body to the heavenly sphere but also points to her objectification in the eyes of the jurors. Phryne resembles a statue that is molded by the gaze of the male jurors. The genius of Hyperides' gesture consists in simultaneously empowering and debilitating the representatives of the law, in turning Phryne into the object of their desire but also subjecting them to her irresistible beauty. By exposing Phryne's body before the eyes of the jurors, the orator exploits law's desire to possess a body, which recalls the writ of *habeas corpus*.[35] What is brought before the absolute jurisdiction

32 Douglas Olson (trans.), *Athenaeus, The Learned Banqueters, Volume VI* (Massachusetts: Harvard University Press, 2010), 13.590d (modified).

33 Anatol Semenov, "Hepereides und Phryne," *Klio*, 28 (1935), 278–9; Cooper, "Hyperides and the trial of Phryne," 317.

34 Athenaeus, *The Learned Banqueters* 13.590f–591a.

35 See Anselm Haverkamp and Cornelia Vismann, "*Habeas corpus*: the law's desire to have the body" in H. De Vries and S. Weber (eds.), *Violence, Identity, and Self-Determination* (Stanford: Stanford University Press, 1997), pp. 223–35; Desmond Manderson, "Klimt's *Jurisprudence*: sovereign violence and the rule of law," *Oxford Journal of Legal Studies*, 35 (2015), 536.

of a court is not a person or a citizen, but a body – an aspect of the legal proceedings that Hyperides throws into sharper relief by objectifying and sublimating his client through the intervisual references of his gesture to statues of Aphrodite.

Building on Foucault, Agamben comments on the concrete ways in which sovereign power penetrates subjects' very bodies and forms of life.[36] Hyperides acknowledges the court's sovereignty and relies on law's desire to possess a body, exposing the more intimate and invasive practices of courtroom procedures.[37] The jurors' eyes fixed on Phryne's naked breasts represent the unblinking surveillance of the law, whose powerful eye can penetrate the bodies subjected to its command. Phryne's body satisfies law's desire to have access to the bare truth, but the evidence of her nudity is illusory because it is invested with the irresistible narratives and images of Greek myth.

The exposure of a body before the court is an ambiguous power play. As Agamben notes, "*corpus* is a two-faced being, the bearer both of subjection to sovereign power and of individual liberties."[38] Phryne's naked figure gives an interesting twist to Agamben's confluence of bare life and sovereign power. As a defendant and a courtesan, Phryne is both subjected to legal procedures and excluded from the juridical order. Her nudity highlights both her defenselessness before the court and her exemption from it. The courtesan occupies an extralegal position at the very moment of her body's submission to the force of law. The law is simultaneously able to possess Phryne's body and incapable of touching it. When Hyperides stopped talking and bared Phryne's breasts, he acknowledged the limitations of forensic speech, forcing the jurors to decide the case on a level of justice that both included and exceeded legal procedure. By being displayed in the proceedings of a trial, Phryne's divine physique exempts her from human laws of ungodliness. Her divine body is sacred and human law cannot violate it. Her defenseless nudity protects her by exposing law's fundamentally carnal desire. Yet like all desires, law's yearning for bodily possession remains unfulfilled. At the same time, Hyperides acknowledges that a foreign courtesan's desire for exposure and legal recognition – to be seen by the law and thus incorporated in the legal system – is the perverse complement to subjection.[39] Phryne's naked figure activates the

[36] Giorgio Agamben, *Homo Sacer: Sovereign Power and Bare Life* (trans. D. Heller-Roazen) (Stanford: Stanford University Press, 1998), p. 5. See also Agamben, *The Use of Bodies* (trans. A. Kotsko) (Stanford: Stanford University Press, 2015).

[37] My argument is here indebted to Manderson, "Klimt's *Jurisprudence*," 535–536.

[38] Agamben, *Homo Sacer*, p. 125.

[39] Manderson, "Klimt's *Jurisprudence*," 536.

interdependence of desire and subjection. The tables are turned as the jurors are subjected to a woman's irresistible body at the very moment of her submission to the supreme power of the courtroom.

Phryne's body, a double symbol of vulnerability and inviolability, is offered to the representatives of the law to destroy or save, without ever fully possessing it or comprehending the source of its irresistible charm. Granting the jurors full power over the body of the courtesan exposes the limits of the judiciary. The coexistence of the tangible and the immaterial, the concrete and the abstract, reason and desire, human law and divine justice lies at the heart of judicial proceedings and literary texts. The fascinating relationship between the fictions of myth and literature and the facts of real life is an issue that is also a main concern in the rituals of law. Reading a legal case, like reading literature, entails not only telling facts from fiction, but also bridging the divide between the two in an endless search for narrative truth. That is why it is more fruitful to examine the literary and mythological background that informs ancient narratives about the trial of Phryne and the ways in which this background can provide a key to interpreting judicial proceedings, rather than attempting to exclude the influence of drama, stereotypical characterizations, and biographical fictions in order to discover the bare facts of Phryne's trial.

There are precedents for the display of Phryne's body both in literature and in legal cases. Besides the mythological example of Helen, Hyperides' gesture is a foil for the common practice of military men to bare their bodies in a trial in order to expose their wounds and thus move jurors to pity with their heroism.[40] In both cases, the body is submitted to court as evidence and its persuasive effect relies on epic narratives. While the display of a wounded body acts as evidence of courage, patriotism, and masculinity, Phryne's impeccable breasts attest to her divine femininity. Female beauty, like male heroism, acts as a barrier that checks the punitive hand of law. The interplay between the heroic bodies of Homeric heroes and Helen's flawless body, which has the power figuratively to wound men with love and literally to kill them in the Trojan War, is transferred to the courtroom in the case of Phryne. From a defendant about to be sentenced to death, Phryne morphs into a fearsome goddess. The courtesan is simultaneously a wretched woman inspiring pity and an awesome goddess inspiring fear (of a superstitious nature, according to Athenaeus) in the jurors, who thus act as spectators or judges of a successful tragedy.

[40] See, for instance, Ovid, *Metamorphoses* 13.262–5 (Ulysses bares his body to show his wounds in the judgment of arms). See also Cooper, "Hyperides and the trial of Phryne," 315.

Phryne is an excellent case study for the interactions between law and literature not only because the narrative of her trial draws on Greek myth, but also because it influenced later literary texts. The second *Mime* of the Hellenistic poet Herodas (third century BCE), for instance, which is a parody of a defense speech in a court, includes a passage that evokes the trial of Phryne. The speaker is the pimp Battarus, who prosecutes a certain Thales, accusing him of breaking into his establishment and battering one of his girls in an attempt to carry her off. Battarus admits that he has no witnesses for his accusations, but produces the body of Myrtale, the girl in question, as evidence for Thales' violence:

> Myrtale, you too, come here; show yourself to all – don't be ashamed before anyone; consider that in these gentlemen you see on the jury you are looking on fathers, brothers. See, gentlemen, her plucked skin, both below and above, how smooth this "innocent" has plucked it, when he was dragging and forcing her.[41]

Part of the *Mime*'s farce consists in Battarus' displaying the naked body of Myrtale to the jurors just as he would do in order to attract possible clients. The pimp tries to win over the jurors by indulging in the practices of his disreputable trade. The reference to Myrtale's smoothly plucked skin, "both below and above," is the pimp's typical exhibition of the finely trimmed body of his "merchandise." The joke is that this "plucking" here refers to the abuse that Myrtale suffered at the hands of Thales, who is ironically described as "innocent." Myrtale's body is simultaneously damaged and alluring and Battarus tries to seduce the jurors by making them feel pity for the plight of his sexy girl. The pimp combines the display of soldiers' wounds in court and the disrobing of a woman's attractive body, and from that perspective he follows Hyperides' lead, or even improves on the orator's use of female flesh as emotive yet hard evidence. It has long been recognized that Herodas stages a travesty of Phryne's disrobing,[42] and also offers a burlesque of the standard displays by victims and their advocates in court.[43] While the persuasive force of Phryne's body relies on a rich mythological tradition, the story of her trial as well as common practices in the courtrooms of classical Greece had a lasting impact on later literature.

41 I. C. Cunningham (trans.), *Herodas: Mimes* (Massachusetts: Harvard University Press, 2003), 2.65–71.

42 See John Arbuthnot Nairn, *The Mimes of Herodas* (Oxford: Oxford University Press, 1904), p. 15.

43 Cooper, "Hyperides and the trial of Phryne," 315.

The trial of Phryne not only pits desire against reason but also exemplifies the deep interconnections between *eros* and *nomos*.[44] The story of her trial is often reported in the context of Hyperides' love affairs: Athenaeus attests that in his speech Hyperides confessed that he was passionately in love with her,[45] and pseudo-Plutarch says that he became her advocate because he was her lover.[46] Ancient biographical tradition views the trial as a quarrel between two lovers.[47] Euthias is the scorned lover who accuses Phryne of impiety and takes her to court in order to avenge himself against her, while Hyperides is the new lover who defends his mistress by successfully using her charm in order to seduce the jurors. The trial of impiety is thus the façade of a love triangle in a court of love.

The Roman poet Ovid (43BCE–17CE) follows the tradition of Phryne's trial in the fifth elegy of his second book of the *Amores*, a collection of love elegies that includes poems which draw heavily on courtroom rhetoric and proceedings.[48] The power play between law and love is a crucial aspect of Ovid's poetry and features prominently in *Amores* 2.5. In this poem, the poet/lover, Ovid's persona in the *Amores*, indulges in the fantasy of a trial after witnessing his mistress first exchanging suggestive signals with another man at a dinner party and then kissing him passionately. In this courtroom drama, the lover plays the role of the prosecutor who brings charges against his unfaithful mistress. Even though he would much rather lose the case, the evidence is compelling since he himself was eyewitness to his mistress' indiscretions. With a clever combination of amatory passion and forensic oratory, the lover exclaims: "Oh, would that my charge were such that I could not win! Wretched me, why is my case so strong?"[49] The dramatic effect of Ovid's forensic rhetoric is exemplary. The prosecutor casts himself as lenient and reluctant to accuse the defendant, a ploy that stresses the indisputable nature of the incriminating evidence and thus ultimately buttresses the prosecution's arguments.

44 The conflict and confluence of law and love is a current trend in legal theory and studies of law and literature. For examples, see Peter Goodrich, *Law in the Courts of Love: Literature and Other Minor Jurisprudences* (London and New York: Routledge, 1996); Paul Kahn, *Law and Love: The Trials of King Lear* (New Haven: Yale University Press, 2000); Renata Grossi and Joshua Neoh (eds.), *Law and Love: Law in Context* (Special Issue) 34(1) (2016).

45 Athenaeus, *The Learned Banqueters* 13.590d–e.

46 *X Oration* 849d–e.

47 cf. Alciphron, *Epistle* 4.5 and 5.

48 See: Edward Kenney, "Ovid and the law," *Yale Classical Studies*, 21 (1969), 241–63; Paul Allen Miller, *Subjecting Verses: Latin Love Elegy and the Emergence of the Real* (Princeton: Princeton University Press, 2004), pp. 160–83; Ulrich Gebhardt, *Sermo Iuris: Rechtssprache und Recht in der augusteischen Dichtung* (Leiden: Brill, 2009), pp. 106–84.

49 Translations of *Amores* 2.5 are from Grant Showerman, *Ovid, Heroides. Amores* (Massachusetts: Harvard University Press, 1914) (with occasional modifications). Here 2.5.7–8.

This maneuver is at home in courtroom rhetoric and attested in declamations (see [Quintilian] *Declamation* 5.5, "Oh unfortunate me for having a good case"). The voice of a lover tormented by his mistress' infidelity converges with the emotive histrionics of courtroom rhetoric.

The typical triangle of love elegy in Ovid's courtroom is similar to the case of Phryne. As a prosecutor, Ovid corresponds to Euthias, Phryne's jilted lover, and his mistress to the famous courtesan. The trial of Phryne as a precedent for Ovid's case is further suggested by the lover's failure to convict the guilty woman. The mistress' guilt is beyond dispute and, besides Ovid's eyewitness testimony, it is confirmed by her blushing at the face of the accusations. The woman's face thus becomes her confession, but her conscious blushing is also what saves her from punishment, because it reveals her beauty along with her guilt. At the sight of such loveliness, the lover is incapable of exacting retribution:

> When I looked on her face, my brave arms dropped; our girl was protected by armor of her own.[50]

In the courtroom drama of *Amores* 2.5, the lover shifts between the roles of prosecutor, eyewitness, and judge.[51] Just like the jurors in the trial of Phryne, even though he is convinced of her guilt, he is incapable of convicting her when he is faced with her stunning looks. The lover/judge in the end is the slave of carnal knowledge and the defendant asserts her position as the domineering mistress. *Amores* 2.5 is a version of the trial of Phryne, further alluding to the way in which the adulterous Helen disarmed Menelaus with her beauty, itself a crucial mythological precedent for the case of Phryne. The lover drops his arms at the sight of the mistress just as Menelaus dropped his sword at the sight of Helen's breasts.[52] The focus on the mistress' face further evokes the scene from *Iliad* 3, the elders' judgment of Helen. The lover/judge surrenders to the superior forces of desire.

In the *Amores*, the desire for the mistress' body is inextricably related to the poet/lover's desire to control and reshape literary tradition. Corinna, the elusive mistress of the *Amores*, is a construct of Ovid's passion for textual and sexual knowledge.[53] Once the angry lover observes the confession of

[50] Ovid, *Amores* 2.5.46–7. [51] Gebhardt, *Sermo Iuris*, pp. 172–5.

[52] Ovid was aware of this version – see *Heroides* 16.249–54. Paris peeks at Helen's lovely breasts at a dinner party and drops his cup, an allusion to Menelaus' dropping his sword.

[53] For the body of the Roman mistress in Latin elegy, see Maria Wyke, *The Roman Mistress* (Oxford: Oxford University Press, 2002). For Ovid's prevarication about Corinna, see Duncan Kennedy, *The Arts of Love. Five Studies in the Discourse of Roman Love Elegy* (Cambridge: Cambridge University Press, 1993), pp. 89–100.

guilt on the face of his mistress, the poem is suffused with images from Greek and Roman poetry that range from Homer to Catullus. The color on the girl's face is "like the sky grown red with the tint of Tithonus' bride, or a maid gazed on by her newly betrothed; like roses gleaming among the lilies where they mingle, or the moon in labor with enchanted steeds, or Assyrian ivory Maeonia's daughter tinctures to keep long years from yellowing it."[54] The color of Dawn (Tithonus' bride) evokes Homer's book opening and the red dye on ivory is a Homeric simile (Menelaus' wound in the *Iliad*), while the blushing of the fiancée recalls Catullus 65.[55] The literary background to Ovid's similes is too complex to be analyzed here,[56] but one of its effects that is relevant to my argument is that it highlights the interdependence of female beauty and literary tradition. If Phryne's nudity is the embodiment of signification by means of intertextual and intervisual allusions, Corinna's very body is made out of multiple layers of literary references. In the end, the similes of Corinna's blush are indistinguishable from the shape and color of her face – in fact, the similes are her face. The blushing is depicted on the intertextual canvass and Corinna's beauty disarms the jealous lover's aggression by fanning the poet's creative desire. *Amores* 2.5 exemplifies the inherent tensions in the power play between law and literature. In Ovid's court of love, the literary evidence that fashions a desirable female body trumps actual evidence – the facts observed by an eyewitness fade away at the sight of poetic splendor.

Barthes compares the unfolding of the narrative in the act of reading to striptease.[57] The desire to know the story's end in the body of the text turns readers into voyeurs. This voyeuristic desire for narrative closure and consummation motivates both readers of literature and jurors in the courtroom; the naked body of Phryne at the end of her trial reflects the shared desires and experiences of readers, spectators, and judges. The trial illustrates the influence of myth, literature, and art on legal narratives as well as the impact of courtroom proceedings on literature. The story of the trial highlights the normative force of the aesthetic on the juridical as well as the dramatic appeal of judicial proceedings. The culmination of the trial resembles the resolution of a drama, a scene of recognition that resolves

[54] Ovid, *Amores*, 35–40.

[55] The echoes of Catullus 65 have been anticipated since the beginning of the poem – compare *Amores* 2.5.6 with Catullus 65.19 and 2.5.33–4 with 65.25. The Homeric references are *Iliad* 11.1–2, *Odyssey* 5.1–2, and *Iliad* 4.141–7, respectively.

[56] For more references, see James McKeown, *Ovid: Amores. Volume III. A Commentary on Book Two* (Leeds: Francis Cairns, 1998).

[57] Barthes, *The Pleasure of the Text.* p. 10.

dramatic tension or an epiphany of a *dea ex machina* that puts an end to dramatic indeterminacy. Arousing strong feelings of pity and fear is the main objective of an advocate and a playwright. Phryne's body symbolizes the unconditional access to bare facts, the very objective of law's desire for truth, but at the same time it becomes the text of mythological narratives and the projector of powerful illusions. Far from ruling out the aesthetic for the sake of the objective, the rituals of law incorporate literary tradition as irrefutable evidence.

CHAPTER 6

The "Parallel Evolutions" of Medieval Law and Literature

Stephen Yeager

Law and literature in the medieval period may be understood to share a parallel evolution in two senses. The first is that suggested by Richard Firth Green in his classic study *Crisis of Truth*. Green explains that he treated medieval law and literature as "parallel forms of discourse, each with its own conventions and traditions," and that he reads between those parallels to determine "how the lawyer's comparatively more formal analysis of mental or social processes can help us understand what the imaginative writer sometimes leaves unspoken or expresses only obliquely."[1] Reading between medieval law and literature provides us with more information about that elusive chimera, the medieval worldview, than a study of just one or the other ever could.

In its second and more fundamental sense, the title of this chapter refers to the evolution of the parallel itself, as the very opposing categories "law" and "literature" are themselves medieval developments. One helpful way of tracing this opposition's origins is through examining the etymologies of the English words. "Law" is a loan word from Old Norse, and its adoption reflects the cultural and political influence of the so-called "Vikings" on English-speaking peoples in the centuries leading up to the Norman conquest.[2] "Literature," meanwhile, is derived from the Latin adjective *litteratus* or "literate." This term referred through much of the medieval period to literacy in its most basic technical sense, and only regains its connotations of erudition with the ascendancy of "humanist" classicism in late medieval clerical culture.[3]

[1] Richard Firth Green, *A Crisis of Truth: Literature and Law in Ricardian England* (Philadelphia: University of Pennsylvania Press, 1999), p. xvi.

[2] On this loan word in Old English, see Sara Pons-Sanz, *Norse-derived Vocabulary in Late Old English Texts: Wulfstan's Works, a Case Study* (Amsterdam: University Press of Southern Denmark, 2007), pp. 68–124.

[3] Michael Clanchy, *From Memory to Written Record: England 1066–1307*, 3rd edn. (London: Wiley-Blackwell, 2013), pp. 228–36.

In the word "law," then, we see a trace of how politics and culture evolved in the early medieval period in response to waves of migration and conquest. In the word "literature," we see the traces of Roman imperialism that would shape the self-conceptions of succeeding waves of assimilated peoples, providing them with the technology of writing that they would adapt and develop to codify those self-conceptions and articulate their aspirations. The parallelism between the forms of law and literature noted by Green is itself a feature of the larger stabilization of cultures in Europe between the fall of Rome and the discovery of America, as the predominately oral traditions of non-Roman peoples grafted on to and transformed the Roman literate infrastructures which had been preserved especially by the institutions of the Church. To see how this stabilization took place, then, we must avoid taking the parallelism of "law" and "literature" for granted, and rely also on hybrid concepts like Emily Steiner's influential notion of a "documentary poetics" in fourteenth-century England.[4]

This chapter will begin by unpacking the shared origins of law and literature, to describe briefly how their oppositional parallelism came to assume its current shape between the eleventh and thirteenth centuries. Among other major developments, the century 1050–1150 saw the first Crusade,[5] the early codification of canon law and entrenchment of the secular church,[6] the foundation of the oldest European universities,[7] the crisis of the investiture controversy,[8] a great outpouring of apocalyptic and visionary texts,[9] and the start of the "twelfth-century Renaissance" in literature and learning.[10] Taken together, these developments may be said

[4] Emily Steiner, *Documentary Culture and the Making of Medieval English Literature* (Cambridge: Cambridge University Press, 2003).

[5] Edward Peters, *The First Crusade: The Chronicle of Fulcher of Chartres and Other Source Materials* (Philadelphia: University of Philadelphia Press, 1971).

[6] James A. Brundage, *Medieval Canon Law* (London and New York: Longman, 1995).

[7] Hilde De Ridder-Symoens (ed.), *A History of the University in Europe: Universities in the Middle Ages* (Cambridge: Cambridge University Press, 1992), vol. 1.

[8] Uta-Renate Blumenthal, *The Investiture Controversy: Church and Monarchy from the Ninth to the Twelfth Century* (Philadelphia: University of Pennsylvania Press, 1988).

[9] Richard K. Emmerson and Bernard McGinn, *The Apocalypse in the Middle Ages* (Ithaca: Cornell University Press, 1992).

[10] See C. Warren Hollister, *Anglo-Norman Political Culture and the Twelfth-Century Renaissance* (Woodbridge: Boydell & Brewer, 1997); Richard Southern, "The place of England in the twelfth-century renaissance" in Richard Southern (ed.), *Medieval Humanism and Other Studies* (Oxford: Basil Blackwell, 1970); Charles Homer Haskins, *The Renaissance of the Twelfth Century* (Massachusetts: Harvard University Press, 1927). Another important summary account of these changes is Susan Reynolds' *Kingdom and Communities in Western Europe 900–1300* (Oxford: Oxford University Press, 1997).

to reflect the codification of the concept of a secular function to literacy, which the people of later eras sought to separate from the religious functions of reading and interpreting the Bible, lest the spiritual be contaminated by the secular or vice versa. The parallelism between law and literature emerging from this period would come to suspend the written apparatus of secular humanism between its poles, the tension between them serving even today to provide shape and rigor to our formal categories of authoritative writing.

In the second section of the chapter, we will demonstrate how the parallel formalisms of "literature" and "law" came to serve as this framework for defining the various secular functions of writing. In the late medieval period, opposition to the political, social, and cultural developments that surrounded the growth and entrenchment of secular literacy deployed a mode that I have referred to elsewhere as "legal-homiletic," which not only resisted the emergence of distinctions between legal and homiletic formalisms but also framed the two as mutually reinforcing.[11] Texts in this vein may be apocalyptic and reformist (like *Piers Plowman*), hagiographic and institutional (like certain works of Lydgate), or anything in between, and while we tend to categorize them today as "literature," this is more of a reflection of the capaciousness of that term in our historical moment than it is of the categories that appear to govern the creation and use of medieval writing.[12]

Modern literary authorship may trace its roots back to the end of the twelfth century, when literary and legal formalisms first began to assume their later forms in first the writings of secular officials, lawyers, and clerks, and then the intellectual output of scholastic theologians and philosophers.[13] The influential love lyrics of the so-called "troubadour" poets were written down in Southern France, Italy, and Spain at the same time and by the same courtiers and notaries who standardized, recorded, and disseminated official laws and legal records in those regions.[14] Ethan

[11] Stephen Yeager, *From Lawmen to Plowmen: Anglo-Saxon Legal Tradition and the School of Langland* (Toronto: University of Toronto Press, 2014).

[12] On law and literature in *Piers Plowman* and the tradition of affiliated texts, see for example: Anne Middleton, "Acts of vagrancy: the c-version autobiography and the statute of 1388" in Steven Justice and Kathryn Kerby-Fulton (eds.), *Written Work: Langland, Labor and Authorship* (Philadelphia: University of Pennsylvania Press, 1997), pp. 208–317. On Lydgate, see Shannon Gayk, *Image, Text, and Religious Reform in Fifteenth-Century England* (Cambridge: Cambridge University Press, 2010), pp. 84–122; Maura Nolan, *John Lydgate and the Making of Public Culture* (Cambridge: Cambridge University Press, 2005).

[13] Alastair Minnis, *The Medieval Theory of Authorship: Scholastic Attitudes in the Later Middle Ages*, 2nd edn. (Philadelphia: University of Pennsylvania Press, 2011).

[14] Simon Gaunt, *The Troubadours: An Introduction* (Cambridge: Cambridge University Press, 1999).

Knapp's study of the poet Thomas Hoccleve, whose intensely self-aware, autobiographical poetry stands in revealing contrast to his anonymous, bureaucratic output, provides one remarkably clear portrait of a figure who follows the pattern set by Italian humanist poet-officials such as Boccaccio and Petrarch and also anticipates later analogues from John Donne to Wallace Stevens.[15] For such figures, formally inventive poetry appears to have been, among other things, an escape from formulaic administrative drudgery, and in their work we see the original distinction between legal and literary authorizing modes that enabled the bureaucratic structure of the modern state to co-evolve with the poetic expression of the modern subject.

But while the divisions between law and literature had started to sharpen in the final decades of the medieval period, the earlier and more synthetic relationship between law and literature persisted even then, to articulate a nostalgic longing for earlier and less rigid political and cultural systems. Though nominally conservative, in fact such nostalgia often enabled innovations to be introduced into systems that abhorred innovation on principle, by framing the novel forms and formulae as revivals of earlier practices.[16] To exemplify this last development, I will cite in my final section some examples of how Geoffrey of Monmouth's quasifactual *Historia Regum Brittaniae* (hereafter *HRB*), famous for popularizing the legends of King Arthur, was deployed as a legal source when the situation demanded it. It is typical of England in this generative period that the *Dialogue of the Exchequer*, the first accounting manual of the medieval West, should appear within decades of Geoffrey's unprecedented incorporation of mythic and romance narratives into the genre of official history.[17] The uses of Geoffrey's *HRB* demonstrate how its legendary, "literary" content was able to play a substantive role in the shaping of legal, political history, and for this reason it is a particularly clear example of how the shared histories of medieval law and literature offered productive resistance to their oppositional, parallel tension, and in this manner shaped their development.

[15] Ethan Knapp, *The Bureaucratic Muse: Thomas Hoccleve and the Literature of Late Medieval England* (University Park: Penn State University Press, 2001).

[16] For a complementary reconsideration of novelty in the medieval period see Patricia Ingham, *The Medieval New: Ambivalence in an Age of Innovation* (Philadelphia: University of Pennsylvania Press, 2015).

[17] Richard Fitz Neal, *Dialogus de Scaccario*, 2nd edn., ed. Charles Johnson (Oxford: Oxford University Press, 1983).

The Emergence of Law and Literature

The coextensive nature of law and literature in preliterate, oral cultures has been recognized since the time of Jacob Grimm himself, who believed that the legendary literature of the pagan, "Germanic" North Atlantic witnessed a common legal vocabulary.[18] Certainly the evidence we have of late antique and preconversion northern Europe suggests that in Britain, Ireland, Denmark, Sweden, and Iceland, laws and histories were metrical and in that sense "poetic." Recent studies have challenged earlier assumptions that, since poetic forms were likely adopted by "law-sayers" (*asega*, as they were called in Old Frisian) because they were easiest to memorize, we may conclude that the law's inherent conservatism is the only thing that hindered early medieval legislators' adoption of clear, precise modern prose.[19] As Patrick Wormald summarizes in the "Legislation as Literature" section of his magisterial survey *The Making of English Law*, "as least as they survive, [the laws'] arrangement can be illogical, their style either quaintly elementary or ponderously rhetorical, their form inconsistent . . . Much of the material is intelligible as statute law in the modern sense. The puzzle is that much is not."[20] To the extent that this puzzle has been solved by Grimm's successors, it has been through consideration of the role played by the Christian Church in the development of literacy in Western Europe.

In the early medieval period, the Church appears to have enjoyed a near monopoly on literate professionalization, though – crucially – not on the actual use of written texts.[21] It is no coincidence that early medieval monarchs such as Charlemagne and Alfred the Great are known not only for the might of their kingdoms but also for their piety, manifest especially in their investments in literacy and education.[22] They recognized that the

[18] Stefan Jurasinski, *Ancient Privileges: Beowulf, Law, and the Making of Germanic Antiquity* (Morgantown: West Virginia University Press, 2003).

[19] For a recent history of this discussion in Old Frisian see Rolf Bremmer, "The orality of Old Frisian law texts" in Rolf Bremmer, Stephen Laker, and Oebele Vries (eds.), *Directions for Old English Philology* (Amsterdam: Rodopi, 2014), pp. 1–48.

[20] Patrick Wormald, *The Making of English Law: King Alfred to the Twelfth Century* (Oxford: Blackwell, 1999), p. 416.

[21] Susan Kelly, "Anglo-Saxon lay society and the written word" in Rosamond McKitterick (ed.), *The Uses of Literacy in Early Medieval Europe* (Cambridge: Cambridge University Press, 1990), pp. 36–65.

[22] On literacy in the Carolingian world, see especially Rosamond McKitterick, *Perceptions of the Past in the Medieval World* (South Bend: University of Notre Dame Press, 2006); *The Carolingians and the Written Word* (Cambridge: Cambridge University Press, 1989). Alfred's literacy and piety are both described in Asser's Life. See Simon Keynes and Michael Lapidge (eds.), *Alfred the Great: Asser's Life of King Alfred and Other Contemporary Sources* (London: Penguin Classics, 1983).

exercise of secular power on the Roman model required institutional archives, and that the easiest way to generate such archives was to work with institutions such as powerful Benedictine monasteries, the foundations of the Augustinians, and the parochial system of the secular clergy. Thus one may see how the (often metrical and poetic) authorizing forms of religious oratory should come to be deployed in legal and documentary texts almost exactly as they were deployed in homilies and poems.

An instructive example from England is the corpus of writing attributed to the archbishop Wulfstan II of York. Wulfstan's most widely anthologized text is his so-called *Sermo Lupi ad Anglos*, which makes the case that the ongoing Danish raids were the result of English sinfulness, and which supplies us with one of the most vivid contemporary descriptions of those raids and the suffering they caused. The sermon deploys the legal forms of testimony interchangeably with the homiletic forms of religious oratory.[23] This appears to be not some holdover of "transitional" orality but, on the contrary, a deliberately cultivated effect of Wulfstan's writing, legal and homiletic.[24] For Wulfstan, the piety of English subjects and the prosperity of English kingdoms are related not only by the cause-and-effect logic of divine retributive justice, but also by the idea that both piety and prosperity are the measure of effectiveness in ecclesiastical institutions.

As the *Sermo Lupi*'s call to repent exemplifies, religious influence over secular affairs was often mediated by the apparatus of the sacrament of contrition.[25] Manuals intended to help confessors determine the necessary acts of contrition occasioned by different sins influenced and were influenced by the standard punishments for crimes, and hence they played a role in developing principles of jurisprudence. The ecclesiastical courts of canon law emerged from this tradition to transform radically in the eleventh and twelfth centuries around three major developments.[26] First, the canons issued by bishops at synods were collected, regularized, and applied to train canon lawyers for service in the burgeoning ecclesiastical court system. Second, the study of Roman civil law began to flourish, and to influence the emergent canon law. Finally, the papacy began to serve

[23] Andrew Rabin, "The wolf's testimony in English: law and the witness in the 'Sermo Lupi ad Anglos'," *JEGP*, 105 (2006), 388–414.

[24] Andy Orchard, "Crying wolf: oral style and the Sermones Lupi," *ASE*, 21 (1992), 239–62. For a recent survey of critical approaches to Wulfstan, see Andrew Rabin, *The Political Writings of Archbishop Wulfstan of York* (Manchester: Manchester University Press, 2014), pp. 44–50.

[25] Stefan Jurasinski, *The Old English Penitentials and Anglo-Saxon Law* (Cambridge: Cambridge University Press, 2015).

[26] Surveyed in R. H. Helmholtz, *Oxford History of the Laws of England: The Canon Law and Ecclesiastical Jurisdiction from 597 to the 1640s*, vol. 1 (Oxford: Oxford University Press, 2004).

increasingly as an appeals court for all of the various local ecclesiastical courts across Europe, and its decisions began to be collected, circulated, and cited as precedent. Commentaries, *summae*, and other paratexts then followed that synthesized and applied these legal principles and precedents, and from this activity emerged the foundations of the European *ius commune* that continues to this day.[27] This law had a complex interrelationship with the secular courts held by kings, royal justices, and the lords of individual estates, as canon law administered not only the punishment of religious crimes such as witchcraft and adultery but also the formalization of contracts, most importantly marriage: Then as now, oaths were often sworn on religious objects and texts, and so it was natural that officers of the Church should participate in proceedings that involved oaths.

In England, of course, another "common law" emerged that diverged from the European legal tradition quite early on, though its precise history is difficult to trace. The trial by jury, for example, is first instantiated in the proscriptions of King Henry II's 1166 Assize of Clarendon, but it may have begun long before that, and in any event the debate by modern historians has been so ideologically loaded that it is difficult to assess the evidence.[28] Legal historians questioning such matters have long used William I's "Norman Conquest" of England as a key dividing line between "early" and "high" medieval periods, though recent scholarship has challenged the fitness of this date quite convincingly. The Norman Conquest of 1066 was only one in a series of ruptures, preceded by Cnut's 1015 "Danish Conquest" and followed by the so-called "Anarchy" in the reign of William's grandson Stephen (1135–54).[29] In any event, as Bruce O'Brien has observed, the refinement of legal literacy in this long period "should be considered the sine qua non of the common law, for without it, the centralization of the courts . . . would have remained a royal fantasy."[30]

There is arguably no more important facet of medieval legal theory and practice than the laws governing the ownership and use of land, and hence no single instance of medieval legal literacy is more important than the

27 Anders Windroth, "The legal revolution of the twelfth century" in Thomas Noble, John Van Engen, Anna Sapir Abulafia, and Sverre Bagge (eds.), *European Transformations* (South Bend: University of Notre Dame Press, 2011), pp. 338–53.

28 On the debate about the jury's origins, see Eric Stanley, *Imagining the Anglo-Saxon Past* (Cambridge: D.S. Brewer, 2000).

29 Elaine Treharne, *Living through Conquest: The Politics of Early English 1020–1220* (Oxford: Oxford University Press, 2012).

30 Bruce O'Brien, "Forgery and literacy in the early common law," *Albion*, 27 (1995), 1–18.

unprecedented survey of English estates, the "Domesday book."[31] Scott Smith's work on "tenurial discourse" in Anglo-Latin documents, Old English dispute narratives, commentaries on the Church Fathers, translations, chronicles, and hagiographic poetry has demonstrated how land law and the anxieties attending its contingency inflect virtually every aspect of early medieval English writing, as the rights of tenure were crucial not only to abstract notions of sovereignty and public debt but also to religious notions of God's dominion.[32] The long history of using threats of excommunication and eternal torment as sanction clauses of property transfers reflects the origins of documentary records in the dominion of the Church, who may well have introduced to English law the very notion of land that may change hands with the transfer of a written document from the old owner to the new.[33] Once this notion took root, it was perhaps inevitable that the Church should lose control over the technology of writing, and it is telling that when the Domesday book finally began to be cited regularly some hundred years after its original creation, it was typically on behalf of tenants and landowners who wished to draw upon the royal prerogative to alienate land from the church.[34] And so, while the process was gradual, we may nonetheless generalize that the rise of both formulaic regularity in legal prose and formal inventiveness in poetry and fiction is a result of the Church's loss of control over the technology of literacy.

The Opposition between Law and Literature

One of the most thorough examinations by a medieval author of preliterate, "oral" legal culture is the Icelandic *Njalssaga*.[35] The text describes in painstaking detail an ongoing feud between two families and the various efforts at settlement by the two patriarchs, who are friends. The story culminates in the deaths of Njal and many of his family in a fire, after which the arsonist is put on trial at the Althing, roughly equivalent to the Icelandic parliament. The two sides of the trial are represented by the two

[31] Clanchy, *From Memory*, pp. 35–8; F. W. Maitland, *Domesday Book and Beyond: Three Essays in the Early History of England* (Cambridge: Cambridge University Press, 1897).

[32] Scott T. Smith, *Land and Book: Literature and Land Tenure in Anglo-Saxon England* (Toronto: Toronto University Press, 2012).

[33] Lester Little, *Benedictine Maledictions: Liturgical Cursing in Romanesque France* (Ithaca and London: Cornell University Press, 1996).

[34] For one dramatic instance see Rosamond Faith, "The 'great rumour' of 1377 and peasant ideology" in R. H. Hilton and T. H. Aston (eds.), *The English Rising of 1381* (Cambridge: Cambridge University Press, 1984), pp. 43–73.

[35] Sveinn Egilsson, *Brennu-Njáls saga. Texti Reykjabókar* (Reykjavík: Bjartur, 2003).

greatest legal minds in all of Iceland, excepting the lawspeaker himself, who serves as judge. Þórhallr, the advocate for Njal's family, has an infection in his leg that has created a large and painful pustule, and so he is forced to relay legal instructions from his tent through an intermediary. The trial proceeds with a series of increasingly complex legal maneuvers, until finally Þórhallr's opponent evokes a rule that may not be circumvented. Upon learning this, Þórhallr picks up a spear, lances his boil, and leaves his tent with blood and pus pouring down his leg. He then leads an attack against the opposing party that engulfs the entire assembly but still does not end the conflict, as the defendant and his friends escape.

The episode is noteworthy because it helps to frame my challenge to the common notion that the evolution of literacy is attended by increasing trust in the new medium.[36] Perhaps, rather, we may imagine the transition as a shift from the contempt borne of one kind of familiarity to a contempt borne of another, which contempt then serves as the engine driving those reforms to the protocols of information production and storage that lead in turn both to a deeper investment in the familiar technology and a deeper, better-informed contempt for it. As Alfred Hiatt demonstrates compellingly, literate historical consciousness and sophistication in forgery are two sides of the same coin, as the fear of forgery drives innovations in protocol which in turn drive innovations in forgery technique.[37] That the author of *Njalssaga* believed there was a similarly inevitable accretion of corruption attending the evolution of Icelandic oral law is suggested by the saga's vivid imagery, in which unsanctioned, extralegal violence is implicitly compared to lancing a boil to let the pus bleed out. This satirical, critical representation of Iceland's political and legal culture anticipates the skepticism and anxiety that will attend to literary representations of written law in later periods, which affective modes will begin and then drive the unending process of institutional, bureaucratic reform that is modernity.

Laura Ashe's work on the later, Norman descendants of Anglo-Saxon legal texts and traditions has demonstrated how literary romance motifs such as exile-and-return in both English and French vernacular romance are conditioned by historical political events in England.[38] Meanwhile

[36] See, for example, Michael Clanchy's chapter "Trusting writing" in his *From Memory* (pp. 295–328).

[37] Alfred Hiatt, *The Making of Medieval Forgeries* (London: The British Library, 2004).

[38] Laura Ashe, *Fiction and History in England 1066–1200* (Cambridge: Cambridge University Press, 2007). Other pertinent studies of nation, history, and romance include Geraldine Heng, *Empire of*

C. Stephen Jaeger has written on how the genre of romance and its surrounding discourse of "courtly love" served a pedagogical function, as it assimilated military heroic values into the courtly, literate realm and thereby established the codes of chivalry.[39] Romance, then, exhibits a particularly close interdependent relationship between chivalric principle and historical precedent, manifest also in the burgeoning of so-called "mirrors for princes" and other advice literature that addressed noble conduct more explicitly.[40] Much of this literature aimed to provide moral instruction to lawmakers and public servants, and for this reason we may identify it with the "homiletic" element of earlier, legal-homiletic writing, though at the same time it is entertaining, diverting, and sometimes satirical.

One predominant feature of romance that deserves special mention is its tendency to be written and transmitted in vernacular languages. So also would the robust systems of royal and imperial law that emerged in the twelfth century begin to allow vernacular languages for debate and even legal record, especially in the English adaption of the dialect that would later be called "Law French."[41] Heterodox reform movements in the wake of Wyclif were particularly keen to target the twin, Latinate evils of civil and canon law, and such criticisms would become a key part of his legacy in England and on the continent.[42] As Maureen Jurakowski has observed, this is perhaps the reason that English common lawyers were particularly drawn to so-called "Lollard" reformist rhetoric.[43] Over time the vernacular became politicized as the language of the

Magic: Medieval Romance and the Politics of Cultural Fantasy (New York: Columbia University Press, 2004); Monika Otter, *Inventiones: Fiction and Referentiality in Twelfth-Century English Historical Writing* (Asheville: UNC Press, 1996); Susan Crane, *Insular Romance: Politics, Faith, and Culture in Anglo-Norman and Middle English Literature* (Berkeley: University of California Press, 1986).

39 Stephen Jaeger, *The Origins of Courtliness: Civilizing Trends and the Formation of Courtly Ideals, 939–1210* (Philadelphia: University of Pennsylvania Press, 1985).

40 Matthew Giancarlo, "Mirror, mirror: princely hermeneutics, practical constitutionalism, and the genres of the English Fürstenspiegel," *Exemplaria*, 27 (2015), 35–54.

41 On French in England, see Jocelyn Wogan-Browne (ed.), *Language and Culture in Medieval Britain: The French of England, c.1100–c.1500* (Woodbridge: Boydell & Brewer, 2009); Ardis Butterfield, *The Familiar Enemy: Chaucer, Language and Nation in the Hundred Years War* (Oxford: Oxford University Press, 2009).

42 On Wycliffite opposition to canon and civil law, see Anne Hudson, *The Premature Reformation* (Oxford: Oxford University Press, 1988), pp. 378–80. On Wyclif's influence, see Patrick Hornbeck and Michael Van Dussen (eds.), *Europe After Wyclif* (New York: Fordham University Press, 2016).

43 Maureen Jurakowski, "Lawyers and Lollardy in the early fifteenth century" in Margaret Aston and Colin Richmond (eds.), *Lollardy and the Gentry in the Later Middle Ages* (New York: St. Martin's, 1997), pp. 155–82.

new, secular, bourgeois world order which set it in contrast to ecclesiastical Latinate authority, though of course the conditions on the ground never quite reflected this conceptual division. In England, vernacular poetic texts such as the so-called *South English Legendaries* collections of saints' lives were instruments of ecclesiastical authority at the same time that Latin and English literature of complaint together spread dissent and even heresy.[44] In both official and unofficial languages, we see literature developing its unique capacity to serve as a moral supplement to – and, when necessary, a critical discourse about – the law.

One example of the new model of secular poet is Geoffrey Chaucer. Chaucer, who was unusual for writing exclusively in English, was himself a product of the emergent urban mercantile class – his father was a vintner and his surname means "shoemaker" – but his brother-in-law John of Gaunt was the uncle of King Richard II and so was enormously influential in Richard's minority.[45] Chaucer was a member of parliament and he worked in the port of London as the controller of Petty Custom, auditing to make sure that the king's duties were properly paid. There is a long history of speculation that he may himself have been a lawyer, encouraged by the fact that the pilgrims of his famous *Canterbury Tales* include a "sergeant of law" and a manciple who procured provisions for the temples at the Inns of Court.[46]

The problem of law and its relationship to literature is a major formal problem in *The Canterbury Tales*. There are many indications that the work was unfinished at the time of Chaucer's death. In the "Man of Law's Introduction," Chaucer assigns a speech to this figure that includes one of his characteristically self-deprecating authorial portraits. The sergeant claims that he can tell no stories of olden times because the prolific Chaucer, who knows little about meter and crafty rhyme, has already told all of them, in the (implicitly rather insufficient) English that he knows.[47] The sergeant then promises to tell a tale in prose,[48] and as near as we can tell, it appears that he is supposed to have told the *Tale of Melibee* that,

[44] On the *South English Legendaries* see Heather Blurton and Jocelyn Wogan-Browne (eds.), *Rethinking the South English Legendaries* (Manchester: Manchester University Press, 2011). On complaint literature in Latin and English see Wendy Scase, *Literature and Complaint in England 1272–1553* (Oxford: Oxford University Press, 2007); Fiona Somerset, *Clerical Discourse and Lay Audience in Late Medieval England* (Cambridge: Cambridge University Press, 1998).

[45] On the poet's life see Paul Strohm, *Chaucer's Tale: 1386 and the Road to Canterbury* (New York: Viking, 2014).

[46] All references to Chaucer are from Larry Benson (ed.), *The Riverside Chaucer*, 3rd edn. (Boston: Houghton Mifflin, 1987).

[47] Chaucer, *Canterbury Tales*, II.46–50.

[48] Chaucer, *Canterbury Tales*, II.96.

in the manuscripts, is rather attributed to the pilgrim-narrator Chaucer himself. It appears further that this revision was undertaken to underscore even more baldly the association of this text with Chaucer's self-satire, as Chaucer the pilgrim only tells the *Tale of Melibee* after his parodic romance, the *Tale of Sir Thopas*, is interrupted by the Host's summary judgment that its "drasty" rhyming "is nat worth a toord."[49] *Melibee*, meanwhile, is a translation of a work by the Italian notary Albertanus of Brescia, in which a wife, Prudence, advises her husband and seeks to mitigate his desire for vengeance and justice.[50]

The prominent Chaucerian Jill Mann has written that at this juncture of the *Tales*, "the authority of the audience becomes absolute; the author is not simply misinterpreted or underappreciated but actually hooted off the stage."[51] Replacing Chaucer's verse is the translated prose of a treatise, written by a lawyer, which affirms a notion not far removed from the implicit moral of *Njalssaga*: namely, that the system of law has a way of perpetuating and magnifying the very sorts of violence it ostensibly exists to prevent. Such criticisms of the gap between the law's aspirations and its practice appear commonly in the province of literature, but here again the distinction is troubled, as the authorial anxiety attending Chaucer's abandonment of verse for prose suggests that "literature" on its own may be unequal to the task of addressing the problems it describes. In this way *The Canterbury Tales* illustrates nicely both the contradictions that emerge and the cultural work that is accomplished when the separate, parallel spheres of medieval literature and law give in to their mutual attraction and collapse into one another.

Nostalgia and Innovation: The Case of Geoffrey of Monmouth

The medieval genre containing the clearest examples of both the emergent parallel between law and literature and the generative reintegration of these oppositional categories is that of the chronicle. The medieval evolution of the chronicle genre in both its local and universal forms may be productively compared to the evolution of Ptolemaic astronomy before the Copernican revolution, as the accretion of new data points stretched the old models for understanding movement and change until they reached

[49] Chaucer, *Canterbury Tales*, VII.930.

[50] William Askins, "Tale of Melibee" in Robert Correale and Mary Hamel (eds.), *Sources and Analogues to the Canterbury Tales* (Cambridge: D.S. Brewer, 2002), vol. 1, pp. 321–408.

[51] Jill Mann, "The authority of the audience in Chaucer" in *Life in Words: Essays on Chaucer, the Gawain Poet, and Malory* (Toronto: University of Toronto Press, 2014), pp. 102–16.

breaking point.[52] Not least among these accretions were the transcribed documents of letters, charters, and papal privileges incorporated into chronicles as primary evidence, alongside local legends and sometimes even poems. The *Anglo-Saxon Chronicle* (*ASC*), for example, is an Old English chronicle copied along parallel trajectories in multiple contexts, until the last thread peters out in the mid-twelfth century: these texts are our only sources both for Old English occasional poems such as *The Battle of Brunanburh* and for detailed accounts of legal disputes and their resolutions.[53] After the conquest, there are chronicles like those by William of Malmesbury that are some of the most remarkable literary achievements of the age, and they survive alongside the so-called "cartulary-chronicle" of Abingdon abbey, which stitches together the abbey's most important documents with only a smattering of historical connective tissue.[54] The chronicle genre serves in this way to preserve not only the facts of history, such as they were, but also the formal heterogeneity of poetic documents and documentary poetry, which precedent later justified the introduction of novel, heterogeneous forms to later legal and literary contexts.

Perhaps no medieval chronicle was more efficacious in introducing novelty than Geoffrey of Monmouth's *HRB*.[55] We will leave to others the task of surveying its enormous literary influence,[56] and rather conclude with a brief survey of the text's political and legal uses, beginning with the abbey of Glastonbury. King Arthur disappears from the *HRB* after he is taken, injured, to the isle of Avalon, which became associated at some point with this monastery.[57] Gerald of Wales describes how in 1191, the monks of Glastonbury claimed that they had discovered Arthur's body.[58] Edward Kennedy has suggested that it is no coincidence that this discovery took place two years after the coronation of Richard I, who had cut off his

[52] Robert Stein, "Making history English: cultural identity and historical explanation in William of Malmesbury and Laȝamon's *Brut*" in Sylvia Tomasch and Sealy Gilles (eds.), *Text and Territory: Geographical Information in the European Middle Ages* (Philadelphia: University of Pennsylvania Press, 1998), pp. 97–115, 97.

[53] On the *ASC* see Thomas Bredehoft, *Textual Histories: Readings in the Anglo-Saxon Chronicle* (Toronto: University of Toronto Press, 2001).

[54] Antonia Gransden, *Historical Writing in England c. 550–c.1307* (London: Routledge, 1974).

[55] Geoffrey of Monmouth, *Historia regum Britanniae.* 1136. Vol. 1 (Woodbridge: Boydell & Brewer, 1985).

[56] See for example Patricia Clare Ingham, *Sovereign Fantasies: Arthurian Fantasies and the Making of Britain* (Philadelphia: University of Pennsylvania Press, 2001); Sian Echard, *Arthurian Narrative in the Latin Tradition* (Cambridge University Press, 1998).

[57] Lesley Abrams, *Anglo-Saxon Glastonbury: Church and Endowment* (Woodbridge: Boydell, 1996), pp. 1–27.

[58] Giraldus Cambrensis, *De principis instructione liber*, ed. George F. Warner. *Giraldi Cambrensis Opera*, RS 21, vol. 8. (London, 1891), p. 28.

father's patronage of Glastonbury to fund his crusade instead.[59] Practical motivations often motivated such "discoveries." What is striking here is that the disinterred body in question was that of a legendary king, but not a saint.

In 1278, Edward I travelled to Glastonbury to commandeer Arthur's remains, and this action was only one indication of this king's regard for his legendary predecessor. In the manner of Glastonbury but on a larger scale, Edward seemed to desire to use an association with Arthur as a way of shoring up his rights.[60] Most strikingly, he cites the precedent of Geoffrey's history in a letter he wrote to the Pope trying to justify his claim over Scotland. The letter did not work, and Edward was arguably grasping at straws: Nonetheless, this use of the text suggests that the king wished for *HRB* to be treated as official history, and the strength of this wish at least partially overcame the skepticism of those historians who almost immediately doubted the *HRB*'s veracity.

The political influence of the *HRB* spread far beyond such explicit citations, not least through the enormous reach and influence of commentaries on and vernacular poetic translations of the enigmatic *Prophecies of Merlin*, which was the first non-Biblical prophecy to acquire the sort of robust commentary tradition that discussed and even shaped historical political events.[61] Even more striking is the influence of Geoffrey's history on a legal treatise called the *Leges Anglorum*, which combined legendary material, forged texts, and genuine law into a single compendium focused on the city of London.[62] As Walter Ullmann demonstrates, passages from Geoffrey's text worked their way from the *Leges Anglorum* into the articles on London in Magna Carta.

As we may see, then, Green was quite right to suggest that we must look at law and literature in tandem if we are to understand the social and political world of the medieval period, as the oppositional framework of

59 E. D. Kennedy, "Glastonbury" in Sian Echard (ed.), *The Arthur of Medieval Latin Literature: The Development and Dissemination of the Arthurian Legend in Medieval Latin* (Cardiff: University of Wales Press, 2011), pp. 109–31.

60 Mark Morris, "Edward I and the Knight of the Round Table" in Sean Cunningham and Paul Brand (eds.), *Foundations of Medieval Scholarship:Records Edited in Honour of David Crook* (York: Borthwick Publications, 2008), pp. 57–76.

61 Julia Crick, "Geoffrey and the prophetic tradition" in Sian Echard (ed.), *The Arthur of Medieval Latin Literature: The Development and Dissemination of the Arthurian Legend in Medieval Latin* (Cardiff: University of Wales Press, 2011), pp. 67–82.

62 Walter Ullmann, "On the influence of Geoffrey of Monmouth in English history" in Clemens Bauer, Laetitia Bohm, and Max Muller (eds.), *Speculum Historiale* (Munich and Freiburg: K. Alber, 1965). See also the web resource "Leges Anglorum Londoniis collectae," Early English Laws: www.earlyenglishlaws.ac.uk/laws/texts (accessed November 14, 2016).

"law" and "literature" serves itself to distort the knotted complexity of the evidence. Geoffrey's history serves as a common point of origin both of the tradition of Arthurian romance that is one of the medieval period's most enduring legacies and of language appearing in a major foundational document of English constitutional monarchy. Far from undermining the text's authority, the blatantly legendary qualities of the *HRB* made it more amenable to the interested parties that would use it as legal precedent, as its resolute secularism was more amenable to the emerging systems of royal government than were the ecclesiastical institutional histories of William of Malmesbury and the *ASC*. Even as historical forces pushed law and literature away from each other and into parallel trajectories, they also kept them in contact with each other, that their combination could serve to introduce innovations to each.

CHAPTER 7

Literature and Equity in Early Modern England

Mark Fortier

Equity is a complicated thing, and perhaps never more so than in early modern England. As a word it has a deceptively simple etymology, derived as it is from the Latin word *aequitas*, which means fairness, impartiality, or evenness; the Latin adjective *aequus* means, among other things, equal or level. The English word, however, is also taken to be the equivalent (though not etymologically related) of the Greek word ἐπιείκεια, which means appropriateness or gentleness. The English word is also used to translate a word from the Hebrew Bible that means uprightness. Moreover, equity is not just a word but also a set of ideas, some related, some more at odds. From Latin sources, especially Cicero, comes a sense of equity as a basic element of human society, the ability to live together by treating others fairly. There is also a rather Stoic notion of equanimity at work. The Greek idea – mainly from Aristotle, especially his *Ethics* – is of a particular correction necessary when the strict application of the law would create an injustice, a necessary exception to the rule in order to realign the law with justice. Often this entails reading for the intention and spirit of the law, rather than the letter strictly construed.[1] Equity can also mean flexibility in judgment and the virtue of showing flexibility, consideration, and tolerance toward others. In the Greek New Testament, equity refers to the gentleness of Christ and his followers and is taken as the principle behind the golden rule – do unto others as you would have them do unto you. Among religious dissenters the equity in the Christian conscience gives justification for opposing secular authority when it runs counter to conscience. Equity in English translations of the Hebrew Bible refers to uprightness of character and to the caring justice God bestows on good people as opposed to the harsh justice he enacts on transgressors. Until the 1870s, the English judicial system was divided into courts of law and

[1] The principal source for Aristotle's notion of equity is section 5.10 of *The Ethics of Aristotle* (Middlesex: Penguin, 1955), pp. 166–8.

courts of equity, such as chancery, which applied pseudo-Aristotelian exceptions to what it took to be miscarriages of justice in common law courts. In common parlance, an equitable judge was also one who was impartial and disinterested. The equity courts were prerogative courts, so equity also came to stand for the king's right to overrule the law for the sake of the wellbeing of the people – and so for royal supremacy over parliament.[2]

This cursory and incomplete account of what lies behind the English word equity points to the complex tensions and alignments at work in early modern English usage. The result of these complexities is to render interpretation and understanding of the use of the word inherently problematic, demanding subtlety and discernment. They also help explain why references to equity were so widespread and variable: Equity had cultural capital and was malleable enough to suit divergent needs and arguments.

Equity in Law, Religion, and Politics

Before turning to literature, it is important to get an overview of equity as it arose in law, religion, and politics. The interconnectedness of law, religion, politics, and literature is very important to recognize in understanding early modern equity, and equity's prominence in other fields of public interest is an important reason for its being taken up so often in literature. Once again, what will become evident is the wide variation in meanings attached to equity.

Two texts from the early sixteenth century set out important ideas concerning the relations between equity and common law. The first, by Christopher Saint German, is *Doctor and Student*, a dialogue between a doctor of divinity and a student of common law. The doctor sets out religious and philosophical grounds for justifying equity's interference in the law: God's law, conscience, natural law, the law of reason. The doctor's main authority is Aristotle and he provides an Aristotelian definition of equity: Since "the deeds and acts of men, for which the laws have been ordained, happen in divers manners infinitely, it is not possible to make any general rule of law, but it shall fail in some case," and so equity is "a right wiseness that considereth all the particular circumstances of the deed, the which also is tempered with the sweetness of mercy."[3]

[2] For a fuller account of these points, see Mark Fortier, *The Culture of Equity in Early Modern England* (Aldershot: Ashgate, 2005).

[3] Christopher Saint German, *The Doctor and Student* (Cincinnati: Robert Clarke & Co., 1874), pp. 44–5.

The doctor and student go into some detail as to the circumstances in which equitable relief could be brought to bear on the law. A very useful example concerns a city guard at night. To protect the city, the law makes it a capital crime to open the city gates after dark. One night the guard sees his city's army in flight toward the city, pursued by vast enemy forces. He opens the gates, lets the city's army in, and closes the gates in time to keep out the enemy. Should he be put to death? The intention of the law was to protect the city and its citizens. Opening the city gates did this. Surely a case such as this was not meant to be covered by the law.

The second early sixteenth-century text is *A Replication of a Serjeant at the Laws of England*, a rebuttal of *Doctor and Student*, which gives expression to the theoretical and institutional suspicion the common law held regarding equity and its courts. To trust to the particular conscience of a chancery judge allowed free rein to undo decisions at law is to create uncertainty and a disrespect for and unraveling of the rule of law, even though "the lawe commaundeth all thing that is good for the commen welthe to bee doon, and prohibitithe all thing that is evill and that is againste the coomen welle."[4] The mistrust of equitable discretion as too personal and idiosyncratic and without guiding principle was most famously expressed by John Selden a hundred years later: "Equity is a roguish thing."[5] These two very different ways of seeing equity and law stand behind much legal conflict throughout the period, and the crisis that was to arise in the early seventeenth century.

At the turn of the century, two treatises elaborated alternative ways of understanding the relation between equity and law. William Lambarde's *Archaeion* of 1591 tries to follow a middle way between Saint German's doctor and the serjeant at the laws. Equity and law are always in conflict. Equity is too unpredictable; law is too rigid. But brought together in the right balance, in a kind of reciprocal restraint, they result in "a most sweete and harmonicall *Iustice*."[6] Lambarde's approach conceives of law and equity largely as they have been since Aristotle, with equity as a particular and occasional corrective to law when unforeseen and unique circumstances render a decision at law unjust. In *Epieikeia*, from 1603, Edward

[4] J. A. Guy (ed.), *Christopher St German on Statute and Chancery* (London: Selden Society, 1985), p. 102.

[5] John Selden, *The Table Talk of John Selden* (London: Quaritch, 1927), p. 43.

[6] William Lambarde, *Archeion or, a Discourse upon the High Courts of Justice in England* (Massachusetts: Harvard University Press, 1957), p. 44.

Hake draws a rather different schematic. For Hake, equity is everywhere present in the law, not its opponent but its lifeblood and soul. Discretion, conscience, and the need for interpretation are everywhere in the law; there is no such thing as a law that interprets itself or does not need to be applied to particular circumstances. Hake recommends that the spirit of equity should guide the law, and equity is "sweetnes, gentleness, goodness, myldnes, moderation and such like."[7] Hake's view held little truck in the relations between equity and law, which continued to be structured on an adversarial model, but his view is compelling, and his notion of equity as gentleness and such like expresses a commonplace view of equity at work in some of the literary works we will examine.

The conflict between courts of equity and common law came to a head in the first part of the seventeenth century, culminating in the events around *The Earl of Oxford's Case* in 1616.[8] The Chancellor Thomas Egerton and the Chief Justice of King's Bench, Edward Coke, each refused to yield supremacy to the other's authority. The issue was ultimately decided by King James himself in *The King's Order and Decree in Chancery*.[9] The position going forward was to be that decisions in equity trump decisions at common law.

James had various reasons for deciding as he did; some were no doubt political, rooted in his absolutist beliefs. Equity courts were prerogative courts, drawing their authority from royal authority. To submit such courts to the law courts would be to submit royal authority to parliament. More generally, James's position was informed by a precept from Cicero: *salus populi lex suprema* (the wellbeing of the people is or should be the highest law – in James's translation, "that the health of the common-wealth be his chiefe law"[10]). In political terms, this idea is the most overarching and basic justification for equitable correction of legal authority. For James this meant that his role as protector of his people gave him the right to overrule the law when, in his conscience, he took the law as harmful to his people. Like equity, however, *salus populi lex suprema* is a rather slippery notion. During the Civil War and Commonwealth it was widely used as a justification for the people rising up against an unjust monarch, so much so that the arch-royalist Roger L'Estrange

[7] Edward Hake, *Epieikeia: A Dialogue on Equity in Three Parts* (New Haven: Yale University Press, 1953), pp. 103–4.

[8] *The Earl of Oxford's Case, The Third Part of Reports of Cases Taken and Adjudged in the Court of Chancery* (London, 1716), pp. 1–16.

[9] *The King's Order and Decree in Chancery, Reports or Causes in Chancery* (London, 1650), pp. 115–36.

[10] James I, *Workes* (London, 1616), p. 203.

could, after the Restoration, use the term "the *Salus-populi-men*" as a general term of abuse for republicans.[11]

At least as much as a legal and political term, equity was, in early modern England, a religious word. As in other fields, English religious thought in the period arose within an international European network. Jean Calvin presented equity, in the form of the golden rule (do unto others, "just and upright dealing" toward one's neighbors[12]), as the basis of Christian community.[13] Equity shines in the Christian heart. Vernacular translations of the Bible proliferated equity in religious texts, no more so than in translations of the Book of Psalms. Psalms were translated many times both within and independent of translations of the Bible as a whole. Psalms played a part in liturgy and worship, in religious song, and in private devotion. Works of casuistry also multiplied in the seventeenth century. Casuistry is concerned with how one follows the dictates of conscience, especially in the face of laws that might seem to run counter. Equity was used repeatedly in these calculations. William Perkins, for example, distinguished between laws of common equity, whose righteousness transcended any particular historical period, and laws of particular equity, limited to a specific historical situation.[14] Casuists varied in the degree to which they condoned equity and the Christian conscience standing against law, but as much as it might be hemmed in, as William Ames wrote: "Nothing but the law of God doth properly, directly, immediately, and by it selfe bind the conscience."[15] Dissenters, especially religious radicals in the 1640s, were much readier to stand against secular and religious authority in the name of individual conscience. In a set of tracts that, not atypically, combine religion and politics, John Warr posits equity and conscience, the golden rule and *salus populi*, as ultimately supplanting all law.[16]

Literature and Equity

A commonplace trope of particular interest to students of law and literature is the invocation throughout the period of an equitable reader.

[11] Roger L'Estrange, *L'Estrange His Apology* (London, 1660), p. 107.

[12] Jean Calvin, *A Harmonie Upon the Three Evangelists, Matthew Mark and Luke* (London, 1584), p. 216.

[13] See Guenther H. Haas, *The Concept of Equity in Calvin's Ethics* (Ontario: Wilfrid Laurier University Press, 1997).

[14] William Perkins, *William Perkins, 1558–1602, English Puritanist* (Nieuwkoop: B. De Graaf, 1966), pp. 12–13.

[15] William Ames. *Conscience with the Power and Cases Thereof* (Amsterdam: Walter J. Johnson Inc., 1975), p. 167.

[16] John Warr, *A Spark in the Ashes: The Pamphlets of John Warr* (London: Verso, 1992).

Especially in dedicatory material, writers routinely ask for an equitable reading – impartial, fair, and generous-hearted. One of the most noteworthy examples is Ben Jonson's dedication of *Volpone* to "THE MOST NOBLE AND MOST EQUALL SISTERS THE TWO FAMOUS UNIVERSITIES" – Oxford and Cambridge. "Equall" here is employed in its common early modern usage to mean equitable. The universities have received his play, presumably in university performances, with "LOVE AND ACCEPTANCE" and have been able to look past a strict and overly rigorous application of laws of comedy to see that Jonson's intention is nonetheless to do the office of the comic poet, "to imitate justice, and instruct to life."[17] Another example can be found in Milton's Latin poem to John Rouse, in which he foresees a day sometime in the future when readers might bring to his controversial positions "Iudicia rebus aequiora" – a more equitable judgment of things.[18] Subha Mukherji notes the importance of the equitable reader, or an audience as equitable jury, as one way in which law and literature conceives of the reader as approaching the displays of justice and injustice one finds in works of literature: The text posits the reader as in a privileged position to decide what is equitable, just, and fair.[19]

In prominent literary works of the period, equity, however variously construed, is explicitly or implicitly a theme or prominent concern. Philip Sidney's *Arcadia*, for instance, culminates in the trials of Palladius and Timopyrus for the murder of the king and rape and kidnapping of his daughters. Euarchus, visiting the city, is asked to judge the cases. Euarchus has a very strong reputation as one who "hath always had his determinations bounded with equity."[20] The two accused are found guilty and condemned to death. At this point it is revealed that they are actually Pyrocles and Musidorus, Euarchus' son and nephew. Euarchus is devastated at the news but decides that justice demands the sentences go ahead. At this moment, the supposed dead king stirs, charges are dropped, and Pyrocles and Musidorus marry the king's daughters.

There is a history of scholarly discussion of Euarchus' equity. The dominant strain rejects the claim that he is really the equitable judge his reputation indicates. In condemning his own son and nephew, he doesn't

[17] Ben Jonson, *Works*, eds. C. H. Herford and Percy Simpson (Oxford: Clarendon Press, 1937), vol. 5, pp. 16–20.

[18] John Milton, *Complete Poems and Major Prose* (Indianapolis: Odyssey Press, 1957), p. 148.

[19] Subha Mukherji, "'understood relations': law and literature in early modern studies," *Literature Compass*, 6(3) (2009), 711.

[20] Philip Sidney, *The Countess of Pembroke's Arcadia* (Middlesex: Penguin, 1977), p. 793.

show the requisite flexibility, clemency, and mercy. A. C. Hamilton, Nancy Lindheim, and Constance Jordan present various versions of this perspective.[21] All draw to some extent upon Aristotle, but it is hard to see, given the evidence presented by the court, that equity demands that the strict law be corrected in this case so that murderers and rapists go unpunished. Rather, the dissatisfaction with Euarchus seems to be based on the fact that he doesn't show a mercy that strict justice might not call for, even when the condemned turn out to be his own flesh and blood. As noted above, however, one of the most common meanings of an equitable judge is a judge who is impartial and disinterested. As Joseph Hall writes: "On the Bench hee is another from himselfe at home; now all private respects of bloud, alliance, amity are forgotten; and if his owne Son come under trial, he knows him not . . . Hee scornes to turn his eye . . . looking onely right forward at Equity."[22] Thus Euarchus declares: "Though strangers then to me, I had no desire to hurt them . . . I weighed the matter which you committed into my hands with my most impartial and furthest reach of reason . . . Now, contrary to all expectations, I find them to be my only son and nephew . . . If rightly I have judged, then rightly have I judged my own children."[23] From this perspective, Euarchus is the epitome of an equitable judge, as painful as that is for him as a father and uncle. Indeed, if, on the discovery of their true identities, he had changed his sentence, he would have been abandoning equity in this sense.

Criticism of Euarchus might be more satisfactorily directed toward the king, Atticus, in the anonymous play *Swetnam, the Woman-Hater*. The king's daughter, Leonida, has been caught out in a romantic dalliance with Lisandro, and one of them must be punished by death. The law, however, allows only one person to be condemned per crime. A court is set up to decide whether the man or the woman is more guilty in such a situation. Misogyny leads to the conclusion that the woman is more guilty. Atticus, resentful of his daughter and concerned for his reputation, declares his impartiality: "But that the world should know our Equitie/Were she a thousand daughters she should die."[24] The king, however, is hardly equitable, concerned more with his reputation than justice, and monstrously

[21] See A. C. Hamilton, *Sir Philip Sidney: A Study of his Life and Works* (Cambridge: Cambridge University Press, 1977), p. 56; Nancy Lindheim, *The Structures of Sidney's Arcadia* (Toronto: University of Toronto Press, 1982), pp. 159–61; Constance Jordan, *Renaissance Feminism: Literary Texts and Political Models* (Ithaca: Cornell University Press, 1990), pp. 234–6.

[22] Joseph Hall, *Characters of Vertues and Vices* (London, 1608), pp. 160–1.

[23] Sidney, *Arcadia*, pp. 841–2.

[24] *Swetnam, the Woman-Hater, Arraigned by Women* (New York: AMS Press, 1970), H3r.

willing to kill a thousand rather than lose face. (In this regard, duplicitous behaviour criticized as pretended equity is another commonplace in the period.) Moreover, the need to punish and the need to punish only the woman are both suspect. Why punish two willing lovers, especially when the suitor is honorable? And even if punishment were necessary, as the more clear-sighted assert: "Both sexes equally should bear the blame."[25] Most striking is Atticus's unnecessary hyperbole that he would kill a thousand daughters if he had to. Cruelty and harshness are his motives. Killing one daughter is horrible enough, even if justified. Killing a thousand is more than monstrous. Indeed, the hyperbole returns us to an issue that equity has a hard time with in these cases: how do we really feel about someone who is willing to condemn his own child? Questions of equity and justice aside, it seems somehow wrong. This may be what is ultimately most disturbing about Euarchus. What seems like equity in the abstract is much more troubling in an actual instance. Of course, both *Arcadia* and *Swetnam, the Woman-Hater* are merciful enough to find us a way out of this situation (in *Swetnam* the king's evil counsellors are exposed and everything comes right). Justice or no justice, we simply don't want to see a father execute his own child. As in Sophocles' *Antigone*, a private allegiance in natural law runs counter to, indeed outweighs, public duty.

Book V of Edmund Spenser's *The Fairie Queene* presents particularly thorny difficulties of interpretation. The book is concerned with justice and continually invokes equity in its understanding of justice. The errant knight meting out justice is Artegall; he is aided predominantly by two others: the iron man, Talus, who is mainly interested in the total decimation of malefactors, and Artegall's lover Britomart, who stands for equity. Equity's purpose is defined early in the book: "to measure out along,/ According to the line of conscience,/When so it needs with rigour to dispence."[26] Later, Britomart is associated with the goddess Isis, who represents equity, which is to say "clemence" that "oft in things amis,/ Restraines those sterne behests, and cruell doomes"[27] of justice, represented by Osiris. Indeed, Isis, as equity, is seen to be in a position of dominance over justice. The idea of mitigating rigor aligns Spenser's sense of equity in part with Aristotle's ἐπιείκεια, but the mitigation is driven by a vague sense of clemency rather than the idea that in certain unforeseen

[25] *Swetnam*, F4r.
[26] Edmund Spenser, *Poetical Works* (London: Oxford University Press, 1970), 5.1.7.
[27] Spenser, *Poetical Works*, 5.7.22.

circumstances the strict application of the law might create an injustice – villains are always guilty and deserving of punishment in Spenser. Spenser's poem, however, shows very little in the way of clemency, even from Britomart. Most often heads roll, limbs are lost, bodies are thrown into rivers or from deadly heights. At one point, Artegall is called "our iudge of equity"[28] and mitigates the punishment of a wrongdoer; Talus, however, takes it upon himself to exact further punishment anyway.

Scholarly literature has dealt with Spenser's inconsistencies in various ways. One way is to act as if there is no problem and the poem is a simple celebration of equity as clemency. This is the argument adopted by T. K. Dunseath.[29] Another group has drawn upon less mainstream understandings of equity to present it as a much harsher force than one might have come to expect, as just severity. Sean Kane and James Nohrnberg adopt this approach.[30] One problem they face is that the text explicitly presents equity as clemency. More recently, Andrew Majeske has argued that Spenser is promoting the idea of equity as uniformity of treatment – treating like cases alike.[31] (Majeske argues that equality of treatment became and remains the dominant, even sole meaning of equity, a position that ignores a vast amount of evidence to the contrary.) Of course, there is a character in Spenser who attempts to make everything equal – the giant in Canto ii who wants to reduce all things to equality. Artegall and Talus make short work of him.

Majeske, therefore, like other scholars of Spenser, has to read against the text itself to come to his position. What really drives his work is a historico-political reading in which Spenser is preparing England for masculine rule after the death of Elizabeth I. Andrew Hadfield similarly reads against the text itself in support of a political interpretation in which Spenser, despite what the text says, is mainly interested in justifying harsh treatment of the Irish.[32]

One other critical attempt to reconcile the discrepancy between the harshness of the poem and its advocacy of equity can be seen in the work

[28] Spenser, *Poetical Works*, 5.3.36.

[29] T. K. Dunseath, *Spenser's Allegory of Justice in Book V of The Fairie Queene* (Princeton: Princeton Univeristy Press, 1968).

[30] Sean Kane, *Spenser's Moral Allegory* (Toronto: University of Toronto Press, 1989); James Norhnberg, *The Analogy of The Fairie Queene* (Princeton: Princeton University Press, 1989).

[31] Andrew Majeske, "Equity in Book V of Spenser's *The Faerie Queene.*" *Law and Literature*, 18(1) (2006), 69–99.

[32] Andrew Hadfield, *Edmund Spenser's Irish Experience: Wilde Fruit and Salvage Soyl* (Oxford: Oxford University Press, 1997).

of Richard Mallette, Robin Headlam Wells, and Jon A. Quitslund.[33] Here a distinction is made between an ideal and a fallen world. What may work for Isis and Osiris is not going to be feasible in our imperfect world. Ideals of equity remain ideals, but they must be set aside in the harsh reality encountered by Artegall. Unfortunately, this view renders the exercise of equity in the world as we know it somewhat moot.

Shakespeare is the early modern literary figure most often taken as dealing with questions of equity. On the one hand this is not surprising – Shakespeare's stature means he is always coming to the fore; on the other, it is surprising inasmuch as Shakespeare uses the word equity very rarely, and not at all in the two plays most regularly taken to be about equity – *The Merchant of Venice* and *Measure for Measure*.[34]

About *The Merchant of Venice*, Daniel Kornstein has written: "The consensus view is that the play dramatizes the struggle in Shakespeare's England for supremacy between the common law courts and the equitable Courts of Chancery."[35] As with any Shakespeare play, it is foolhardy to suggest a consensus view. Relatively recently, for example, two American judges looking at the play were able to discuss its legal issues without once invoking equity,[36] and a striking thing for a student of law and literature is the great variety of legal issues addressed in the play. Nonetheless, it is not difficult to argue that issues of equity arise in several ways. Most obvious is the focus on mercy over the strict demand for one's rights. On a complicated and arguably anti-Semitic note, mercy is given a Christian value which the Jew, Shylock, rejects, although Shylock states eloquently that for better and for worse he is the same as the Christians around him. As we shall also see in *Measure for Measure*, Shakespeare's judges (Portia, Angelo, Vincenzio) are anything but impartial in the way called for by equity. It has often been noted that Portia's strict adherence to the letter of the law runs counter to equity's focus on its intention and spirit.[37] One remedy

33 Richard Mallette, "Book V of *The Fairie Queene*: An Elizabethan Apocalypse," *Spenser Studies*, XI (1994), 129–59; Robin Headlam Wells, *Spenser's Fairie Queene and the Cult of Elizabeth* (London: Croom Helm, 1983); Jon A. Quitslund, *Spenser's Supreme Fiction: Platonic Natural Philosophy and The Fairie Queene* (Toronto: University of Toronto Press, 2001).

34 William Shakespeare, *The Riverside Shakespeare*, ed. Gwynne Blakemore Evans (Boston: Houghton Mifflin, 1974), pp. 254–83, 550–85.

35 Daniel J. Kornstein, *Kill All the Lawyers? Shakespeare's Legal Appeal* (Princeton: Princeton University Press, 1994), p. 66.

36 Richard A. Posner, "Law and commerce in *The Merchant of Venice*" and Charles Fried, "Opinion of Fried, J., concurring in the judgment" in Braddin Cormack, Martha C. Nussbaum and Richard Strier (eds.), *Shakespeare and the Law: A Conversation among Disciplines and Professions* (Chicago: University of Chicago Press, 2013), pp. 147–55; 156–63.

37 See, for example, Gary Watt, *Equity Stirring* (Oxford: Hart Publishing, 2009), pp. 214–16.

only available in equity is specific performance, whereby the court is able to decree that a certain thing be done or a certain piece of property exchange hands, as opposed to the monetary damages more usual in the common law. Shylock's demand for the pound of flesh rather than any economic compensation is a demand for specific performance. Whatever Shylock's right to the pound of flesh, his demand casts specific performance in a rather unsavory light. Moreover, Brian Jay Corrigan has unpacked the arrangements as to property given in use to Antonio in the court's final decision: The trust, in which something is given to someone (Antonio) to use for the benefit of another (Shylock and then indirectly Lorenzo and Jessica), is a remedy only available in equity.[38] This jumble of equitable issues is difficult to draw into a straight line. The call for the quality of mercy over strict insistence on one's rights would appear to be the high-water mark of equity in the play, but that happens relatively early in the trial scene and by the end we are firmly in the realm of strictness and rigor, which carry the day. One of the major defenders of equity in the Aristotelian sense, Gary Watt, argues that *The Merchant of Venice* is a call for equity, but largely because of its absence in the play, which is a critique of a dominant and oppressive legal formalism.[39]

Measure for Measure works with many legal issues that need explication – the play is, in broad outline, an examination of the entire criminal justice system, an early modern *Law and Order*. B. J. and Mary Sokol and Brian Jay Corrigan have studied marital contract law to understand how the various arrangements in the play are supposed to work.[40] *Measure for Measure* has also regularly been taken to be a play about equity: Debora Kuller Shuger, Joel Levin, Stephen Cohen, and David Bevington have all done so in relatively recent scholarship.[41] In addition to questions of mitigation and mercy versus rigor and how to deal with an overly harsh

[38] Brian Jay Corrigan, *Playhouse Law in Shakespeare's World* (Madison: Fairleigh Dickinson University Press, 2004), pp. 103–10.

[39] Watt, *Equity Stirring*, p. 195.

[40] B. J. Sokol and Mary Sokol, *Shakespeare, Law, and Marriage* (Cambridge: Cambridge University Press, 2003); Brian J. Corrigan. *Playhouse Law in Shakespeare's World* (Madison: Fairleigh Dickinson University Press, 2004), pp. 134–90.

[41] Debora Kuller Shuger, *Political Theologies in Shakespeare's England: The Sacred and the State in Measure for Measure* (Basingstoke: Palgrave, 2001); Joel Levin, "The measure of law and equity: tolerance in Shakespeare's Vienna" in Bruce L. Lockwood (ed.), *Law and Literature Perspectives* (New York: Peter Lang, 1996), pp. 193–207; Stephen Cohen, "From mistress to master: political transition and formal conflict in *Measure for Measure*," *Criticism* 41(4) (1999), 431–64; David Bevington, "Equity in *Measure for Measure*" in Braddin Cormack, Martha C. Nussbaum, and Richard Strier (eds.), *Shakespeare and the Law: A Conversation among Disciplines and Professions* (Chicago: University of Chicago Press, 2013), pp. 164–73.

law, critics have focused on the equitable wisdom and authority bestowed upon the monarch (a connection is made between the Duke and James I). As with discussions of the Duke, views vary as to whether monarchical equitable authority is to be admired (Shuger) or seen as a colorable tool of the powermonger (Cohen).

Shakespeare's main source for *Measure for Measure* is George Whetstone's two-part play, *Promos and Cassandra.* Unlike Shakespeare's play, *Promos and Cassandra* does feature the word equity. First, there is talk of the balance of justice and pity needed "to Judge with equity."[42] Second, the play, like Shakespeare's, concerns a self-interested judge: Promos uses the law to attempt a seduction of Cassandra as Angelo does with Isabella. Following on this, equity in Whetstone's play is focused on the equitable, impartial judge, or the lack thereof. Shakespeare's Angelo is a similarly partial and inequitable judge. The complication in Shakespeare is that, while the King in Whetstone is an equitable and impartial judge, preferring "the general benefit of the cõmon weale"[43] (*salus populi*) before any personal inclination, the Duke in Shakespeare, with his proposal to Isabella, shows himself to be just as interested as Angelo. This circumstance casts special scrutiny on the Duke: Is his judge unjust and inequitable because he is not impartial, or does Shakespeare's play open the possibility that a partial judge is not always a bad thing? The possibility of beneficial partiality hints at a bigger question posed by Shakespearean comedy and problem play: Do we really trust the law or are we better off putting our faith in extrajudicial justice, in misrepresentation, disguise, tricks, and pretended legalism? Such a position presents a very basic challenge to the rule of law itself. Shylock asserts that if the court doesn't give him exactly what the contract calls for, it undoes the rule of law; however, Portia's self-interested fraud is a much deeper undermining of law, for better or worse. Law and literature as an interdiscipline has been founded on a mutual interest, even a basic trust, in law. It may be, however, that many prominent literary works, in their search for justice, eschew law and work extrajudicially: through revenge, vigilantism, fraud, disguise, the harboring of outlaws, the giving of aid to criminals. Many literary narratives exhibit a very strong disrespect for the law.

The texts by a major early modern literary figure that most systematically and carefully utilize the basic notions of Aristotelian equity are perhaps

42 George Whetstone, *The Right Excellent and Famous Historye, of Promos and Cassandra* (New York: AMS Press, 1970), C1r.

43 Whetstone, *Promos and Cassandra*, L3v.

the divorce tracts of John Milton. Equity appears in passing in other works by Milton, including *Paradise Lost* and *Paradise Regained*, but the only sustained usage is in his advocacy for freedom to divorce.

Behind Milton's position is a dissenter's belief in the equity of the Christian conscience, which gives one the authority to make one's own decisions on issues of personal morality; religious and secular authorities should impinge as little as necessary on the decisions of the good Christian man. The trouble Milton's arguments for divorce face is that the Bible explicitly forbids divorce, especially in the New Testament. The importance of biblical text in religious disputation is nearly impossible to overemphasize, although these texts are open to a range of interpretation. God's word and laws, however, cannot be read equitably in the way human laws can be. God foresees all things, so one cannot argue that a particular case is not something the law planned for; nor is God's justice imperfect and in need of correction. Within these parameters, Milton undertakes an equitable reading of sacred text on divorce.

There are four important biblical passages on divorce, but focusing on two will suffice. The first is Deuteronomy 24.1: "When a man hath taken a wife, and married her, and it come to pass that she find no favour in his eyes, because he hath found som uncleanness in her, then let him write her a bill of divorcement, and give it in her hand, and send her out of his house." Matthew 5.31–2: in Milton's version, "It hath beene said whosoever shall put away his wife, let him give her a writing of divorcement. But I say unto you that whosoever shall put away his wife, &c." Here is the "&c": "saving for the cause of fornication, causeth her to commit adultery: and whosoever shall marry her that is divorced committeth adultery." What Milton tries ineffectually to sweep under the "&c" is a strong condemnation of divorce. Typically, the New Testament loosens older prohibitions placed on the believer, as in the case of dietary restrictions; in the case of divorce the situation is reversed, and Christ is a tougher taskmaster than Moses. Divorce in this situation is not an easy sell. What Milton attempts is to find "the best and equalest sense" of scripture against "the strictness of a literal interpreting" in which meaning is "blockt up within their owne letters from all equity and fair deduction."[44]

Milton undertakes several moves of equitable interpretation. First he turns from what the Bible says about divorce to what it says, in the beginning, about marriage. What is the purpose of marriage and the laws

[44] John Milton, *Complete Prose Works* (New Haven: Yale University Press, 1959), vol. 2., pp. 242, 244, 327.

that serve it? In Genesis 2:18, God, seeing Adam before the creation of Eve, declares, "*It is not good*, saith he, *that man should be alone; I will make him a help meet for him.*" From this passage Milton concludes that "in Gods intention a meet and happy conversation is the chiefest and the noblest end of marriage."[45] Since no law, especially God's, should be taken to contradict its own purpose, all laws relating to marriage, and by extension to divorce, serve this intention. If a man, however – especially an innocent, pure, and inexperienced one – should find himself married to someone with whom a meet and happy conversation is impossible, would God, in his kindness, want that man to stay in that marriage, if it even is a marriage, given that it contravenes the purpose of marriage? (The situation is analogous to that of the city guard in the example above from Saint German.) Isn't this an even crueler situation than Adam in his loneliness, in that one is tied to a hateful companionship without any hope of release or any expectation, though bitterly aware of the difference, of real marital comfort? It is not good. Could God really want that? Human life is hard enough already.

Deuteronomy is some help to Milton, allowing as it does for divorce. And if one reads uncleanness broadly and equitably to mean anything that prevents a meet and happy conversation ("exceptions that arise from natural equity are included silently under general terms"[46]), it goes most of the way to where Milton wants it to go. But Matthew 5:31–2 still stands in the way. Milton employs several ideas to attempt to reconcile Deuteronomy and Matthew. First, he discounts that God could mean to make the Jews freer than Christians. Equity protects the innocent and righteous; how could it be harsher on the gentle Christian than on the unbelieving Jew? Next he reads Matthew in context. Jesus was a teacher and a persuader and spoke to those ends. Sometimes he got angry. If these ideas are put together, it is possible to argue that Jesus was overstating something to make a point. He was condemning a too easy recourse to divorce, rather than divorce as a necessary action by the pure of heart. Jesus does seem to condone divorce in the case of fornication. If fornication is read equitably, to include in addition any uncleanness that truly undermines marital communion (a couple might be capable of moving past adultery but not past irreconcilable differences of another sort), then Jesus is supporting something like Milton's position on divorce, what Milton asserts to be "unabolishable equity."[47]

[45] Milton, *Complete*, pp. 245–6. [46] Milton, *Complete*, 330. [47] Milton, *Complete*, 651.

Milton's arguments from equity raise two abiding issues. First: Perhaps not for Milton, but for us, his arguments raise more recent concerns of gender equity. Both the passages from Deuteronomy and Matthew, curiously enough, are about what happens to the woman when a man seeks divorce, but that is not Milton's concern, which stays largely with the male. He equivocates about the right of women to seek a divorce: Divorce should be allowed with "the will and consent of both parties, or of the husband alone."[48] The suggestion from another writer that wives but not husbands can sue for divorce he finds "palpably uxorious": "woman was created for man," not man for woman.[49] Milton's equity only takes him so far. He would not, we can be sure, condone or support same-sex marriage as we are doing in our time, even though if the purpose of marriage is "meet and happy conversation" and one can get this from a person of the same sex, it would be equitable by his criteria to accept that as marriage.

The second issue is more basic and difficult. Self-interest runs counter to the disinterest equity looks for in a judge. As we have seen, Shakespeare is, contrary to this basic equitable precept, relatively open to self-interested judges and legal decision makers. It is sometimes held against Milton that his arguments are self-serving: The assumption is that he himself was interested in a divorce from the wife who had abandoned him and returned to her parents. His self-interest somehow taints his argument. On the other hand, our adversarial justice system works by positioning the parties in a case, though not the judge, to assert their self-interest. No one expects them to be neutral. Moreover, in various rights movements, it is assumed that those seeking rights for people like themselves are best positioned to assert those rights and to understand their need. There is valid suspicion when someone from outside seeks to speak on behalf of an oppressed group. Is equity opposed to arguing from self-interest or is it only opposed to interestedness in judges? If disinterest is good for judges (*pace* Shakespeare), why not for those who speak on behalf of a cause? Don't we trust salespeople more if they aren't working on commission? Gordian knot or hornets' nest, the conflicting relations between equitable disinterest, an interest in what's fair just because it's fair, and the drive to assert and argue for one's own interest are basic in working toward justice, and not easily worked through.

[48] Milton, *Complete*, 344. [49] Milton, *Complete*. 324.

CHAPTER 8

Gender, Law, and the Birth of Bourgeois Civil Society

Cheryl Nixon

The Juridical Imagination: The Domestic Novel and Domestic Relations

Eliza Haywood's proto-novel *The Rash Resolve* (1724) features an orphan, Emanuella, left in the care of an uncle "who by her Father's Will, and her own Consent was made her Guardian, having the vast Fortune left her in his Possession, could not think of parting with it so easily."[1] In her construction of this guardian/ward family, Haywood is careful to note the father's last will and the ward's consent, emphasizing that this is a legal relationship in addition to a familial one. The dramatic possibilities of the legal family are clear: The uncle, Don Pedro, supervises Emanuella's person and estate – and he is loath to give up that power. *The Rash Resolve* details Emanuella's attempts to escape Don Pedro's control after he confines her in his house and attempts to force her to marry his son, Don Marco. The narrative builds to a legal confrontation in which both characters argue their case before the King of Spain in Madrid. Don Marco makes a formal complaint against Emanuella, which takes the textual form of "A brief Abstract of the Crimes alledged against Donna Emanuella."[2]

In contrast, Emanuella advances her legal case by telling a compelling story. She opens her case by exclaiming, "Wonder not, Royal Sir! ... I [will] not await the dull Formalities of Law ... but here presume to make my own Defence unaided but by Truth – Permit me then, great King! To unfold a Story [that] must make my vile Accuser's Heart grow cold within him, tho' warm'd with all the Fires from Hell."[3] She continues to "relate the whole Affair with the greatest Truth and Exactness."[4] Her only support is this narrative evidence, which wins over many of the audience

[1] Eliza Haywood, *The Rash Resolve, Or, The Untimely Discovery* (London: D. Browne and S. Chapman, 1724), p. 4.

[2] Heywood, *Rash Resolve*, p. 33.

[3] Heywood, *Rash Resolve*, p. 33.

[4] Heywood, *Rash Resolve*, p. 33.

who were "confident of her Sincerity."[5] However, Don Pedro's material evidence is substantial, and it is "very near carrying the Cause against her" when Don Marco bursts into the trial to provide dramatic proof of Emanuella's innocence. After "confirm[ing] all Emanuella had averr'd,"[6] he draws his sword and falls on it, making the dying proclamation: "Thus! I hope convince your sacred Majesty, and the yet unbelieving World, that it contains not a Jewel of more worth that Emanuella! – Hear, and believe me, Sir!"[7] The stunned Don Pedro admits his guilt and Emanuella is "dismiss'd with those Encomiums which her modest, but courageous Behaviour merited."[8] The scene ends by noting that "This Adventure engross'd the whole Discourse of the Town for a great while," so that even those who did not know Emanuella "were perfectly well acquainted with her by Report."[9]

Haywood's proto-novel obviously provides an example of "law in literature," in which the legal process is represented in and offers compelling structure to fictional narrative. More interestingly, it provides an example of how the developing novel articulates new possibilities for justice by imagining idealized applications of the law. *The Rash Resolve* depicts the law as fulfilling its promise to determine innocence – but only because it provides a space for the woman's voice to be heard and embraces her storylike narrative as a form of truth. As this short scene demonstrates, the eighteenth-century novel dramatizes juridical subjectivity, or the individual's perception of reality as mediated by his or her understanding of the processes, goals, and ideals – both the form and the content – of the law. Furthermore, the novel encourages the new development of a popular juridical imagination that embraces the most idealistic aspirations of the law, asserting the importance of concepts such as truth, justice, honesty, innocence, and morality by demonstrating that they often remain unrealized by the law.

This chapter explores how domestic fiction stimulates the juridical imagination by drawing on multiple forms of law, including common law, canon law, and equity, in order to express the possibility of a just, moral civil society. Although critics such as John Bender, John Zomchick, and Hal Gladfelder connect the developing novel to the individualism and realism of the criminal law, a different alignment of eighteenth-century law and literature is possible: The domestic novel, with its popular plots of

[5] Heywood, *Rash Resolve*, p. 33.
[6] Heywood, *Rash Resolve*, p. 33.
[7] Heywood, *Rash Resolve*, p. 35.
[8] Heywood, *Rash Resolve*, p. 36.
[9] Heywood, *Rash Resolve*, p. 36.

courtship, marriage, and family conflict, can be connected to the multiple legal systems that address what the eighteenth-century law labels "domestic relations."[10] The eighteenth century's legal definitions of parent–child and husband–wife relationships provide the foundation for what the twentieth century came to term "family law."[11] As fully explored in well-known studies by critics such as Nancy Armstrong, Helen Thompson, and Eve Tavor Bannet, domestic fiction – rooted in the romance, and ranging from early amatory fiction to seduction and courtship novels to novels of sensibility and manners – positions the woman as defining domestic life and the moral structuring of its relationships; because the woman cannot fully access the law as part of that activity, these novels often feature provocative reimaginings of the law's role in these relationships.[12] Many of the best-known eighteenth-century novels, from *Betsy Thoughtless*, *Tom Jones*, and *Clarissa* to *Cecilia*, *A Simple Story*, and *Sense and Sensibility*, feature characters who negotiate the legal difficulties of the parent–child relationship, including custody, guardianship, and inheritance, only to move on to the legal difficulties of the marriage relationship, including the proper forms of consent and correct transfer of property and name. Following the demands of the domestic plot, many of these novels close with truth revealed and virtue rewarded, or, to use terms that can be affiliated with the common law, canon law, and equity courts, justice preserved, morality upheld, and equity achieved.[13] Even when the law is overtly critiqued, the novel's concluding scenes of family reunion, community balance, and happy marriage signal that civil society has been achieved.

The novel's reimagining of the "real" law posits an idealized law that springs from perfected domestic relations, offering a popular articulation of

[10] John Bender, *Imagining the Penitentiary: Fiction and the Architecture of Mind in Eighteenth-Century England* (Chicago: University of Chicago Press, 1987); John Zomchick, *Family and the Law in Eighteenth-Century Fiction: The Public Conscience in the Private Sphere* (Cambridge: Cambridge University Press, 1993); Hal Gladfelder, *Criminality and Narrative in Eighteenth-Century England: Beyond the Law* (Baltimore: Johns Hopkins University Press, 2001).

[11] Janet Halley, "What is family law? A genealogy, Part I." *Yale Journal of Law & the Humanities*, 23(1) (2011), 2, 7–10.

[12] Nancy K. Armstrong, *Desire and Domestic Fiction: A Political History of the Novel* (Oxford: Oxford University Press, 1987); Helen Thompson, *Ingenious Subjection: Compliance and Power in the Eighteenth-Century Domestic Novel* (Philadelphia: University of Pennsylvania Press, 2005); Eve Tavor Bannet, *The Domestic Revolution: Enlightenment Feminisms and the Novel* (Baltimore: Johns Hopkins University Press, 2000).

[13] Michael McKeon sees the novel as addressing essential "questions of virtue and questions of truth." See *The Origins of the English Novel 1600–1740* (Baltimore: Johns Hopkins University Press, 1987), p. 20.

the philosophical ideals of natural law and civil society. In the eighteenth century, this reimagining aligns with the growth of what Jürgen Habermas has famously and controversially labeled a bourgeois "public sphere."[14] As Habermas theorizes, the eighteenth century can only create a public sphere defined by political and economic life by imagining its counterpoint: a private sphere defined by the "humanity of intimate relationships" that "raised bourgeois ideology above ideology itself."[15] Importantly, Habermas positions the novel as one of the most powerful conveyors of this new bourgeois ideology.

If the eighteenth-century novel creates a popular juridical imagination that shapes civil society, how best can we uncover that activity and its influence? This chapter explores how the novel reimagines the law and to what ends, proposing that the domestic novel offers a clear answer: The novel shapes popular understandings of the law by dramatizing the ways in which the law fails women and the ways in which women remedy that failure by perfecting domestic relations. Brief explorations of Frances Burney's *Evelina* (1778), Charlotte Smith's *The Old Manor House* (1793), Mary Wollstonecraft's *The Wrongs of Women: or, Maria* (1798), and Sarah Scott's *Millenium Hall* (1762) provide examples of the wide range of strategies the novel uses to rewrite the law's regulation of familial relationships. The domestic novel also reveals how the novel gives those rewritings cultural power. In addition to replotting specific elements of the law, the novel plays a powerful role in shaping the eighteenth-century understanding of the law by synthesizing the law's multiple, often contradictory forms into a coherent narrative about the woman's position within the law. And the novel is able to circulate that account much more widely and quickly than the law itself. Just as is dramatized in *The Rash Resolve*, the novel can "unfold a Story" about a woman's legal plight in a way that the law's "dull Formalities" cannot – and it can circulate that dramatic story widely, ensuring it "engross[es] . . . the Town."[16]

Reimagining the Family: Enacting the Law beyond the Law

The juridical imagination confronts a legal system that does not uphold its promises. Most obviously, the rights promised within eighteenth-century civil society are unequally apportioned between the genders. The domestic

[14] Jurgen Habermas, *The Structural Transformation of the Public Sphere: An Inquiry into a Category of Bourgeois Society* (Cambridge: MIT Press, 1991).

[15] Habermas, *Structural Transformation of the Public Sphere*, 48.

[16] Heywood, *Rash Resolve*, p. 36.

novel takes this failure as its central topic and often offers surprisingly radical critiques of the law's inability to provide rights to women. The novel positions the female character – typically an underage and unprotected daughter figure – as the source of this critique. This character variously submits to, questions, confronts, and circumvents the processes of the law in order to ultimately secure a moral form of justice that awards her power to create a more equitable civil society. The novel's use of the disempowered young women to express the ideals of justice, equity, and morality is all the more striking when the real legal position of the eighteenth-century women is considered.

At the same time that the domestic novel was depicting the woman as an agent of legal and civic transformation, the legal rights of women, especially within structures of property and marriage, were being eroded. For example, Amy Erickson determines that women's increasing reliance on common law "cut serious inroads into women's already severely restricted entitlement to property."[17] Susan Staves shows how changes in eighteenth-century practices of dower, jointure, pin money, and maintenance worked to disempower wives by evading common law property provisions for them.[18] Eileen Spring agrees, arguing that common law property rights for women eroded and concluding, "When the histories of the heiress, widow, and younger children are considered together, the most striking feature is the decline of women's rights over land."[19] Ruth Perry connects this "great disinheritance" to the increased privatization of marriage that happened after passage of Lord Hardwicke's Marriage Act in 1753, explaining, "Privatized marriage put women increasingly in the power of their husbands as if marriage has the alchemical effect of transforming them into property at the same time as it made over property that they owned to their new masters."[20]

The popular juridical imagination thus imagines a civil society that does not yet exist for women, but that bourgeois culture positions as dependent on the woman and her domestic abilities. The domestic novel draws on these legal realities, counters them with legal possibilities, and demands

17 Amy Louise Erickson, *Women and Property in Early Modern England* (London: Routledge, 1993), p. 230.

18 Susan Staves, *Married Women's Separate Property in England, 1660–1833* (Massachusetts: Harvard University Press, 1990).

19 Eileen Spring, *Law, Land, and Family: Aristocratic Inheritance in England, 1300 to 1800* (Chapel Hill: University of North Carolina Press, 1993), p. 93.

20 Ruth Perry, *Novel Relations: The Transformation of Kinship in English Literature and Culture* (London: Cambridge University Press, 2004), p. 195.

that the law to be true to its ideals. As Robin West argues, "Imaginative literature tells us something that law itself cannot . . . about the meanings of law in the lives of those whom law willfully ignores, subjugates, marginalizes, or excludes."[21] The novel can posit a perfected law that shapes a perfected civil society. As West continues to explain, "literature might somehow have the force of law . . . there may or may not be a firm distinction, in other words, between the law that is, was, or could be and the various products of our literary imagination."[22] The novel's juridical imaginings surely helped to create new cultural critiques of the legal structuring of domestic relations. As Alison L. LaCroix and Martha C. Nussbaum argue, in striking terms, "Overwhelmingly, the eyes of the law were opened by novels."[23]

An emphasis on the juridical imagination reveals the novel's interest in multiple forms of legal ideology and process. John Bender shows how eighteenth-century criminal law supports what he terms the "juridical novel," in which the novel and the law operate through systems of control that become increasingly abstracted and internalized.[24] John Zomchick counters Bender's equation of the law with discipline by uncovering the "juridical subject," a figure that "owes its coherence to a system of legal beliefs, principles, and practices."[25] Although this figure would seem to be controlled by the law, Zomchick argues that it is "a subject empowered by her or his internalization of [the] law," which allows a "rehabilitation of the subject . . . as an active agent capable of carving out a space of freedom and enjoying it."[26] Susan Sage Heinzelman furthers this emphasis on the novel's articulation of freedom by exploring connections between early amatory fiction and a "flexible legal sphere."[27] She explains that "the amatory and the juridical are intertwined and create an imaginary (but not, therefore an unreal) space that is neither public nor private, neither masculine nor feminine and which lies outside of the jurisdiction of either literature or law," and continues, "This imaginary space is precisely where law happens and literature simultaneously records the consequences."[28]

[21] Robin West, "Literature, culture, and law at Duke University" in Austin Sarat, Cathrine O. Frank, and Matthew Anderson (eds.), *Teaching Law and Literature* (New York: MLA, 2011), p. 100.
[22] West, "Literature, Culture, and Law," p. 98.
[23] Alison L. LaCroix and Martha C. Nussbaum (eds.), *Subversion and Sympathy: Gender, Law, and the British Novel* (Oxford: Oxford University Press, 2013), p. 4.
[24] See Bender's chapter 6, "Fielding and the juridical novel," in *Imagining the Penitentiary*, pp. 165–200.
[25] Zomchick, *Family and the Law*, p. xi. [26] Zomchick, *Family and the Law*, pp. xi, xv.
[27] Susan Sage Heinzelman, *Riding the Black Ram: Law, Literature, and Gender* (Stanford: Stanford University Press, 2010), p. 48.
[28] Heinzelman, *Riding the Black Ram*, p. 66.

Because it often focuses on the figure of the mistreated woman who has no access to the law, the juridical imagination proposes forms of justice, equity, and morality that operate outside of legal forms and structure. The novel interrogates the legal structuring of the woman's place in domestic relations, even when it avoids depicting and dramatizing the court and its legal procedures. A brief examination of Burney's well-known *Evelina* illustrates how the popular novel engages with family law by embedding its legal concerns within a compelling domestic plot.[29] As with many domestic novels, *Evelina* features a disrupted family structure, one that allows the law to enter into the seemingly private realm of the family. At the center of the novel is an injustice: Evelina has been disowned by her biological father, Sir John Belmont, and must live with a guardian, Reverend Arthur Villars. The novel uses this legal guardian/ward structure to reveal and remedy the injustices that it finds in the family's treatment of the underage daughter.

Legally, the guardianship of a child contains two distinct responsibilities: the guardianship of the person and the guardianship of the estate. Not only are these powers repeatedly referenced in *Evelina*, but they also structure the novel's central conflicts and dramatic arc. *Evelina* is clearly informed by a legal understanding of these powers, which are consistently defined in the contemporary legal treatises. For example, under the heading "The Power of a Guardian," Sir John Comyns' *A Digest of the Laws of England* (1762–7) explains that a father can give to a guardian "the custody and tuition of this child or children till their age at twenty-one" and the "management of their personal estate, till their age of twenty-one."[30] In *A General Abridgment of Law and Equity* (1741–58), Charles Viner simply creates two headings to divide up the powers of the guardian: "Power of the Guardian over the Estate of the Infant" and "Power as to the Person, of the Infant."[31] In his *Commentaries* (1765–9), William Blackstone explains the source of this division, "The guardian ... performs the office both of the *tutor* and *curator* of the Roman laws ... according to the language of the court of chancery, the tutor was the committee of the person, the curator the committee of the estate."[32]

29 Frances Burney, *Evelina* (Oxford: Oxford University Press, 2002).

30 Sir John Comyns, *A Digest of the Laws of England. By the Right Honourable Sir John Comyns... The Fourth Edition, corrected, and continued to the present time, by Samuel Rose*, 2nd edn. (London: Strahan, 1800), pp. 522–3. The first edition is published in 1762–7.

31 Charles Viner, *A General Abridgment of Law and Equity* (Aldershot: The Author, 1741–1758), vol. 7, pp. 180–3.

32 William Blackstone, *Commentaries on the Laws of England* (Oxford: Clarendon Press, 1765), vol. 1, p. 448.

Before we even meet Evelina, the novel emphasizes the two concerns – person and estate – that legally define the underage daughter and her domestic relations. The novel's first letter dramatizes a claim to Evelina's person: Evelina's grandmother Madame Duval plans to take custody of Evelina and bring her to Paris. The novel's fourth letter, written by the guardian Villars, emphasizes Evelina's denied estate; he explains that she can expect only a "very moderate fortune" although she is "legally heiress of two large fortunes."[33] Evelina's conflicted bodily custody becomes dramatized in the Duval relationship and her conflicted estate inheritance becomes dramatized in the Belmont relationship, while Villars works to fulfill and resolve both familial functions, overtly stating, "My plan, therefore, was not merely to educate and to cherish her as my own, but to adopt her as the heiress of my small fortune and bestow her on some worthy man."[34] Before being able to marry her beloved Lord Orville, Evelina must gain control over her person by leaving Duval and gain control over her estate by reclaiming her relationship with her father.

Evelina dramatizes the legal remedies that the woman enacts outside of the forms of law. Villars explains why Evelina's father refuses to recognize her: Before dying in childbirth, Evelina's mother "consented to a private marriage with Sir John Belmont," who later "denied that they had ever been united."[35] If Evelina gains her father's recognition, she not only secures her legal parental relationship, but retroactively secures her mother's legal spousal relationship and her own future spousal relationship. Evelina corrects her mother's failed marriage, which pointedly happened outside of the law, through her own "extralegal" actions that remind her father of the higher moral values that should be expressed by law but often are not. The novel calls attention to the woman's inability to use the formal mechanisms of the law and her ability to replace those mechanisms with more effective actions. Duval urges a lawsuit be taken up against Belmont, forcing him to claim Evelina as his legitimate daughter; Evelina explains that Duval "would have nothing to do with any *round-about ways*, but [would] go openly and instantly to law, in order to prove my birth, real name, and title to the state of my ancestors."[36] Villars will not allow this lawsuit, stating, "The law-suit . . . I wholly and absolutely disapprove," and continues to protest, "Never can I consent to have this dear and timid girl brought forward to the notice of the world by such a method; a method, which will subject her to all the impertinence of curiosity . . . And for what? – the

[33] Burney, *Evelina*, pp. 18, 20. [34] Burney, *Evelina*, p. 141. [35] Burney, *Evelina*, p. 15.
[36] Burney, *Evelina*, p. 136.

attainment of wealth, which she does not want, and the gratification of vanity, which she does not feel. – A child to appear against a father!"[37] Asserting his understanding of Evelina's estate and person, Villars clearly believes such an act – a daughter proceeding in a lawsuit in a public courtroom against her father – will not succeed.[38]

Belmont eventually agrees to see Evelina, who forces him to read the most personal, emotional narrative provided in the novel: the letter from Evelina's mother written on her deathbed. A climactic scene of mutual reclamation results, featuring Belmont accepting Evelina as "my child, my child," kneeling before Evelina, and asking to be accepted by her. She cries out, "reverse not the law of nature" and kneels to him in return.[39] What the lawsuit could not achieve, then, the "round-about ways" of a female-authored narrative and female-centered action can. Although (unlike *The Rash Resolve*) it cannot envision a woman in a courtroom, *Evelina* desires the familial restructuring offered by the law and ultimately awards Evelina the benefits such a lawsuit would bring. Secured outside the law, that resolution relies on a woman's writing (the mother's letter) and a woman's actions (Evelina's visit with her father). The domestic novel is able to restructure domestic relations; a father and daughter kneel before each other rather than appear against each other in court. This just, equitable, and moral resolution is imagined through the novel rather than the law.

Restructuring the Court System: Synthesizing the Law

The eighteenth-century novel is not only able to reimagine the law, but is also able to give those reimaginings cultural power. An important aspect of the juridical imagination is that it is a synthetic imagination. The eighteenth-century novel creates a coherent understanding of the law out of a complex and fragmented court system, creating an image of the law that is more powerful than the law's own self-definitions. The eighteenth-century subject would not have experienced the law as a monolithic institution, but would have understood it to be an inefficient, bureaucratic system that encompassed several overlapping and competing court systems. Each court system practiced a distinct form of law with differing

[37] Burney, *Evelina*, pp. 142–3.

[38] Susan Greenfield examines this potential lawsuit, arguing that "the suit is unlikely to succeed not simply because of the problems surrounding Caroline's marriage but because the law is unresponsive to women's victimization" (p. 47). See *Mothering Daughters: Novels and the Politics of Family Romance, Frances Burney to Jane Austen* (Detroit: Wayne State University Press, 2002).

[39] Burney, *Evelina*, p. 428.

ideological goals. In addition, each system followed different forms, with unique procedures for initiating and pleading a case, presenting evidence and witnesses, deciding a case by judge or jury, and maintaining and referring to legal records. If an individual sought legal redress, it was often unclear exactly which court system to use and, even after a court was selected, what procedural forms to use to advance the case. The well-known historian Lawrence Stone explains: "The eighteenth-century legal system – if system it can be called – was ... a dense, complex, and bewildering jungle, full of contradictions, anomalies, legal fictions, and downright foolishness. Natural justice seems even more remote from the law than is usually the case."[40] He concludes with a warning, "To enter the eighteenth-century machinery of the law is to penetrate the heart of darkness."[41]

The novel brings light to this darkness, synthesizing these court systems by incorporating them into familiar narrative structures. Even when critiquing them by calling attention to their duplication and fragmentation, the novel gives them an order and coherence they lack. A brief review of the five court systems that comprised eighteenth-century law reveals why the juridical imagination is needed.

First, the common law upholds Britain's traditional or customary understandings of justice. Famously uncodified – not written down as a comprehensive set of rules – common law is created through the accretion of precedent-setting cases that are decided by a judge and jury and affirmed as binding for similar cases. The common law courts included the King's (or Queen's) Bench, the Court of Common Pleas, and the Court of Exchequer, which determined criminal law and several forms of civil law. Second, common law was supplemented by equity, a form of justice practiced in the Court of Chancery. Developed to remedy the failings of the common law, equity was founded as a court of conscience that exists outside of or beyond the law. It did not use a jury, but relied on the discretion of the Chancellor to determine the correct application of justice. Equity claimed jurisdiction over trusts, which structured many domestic relationships, including guardianship.[42] Third, ecclesiastical law was founded on canon law; unlike precedent-based common law and equity, ecclesiastical law implemented written laws that originated in Roman law.

40 Lawrence Stone, *Road to Divorce: England 1530–1987* (Oxford: Oxford University Press, 1992), p. 27.

41 Stone, *Road to Divorce*, p. 27.

42 J. H. Baker, *An Introduction to English Legal History* (Oxford: Oxford University Press, 2005).

Canon law emphasized the collection and recording of evidence, including extensive witness testimony, which was reviewed by a Chancellor. The ecclesiastical courts oversaw moral and spiritual matters as embodied in civil law, including marriage law and the probate administration of a deceased person's estate. Fourth, statutory law was created by legislation passed by parliament, providing the written laws of the country. In addition to these Public Acts, statutory law also took a private form – parliament hears and passes Private Acts that remedy individual complaints.[43] And, finally, at the opposite end of the spectrum was a fifth form of local law: manorial and customary law that empowered the lord of an estate to resolve local disputes. Rooted in feudal law, manorial law granted a lord jurisdiction over conflicts between tenants and property improvements or transactions.

The novel recognizes these often contradictory structures and uses them to dramatic effect. For example, the climax of Smith's *Old Manor House* features the hero Orlando's attempt to prove that he is the rightful heir to Rayland Hall by engaging with common law, equity, and canon law. He wants to secure a home for himself and his beloved Monimia, who had lived in Rayland Hall as a ward under her great-aunt Mrs. Lennard. As he advances his legal case, Orlando attempts to help his brother Philip, who has incorrectly entered cases in both common law and Chancery.[44] Orlando's lawyer, Carr, explains, "all your elder brother's proceeding have been wrong, and will only mar ours . . . we must begin again, and file a bill of discovery."[45] Carr and Orlando then confront a series of dishonest lawyers (Roker, Fisherton, and Darby), who each represent a different facet of the law. As they attempt to prove a case that looks increasingly hopeless, Orlando's actions are structured by the inefficiencies of the law: He attempts to track down witnesses to a revised will and counter an uncle's pressure to secure a new lawyer,[46] while "another Term was almost wasted in those contrived delays which destroy all the boasted energy and simplicity of the British laws."[47]

Smith creates a coherent narrative out of the eighteenth century's complex multicourt system in order to criticize it. The disappointments

[43] See my explanation of Public Acts and survey of Private Acts: Cheryl Nixon, *The Orphan in Eighteenth-Century Law and Literature: Estate, Blood, and Body* (Burlington: Ashgate, 2011), pp. 73–5, 90–9.

[44] Charlotte Smith, *The Old Manor House*, ed. Anne Henry Ehrenpreis (Oxford: Oxford University Press, 1989), pp. 446–51.

[45] Smith, *Old Manor House*, p. 449.

[46] Smith, *Old Manor House*, pp. 448–506.

[47] Smith, *Old Manor House*, p. 494.

of this legal world are overtly contrasted with the virtues of domestic relationships: "amid all the fatigue and disappointments of the law's delay . . . the tenderness, the sweetness of Monimia soothed and tranquilized his trouble spirits; and when he returned to her of an evening, wearied with the contradictory opinions of counsel, or tormented by trifling and unnecessary forms, he seemed to be transported from purgatory to paradise."[48] At the end of the novel, the domestic realm provides not just a refuge from the law, but the resolution to its failings. The novel imagines a moral ending in which a woman comes forward to help secure Orlando's estate, overtly stating that she does so "for the sake of justice."[49] Mrs. Lennard, Monimia's aunt and guardian, has been hiding the revised will that proves Orlando's inheritance. Even though she is married to the lawyer that Orlando is suing, she feels the sting of conscience and writes Orlando a letter directing him to a copy of the will hidden in a staircase. Following common law, Orlando uses a search warrant to secure the will with the help of a constable, and, following ecclesiastical law, he brings the will to London to have it opened and proven. With Orlando able to reclaim his estate, the novel ends with the virtuous domesticity of Orlando and Monimia rewarded. Justice is advanced by the morality of domestic relationships – not the contradictory structures of the law.

Replacing the Legal Record: Circulating the Law

Having reimagined the law, the eighteenth-century novel circulates those reimaginings more efficiently than the law itself. Just as it brings order to the multicourt structure of the law, the juridical imagination lends coherence to the chaotic recordkeeping of these many court systems. Eighteenth-century law was a manuscript institution, with each court keeping voluminous manuscript records that took a bewildering number of forms. Importantly, while the novel could incorporate the individuals' interactions with the law into a coherent narrative of domestic relations, the manuscript records for an individual case in common law, equity, or canon law did not cohere into a unified record that narrates the case from beginning to end. In addition, eighteenth-century recordkeeping practices were not organized with print in mind, and legal publishing was characterized by the struggle to translate these manuscript records into a print form that would document important case decisions for an increasingly precedent-dependent law. *The Old Manor House* provides multiple examples

[48] Smith, *Old Manor House*, p. 494. [49] Smith, *Old Manor House*, p. 524.

of how the inefficiencies of this manuscript practice complicate the search for justice: Orlando's brother is imprisoned while his dishonest lawyer refuses to return the papers central to his case;[50] Orlando "accidentally" casts his eyes upon "bundles of papers" relating to law cases and sees one relating to an old friend's wife who is being unfairly sued;[51] Orlando visits witnesses to secure written testimony because they did not keep correct manuscript records of the revised will.[52] Most obviously, multiple and contradictory manuscript wills undermine Orlando and Monimia's ability to secure the domestic circle they so obviously deserve.

Contrasting the manuscript culture of the law is the print culture of the novel. While the publication of case law was not regularized until the nineteenth century, the eighteenth century developed what George Justice provocatively terms "novel culture."[53] The novel achieved a wide and eager readership, a phenomenon produced by a rapidly developing popular press, furthered by new publishing practices such as reprinting and anthologizing, and supported by institutions such as lending and circulating libraries.[54] Ironically, then, ideas about the law circulated more quickly and more widely in the novel than in the official legal record. Additionally, the novel explored the law within increasingly effective narrative forms that made its critiques emotionally resonant and intellectually compelling.

The interconnected growth of the publishing industry, literacy, and the novel is the subject of numerous detailed studies, and a few key facts can be rehearsed here. James Raven explains that "[t]he fundamental story remains that of the complex penetration of print throughout eighteenth-century society," and demonstrates that "[p]rior to 1700 up to about 1800 different printed titles were produced annually; by 1800 this had risen to over 6000."[55] A small but growing number of novels contributed to this expanding print culture: Raven finds that while only a "handful of works, recognizable as novels" were published in 1700, "nearly one hundred self-proclaimed 'novels'" were published in 1769.[56] In *The English*

50 Smith, *Old Manor House*, p. 447.

51 Smith, *Old Manor House*, p. 450.

52 Smith, *Old Manor House*, p. 454.

53 George Justice, *The Manufacturers of Literature: Writing and the Literary Marketplace in Eighteenth-Century England* (Newark: University of Delaware Press, 2002), pp. 154–7.

54 Alvin Kernan cites figures that show the number of printing presses in London rising from 65 in 1668 to 625 in 1818. St. Clair charts the growth of circulating libraries in London from nine in 1740–50, to nineteen in 1770–80, to twenty-six in 1790–1800 (p. 665).

55 James Raven, "The book trades" in Isabel Rivers (ed.), *Books and Their Readers in Eighteenth-Century England: New Essays* (London: Continuum, 2001), pp. 1–2.

56 James Raven, *British Fiction, 1750–1770: A Chronological Check-List of Prose Fiction Printed in Britain and Ireland* (Newark: University of Delaware Press, 1987), p. 10.

Novel, 1770–1829, Garside, Raven, and Schowlering find that sixty novels were produced in 1771, followed by a short lull in production.[57] Building on these findings, William St. Clair analyzes the growth of novel publication after the 1774 abolition of perpetual copyright, explaining that approximately 3,000 new prose titles were published between 1790 and 1830.[58] Additionally, this period is characterized by the extensive reprinting of older titles, a trend of anthologizing and abridging analyzed by Leah Price.[59] This expansion of print culture followed and furthered the expansion of literacy rates. Vivian Jones explains that, in 1640, 10 percent of women and 33 percent of men could sign their names (the traditional indicator of literacy); by 1700, these figures rose to 30 percent of women and 50 percent of men; and by 1760, they reached 40 percent of women and 60 percent of men, at which levels they remained until the end of the century.[60]

While the eighteenth-century novel could circulate a compelling dramatization of the individual's interactions with the law, the legal record could not. Whereas the novel experienced rapid advances in publication and circulation, the law was bound by its manuscript practices and underwent a slow and disorderly translation into print. The sheer amount and variety of manuscript material generated by any one case was the largest obstacle to creating a unified narrative of an individual case.[61] To take the Chancery Court as an example, a single case consists of a bill and answer known as the "pleadings"; depositions and interrogatories; exhibits or evidence; affidavits; the masters' reports; and the final decree and official registering of this decision in the books of orders and the minute books.[62] The case's records were not held together as a unified whole, but spread across different manuscript collections, organized according to each of these steps. Henry Horwitz and Amy Erickson, historians who have worked

[57] Peter Garside, James Raven, and Rainer Schowerling (eds.), *The English Novel, 1770–1829: A Bibliographical Survey of Prose Fiction Published in the British Isles* (Oxford: Oxford University Press, 2004), vol. 1, p. 26.

[58] William St. Clair, *The Reading Nation in the Romantic Period* (Cambridge: Cambridge University Press, 2004).

[59] Leah Price, *The Anthology and the Rise of the Novel from Richardson to George Eliot* (Cambridge: Cambridge University Press, 2000). Also see St. Clair, *The Reading Nation*, pp. 135, 172–3.

[60] Vivian Jones (ed.), *Introduction to Women and Literature in Britain, 1700–1800* (Cambridge: Cambridge University Press, 2000), p. 3.

[61] Baker, *An Introduction*, p. 129.

[62] Henry Horwitz, *Chancery Equity Record and Proceedings, 1600–1800* (Kew: Public Records Office Publications, 1998). Horwitz provides a clear description of the stages of a Chancery case: see chapter I, 8–29.

extensively with chancery records, explain that these manuscript sources are so complex that they have been little used.[63]

The eighteenth-century legal print record was equally disorganized.[64] Precedent-setting or principle-affirming cases were recorded in notes circulated among judges, court reporters, law students, and interested lawyers.[65] A very small number of these records made their way into irregularly printed court "reports," which become the quasi-official record of case law. Reports appeared in print years or even decades after the cases were decided. To again take the Chancery Court as an example, only twenty-three collections of reports were published in the eighteenth century and the yearly publication of reports did not occur until the nineteenth century. In the reports, brief summaries of cases were provided, but they focused on narrow points of legal interpretation rather than providing a clear or compelling narrative of the case. Clyde Croft emphasizes the inadequacy of the print record, explaining: "the state of reporting of Chancery decisions in the eighteenth century was, as with common law decisions, unsatisfactory both in terms of quality and the number of printed reports available."[66]

These trends in print and manuscript circulation contributed to a popular culture of reading and writing that focused on the novel rather than the official records of the law. The domestic novel became an increasingly institutionalized as well as an increasingly powerful conveyor of social meaning. The expansion of print created a new and growing space for conversation about the law's role in forming society, and, because it was able to give the law both narrative order and circulation, the novel led that conversation.

Reimagining the Law: Prison or Utopia?

By concluding with a brief comparison of two novels that reimagine the law in radically different ways, this chapter hopes to gesture toward the

[63] Erickson, *Women and Property*, p. 114.

[64] The standard reference text to the history of the British court system remains Sir William Holdsworth's seventeen-volume *A History of English Laws* (London: Methuen, 1903, reprinted 1971). Holdsworth provides a comprehensive description of the uneven quality of eighteenth-century reporting in vol. 12 (pp. 101–46).

[65] John Baker, *Why the History of English Law Has Not Been Finished* (Cambridge: Cambridge University Press, 1999), pp. 21–2. Baker provides a concise overview of the many forms of manuscript legal materials in use from the medieval period through the eighteenth century.

[66] Clyde Croft, "Lord Hardwicke's use of precedent in equity" in Thomas G. Watkin (ed.), *Legal Record and Historical Reality: Proceedings of the Eighth British Legal History Conference* (London: Hambledon Press, 1989), pp. 125–6. Also see Staves, *Married Women's Separate Property*, p. 13.

wide range of forms assumed by the eighteenth-century juridical imagination. Both Wollstonecraft's *Maria* and Scott's *Millenium Hall* overtly critique the legal formulation of the woman's position within the family. Wollstonecraft criticizes the law by showing how it encourages the perversion of domestic relations and undermines the civil society those relationships represent. The victim of a failed marriage, Maria is reduced to insanity and the narrative itself is left incomplete, trailing off into fragments. Scott offers to the law an opposing strategy for reimagining. Rather than critiquing the law by depicting its failings, she imagines a society that is able to invent new forms of law that replace the family with perfected domestic relations. This idealistic rewriting of the law allows the creation of a utopian "sisterhood" dedicated to community, education, charity, and benevolence, achieving a truly civil society. Scott's narrative reflects the orderly structure of these ideas, offering lists of rules that define the sisterhood, for example.

Echoing Wollstonecraft's philosophical writings, *Maria* presents a cogent critique of marriage law. In the fully drafted first half of the novel, Maria is physically imprisoned in a madhouse by an unfaithful, gambling, dissolute husband, George Venables, who has both wasted her inheritance and stolen her child. She is unable to escape his control and spends her days miserably longing for the daughter she believes is dead. Maria famously explains that "Marriage had bastilled me for life," and continues to detail "the laws enacted by men" that "lay a stress on the dependent state of a woman" and to emphasize "the compassion I feel for many amiable women, the *out-laws* of the world."[67] After she leaves her husband, Maria becomes the "out-law" she describes. The fragmentary second half of *Maria* details a divorce trial that results from Maria's adulterous affair with Henry Darnford. Although these scenes are described in limited passages, Maria takes on a surprisingly active courtroom role. Her private critique of marriage becomes a public argument, as "she wrote a paper, which she expressly desired might be read in court."[68] The paper condemns the laws that "make women the property of their husbands," and pleads, "If I am unfortunately united to an unprincipled man, am I for ever to be shut out from fulfilling the duties of wife and mother?"[69] In the final chapter, when she nearly succumbs to the despair caused by her failures as wife, lover, and mother, she eventually succeeds in reuniting with her child and plans a maternal life.

[67] Mary Wollstonecraft, *Maria*, ed. Janet Todd (London: Penguin, 1992), pp. 115–16.
[68] Wollstonecraft, *Maria*, p. 142. [69] Wollstonecraft, *Maria*, pp. 143–4.

Unable to secure legal success, Maria retreats into a domestic realm that offers an escape from failed civil society.

Like *Maria*, *Millenium Hall* criticizes the law as an institution that creates dependent women; unlike *Maria*, it positions the law as a tool that can be restructured by women to create a just civil society. *Millenium Hall* features a series of domestic narratives that detail the founders' family histories and provide examples of failed marriage, parenting, and education. Rather than entrapping these women, as dramatized by *Maria*, these experiences encourage the founders' creation of their utopian society, and reveal a hope that lies at the heart of the domestic novel: Reimagining the law's treatment of women can construct not just a better family, but a better society. The novel is built on the conceit that two male visitors have inadvertently discovered Millenium Hall and ask for a tour; the narrative intersperses the founders' stories with descriptions of the Hall and its charitable institutions, including schools, factories, and communal homes. The Hall's leader, Mrs. Maynard, is repeatedly asked to explain the principles that structure the society. For example, in one dialogue, she asserts that the society is "founded in reason ... What I understand by society is a state of mutual confidence, reciprocal services, and correspondent affections; where numbers are thus united, there will be a free communication of sentiments."[70] Mrs. Maynard continues to detail an ideal society in which people engage in "rational conversation," "reflection on the motives for, and consequences of, their actions," and "pleasures [that are] real and permanent, and followed neither by repentance nor punishment."[71] Lamont questions if this society works to "make us all slaves to each other."[72] In response, Mrs. Maynard explicates her philosophy of reciprocity – the "reciprocal communication of benefits" – in which the wealthy give to the poor, but the poor give the wealthy the "pleasure" and "gratification" of charity.[73] The ideals of justice, equity, fairness, and conscience are encapsulated in dialogues such as this and amplified by each of the projects of the Hall.

Although they present very different experiences of the law, Scott and Wollstonecraft's female protagonists express the hope that reimagined domestic relationships can reform the law. The domestic novel, represented here by *Evelina*, *The Old Manor House*, *Maria*, and *Millenium Hall*, develops a popular juridical imagination that embraces the most idealistic

70 Sarah Scott, *Millenium Hall*, ed. Gary Kelly (Peterborough: Broadview Press, 1999), p. 111.
71 Scott, *Millenium Hall*, p. 112. 72 Scott, *Millenium Hall*, p. 112.
73 Scott, *Millenium Hall*, p. 113.

aims of the law, using the figure of the disempowered woman to assert the importance of innocence, virtue, truth, equality, and morality. It is a short step to imagining a resulting society that would legally recognize and even empower the woman. Able to dramatize, synthesize, and circulate the law, the novel positions "literature as law" as it helps to create bourgeois civil society. The eighteenth century's domestic laws are given their most powerful expression – and most powerful revision – in the domestic novel.

CHAPTER 9

Romanticism, Gothic, and the Law

Bridget M. Marshall

Crime, incarceration, and inheritance: these are three major concerns of modern legal systems. They are also three primary fixations of the Gothic. Legal issues feature prominently in popular recipes for the Gothic, such as one written by Samuel Taylor Coleridge in 1810 in which he specified ingredients such as "A Baron or Baroness ignorant of their Birth, and in some dependent situation – Castle . . . a written record – blood on it! – A wonderful Cut throat – &c. &c. &c."[1] The legal possibilities of this and similar recipes are legion: personal and legal identity must be established to enable proper inheritance for the baron or baroness; real estate lawyers must establish and document ownership of the castle; murders must be investigated; written records must be reviewed and notarized; assassins must be detected, apprehended, and imprisoned. Portrayals (and critiques) of various legal systems – including civil law, common law, statutory law, and religious law – appear in the plotlines of almost any Gothic novel. Gothic novels consistently feature three major legal elements in their storylines: trials (of many sorts), imprisonment (both legal and extralegal), and legal documents (both real and forged). Moreover, Gothic novels themselves also frequently have a legalistic form: The frame narratives and inserted texts that are a hallmark of the Gothic create an evidentiary or legalistic narrative. The struggle for narrative authority that is central to a legal trial is also central to a Gothic novel. The Gothic forces the reader to question the efficacy and value of the law, and to contemplate questions about the legal, judicial, and penal systems. In both content and form, the Gothic repeatedly provokes and probes questions about the ability of law – of legal processes, personages, or documents – to achieve justice.

Critic David Punter asserts in *Gothic Pathologies: The Text, The Body and the Law* that the Gothic "is obsessed with the law, with its operations,

[1] Samuel Taylor Coleridge, "Coleridge: a letter to Wordsworth" (1810) in John O. Hayden (ed.), *Walter Scott: The Critical Heritage* (London and New York: Routledge, 1970), p. 59.

justifications, limits."[2] Gothic authors' obsession with legal themes is perhaps less surprising when one considers the suspiciously large number of authors of key Gothic texts who had training at law, or were related to lawyers: Major Gothic authors including Thomas Gray (*Elegy Written in a Country Churchyard*), Horace Walpole (*The Castle of Otranto*), Charles Brocden Brown (*Edgar Huntly* and several others), Sheridan LeFanu (*Uncle Silas, Carmilla*), E. T. A. Hoffman (*The Sandman*), Robert Louis Stevenson (*Jekyll and Hyde*), George Brewer (*The Witch of Ravensworth*), and Samuel Warren (*Diary of a Late Physician*) all had formal law training, and Ann Radcliffe's husband, William Radcliffe, was a lawyer. These and other authors of the Gothic employ legal language and depict legal processes in ways that suggest both an understanding of the law and a deep skepticism about any legal system's ability to consistently achieve justice. The Gothic manifests a concern for rights and liberty (and the violation thereof) that is also an essential element of the emerging discourse of Romanticism. The rhetoric of law and that of the Gothic are frequently intertwined; eminent British barrister and judge William Blackstone, in his *Commentaries on the Laws of England* (1765–9), made the connection between the Gothic and the law explicit in his famous claim:

> Our system of remedial law resembles an old Gothic castle, erected in the days of chivalry, but fitted up for a modern inhabitant. The moated ramparts, the embattled towers, and the trophied halls, are magnificent and venerable, but useless, and therefore neglected. The inferior apartments, now accommodated to daily use, are cheerful and commodious, though their approaches may be winding and difficult.[3]

This metaphor of the legal system as a Gothic castle provokes consideration of the ways in which the law is always already out of date, and of how the past haunts the present, particularly within inheritance law, which is frequently central to the plot of the Gothic. Inheritance law is rife with Gothic language and concepts, such as the legal term "mortmain," which literally translates to "dead hand," but in law refers to a perpetual ownership of real estate that forever prevents its sale or transfer to another party. The ways in which the legal system enables (and requires) property to be passed from one generation to the next are frequently sources of conflict in Gothic novels; as Natasha Tessone points out, the laws surrounding

[2] David Punter, *Gothic Pathologies: The Text, the Body and the Law* (London: Palgrave Macmillan, 1998), p. 19.

[3] Sir William Blackstone, *Commentaries on the Laws of England: In Four Books* (New York: J.B. Lippincott, 1859), p. 268.

inheritance can be seen as Gothic in the way that they "authorize the posthumous control by the dead over the future inheritors of property."[4] The law in such cases is a haunting force, inflicting the will of individuals from the past (both those who established a community's laws and those who dictated their individual wills) to control the lives of those in the present. As Leslie Moran explains, "the law appears as the archaic and the dark, a vestigial shadow that haunts the legal and social order of the enlightenment and of modernity."[5] The genre of the Gothic allows for exploration and contemplation of the darkness and chaos that is present in the presumed or imagined light and order intended in the codification of legal systems.

While the Gothic typically suggests the ways in which the hold of the past over the present can be dangerous and destabilizing, Blackstone's famous analogy suggests that the Gothic castle of the law is in fact a positive feature; he proposes that the law, like an older building, merely needs to be improved and renovated to make its old façade accommodate the current generation. Edmund Burke, likewise, admired the "noble and venerable castle" of the pre-revolutionary French constitution.[6] Both Blackstone and Burke suggest the positive, conservative nature of the Gothic castle; it represents traditional reverence for the beauty and wisdom of the past, which, though perhaps out of fashion, is ultimately a strong and well-built guide to the present. While the well-worn metaphor of the law as a Gothic castle was popular, not everyone agreed that the best path forward was to renovate. Mary Wollstonecraft (author of the Romantic Gothic novel *Matilda*, and mother of Mary Shelley) questioned why we should "repair an ancient castle, built in barbarous ages, of Gothic materials? Why were the legislators obliged to rake amongst heterogeneous ruins; to rebuild old walls . . . ?"[7] Wollstonecraft questions the value and integrity of the Gothic castle of the law, advocating that citizens abandon such tradition and build a system that will create real justice for the contemporary world, without reference to the past. Like Wollstonecraft, American author Charles Brockden Brown, in his novel *Ormond; or, the*

[4] Natasha Tessone, *Disputed Titles: Ireland, Scotland, and the Novel of Inheritance, 1798–1832* (Lewisburg: Bucknell University Press, 2015), p. 17.

[5] Leslie J. Moran, "Gothic law," *Griffith Law Review*, 10(2) (2001), 75.

[6] Edmund Burke, *Reflections on the Revolution in France*, ed. Leslie George Mitchell (Oxford: Oxford University Press, 1999), p. 35.

[7] Mary Wollstonecraft, "Vindication of the rights of men" (1790) in Janet Todd (ed.), *A Vindication of the Rights of Men; A Vindication of the Rights of Woman; An Historical and Moral View of the French Revolution* (Oxford: Oxford University Press, 1999), p. 41.

Secret Witness (1799), also deploys the metaphor as a condemnation rather than a celebration, describing the legal system as "made up of the shreds and remnants of barbarous antiquity, polluted with the rust of ages, and patched by the stupidity of modern workmen, into new deformity."[8] While Blackstone and Burke use the Gothic castle as a positive metaphor for the law, Wollstonecraft and Brown employ the same metaphor as a negative depiction of it, revealing the malleability of the metaphor. Jeremy Bentham suggested that Blackstone should have "kept clear of allegories" and not "turn[ed] the Law into a Castle,"[9] a powerful image that can be interpreted in different – and conflicting – ways. The fact that some critics depicted the law's Gothic nature as a virtue while others saw it as a curse is also suggestive of the way in which the Gothic genre itself has been read by critics as both a conservative and a revolutionary genre. In the hands of some authors (Ann Radcliffe, for instance), the Gothic ultimately suggests the importance of "traditional, conservative values";[10] in the conservative Gothic, homes are restored to their rightful inheritors and crimes are (eventually) punished appropriately, and thus the law's Gothic nature is a positive feature, ultimately restoring order. Other authors (William Godwin, for instance) deploy the Gothic to critique tradition and power structures (especially those based on gender and class), and to demonstrate the necessity of destroying oppressive systems, including the law. Gothic novels (and their interpreters) are ultimately mixed on whether or not the legal system is a horribly haunted mansion that should be condemned and torn down, or simply an old "fixer-upper" with character and integrity that should be preserved, restored, and improved. In *The Gothic and the Rule of Law, 1764–1820*, Sue Chaplin asserts that "the Gothic poses a challenge, or at the very least a question, to the law," frequently contesting the law's legitimacy and "exposing its hidden violence"; she suggests the Gothic in part serves to expose the problematic nature of the law.[11] In its depictions of deeply flawed trials, unjust imprisonment, and problematic legal documents, the Gothic repeatedly shows that the law's aims, though lofty, are rarely achieved through extant legal processes, and that in fact

[8] Charles Brockden Brown, *Ormond, Or, The Secret Witness: With Related Texts*, eds. Philip Barnard and Stephen Shapiro (Indianapolis: Hackett Publishing, 2009), p. 15.

[9] Jeremy Bentham, *Bentham: A Fragment on Government*, eds. J. H. Burns and H. L. A. Hart (Cambridge: Cambridge University Press, 1988), p. 20.

[10] David Durant, "Ann Radcliffe and the conservative Gothic," *Studies in English Literature 1500–1900*, 22 (1982), 520.

[11] Susan Chaplin, *The Gothic and the Rule of the Law, 1764–1820* (London: Palgrave Macmillan, 2007), p. 2.

legal systems prove to be Gothic labyrinths, confusing, confounding, and often punishing those who seek justice.

Depictions of Trials in the Gothic

Gothic novels frequently depict trials meant to settle intractable problems such as disputes over inheritance or the determination of an appropriate punishment for a criminal act. Given the array of time periods, countries, and cultures in which Gothic novels are set, they portray a diverse range of kinds of courts, from ecclesiastical courts, to state-sponsored courts, to trial by combat. But again and again, Gothic novels portray judicial systems (whether located in churches, in courtrooms, or on battlefields) as sites where justice is not achieved. These portrayals in fact mostly serve to undermine any sense of hope a reader might have that justice can be accomplished through any established judicial process.

Ecclesiastical courts – particularly the ones within the Catholic Church during the Inquisition – were a significant source of material to fill Gothic novels with suitably scary scenes of trials. Archetypal Gothic novels such as Matthew Lewis's *The Monk* (1796) and Ann Radcliffe's *The Italian, or the Confessional of the Black Penitent* (1797) reveal considerable cultural anxiety about what happened during the Inquisition and the way that corrupted courts of the Church were used to torture innocents and otherwise violate justice. In *The Monk*, Lewis's narrator explains the Inquisition thus: "in these trials, neither the accusation is mentioned, nor the name of the accuser. The prisoners are only asked, whether they will confess. If they reply, that, having no crime, they can make no confession, they are put to the torture without delay."[12] Readers of Lewis's time would have understood this as an unjust trial. As Diane Long Hoeveler notes, the practices of the Inquisition were "the very antithesis of modernity's legal reforms and due processes."[13] Although Ambrosio is, as the reader well knows, guilty of rape and murder, the narrator notes that the inquisitors were "determined to make him confess not only the crimes which he had committed, but those also of which he was innocent."[14] Lewis's narrator further notes that the judges of the Inquisition are less interested in achieving justice than in giving "a striking testimony of their vigilance."[15]

[12] Matthew Gregory Lewis, *The Monk* (Peterborough: Broadview Press, 2003), p. 349.

[13] Diane Long Hoeveler, "Anti-Catholicism and the Gothic imaginary: the historical and literary contexts" in Brett C. McInelly (ed.), *Religion in the Age of Enlightenment* (Brooklyn: AMS Press, 2012), vol. 3, p. 2.

[14] Lewis, *The Monk*, p. 350.

[15] Lewis, *The Monk*, p. 349.

The inquisitorial system values performance and appearance over actual justice. Even though Ambrosio should be tried (and convicted) for his crimes, the novel demonstrates the deep flaws and ultimate failure of the Inquisition as a means of reaching justice. In *The Italian*, Radcliffe takes this critique of the Inquisition further. While Lewis has the villain detained by the Inquisition, Radcliffe has her heroine, Ellena, and her hero, Vivaldi, experience the torments of the Inquisition, further demonstrating the dangerous power – particularly over the innocent – of this institution. Radcliffe's narrator suggests that even though such systems as the Inquisition cause men to "boast . . . of [their] sense of justice," it is clear that they are actually perpetrating "the most terrible extremes of folly and wickedness."[16] While Radcliffe's portrayal of the Inquisition is certainly a critique of that specific system, given the many ways in which her novel is anachronistic and vague about both the time and place of its setting, the text suggests a critique not only of the Inquisition (which was largely over when Radcliffe was writing her novel) but of other, more contemporary judicial systems. As Sue Chaplin has suggested in *Law, Sensibility, and the Sublime in Eighteenth-Century Women's Fiction: Speaking of Dread*, Radcliffe's portrayal of the Inquisition "cannot be attributed wholly to anti-Catholic sentiment."[17] Radcliffe is likely reflecting on the horrors committed by France's Revolutionary Tribunal court and possibly even on England's own "Bloody Code," which imposed a punishment of death for more than 200 offences. In their representations of the courts of the Inquisition, Gothic authors were frequently also commenting more generally on the inability of all kinds of court systems to get at the truth and come to just rulings.

In addition to its terrifying portrayals of the Inquisition, the Gothic exposes other court systems as similarly corrupt and unable to provide justice. Horace Walpole's founding Gothic novel, *The Castle of Otranto* (1764), features a deeply corrupt trial in which Manfred – who rules Otranto because his grandfather secretly murdered the true monarch and altered his will – demands that Theodore (the rightful heir of the kingdom) submit completely to his authority. Manfred attempts to mete out justice, but it is patently clear to Theodore (and to the reader) that such justice is no justice at all, and only supernatural interventions can reinstate

[16] Radcliffe, Ann, *The Italian, or the Confessional of the Black Penitents: A Romance*, ed. Frederick Garber (Oxford: Oxford University Press, 1986), p. 198.

[17] Susan Chaplin, *Law, Sensibility, and the Sublime in Eighteenth-Century Women's Fiction: Speaking of Dread* (Burlington: Ashgate, 2004), p. 130.

the rightful heir to the kingdom. Theodore's "crime" is that he openly suggests that the giant helmet that fell upon and killed Manfred's son Conrad looks like the helmet that appears on a statue of Alfonso the Good. Manfred calls this remark "treason," and insists that Theodore's "life shall pay for it."[18] After Manfred has Theodore in custody, he claims that Theodore is in fact a wizard who killed Conrad with the helmet and proclaims that "the young man was certainly a necromancer, and that till the church could take cognizance of the affair, he would have the magician, whom they had thus detected, kept prisoner."[19] Notably, although Theodore and even Manfred's friends "endeavor[ed] to divert him from this savage and ill-grounded resolution," the people in the community "were charmed with their lord's decision, which to their apprehensions carried great appearance of justice."[20] Walpole's general disregard for the common man here shines through, but also highlights the problematic nature of justice; what Manfred and the crowd find appropriate (and even charming), Manfred's friends and Theodore (and likely the reader) believe unjust. Even Manfred knows full well that Theodore is no criminal, as the narrator acknowledges by saying that Manfred "even felt a disposition toward pardoning one who had been guilty of no crime";[21] nonetheless, Manfred is carried away by his passion for Isabella, and cannot act justly because of his own self-interest. Manfred uses the legal system – his own legal powers and the ecclesiastical courts – to further his own ends, not to actually achieve a just resolution. As Sue Chaplin explains in *The Gothic and the Rule of Law, 1764 – 1820*, "*Otranto*, like the *Commentaries*, is a text obsessed by questions of legal origin, authority, and authenticity."[22] Walpole's novel portrays Manfred's civil court as corrupt and unjust due to Manfred's illegitimacy and biases, and shows that the church's ecclesiastical court is similarly corrupted by its reliance on Manfred's financial support.

Manfred knows that the corrupted ecclesiastical court will favor his side, but, curiously, he also seems to genuinely believe that despite being a usurper, he is on the side of right. When Frederick arrives (in disguise) he challenges Manfred to "single combat to the last extremity,"[23] an ancient form of trial in which a battle (to either death or surrender) decides a legal question. Manfred exclaims that "heaven [will] befriend the juster side,"[24]

[18] Horace Walpole, *The Castle of Otranto and The Mysterious Mother* (Peterborough: Broadview Press, 2003), p. 76.

[19] Walpole, *Otranto*, p. 77. [20] Walpole, *Otranto*, p. 77. [21] Walpole, *Otranto*, p. 87.

[22] Chaplin, *The Gothic and the Rule of Law*, p. 48. [23] Walpole, *Otranto*, p. 114.

[24] Walpole, *Otranto*, p. 118.

a principle that was indeed the intention of trial by combat. Although *Otranto*'s trial by combat never materializes, Clara Reeve's *The Old English Baron* (1778), which she claimed she modeled on *Otranto*, features a trial by duel that does yield a just result. The majority of the novel's plot revolves around seeking due punishment for a man who has murdered and usurped the kingdom of the rightful Lord Lovel. The plot depicts a quite long and drawn-out description of the duel between Sir Philip Harclay (a friend of the murdered Lovel) and the new (usurping) Sir Walter Lovel, including formal letters between the aggrieved parties, the terms and specific people present for the adjudication of the combat, and the formal legal language invoked by both the accuser and the accused as they prepare for a battle wherein they expect that "God [will] defend the right."[25] Armed with a lance and sword, Sir Philip brings the usurping Walter Lovel to the brink of death, and then demands he confess to his crimes or die. Both men believe that the outcome of the battle has revealed a just edict from a higher power: Philip exclaims, "Heaven, by my hand, has chastised him; he has confessed the fact I accuse him of,"[26] while Walter acknowledges, "At length I am overtaken by justice."[27] This premodern form of determining justice, at least in this case, is successful, with the outcome of the duel according with the truth. As Sir Clifford writes in a letter detailing the duel, "you will unite with us in wondering at the ways of providence, and submitting to its decrees, in punishing the guilty, and doing justice to the innocent and oppressed";[28] thus this trial by combat is portrayed as achieving a divine justice. As Diane Hoeveler and James Jenkins note, both *Otranto* and *Baron*'s use of the duel to determine a legal outcome "reifies the early gothic's loyalist posture, suggesting that the shame of a public trial is more than an aristocrat should or could bear."[29] Both of these novels are resolved with the restoration of the original aristocratic line, and thus present a more conservative version of the Gothic, suggesting that ancient orders and hierarchies are just. While such "divine justice" does restore hierarchies, as the Gothic continued to develop it increasingly portrayed man-made laws and legal systems as distinctly unjust, frequently resulting in imprisonment or death for the innocent.

[25] Clara Reeve, *The Old English Baron*, eds. James Trainer and James Watt (Oxford: Oxford University Press, 2003), p. 87.

[26] Reeve, *The Old English Baron*, p. 89.

[27] Reeve, *The Old English Baron*, p. 93.

[28] Reeve, *The Old English Baron*, p. 96.

[29] Diane Long Hoeveler and James D. Jenkins, "Where the evidence leads: Gothic narratives and legal technologies," *European Romantic Review*, 18(3) (2007), 323.

Depictions of Imprisonment in the Gothic

As Foucault reminds us, imprisonment was not, historically, the default means of punishment. Nonetheless, Gothic novels repeatedly feature characters who are incarcerated; for some characters, this is rightful punishment for criminal offences they have committed, but many more are held captive due to mistaken identity, or because of nefarious schemes typically devised by powerful men. In Matthew Lewis's *The Monk*, Antonia is imprisoned beneath a monastery by the titular monk, and the pregnant Agnes is confined to a subterranean vault (where her newborn baby dies) by the evil Prioress of the convent. Radcliffe's heroines are frequently held captive by their fathers, guardians, or suitors, and occasionally her male characters (such as Vivaldi in *The Italian*) are also imprisoned. All of these depictions dwell, to varying degrees, on the horrible conditions of confinement, particularly when such confinement is unjustified. William Godwin's *Caleb Williams* (1794) is perhaps one of the most significant Gothic novels in its detailing of unjust imprisonment; the novel is often considered to be a dramatization of Godwin's philosophical and political text, *An Inquiry Concerning Political Justice* (1793). Emily Melville is the novel's first and more traditional Gothic prisoner; when she refuses the objectionable man whom her legal guardian, her Uncle Tyrrel, demands she marry, he first confines her to the estate, and Emily laments that she must live in "a house which was now become her dungeon."[30] Tyrrel orders her "to be closely confined to her apartment, and deprived of all means of communicating her situation."[31] Although Emily resolutely defies him – "You may imprison my body, but you cannot conquer my mind"[32] – she remains confined against her will, despite interventions by rescuers. After Emily manages to escape, Tyrrel escalates his power to imprison from the domestic to the state level, by commanding the local bailiff to have her arrested based on a wildly unjust financial claim. The legal figures within the novel (a lawyer and a bailiff) are horrified by Tyrrel's misuse of the law, but nonetheless they follow his demand and have her arrested and imprisoned for debt. Despite the horrified reactions of both the general public and the public figures involved in the arrest, Tyrrel insists, "the law justifies it. – What do you think laws were made for? I do nothing but right, and right

30 William Godwin, *Caleb Williams*, ed. Gary Handwerk and A. A. Markley (Peterborough: Broadview Press, 2000), p. 114.

31 Godwin, *Caleb Williams*, p. 119.

32 Godwin, *Caleb Williams*, p. 120.

I will have."[33] Tyrrel uses the law in villainous ways, revealing the law itself as an abuse of power. Godwin goes even further in *Caleb Williams* to demonstrate the extreme horrors of state-sponsored physical imprisonment, and to highlight not just the physical, but also the mental, emotional, and spiritual toll of imprisonment.

While Emily insisted that despite her physical imprisonment, her mind was free, Caleb admits that despite his physical freedom (he is not yet literally imprisoned), his mind is held captive by his fear of Falkland and his commitment to the oath that he will keep his secret. Caleb explains, "I had made myself a prisoner, in the most intolerable sense of that term, for years – perhaps for the rest of my life."[34] Caleb here suggests that the "most intolerable" sense of imprisonment is not physically being imprisoned (as Emily was and as he will soon be), but feeling imprisoned mentally (in his case by the powerful figure of Falkland). Although Caleb emphasizes the horror of such mental subjugation to the will of another – constrained by what William Blake referred to as "mind-forged manacles"[35] – the novel is also deeply concerned with the physical conditions of imprisonment: Godwin went so far as to footnote his text to explain the ways in which his fictional depiction of Caleb's woes was in fact based on the actual conditions of prisons where real people – often innocent people – were imprisoned. Once Caleb is actually confined, he details his experience, noting that "it is impossible to describe the sort of squalidness and filth" and the "putridity and infection" that appear everywhere.[36] Caleb proclaims, "he that has observed the secrets of a prison, well knows that there is more torture in the lingering existence of a criminal, in the silent intolerable minutes that he spends, than in the tangible misery of whips and racks!"[37] Perversely, Caleb emphasizes the ways in which the physical tortures of the inquisition (which are part of the standard fare of Gothic novels) are more tolerable for prisoners than the truly all-encompassing horror of the real physical conditions of imprisonment. Here he suggests that the Gothic nightmares of Lewis and Radcliffe are not truly the source of horror; rather, the reality of British prisons is far worse than the Gothic imagination ever conjured. As criminologist David Wilson explains, prisons at this time were "largely custodial in function"[38] – they were

[33] Godwin, *Caleb Williams*, p. 149. [34] Godwin, *Caleb Williams*, p. 217.

[35] William Blake, "London" in *William Blake: The Complete Illuminated Books* (London: Thames & Hudson, 2000), p. 88, line 8.

[36] Godwin, *Caleb Williams*, p. 262. [37] Godwin, *Caleb Williams*, p. 265.

[38] David Wilson, *Pain and Retribution: A Short History of British Prisons 1066 to the Present* (London: Reaktion Books, 2014), p. 13.

not the punishment, but a waiting place for the accused until actual punishment could be determined. The conditions in these places of imprisonment varied widely, and both innocent and guilty, tried and untried individuals were held together in frequently unpleasant and often dangerous environments. Caleb provides specific descriptions of his cell, where he and sometimes three other inmates are confined "for fourteen or fifteen hours out of the four-and-twenty": he notes that it measured only "7 feet by 6," and was located "below the surface of the ground, damp, without window, light, or air, except from a few holes."[39] Godwin includes several footnotes in his text referring the reader to the Newgate Calendar and to prison reformer John Howard's *The State of the Prisons in England* (1777), which documented (and strongly criticized) the conditions in British prisons. In *Caleb Williams*, Godwin engages in contemporary debates about the conditions of state-sponsored prisons, but also delves deeper to question the larger structures of power that put men and women into prison. *Caleb Williams* again and again shows how the legal system benefits those with power and further victimizes those without it – in particular women and the poor. As Caleb notes, "Wealth and despotism easily know how to engage those laws as the coadjutors of their oppression, which were perhaps at first intended (witless and miserable precaution!) for the safeguards of the poor."[40] With its specific documentation of prison conditions and its larger argument against a legal and judicial system that is stacked against the poor and the powerless, Godwin's *Caleb Williams* engages with the Gothic motif of unjust imprisonment, part of what Foucault called the later eighteenth century's "fear of darkened spaces."[41] The Gothic thus documents the problems of the legal system and demonstrates the failures and unfinished work of Enlightenment movements that sought to modernize criminal law and punishment by making them more humane. As Victor H. Brombert explains in *The Romantic Prison*, "the link between enclosure and inner freedom is at the heart of the Romantic sensibility."[42] While many Romantic texts (like Coleridge's "This Lime-Tree Bower My Prison") suggest the romantic possibilities for spiritual or mental freedom in spite of physical constraint, the Gothic darkly asserts that imprisonment of the mind is all too often concurrent with physical

[39] Godwin, *Caleb Williams*, p. 266. [40] Godwin, *Caleb Williams*, p. 137.

[41] Michel Foucault, "The eye of power" in *Power/Knowledge: Selected Interviews and Other Writings, 1972–1977* (New York: Pantheon Books, 1980), p. 153.

[42] Victor H. Brombert, *The Romantic Prison: The French Tradition* (Princeton: Princeton University Press, 1978), p. 4.

confinement, whether that is literally, in a prison cell, or metaphorically, through the constraints of a society's legal system and social structures.

Depictions of Legal Documents and the Gothic as Documentary

Many Gothic novels feature key legal documents – in particular, wills, deeds, financial documents, and confessions – which are lost, found, manipulated, contested, or otherwise important to initiating, unfolding, or resolving the plot. But more than just plot devices, such documents are frequently presented as a part of the novel, often as inserted narratives, creating for the reader an experience of reviewing legal documents or evidence. As Leslie Moran writes, numerous Gothic novels "construct their truth through the presentation of an accumulation and an incomplete consolidation of fragments," which ultimately leaves the reader with "an experience of both the legal process and the Gothic text as a labyrinth."[43] From the earliest Gothic novels, documents – particularly wills, confessions, and letters – are hidden; it is only their discovery and revelation that brings order back to the disrupted family or community. But the chaos of the Gothic does not mesh well with the orderliness of the legal system. The real legal documents that appear in the Gothic most typically do not resolve situations, and quite frequently the documents prove to be forgeries (such as the forged will in *The Castle of Otranto*), further undermining the ability to assess authentic narratives. In Charles Brockden Brown's *Ormond; or, the Secret Witness*, counterfeit bank notes and forged business and personal letters financially ruin the Dudley family. When the Dudleys then turn to the law for protection, they are instead further bankrupted by the legal system, which is operated by "men, who squared their actions by no other standard than law."[44] When Mr. Dudley takes a job copying documents in an office, he finds himself "perpetually encumbered with the rubbish of law, and [he] waded with laborious steps through its endless tautologies, its impertinent circuities, its lying assertions, and hateful artifices."[45] *Ormond*'s plot suggests the uncertainty of supposedly "authentic" documents, and further highlights the deeply destructive nature of the legal system for those without power or money.

Legal documents (and forgeries thereof) are easily found within a typical Gothic novel, but starting from the very beginning with *Otranto*, Gothic novels are frequently embedded in frames (like prefaces and introductions) attesting to a (false) authenticity. As Chaplin notes,

[43] Moran, "Gothic law," 77. [44] Brown, *Ormond*, p. 13. [45] Brown, *Ormond*, p. 15.

Otranto is, "like [Blackstone's] *Commentaries*, a narrative that is almost overshadowed by its prefaces."[46] The numerous frame narratives that surround the tale of Otranto seem to be set up to be read as evidence of the truth of the story within. Such framing prefaces or introductions, as well as inserted letters, frequently add a legalistic form to the Gothic's already legal-driven plot. Radcliffe's *The Italian* opens with a brief narrative describing a group of English travelers in Italy who receive a volume (the novel itself) from a friar detailing the story that began in the confessional of the church; the frame suggests that the story is a religious and possibly legal confession, recounting real events and tied to a real place. As David Punter explains, Gothic novels are filled with and often framed as "cases" with confessions and testimonies; he hypothesizes that Gothic fiction "deals with those moments when we find it impossible, with any degree of hope, for our 'case to be put,'"[47] thus highlighting a central problem of the law: it requires stories to be told, and yet some stories are untellable. *Caleb Williams* is particularly notorious on this count, for the ways in which Caleb's testimony breaks down completely in the final scene, leaving the reader to sort out truth by judging the testimony and evidence. As the Gothic lingered into the late nineteenth century, its legal obsessions became even more apparent. In classic Victorian Gothic texts such as *The Strange Case of Jekyll and Hyde* (1886) and in Bram Stoker's *Dracula* (1897), the legal focus continues to be central, with the legalistic presentation of pieces of evidence (including letters, confessions, diaries, and newspaper clippings) and the central importance of characters who are lawyers, such as Mr. Utterson in *Jekyll and Hyde* and Jonathan Harker in *Dracula*.

Conclusion: Impossible Justice

In their portrayals of trials, punishments, and documents, as well as in their use of legalistic or evidentiary forms, Gothic novels repeatedly portray justice as ultimately unattainable; victims typically are not served by the justice system, and in many cases they are victimized a second time by the justice system's procedures. Percy Shelley's Gothic drama *The Cenci* (1819) is perhaps the most compelling portrayal of the devastating nature of Gothic justice. After her father has raped her, Beatrice Cenci is unable to achieve justice through the courts, and she ultimately participates in a plot to arrange her father's murder; however, following this retributive

[46] Chaplin, *The Gothic and the Rule of the Law*, p. 48.
[47] Punter, *Gothic Pathologies*, p. 5.

vengeance, she still feels that justice has not been done. She laments: "— O! In this mortal world/There is no vindication and no law/Which can adjudge and execute the doom/Of that through which I suffer."[48] Beatrice understands that her father's act of rape and her act of parricide are both crimes, and both require punishment; however, she cannot envision how to resolve the situation justly. Her act of parricide did not enable justice for his act of rape, nor does the punishment of her brother for his involvement in the parricide constitute justice. As Laurence Lockridge explains, "Retributive justice, instead of balancing and cancelling, is inefficient; it compounds the original crime, and makes the avenger vulnerable to the powers she challenges."[49] But the play does not offer a solution to this problem of justice out of balance; as Michael Scrivener explains, "The play forces the reader to play the role of a juror whose impossible task mirrors Beatrice's impossible task, for the reader must judge what eludes judgment."[50] Readers of the Gothic must sift through the evidence to assess guilt and innocence, and imagine an appropriate and just solution to the wrongs committed by the characters. Although the narrator of Ann Radcliffe's *The Romance of the Forest* (1791) intones that "Justice, however long delayed, will overtake the guilty,"[51] the Gothic generally does not uphold such a satisfying conclusion. While kingdoms may be restored to their rightful heirs, and separated lovers may be reunited, murdered fathers cannot be brought back to life and raped women cannot stop or redress their violation. Perpetrators of villainy are frequently (though not always) punished in the Gothic, but it ultimately is not satisfying, and frequently it is not just. For example, although Matthew Lewis' monk, Ambrosio, is condemned to horrendous torture as a result of his crimes, his punishment does not erase his rape and murder of his sister Antonia or his murder of his mother Elvira. As Robert Miles suggests, the ending of *The Monk*, with its extended torture of Ambrosio narrated in horrifying, excessive, and what contemporary readers saw as blasphemous detail, "calls into question the divine justice that has inflicted such gruesome torments." Miles explains that "it appears less divine than pagan, brutal, and arbitrary."[52]

48 Percy Bysshe Shelley, *The Cenci: A Tragedy in Five Acts* (New York: Phaeton Press, 1970), p. 37.

49 Laurence S. Lockridge, *The Ethics of Romanticism* (Cambridge: Cambridge University Press, 1989), pp. 320–1.

50 Michael Scrivener, "Trials in Romantic-era writing: modernity, guilt, and the scene of justice," *The Wordsworth Circle*, 25 (2004), 132.

51 Ann Radcliffe, *The Romance of the Forest*, ed. Chloe Chard (Oxford: Oxford University Press, 1986), p. 343.

52 Robert Miles, "Ann Radcliffe and Matthew Lewis" in David Punter (ed.), *A New Companion to the Gothic: Blackwell Companions to Literature and Culture* (Chichester: Wiley-Blackwell, 2012), p. 106.

In fact, Ambrosio's gruesome death most clearly echoes an earlier death in the novel, that of the Prioress, who suffers a horrifying fate at the hands of a crowd of angry rioters. Although Lorenzo seeks justice for the death of his sister Agnes, who was murdered by the Prioress, even Lorenzo seeks to protect the Prioress from the rioting crowd, urging that "she had undergone no trial, and advised them to leave her punishment to the Inquisition."[53] Lorenzo is deeply disturbed by the way the crowd inflicts vigilante justice: "Though regret for his sister made him look upon the prioress with abhorrence, Lorenzo could not help pitying a woman in a situation so terrible."[54] These scenes of violence only beget more violence, and the Gothic repeatedly suggests that righting a wrong is far more difficult than simply having a trial and inflicting a punishment. In the Gothic, the scales of justice are eternally out of balance; the Gothic's rather bleak perspective serves to provoke the kind of anxiety in the reader that is central to the genre. While laws and courts are intended to preserve and restore order, the Gothic suggests that legal systems, whether ancient or remodeled, are deeply flawed and predominantly serve to perpetuate injustice. The Gothic allows for the notion that legal systems – even those that aspire to transparency and equity – are often impervious to reason, perverting truth and preventing justice.

[53] Lewis, *The Monk*, p. 301. [54] Lewis, *The Monk*, p. 302.

CHAPTER 10

Strange Cases in Victorian England

Kieran Dolin

Introducing his 1906 collection of trial narratives, *Notable Trials: Romances of the Law*, barrister Richard Storry Deans observes that "there is nothing to surpass, in human interest, the records of the Law Courts," and that "Many a writer of fiction has founded his romances on these records; and many another has spent much ingenuity in inventing plot and incident not half so weird or so striking as hundreds to be found in the pages of the 'State Trials,' the brief reports of the 'Annual Register,' or the columns of the *Times*."[1]

In advancing his claim for the narrative and dramatic power of legal cases, Deans overlooks any number of violent, transgressive, or mysterious stories from the Victorian era: Robert Browning's *The Ring and the Book*, Emily Bronte's *Wuthering Heights*, or Wilkie Collins's *The Woman in White*, for example. While the dominant canons of literary realism inclined writers and critics toward mainstream rather than extreme situations, and a system of formal and informal censorship restricted the representation of sexual and other passions, the "weird" and disturbing side of human conduct found expression in poetry, sensation novels, and the aesthetic or decadent writing of the 1890s. The nineteenth-century literary fascination with cases, real and imagined, is well known, and Deans cites Scott, Dickens, Collins, and Stevenson as examples, but insists nonetheless that truth is stranger than fiction. My aim in this chapter is not to adjudicate on his claim, but to trace the relations between law and literature in the culture of Victorian England, and to explore the cross-disciplinary interest in "cases."

As part of a series of rhetorical questions, Deans alludes to one of the most sensational cases of the century, the Tichborne affair: "Is there, in all fiction, any story of imposture equal to that of Orton, the butcher's son, who cozened half England that he was the rightful heir of one of her most

[1] R. Storry Deans, *Notable Trials: Romances of the Law* (London: Cassell, 1906), p. vii.

ancient families?"[2] In fact, there is evidence that Orton was inspired, in devising his fraudulent claim to be Sir Roger Tichborne, by reading the sensation novels of Mary Elizabeth Braddon: A quotation from *Aurora Floyd* was found in his pocketbook and read out at his final trial, and Braddon's earlier novel, *Lady Audley's Secret*, is a "story of imposture."[3] In its turn, the Tichborne craze inspired a number of novels, including Anthony Trollope's *Is He Popenjoy?* and *Ralph the Heir*, Marcus Clarke's *His Natural Life*, and Charles Reade's *The Wandering Heir*.[4]

I begin with Deans because he exemplifies the close proximity and potential exchanges between the legal and literary spheres in this period. His book represents a genre of popular legal history that celebrated the English legal system through retellings of its famous trials. Such "juridical nationalism" strengthened attachment to the inherited ideology of the rule of law.[5] More broadly, however, works such as Deans' demonstrate the Victorians' obsession with law and legality, their emotional and intellectual investment in law as the basis of their achievements and their identity.[6] Legal values and concepts were among the most significant components in Victorian culture. Literature was embedded in that broader cultural field, and consequently relations between these two domains were intricate and interdependent.[7]

A Culture of Legality

Reigning from the 1830s to the beginning of the new century, Queen Victoria presided over "an age of swift transition," dominated by the Industrial Revolution at home and the imposition of British imperial rule abroad.[8] Law functioned as one of the instruments of change, both through reformist

[2] Deans, *Notable Trials*, p. viii.

[3] On *Aurora Floyd* see Robyn Annear, *The Man Who Lost Himself: The Unbelievable Story of the Tichborne Claimant* (London: Robinson, 2003), p. 335. For a broader study of literary links to the case, see Patrick Morgan, "The reading habits of the Tichborne claimant," *Margins* (November 2003), www.thefreelibrary.com/The+fiction+reading+habits+of+the+Tichborne+claimant.-a0111856221.

[4] Jan-Melissa Schramm, *Atonement and Self-Sacrifice in Nineteenth-Century Narrative* (Cambridge: Cambridge University Press, 2012). See Chapter 5 for a discussion of these and other texts inspired by the case.

[5] Peter Fitzpatrick, *The Mythology of Modern Law* (London: Routledge, 1992), p. 114.

[6] W. Wesley Pue, 'Book Review: *The Law of Evidence in Victorian England* by Christopher Allen,' *Victorian Studies*, 43 (2001), 336.

[7] This formulation draws on Christine L. Krueger, *Reading for the Law: British Literary History and Gender Advocacy* (Charlottesville: University of Virginia Press, 2010), p. 2.

[8] The quoted phrase is from G. M. Young, *Victorian England: Portrait of an Age* (Oxford: Oxford University Press, 1936), p. 156.

legislation and through developments in the common law. Innovative statutes such as the New Poor Law and the Corn Law Reform sought to create an industrial capitalist economy and society; the utilitarian "spirit of reform" that inspired these acts was also brought to bear on the analysis and statutory amendment of many aspects of the inherited legal system. A similar strategy was adopted by humanitarians and conservatives – that of introducing legislation such as the Factories Acts in order to limit child labor and to mitigate the social consequences of economic individualism.[9] The resources of imaginative literature, including popular narrative modes such as melodrama, were quickly recruited to the cause, as Dickens's *Oliver Twist* and Gaskell's *Mary Barton* show. In the common law, its case-by-case method could deliver the gradual expansion of inherited doctrines and remedies, as precedents were applied in new situations thrown up by industrialism: Brian Simpson's historical narrative collection, *Leading Cases in the Common Law*, includes a number of "cases of first impression," unprecedented circumstances submitted to the courts for judgment that demonstrate this adaptive capacity in the Victorian courts.[10] In the nineteenth century, as Ayelet Ben-Yishai has shown, this evolutionary tendency was nevertheless contained by a shift in the meaning assigned to the word "precedent," which changed from "a convention that was evidence of *custom*, which was the law" to a situation wherein "precedential cases were regarded as *rules* made by judges."[11] For Ben-Yishai, this change helped to consolidate the authority of the common law at a time when the legislative program of Parliament was expanding and assuming a dominant position in jurisprudence. At the same time, precedential thinking began to be understood as a specifically English habit of mind, a way of understanding the present in terms of past situations that was operative in cultural domains other than the law. She traces its influence in the novels of Anthony Trollope, George Eliot, and Wilkie Collins.

Not only were these novelists fascinated by law as a subject for fiction, but they also used analogies drawn from trial procedure to describe their preferred narrative forms. Trollope's logical method of narration owes

[9] See Patrick Brantlinger, *The Spirit of Reform: British Literature and Politics, 1832–1867* (Cambridge: Harvard University Press, 1977); Josephine M. Guy, *The Victorian Social Problem Novel* (Houndmills: Macmillan, 1996); Amanda Claybaugh, *The Novel of Purpose: Literature and Social Reform in the Anglo-American World* (Ithaca: Cornell University Press, 2007).

[10] A. W. Brian Simpson, *Leading Cases in the Common Law* (Oxford: Clarendon Press, 1995).

[11] Ayelet Ben-Yishai, *Common Precedents: The Presentness of the Past in Victorian Law and Fiction* (Oxford: Oxford University Press, 2013), p. 35. Italics in original.

much to the form of legal pleadings, as Rowland McMaster demonstrates.[12] In *The Eustace Diamonds* Trollope inserts a barrister's opinion into the narrative, the legal reasoning of which presents no discernible departure from his normal narrative voice.[13] In chapter 17 of *Adam Bede*, Eliot likens her narrative stance to that of a witness in a court, aiming "to give a faithful account of men and things as they have mirrored themselves in my mind. The mirror is doubtless defective . . . but I feel as much bound to tell you as precisely as I can what that reflection is, as if I were in the witness box narrating my experience on oath."[14] And Collins constructs his sensation novel, *The Woman in White*, as a series of statements by different witnesses, "just as the story of an offence against the laws is told."[15]

While Eliot and Collins may have sought to add the cultural prestige of the law to their fictional experiments, these varied examples suggest underlying commonalities between the form of the legal trial and that of the Victorian novel. Critics studying the intersections between law and literature in the period have built on Ian Watt's comparison between the realist representational procedures of the eighteenth-century novel and the work of jurors in a court of law: "both want to know all the particulars of a given case."[16] Alexander Welsh has shown how arguments in favor of circumstantial evidence circulated in philosophy, theology, and the law of evidence, and became foundational to the dominant literary realism in the eighteenth and nineteenth centuries.[17] In a study that complements Welsh's, Jan-Melissa Schramm argues for the importance of witness testimony and of advocacy in legal trials and fiction, linked to reforms in the criminal trial allowing prisoners to give evidence and be represented by counsel. So interested in these procedures were writers that trials in the Victorian novel often represent the law's failures of justice, leading Schramm to propose that literature saw itself as a rival to law's normative authority.[18] As well as these similarities in narrative resources, there are differences. Noting that both law and literature have a deep investment in

[12] Rowland McMaster, *Trollope and the Law* (London: Macmillan, 1986).

[13] See Marco Wan, "*Stare decisis,* binding precedent and Anthony Trollope's *The Eustace Diamonds*" in Marco Wan (ed.), *Reading the Legal Case: Cross-Currents between Law and the Humanities* (Abingdon: Routledge, 2012), p. 206.

[14] George Eliot, *Adam Bede* (Oxford: Oxford University Press, 1996 [1859]), p. 175.

[15] Wilkie Collins, *The Woman in White* (London: Penguin, 1985 [1860]), p. 33.

[16] Ian Watt, *The Rise of the Novel* (London: Chatto and Windus, 1957), p. 31.

[17] Alexander Welsh, *Strong Representations: Narrative and Circumstantial Evidence in England* (Baltimore: Johns Hopkins University Press, 1992).

[18] Jan-Melissa Schramm, *Testimony and Advocacy in Victorian Law, Literature and Theology* (Cambridge: Cambridge University Press, 2000).

the mental states of individuals, especially the intentions underlying their acts, Lisa Rodensky notes how the novelist has an advantage over a judge or jury because of the genre's techniques for representing consciousness, including omniscient narrative and free indirect speech.[19] In their studies, Welsh, Schramm, and Rodensky all analyze narratives and reports of famous cases as well as literary texts.

Thus legal notions such as precedent and evidence became "traveling concepts," commitments taken up in the wider culture, strongly suggesting the "signifying power" of legal discourse, its capacity to produce or control meaning.[20] At the same time, these examples also show law operating in dialogue with other elements in the culture. Law should also therefore be considered an "expression of culture," in that it formed one element in the negotiation over possible actions and identities in the society.[21] In the gradually evolving democracy of Victorian England, this meant that legal, social, and political issues were debated in the public sphere, especially in the newspapers, periodicals, books, and pamphlets afforded by a rapidly expanding literary marketplace. With growing literacy rates and cheaper paper and printing costs, a socially formative and responsive "print culture" developed, entailing not merely debates about ideas, but also "a struggle over the symbols through which the social world [was] defined."[22] That culture opened up opportunities for writers to earn a living, including many young barristers and law students, but it also provided a space in which subordinated social groups could articulate their claims for political and legal rights, and build their collective identities. Thus, in the 1840s, Chartist journals were a forum in which working-class people could contest hegemonic definitions of crime and tell stories that would not be heard by the courts, and defend their economic rights and imagine alternative futures in the media of poetry and fiction.[23] Similarly, a sustained contest over the rights of married women was conducted across all the media of print

[19] Lisa Rodensky, *The Crime in Mind: Criminal Responsibility and the Victorian Novel* (New York: Oxford University Press, 2003).

[20] See: Mieke Bal, *Travelling Concepts in the Humanities* (Toronto: University of Toronto Press, 2002); and Krueger, *Reading for the Law*, p. 22, quoting the words of Rosemary Coombe.

[21] David Theo Goldberg, Michael Musheno, and Lisa C. Bowers (eds.), *Between Law and Culture: Relocating Legal Studies* (Minneapolis: University of Minnesota Press, 2001), p. xxiv. Cited in Regina Hewitt, "Utopianism and Joanna Baillie: a preface to converging revolutions," *Romantic Circles*, www.rc.umd.edu/praxis/utopia/hewitt_preface/hewitt_preface.html, para 24.

[22] Barbara Leckie, *Culture and Adultery: The Novel, the Newspaper and the Law, 1857–1914* (Philadelphia: University of Pennsylvania Press, 1999), p. 4.

[23] See Simon Joyce, *Capital Offences: Geographies of Class and Crime in Victorian London* (Charlottesville: University of Virginia Press, 2003), p. 84.

culture, through fictional and autobiographical stories of women's lives under the inherited law, in new feminist periodicals such as the *English Women's Journal* and the *Victoria Magazine*, as well as in the *Westminster Review* and other established journals.[24]

Within this system of print culture, "law's power over signification" was asserted to limit the scope of representation through formal and informal regimes of censorship.[25] Legal categories of obscenity, blasphemy, and sedition and the requirement that play scripts be licensed by the Lord Chamberlain curtailed the expression of radical ideas on religion, sexuality, and politics in printed forms and on stage, and limited the representation of sexual relations to a largely metaphoric register. Despite the strength of liberal values in this culture and the emergence of what Barbara Leckie has called a "democracy of print," these legal mechanisms reflected dominant community opinion.[26] The period saw major prosecutions brought for the "word crimes" of blasphemy and obscenity, while circulating libraries' and religious organizations' supplementary enforcement of moral norms in their selection and review of books inhibited the literary exploration of unpleasant realities such as adultery.[27] However, as Leckie has shown, drawing on the work of Michel Foucault, such "expurgations" are accompanied by the production of discourses that license certain kinds of statements, certain speaking positions.[28] As a result, "adultery *was* represented. And it was precisely the discourses and institutions designed to subdue adultery that contributed most forcefully to the categories of perception through which it was rendered legible," especially the divorce court, law reporting, and medicine.[29] Once in circulation, the vocabularies and images of those discourses were available for rehearsal and adaptation by imaginative writers, in genres such as the realist or the sensation novel. While some writers worked within the limits allowed by this legal and extralegal censorship, creatively exploiting the value of implication through metaphor and

24 For excellent accounts of aspects of this movement, see Lisa Surridge, *Bleak Houses: Marital Violence in Victorian Fiction* (Athens: Ohio University Press, 2005); Krueger, *Reading for the Law*; Leckie, *Culture and Adultery*; Kelly Hager, *Dickens and the Rise of Divorce: The Failed-Marriage Plot and the Novel Tradition* (Farnham: Ashgate, 2010); Tim Dolin, *Mistress of the House: Women of Property in the Victorian Novel* (Aldershot: Ashgate, 1997); and Hilary Fraser, Judith Johnston, and Stephanie Green, *Gender and the Victorian Periodical* (Cambridge: Cambridge University Press, 2008).

25 Krueger, *Reading for the Law*, p. 22, quoting Coombe.

26 On "democracy of print," see Leckie, *Culture and Adultery*, chapter 1.

27 Joss Marsh, *Word Crimes: Blasphemy, Culture and Literature in Nineteenth-Century England* (Chicago: University of Chicago Press, 1998).

28 Leckie, *Culture and Adultery*, p. 3f.

29 Leckie, *Culture and Adultery*, p. 251f.

allusion, from the 1880s and 1890s a new generation, which included Thomas Hardy, felt compelled to adopt a more candid approach to the representation of sexuality and religious belief.[30]

Thus, law exerted a pervasive influence in Victorian culture, while cultural forms were consistently mobilized to uphold or reshape the discourses of the law. So deep and manifold were the connections between these two domains of culture that law and literature may be said to have existed in a "mutually constitutive" relation.[31] That relation was well illustrated by the Copyright Act 1842, which drew its justification for extending the term of copyright protection from Wordsworthian ideas of literary authorship as a form of inspired, original creation, and which, once enacted, helped to entrench literature as an elevated vocation, a protected sphere of art.[32] Dickens, Anthony Trollope, and George Eliot participated in later debates over international and domestic copyright laws. Clare Pettitt has related these literary concerns to a broader context of debates concerning property, work, and value, suggesting that advances in copyright law in turn helped establish literature as a possible profession.[33]

Another materialization of that mutuality may be seen in cases that captured the public attention, such as the trials of Oscar Wilde or the Tichborne affair cited earlier, in which a working-class butcher from Australia claimed to be the long-lost baronet Sir Roger Tichborne. While Deans ascribes to credulity the wide popular support for the claimant, recent scholars have pointed to the indispensable role of print culture in cultivating this *cause célèbre*, and have argued that the legal issues were not the only matters at stake in the Tichborne craze. Jan-Melissa Schramm demonstrates how contemporary commentators reflected on the way in which this imposture raised concerns about the nature and proof of identity.[34] Others have argued that the case became a radical popular cause and a lightning rod for working-class discontent with

30 See Nora Gilbert, *Better Left Unsaid: Victorian Novels, the Hays Code and the Benefits of Censorship* (Stanford: Stanford University Press, 2013); Thomas Hardy, "Candour in English fiction" in Harold Orel (ed.), *Thomas Hardy: Personal Writings* (London: Macmillan, 1967), pp. 125–33.

31 Ben-Yishai, *Common Precedents*, p. 10 (where the phrase is used in a slightly different context).

32 See Martha Woodmansee, "The romantic author" in Isabella Alexander and H. Tomás Gómez-Arostegui (eds.), *Research Handbook on the History of Copyright Law* (London: Edward Elgar, 2016), pp. 53–76. Paul K. Saint-Amour offers a study of the literary mediation of copyright in *The Copywrights: Intellectual Property and the Literary Imagination* (Ithaca: Cornell University Press, 2003).

33 Clare Pettitt, *Patent Inventions: Intellectual Property and the Victorian Novel* (Oxford: Oxford University Press, 2004), chapter 1.

34 Schramm, *Atonement and Self-Sacrifice*, pp. 194–203.

liberal politics.[35] For Rohan McWilliam, "the Tichborne cause was a form of popular theatre," which mingled discourses from radical politics and cultural genres such as melodrama.[36] In Victorian England as much as today, major legal cases assumed cultural significance, and distilled larger ideological contests. Their circulation brought forth fictional examinations of the phenomenon of the sensational trial such as Trollope's *The Eustace Diamonds.* They also helped to constitute the enduring genre of the detective novel, early versions of which were often formally modeled on a brief of evidence.[37] This circulation of real and fictional cases in turn reinforced the cultural image of the trial as an instrument of justice by creating a discourse of famous cases or "notable trials" that could be narrated as popular legal history in collections such as that by Deans.

The Case as a Cultural Form

Thus far we have discussed the "case" in terms of circumstantial particularity, drawing on Ian Watt's analogy between the novel reader and the jury in a legal trial. Recent scholarship on cases and the nineteenth-century novel has emphasized Adam Smith's *Theory of Moral Sentiments* as a key influence. Rae Greiner and James Chandler have both drawn on Smith's use of cases in developing his account of sympathy and moral judgment. Greiner argues that, "Moving us between minds, the sympathetic case helps activate the impression of realism" by soliciting readers to a form of "fellow-feeling" with characters and their situations.[38] Chandler too places "moving" at the heart of his account, arguing that "sympathetic imaginative mobility" is an animating premise of nineteenth-century fiction, especially in its experiments with point of view – "how a novelist moves (and moves a reader) from one standpoint on the story, or in it, to another."[39] Chandler had generated renewed interest in the case as a form

[35] Rohan McWilliam, "Radicalism and popular culture: The Tichborne case and politics of 'fair play,' 1867–86" in Eugenio F. Biagini and Alastair J. Reid (eds.), *Currents of Radicalism: Popular Radicalism, Organised Labour and Party Politics in Britain 1850–1914* (Cambridge: Cambridge University Press, 1991), 44–64; David Wayne Thomas, *Cultivating Victorians: Liberal Culture and the Aesthetic* (Philadelphia: University of Pennsylvania Press, 2004), chapter 3.

[36] McWilliam, "Radicalism," 45.

[37] Lauren Berlant, "On the case," *Critical Inquiry*, 33 (2007), 663–72. See for instance Collins, *Woman in White* and Charles Warren Adams, *The Notting Hill Mystery* (London: British Library, 2012 [1862–3]).

[38] Rae Greiner, "The art of knowing your own nothingness," *ELH*, 77 (2010), 899.

[39] James Chandler, "On the face of the case: Conrad, *Lord Jim*, and the sentimental novel," *Critical Inquiry*, 33 (2007), 842–3.

by appropriating Andres Jolles' 1929 theory that the "case" was a "simple form," a transcultural genre along with legend, myth, the riddle, the fairy tale and others. As translated by Chandler, Jolles argued that "the peculiarity of the case form lies precisely in that it poses a question without being able to give an answer, that it imposes on us the obligation to decide without containing the decision in itself."[40] In a recent overview of the attraction of the case for various fields of study, Lauren Berlant defines it more pithily: "The case represents a problem-event that has animated some kind of judgment. Any enigma could do – a symptom, a crime, a causal variable, a situation, a stranger."[41] In *The Eustace Diamonds*, for example, the plot centers on the ownership of the eponymous jewelry – whether the necklace is a family heirloom or whether it was a gift outright to Lady Eustace by her late husband, and thus part of her "paraphernalia." To the shock of the family solicitor, a very learned barrister's opinion concludes that they are paraphernalia. Even with that ruling, the lost diamonds remain elusive, and conflicts between the characters multiply, prompting further recourse to law and judgments across the social spectrum.[42]

In both legal and literary forms, the case involves a process of abstracting from the particular to the general, and vice versa.[43] Ayelet Ben-Yishai also frames the process of legal judgment in terms of the interplay between the general rule and the individual case. While it is readily understandable when the rule is encoded in a statute and applied to the particular circumstances before a court, Ben-Yishai shows that in a common law system based entirely on precedent cases the situation is more complex: In this context the general rule has first "to be abstracted from one specific instance and then applied to another" in an "active and dynamic process" that makes law in the act of applying it.[44] Hence, Ben-Yishai argues, the appeal of strengthening the inherited concept of precedent as a means of limiting this dynamism in an age when technology and urbanization were increasingly creating new situations.

James Ram, whose 1834 treatise *The Science of Legal Judgment* has been called "the first systematic work on the case law method," was alive to the perception that this "dynamic process" created uncertainty in the common

[40] James K. Chandler, *England in 1819: The Politics of Literary Culture and the Case of Romantic Historicism* (Chicago: University of Chicago Press, 1998), p. 208.

[41] Berlant, "On the case," 663.

[42] See Ben-Yishai, *Common Precedents*, chapter 3; Randall Craig, *Promising Language: Betrothal in Victorian Law and Fiction* (Albany: State University of New York Press, 2010), pp. 240–4.

[43] See Greiner, "The art of knowing," 899.

[44] Ben-Yishai, *Common Precedents*, pp. 75, 77.

law.[45] He opens his textbook by attempting to explain its causes, notably that no two cases are exactly alike, that there are likely therefore to be conflicting precedents, and that the interpretation of circumstances has a subjective element, so that witnesses may well see things differently.[46] Despite the appeal to science in his title, Ram offers a descriptive account of how common law practitioners and judges discuss, reason from, and use cases. His frame of reference is professional practice, and so his book is dominated by examples drawn from cases. Compared with treatises that show the influence of Bentham, Ram's writing lacks a critical analysis of its subject; rather, it offers an insider's guide to the professional discourse on cases – ways of arguing that individual cases are analogous to earlier decided cases or are distinguishable from such possible precedents, or even that they must be decided on their own particular circumstances.[47] William Cornish regards Ram as a writer who "treated the rules for finding and using the law ... with a new sophistication," pointing out that he offered thirteen ways of arguing in favour of a case as a precedent, and twenty-one arguments for discounting it.[48] Yet this very fluency was indicative of a larger problem in the common law that Ram recognized: the multiplication of instances, and the danger of uncertainty. As Cornish puts it, "the need to generalise gained a new urgency," impelling the emphasis on precedent, the production of textbooks, and the identification of certain cases as "leading cases."[49]

Ram's final book, *A Treatise on Facts as Subjects of Inquiry by a Jury*, is a primer on the law of evidence written for potential jurors. It begins with a capacious definition of fact: "If anything is seen or heard, the seeing or hearing of it is a fact. If any emotion of the mind is felt, as joy, grief, anger, the feeling of it is a fact."[50]

Ram exemplifies these possibilities by reproducing Wordsworth's poem "Lucy Gray" in full. He offers no evidentiary commentary on the text, only an apology for using such a "tender" and "sad" poem "as a mere example of facts."[51] Wordsworth's lyrical ballad might well be what Chandler calls a case in the "sentimental form" – one that preserves an exemplary instance

[45] John H. Farrar, "Reasoning by analogy in the law," *Bond Law Review*, 9 (1997), 151.

[46] James Ram, *The Science of Legal Judgment* (London, 1834), p. 2.

[47] Ram, *Science*, pp. 25, 248, 256.

[48] William Cornish, "The sources of the law" in William Cornish et al. (ed.), *The Oxford History of English Law* (Oxford: Oxford University Press, 2010), vol. XI, p. 41, 49.

[49] Cornish, "Sources," 66; Simpson, *Leading Cases*, "Introduction."

[50] James Ram, *A Treatise on Facts as Subjects of Inquiry by a Jury* (London, 1861), chapter 1.

[51] Ram, *Treatise on Facts*, chapter 1. Later editions, including those available via the Internet Archive, do not include the poem.

of the hazards of life, the grief experienced upon the accidental death of a child.[52] Throughout the text, Ram intersperses legal and literary examples, demonstrating the traffic between these two spheres of the culture. More particularly, it opens up the possibility of seeing literary narratives as imagined cases. Yet this possibility is largely unrealized, as Ram tends to use his literary examples to illustrate a rule, or to support a particular usage of a word. In other words, he invokes writers as "authorities," linguistic precedents.[53] This approach affords a circumscribed example of "literature as law," something akin to the illustrative passages that support meanings in a historical dictionary, but it sacrifices the possibility of "sympathetic imaginative mobility" that a fuller engagement with the facts of "Lucy Gray" might have allowed. It also suggests why Ram saw tenderness and facts as antithetical even while arguing that emotions could be facts.

In the literary sphere, novelists and poets embraced the kind of complex fact situations that were found in legal cases, or derived from them. Space permits me to discuss only a couple of examples here, one broadly realistic and one more sensational in its elements.

Anthony Trollope's *The Warden* provides a well-known example of a novel based on a real lawsuit. Set in the cathedral city of Barchester, the novel concerns a dispute raised over the correct interpretation of a medieval charitable trust, which has paid for the support and accommodation of twelve elderly men and their chaplain, Mr. Harding. In the centuries since the trust was set up, the value of the land from which it gains its income has greatly increased. The twelve pensioners are still paid the sum set out in the will, but their chaplain, the Warden of the title, receives the bulk of the revenue for his house and stipend.

Similar appropriations led to campaigns of protest against the Church's abuse of trusts in the early nineteenth century, and to litigation in the 1850s. Trollope draws on the case of *Attorney-General* v. *St Cross* and another notorious instance at Rochester in framing his plot, and alludes to these events in the exposition of his fictional dispute. A young doctor, John Bold, confidently files suit in the name of the old men, seeking a fairer distribution under the trust. In the ensuing litigation, Mr. Harding, who, unlike the Master at St. Cross Hospital, undertakes his duties conscientiously, is caught between the reformers on one side and the institutional Church defending its property on the other. Morally, he feels the force of the men's claim, but the Church's legal

[52] See particularly Chandler, "On the face of the case," 837, 841.
[53] See, e.g., Ram, *Treatise*, pp. 37, 285.

advisers mount a strong defense on his behalf, briefing the Attorney-General as counsel. Personal ties complicate Harding's dilemma, as John Bold loves his daughter Eleanor, while the major force in the diocese, Archdeacon Grantly, is his son-in-law.

As the dispute intensifies, the Warden travels to London naïvely hoping to gain assurances about the justice of his position from the Attorney-General, Sir Abraham Haphazard. The name Haphazard echoes the etymology of the word "case," which is derived from the Latin *casus*, meaning "the fall in and through chance."[54] Trollope portrays Sir Abraham as a "machine with a mind," so imbued with the adversarial culture of the common law trial as to be interested only in "legal victory over an opposing party."[55] Having identified a procedural flaw in the claimant's case, he does not turn his mind to the justice of their cause or of the defense. Bold withdraws the case, but, while other clerics are satisfied, Mr. Harding feels bound by his conscience to resign the Wardenship. The legal case is thus superseded by a moral one, but this outcome leaves the plot in a stalemate, as no new warden is appointed and the charity gradually falls into abeyance. The question regarding a just interpretation of the trust deed and the proper payment of all parties is left unresolved. In the case of *Attorney-General* v. *St Cross*, by contrast, the court ruled that the customary practices of the Master were "a glaring and . . . discreditable breach of trust."[56] However, it also determined that the Master, who acted within established custom, should not have to account for the funds retrospectively.[57] This containment of the change effected by the judgment is paralleled by the outcome of Trollope's plot. James Fishman rightly argues that Trollope recast the case into one of moral ambiguity, but doing so allowed him to enlist the Attorney-General on the side of the defense, rather than in the interest of the charitable trust, as in the original case. *The Warden* ends in an impasse, and even implies that the attempt to ameliorate the pensioners' conditions was ill founded. Trollope's moral realism has blocked the argument for institutional reform in favor of the ethical performance of traditional roles.

The Warden reveals the ordinary norms of the Victorian culture of legality; by contrast, Robert Browning presents "a most peculiar case" in

[54] Jean-Luc Nancy, *A Finite Thinking*, ed. Simon Sparks (Stanford: Stanford University Press, 2003), pp. 157.

[55] Anthony Trollope, *The Warden* (Oxford: Oxford University Press, 1998), pp. 230, 109.

[56] *Attorney-General* v. *St. Cross* (1853) 51 English Reports, 1114.

[57] For a detailed historical account, see James J. Fishman, "Charity scandals as a catalyst of legal change and literary inspiration," *Michigan State Law Review* (2005), 369–416.

his verse-novel of 1875, "Red-Cotton Night-Cap Country."[58] Based on recent events in Normandy, it tells the story of a Parisian jeweler, Léonce Miranda, who oscillates between the competing demands of religious duty and sensual pleasure, between a fervent Catholicism and the earthly love of his mistress, Clara de Millefleurs. Racked with guilt that the sudden death of his mother was a result of his immoral life, he reads Clara's letters a final time, then slowly places them in the fire, burning his hands along with the correspondence. After a short attempt at renunciation, he returns to live with Clara, but remains conscious of the religious law:

> No prejudice for old profound respect
> For certain Powers! I trust they bear in mind
> A most peculiar case, and straighten out
> What's crooked there, before we close accounts.
> Renounce the world for them – some day I will:
> Meantime, let her to me become the world!

This conflict between desire and the law plays out in a tragic key. Unable to leave Clara, Miranda becomes increasingly prone to compensatory behaviour, including extraordinary donations to the Church and the poor, conspicuous acts of public devotion, and fantasies about the miraculous resolution of his predicament. In a leap of faith, he throws himself off the tower at his country house, believing that the Virgin Mary will assist him to fly to a nearby church – a miracle that would be witnessed by thousands – and demonstrate the truths of Christianity to secular, skeptical France. After "tragic death befell" him, a court case ensues to determine his sanity and the validity of his will, which bequeathed all his property to the Church, with a life interest for Clara.

Browning reconstructs the narrative from evidence given in the lately decided court case, and from his own knowledge of the region. He reflects on how to represent the mental processes that led to Miranda's "sublime spring from the balustrade":

> Along with every act – and speech is act –
> There go, a multitude impalpable
> To ordinary human faculty
> The thoughts which give the act significance.
> Who is a poet needs must apprehend

[58] "Red-Cotton Night-Cap Country," in *Robert Browning: The Poems* II, ed. John Pettigrew (Harmondsworth: Penguin, 1981), line 1800.

Alike both speech and thoughts which prompt to speak.
Part these and thought withdraws to poetry:
Speech is reported in the newspaper.[59]

As the prelude to a dramatic monologue by Miranda in the tower, these lines also recall James Ram's insistence on mental and emotional "facts": "If the operation of the mind is productive of an effect, as intention, knowledge, skill, the possession of this effect is a fact."[60] Browning represents Miranda's delirious reasoning as speech, offering him a form of testimony which is only available in literary modes, and allowing readers to understand, but also to judge, him. For James Chandler, "a tension develops between sympathy and judgment" in the nineteenth century, which is registered with great clarity in the dramatic monologue.[61] Although Miranda's vision of the Virgin was delusory, Browning denies he was mad: "Such being the conditions of his life/Such end of life was not irrational."[62] There follow dramatic monologues by one of Miranda's cousins and by Clara, which give different perspectives on his behavior and which are supplemented by Browning's very different, measured judgment on their characters.

Browning self-consciously adopts the forensic model for his exposition. As the conflict crystallizes, he frames a question for judgment, with the words "Here's our case":

Monsieur Léonce Miranda asks of God,
– May a man, living in illicit tie,
Continue, by connivance of the Church,
No matter what amends he please to make
Short of forthwith relinquishing the sin?[63]

His own answer to this question is guided by precedential thinking, as he invokes an historical example involving a happily married couple who desired to enter religious orders. Although the situation was different, their case discloses the legal principles to be applied, and facilitates a detached judgment on the conduct of Miranda, Clara, and the representatives of the Church. Although espousing a vision of art as socially radical ("Artistry being battle with the age/It lives in!"[64]), Browning does not endorse the "illicit tie" between Miranda and Clara as an exercise of personal freedom and love. Rather he defers to contemporary standards of morality, assuring

59 Browning, "Red-Cotton," 3277–84. 60 Ram, *Treatise on Facts*, chapter 1.
61 Chandler, "On the face of the case," 856. 62 Browning, "Red-Cotton," 3604–5.
63 Browning, "Red-Cotton," 3040. 64 Browning, "Red-Cotton," 2081–2.

readers, "I will not scandalise you."[65] Although the Court found Miranda had died by an accidental fall, Browning concurs with its overall judgment of his sanity and the validity of his will. His poetic account of the case highlights the mental and moral extremes felt by Miranda; however, Browning reveals their underlying relationship to the century's conflict between faith and doubt, and its competing ethical systems.

Both these cases show an inherited culture of legality placed under stress by new conceptions of right, or transgressive desire. In *The Warden*, the substantive legal issue raised by the reformers remains moot, Trollope preferring to cultivate normative uncertainty rather than following the judicial compromise crafted in *A-G* v. *St Cross*. In "Red Cotton Night-Cap Country," Miranda's case incarnates the struggles of a society that extols personal freedom while still being psychically subject to the authority of traditional law. If, as Lauren Berlant argues, cases are "always pedagogical," their appeal for Victorian writers and readers as a tool for navigating their rapidly changing world is unsurprising. For readers reflecting on law and culture today, the Victorian impulse to "put the case" provides a powerful heuristic for understanding the conflicts of the period and their relevance to our own.

[65] Browning, "Red-Cotton," 2734.

CHAPTER 11

Forming the Nation in Nineteenth-Century America

Nan Goodman

In *Nationalism: Five Roads to Modernity*, the historical sociologist Liah Greenfeld describes America as "an ideal nation" in which "the national element . . . is challenged by the fewest counterinfluences." According to Greenfeld, it is possible to describe America in this way because, unlike England, France, Russia, or Germany – the other four nations she examines in her book – America was always a nation, even before it officially declared itself one. Greenfeld's argument about America depends on her characterization of the white colonial settlers, who in her view understood themselves from the start as subjects of a nation – in their case, England – and who came to the New World already invested in nationalism as a legal concept. That the nation that emerged 150 years after they arrived was American rather than English prompts Greenfeld to admit that a certain amount of "tweaking" had to be done, but this, she suggests, paled in comparison to the work required for nation formation in other countries where beliefs needed to be wrenched around to put a nationalist ideology into place. America, Greenfield concludes, "is a purer example of a national community than any other."[1]

To speak about America in Greenfeld's terms, however – as always already a nation – presents a number of difficulties. Chief among these is that it erases America's indigenous and colonial pasts – a critique leveled at Greenfeld's work from many quarters.[2] Still, Greenfeld's comments provide a fruitful starting point for our examination of the development of the American nation because they exemplify a strain of American

[1] Liah Greenfeld, *Nationalism: Five Roads to Modernity* (Massachusetts: Harvard University Press, 1992), p. 403.

[2] For a sampling of critiques of Greenfeld's book, see, for example, John A. Armstrong, "Nationalism: five roads to modernity," *History and Theory*, 33(1) (1994), 79–95; Juan Diez Medrano, "Nationalism: five roads to modernity," *American Journal of Sociology*, 99(4) (1994), 1443–5; Raymond Pearson, "Nationalism: five roads to modernity," *The Journal of Modern History*, 67(4) (1995), 903–4.

exceptionalism – the notion that America was always different from other nations – that has lingered longer than any other. In the past, people have argued that America was exceptional because it was bigger, newer, or more diverse than other nations, but these assertions have almost all yielded to recent and more nuanced counterarguments that link America to comparable forms of difference in the development of nationhood in other parts of the world.[3] Rooted however not in size, novelty, or demographics, but rather in the assumption that the Anglo-American law that helped to bring the American nation into being was unusually just, equal, and democratic, Greenfeld's strain of American exceptionalism has proved especially intractable, leading many to think of the American nation as legally different and "ideal" even today.[4]

Taking Greenfeld's assumption about American law and nationalism seriously, this chapter tries to unsettle it by examining the development of Anglo-American law from the prerevolutionary period to the end of the nineteenth century. While there can be no question that the prenational and national legal systems embodied in Anglo-American common law and the Constitution contained many democratic precepts, it is also true that we cannot adequately understand the process of nation formation in America unless we analyze the gap between these principles and their implementation. As Saidiya Hartman explains, the articulation of the principles of equality and freedom in the U.S. Constitution that seemingly set it apart from other legal systems did not necessarily ensure their realization as the law moved from theory to practice. Indeed, the fact that these principles were enshrined in the language of the Constitution, Hartman suggests, seems to have been taken at times as sufficient evidence of their existence, opening the door to the enforcement of inequality and injustice, their antitheses.[5] Paying lip service to the national goal of securing "the Blessings of Liberty to ourselves," the preamble to the U.S. Constitution, for example, made it possible for those in power to define the reflexive

[3] For examples of Americanist scholarship that have abandoned exceptionalism in favor of transatlantic, hemispheric, and global contexts, see William C. Spengemann, *A New World of Words: Redefining Early American Literature* (New Haven: Yale University Press, 1994); Wai Chee Dimock, *Through Other Continents: American Literature across Deep Time* (Princeton: Princeton University Press, 2008); David Armitage, *The Declaration of Independence: A Global History* (Cambridge: Harvard University Press, 2007); Thomas Bender, *A Nation Among Nations: America's Place in World History* (Boston: Hill and Wang, 2006).

[4] See Donald Pease, "Rethinking American studies after exceptionalism," *American Literary History*, 21(1) (2009), 21, for an acknowledgment of the "rule of law" as one of the core tenets of American exceptionalism and a possible source of its perpetuation.

[5] See Saidiya V. Hartman, *Scenes of Subjection: Terror, Slavery, and Self-Making in Nineteenth-Century America* (New York: Oxford University Press, 1997), p. 116.

pronoun "ourselves" in exclusionary ways, leaving theory alone to unite the "imagined community" of the nation.[6] As the American nation developed in the nineteenth century, however, those who were left out of the founders' vision, including slaves, immigrants, women, and manual laborers, began to speak for themselves, making nation formation in nineteenth-century America a variation of the process known in music as "call and response."

A sequence of musical phrases in which the second phrase responds to and comments on the first, the pattern of call and response can be found in several musical traditions. Its prominence in the African-American tradition, however, makes it an especially apt tool for understanding nation formation in the nineteenth-century United States in which slavery was such a divisive issue. Following the musical form, the legal "call" in nineteenth-century America often came, unsurprisingly, from the government in the form of court-made law or legislation. These legal calls typically prompted a "response" from the people to whom the law addressed itself, often in the form of protests, strikes, or literary, religious, and philosophical expression. Just as often, however, the roles of the law and popular expression were reversed, revealing the extent to which nation formation was a two-way street with the people and the law calling and responding at various times. As this culturally reciprocal call-and-response model suggests, while the law as understood by lawyers and judges emerged as determinative from time to time, it was typically in dialogue with a variety of discursive partners, including the arts, the humanities, and the social sciences. As the fledgling republic developed into a nation, all of these discourses were soon engaged in a multidirectional call-and-response communication about what shape the new nation should take.

Of the many discourses involved in this nineteenth-century debate with the law, perhaps the most prominent was the literary. Aside from the fact that many novelists were also lawyers – a fact which made the relationship between fiction and the law especially close – poets and novelists often seemed more visibly concerned than others with describing the contours and trajectories of the new nation. In a representative government in which people elected others to speak on their behalf, it followed that those directly involved with expression would be central to the task. When Ralph Waldo Emerson, for example, called for an American poet who would not merely repeat the truisms of English literature but attend to the "literature

[6] The phrase is from Benedict Anderson, *Imagined Communities: Reflections on the Origin and Spread of Nationalism* (London: Verso, 2006).

of the poor, the feelings of the child, the philosophy of the street, the meaning of household life," he was acknowledging that the law alone could not satisfy the mandate to represent the nation.[7] And when Walt Whitman wrote in *Leaves of Grass* (1855), close to twenty years later, that he was "the poet of the Body and . . . the poet of the Soul" and "the poet of the woman the same as the man," he answered Emerson's call by deferring to every American as an author of the nation. Indeed, it was often the early American popular novel – the cowboy Western, the seduction tale, the slave story, the sea story, among others – that proved a testing ground for national potential. Learning through fiction about what others believed, needed, or desired when those same voices could not always make themselves heard in the law often brought together people who would otherwise not have found common ground. Jeannine DeLombard calls our attention to one such literary partnership between abolitionists and nonabolitionist white northerners, who discovered in the discourse of abolitionism, which had yet to receive legal sanction but was given its due in newspaper articles and novels, an indignation about the absence of rights for slaves that resonated with their own perceived losses.[8]

In reflecting on the many questions that nineteenth-century Americans asked about what the new nation should look like, three stand out in the intersecting realms of law and literature: Who was entitled to citizenship and the rights and liberties the Constitution promised? What would nationalization do for people's incomes and the livelihood of workers? How would nationhood alter Americans' relationships with people in other nations across the world? These three questions animate the discussion below, which is divided into sections that correspond roughly with these categories: in the first case, membership; in the second case, labor; and in the third case, foreign relations.

Membership

The subject of membership in the new nation tells a story of inclusion and exclusion, of a nation wrestling with a heterogeneous population in terms of race, ethnicity, gender, religion, and socioeconomic class. The threshold question for a nation forming under such circumstances was who was in

[7] Ralph Waldo Emerson, "The American scholar" in *The Essential Writings of Ralph Waldo Emerson* (New York: Random House, 2000), p. 57.

[8] See Jeannine Marie DeLombard, *Slavery on Trial: Law Abolitionism, and Print Culture* (Chapel Hill: University of North Carolina Press, 2007), p. 40.

and who was out. Arguably all communities, national or otherwise, share this concern, but the pressures generated by a declaration of nationhood made this question even more pressing. When the U.S. Constitution, for example, referred to the nation that was forming as "a more perfect union," it suggested that the organization that had united people living in America before 1789 was soon to improve. There were of course many who had sided with England during the Revolutionary War and who did not think the union that followed the war would be "more perfect." This Anglophilic and nostalgic sense of nationalism, best exemplified by Hector St. John de Crevecoeur's *Letters from an American Farmer* (1783), raises questions about Liah Greenfeld's assertion that the only change needed after America became an official nation was a mere "tweaking" of the national ideology. For Farmer James, the protagonist of *Letters*, the "perfect union" that was America before the war disintegrates when nationhood is declared and the tranquility that was possible for Americans living under the distant and relatively benign rule of King George is shattered. Before the nation takes official shape, Farmer James revels in being an American. For Farmer James, prenational America is a place where liberty and equality is already secure, and where, in Crevecoeur's words, "individuals of all races are melted into a new race of man, whose labors and posterity will one day cause great changes in the world."[9] After the revolution this equality vanishes, and Farmer James returns to Europe, horrified by what the declaration of nationhood has ushered in.

Regardless of whether people supported nationhood or were disgusted by it, most agreed that making a nation out of what had formerly been a group of colonies, and then a province, would make a visible difference. Even this, however, was in doubt at the beginning of the nineteenth century, when some of the nation's detractors believed that it was nothing more than a colony or province ruled by monarchical principles under a different name. In his celebrated tale "Rip Van Winkle," Washington Irving takes up this issue in telling the story of a man who falls asleep in the forest for twenty years and wakes up after the new nation has been formed. As Rip Van Winkle trudges back to his village, unaware that he has slept through the revolution, he notices that things look altered but also strangely the same. One of the first things Rip notices is the old hotel, where, as Irving remarks:

[9] J. Hector St. John de Crevecoeur, *Letters from an American Farmer and Sketches of Eighteenth-Century America*. Ed. Albert Stone (New York: Penguin Group, 1981), p. 70.

> He recognized on the sign ... the ruby face of King George, under which he had smoked so many a peaceful pipe, but even this was singularly metamorphosed. The red coat was changed for one of blue and buff, a sword was stuck in the hand instead of a scepter, the head was decorated with a cocked hat, and underneath was painted in large characters, GENERAL WASHINGTON.[10]

Here Irving suggests that the shift from colony to nation entailed a mere shift in the different Georges in power, for where King George III had once held sway by means of his scepter, now George Washington, the first president of the United States, ruled by means of his sword. The implications for the new nation are disturbing, for, in revealing the similarity between the faces of the two Georges, Irving implies that Washington, the leader of the new, democratic nation, is every bit the monarch his predecessor was.

These early literary expressions of ambivalence about the new nation soon gave way to more charged interactions between law and literature over the membership and later citizenship of two groups in particular: slaves and women. Second only to the revolution itself, the Civil War, which divided the nation over the issue of slavery, raised serious questions about the viability of the nation as a whole. If the South and its institution of slavery managed to secede from the Union, it would, many reasoned, no longer be clear what held the Union together, or what it meant to be an American. This divisiveness received its most prominent legal expression in the Fugitive Slave Act of 1850, a compromise measure promoted by Henry Clay to heal the nation's wounds and to make sure the Union would survive. The Act, which provided that any slave captured in the free states of the North had to be sent back to the South as missing property, was viewed by most Northerners as an attack on the right of states to make laws for their own citizenry. This sense of deprivation had the unintended consequence of galvanizing the North against slavery. More curious still from a law and humanities point of view was that while the Fugitive Slave Law represented the power of the law, it was received by many as a moral rather than a legal proclamation, provoking outrage among those who felt that the nation's laws should adhere to the moral principles of equality and liberty on which they had ostensibly been built. This, as Gregg Crane argues, brought literature and the law even closer. "[T]he barest sketch," Crane writes, "of the decent citizen forbidden by law from aiding the

[10] Washington Irving, "Rip Van Winkle" in *The Legend of Sleepy Hollow and Other Stories from the Sketchbook* (New York: Signet, 2006), p. 53.

shivering fugitive ... created a special role for literary renderings of the jurisprudential crisis."[11] As Crane suggests, this opened the way for what ultimately became paralegal literature, such as Harriet Beecher Stowe's novel, *Uncle Tom's Cabin*, which worked alongside the law, influencing the further development of slave law by appealing to basic human sentiments and turning the populace against slavery through depictions of slavery's cruelty and abuse.

While Harriet Beecher Stowe's bestselling novel influenced the law through the backdoor of sentiment, works by and about women and slaves entered into a more direct struggle with the law to define the nation's members. Frederick Douglass was perhaps the most prominent black abolitionist speaker and writer to directly engage the language of the law and, in doing so, revise it. After the decision in *Dred Scott* v. *Sanford*, the Supreme Court case that openly excluded black people from citizenship because they were, in Justice Taney's words, "of an inferior order," Frederick Douglass addressed the American Anti-Slavery Society to offer a counterargument.[12] Not content with pointing out the case's logical deficiencies, of which there were many, Douglass directly addressed the implication of his inferiority by referring to himself "as a man, an American, a citizen, a colored man of both Anglo-Saxon and African descent."[13] To speak as a citizen – as did many of the authors of slave narratives, including Harriet Jacobs, who wrote the widely read *Incidents in the Life of a Slave Girl* (1860) – in prestigious literary forums was the first step in countering the Taney decision.

Extending citizenship no further than to white landowning men meant that women were excluded as well. Like the abolitionists with whom they often joined forces, many women were defiant in the face of this exclusion. While some took their cue from Stowe and aimed to exercise authority from within the sentimental and domestic realms, others took up a more strident position, working toward a platform of women's rights which was finally presented to the world at the first women's rights convention in Seneca Falls, New York in 1848. Called the "Declaration of Sentiments" in deference to the prevailing sentimental ideology, the document that issued

[11] Gregg D. Crane, *Race, Citizenship, and Law in American Literature* (Cambridge: University of Cambridge Press, 2002), p. 17.

[12] *Dred Scott* v. *John F.A. Sanford* 60 U.S. 393 (1857).

[13] Frederick Douglass, "The Dred Scott decision: speech delivered before American Anti-Slavery Society, New York, May 14, 1857" in Philip S. Foner (ed.), *Frederick Douglass: Selected Speeches and Writings* (Chicago: Lawrence Hill Books, 1999), p. 355. For more on this counter attack, see DeLombard, *Slavery on Trial*, p. 103.

from the Seneca Falls Convention was its own Bill of Rights, outlining women's demands for equal rights with men, including the vote, married women's property rights, and divorce. Although the document itself did not have the force of law, its use of legal language made the legal domain more accessible to those who had for too long been barred from it, and by definition expanded the category of those working to make law in America. One especially gifted proponent of women's rights, Margaret Fuller, was notable for adapting her arguments on behalf of women into a legal language that resonated with both men and women. Her monumental brief for women's equality, "The Great Lawsuit: Man versus Men, Women versus Women," drove home one of the essential drawbacks of American law – its tendency to speak in abstractions of equality without ensuring their enforcement and distribution. What good was the abstraction of Man, or for that matter Woman, Fuller asked, when individual men and women were treated unfairly?

Labor

The disparity that Fuller, Douglass, and others perceived between the theory and practice of American law also had implications for those reflecting on the nation's economy and its central instrument of productivity and equality – the contract. Often described as "a meeting of the minds" allowing for independent financial arrangements that would in turn stimulate economic growth, the contract was so valorized in the nineteenth century that more than one legal historian has referred to the period as America's "golden age of contract law."[14] Contract had a particularly salient place in the development of the American nation, stemming from the Biblical concept of the covenant – a contract, essentially, between the Jews and God – which was later adopted by the New England Puritans, who thought of themselves as the surrogate Jews. This Biblically inspired covenant, which depicted a model of legal and political association based on the voluntary consent of its adherents, also became the model of the social contract that guided the emergence of republican governments in the Enlightenment and beyond.

From a legal point of view, contract was the perfect instrument to ensure equality because it required that both parties to the contract express themselves in open and voluntary terms. As the liberalizing agent that

[14] See Lawrence M. Friedman, *A History of American Law: Third Edition* (New York: Simon & Schuster, Inc., 2005), p. 405.

allowed capitalism and free markets to thrive, however, contract often fell short of this ideal, as even after the passage of the Thirteenth Amendment, which abolished slavery, several Southern states continued to pass laws that concealed forms of involuntary servitude under the veil of contract. These laws, often referred to as the peonage laws, forced employees, typically former slaves, to work to pay off debts and went so far as to criminalize their behavior if they sought better contractual terms elsewhere.[15] These lapses in fairness tolerated and perpetuated by contract law only increased throughout the nineteenth century as even the pretense of evaluating a contract on the basis of fairness disappeared from most judicial decisions. In fact, it was not until the early years of the twentieth century that peonage laws were finally held to be unconstitutional.

Too often determined by the coercive terms of agreements made between employer and employee, contract had a heinous effect in the northern urban workplace as well. Herman Melville's "Bartleby the Scrivener" exposes these inequities in the celebrated portrait of the wage laborer Bartleby, whose ability to work as a copyist in an elderly lawyer's office diminishes over time along with his desire and ability to express himself, until all he can say when asked why he will not finish his tasks is "I would prefer not to."[16] Inherent in Bartleby's response to the lawyer's seemingly polite request that he fulfill the terms of the contract he signed is the fallacy of the law's assumption that contractual relations were always fair in the first place. What Bartleby's contract purports to be in theory – a meeting of the minds between two or more free and equal negotiators – is in practice a statement of the rights of the more powerful partner to demand productivity and the obligations and duties of the less powerful partner, who must agree to the stated terms or, in many cases, starve. In depicting the struggle between employer and employee with the language of polite request on the employer's part and polite resistance on the employee's part, Melville critiques legal language for a gentility that obscures a harsh reality. Bartleby does not simply "prefer" not to work; he is physically unable to do his work because his sight is failing, and he can no longer see the words he has been asked to copy. The terms of contract law, however, were not designed to acknowledge this.

A growing recognition that fewer and fewer contracts were the genuine expressions of equality they were intended to be led laborers to band

[15] "Full text of the Peonage cases," www.archive.org/stream/jstor-1109963/1109963_djvu.txt.

[16] Herman Melville, "Bartleby the scrivener" in *Billy Budd, Bartleby, and Other Stories* (New York: Penguin Random House, 2016), p. 25.

together in collective bargaining units to overcome the disproportionate power given to the employer. Fear of recrimination by employers led many of these early unions to take the form of secret societies, such as the notorious Molly Maguires, a group popular with coal miners in Pennsylvania in the 1870s. Violent clashes between labor groups such as the Molly Maguires and the Pinkerton detective agency, which had been hired by the president of the Philadelphia and Reading Railroad to break up the Mollies, led to a series of lurid trials in which more than twenty alleged members of the Mollies were executed. Reinforcing the link between law and literature in this period was the accompanying explosion of writing about the Mollies before and after these trials, including accounts that took the form of histories, newspaper stories, and detective fiction, some of it authored by Alan Pinkerton, the founder of the famous detective agency himself. In his 1877 novel *The Molly Maguires and the Detectives*, for example, Pinkerton told a story based loosely on the experiences of the Pinkerton Agent, James McParlan, who had been sent to live among and infiltrate the Mollies over the course of two years. Even though McParlan's infiltration of the society resulted in his own occasional complicity in what the Pinkertons believed were unlawful acts, Pinkerton represents the detective's work as supremely honorable. In the scene in which he first explains the assignment, Pinkerton reassures McParlan that his "refusal to accept the responsibility – while I can but acknowledge it would prove a disappointment – will not injure you in my estimation, or prevent your employment by me in the future.'" To this caution, however, McParlan responds dismissively. "Mr. Pinkerton," he says, "rising from his chair, 'I am not in your Agency to object to such a thing as this seems to be.'"[17] In reiterating his readiness to take on whatever work his employer throws his way, in other words – including the dangers of infiltrating an allegedly violent secret society – McParlan gives voice to the views of management, which saw its own terms of employment as far more honorable than those of labor. Not surprisingly, this scene stands in stark contrast to several later scenes in the novel, which portray the Mollies as dishonorable, violent, and adhering to no perceptible understanding of fairness at all.

When it came to violence, Pinkerton's depiction of the Mollies was especially unfair, since there was often violence on both sides – on the part of the striking workers and on the part of the police who were called in to disperse the crowds on the grounds that unions were themselves

[17] See Allan Pinkerton, *The Molly Maguires and the Detectives* (New York: G.W. Carleton and Co., 1876).

unlawful. In a demonstration of the salutary influence of unions, however, in *Commonwealth* v. *Hunt* (1842) the Massachusetts Supreme Court sanctioned the formation of labor unions and allowed them to operate without interference by the police or the law. As the nineteenth century drifted toward the twentieth, an increasing number of novels, from Rebecca Harding Davis's lyrical portrait of the soul-crushing effects of factory life in *Life in the Iron Mills* (1861) to Upton Sinclair's graphic depiction of the Chicago meatpacking plants in *The Jungle* (1906), joined the court's effort to shore up the unions by revealing the harsh working conditions of factory laborers. A novel written in the form of an exposé, *The Jungle* was replete with details of a factory floor "half an inch deep with blood" and filled with "a sickening stench, which caused the visitors to hasten by, gasping."[18] Such details contributed directly to the passage of legal reforms, including protective measures for employees and prohibitions on child labor. In these novels, literature was used for social ends, deploying an aesthetic form for the purposes of political emancipation and further blurring the lines between law and literature.

A Nation among Nations

As Thomas Bender, David Armitage, and others have recently pointed out, the history of American nation formation has for too long been studied in isolation. This phenomenon has contributed to a tendency toward exceptionalism within American historiography, with many scholars promoting the belief that America was bigger, newer, better than other nations. In Bender's corrective terminology, however, America was not alone but "a nation among nations," established with an awareness of other nations undergoing nationalistic struggles, including eighteenth-century France (1789) and Haiti (1791–1804), as well as nineteenth-century Germany, Italy, Denmark, Brazil, the Hapsburg Empire, and Sweden, among others. Indeed, so many countries were experiencing national crises that the period is often called the "springtime of nations."[19]

Although it has not been adequately emphasized, the legal documents that first articulated American nationalism bore the marks of this national "springtime." Both the Declaration of Independence and the Constitution were outward-looking documents in ways that have yet to be fully

[18] Upton Sinclair, *The Jungle* (New York: Dover Thrift Editions, 2001), p. 31.

[19] It is also referred to as the "Spring of Peoples." See, for example, Mike Rappaport, *1848: The Year of Revolution* (New York: Basic Books, 2009), p. 112.

appreciated. Far from a dominant power, America was at the time of its revolution, and for decades afterward, relatively weak and untried. Yet it was imperative for the founders to create a nation that would hold its own in the international sphere.[20] Two scholars of the global context in which the American nation was formed go so far as to argue that the purpose of the U.S. Constitution was first and foremost to facilitate the admission of the new nation into the European-centered community of "civilized states."[21] Toggling between the mandates of international recognition and domestic cohesion, the American nation tackled a variety of issues and ideologies that had both outward and inward-looking consequences, including the so-called "Indian problem," immigration, territorial expansion, and manifest destiny.

Declaring its adherence to the law of nations, which governed international relations at the time of America's founding, enabled America to gain initial recognition in the global sphere. As it soon discovered, however, to ensure that recognition over time, America had to expand. As newer nations were struggling to define themselves, older nations, such as England and France, were asserting their dominance through nineteenth-century programs of expansion. America did not want to fall behind. The first avenue for American expansion was westward across its own continent. The initial thirteen states lay on the Eastern seaboard, but the ideology of nationalism urged Americans to occupy and settle what they assumed, mistakenly, to be unsettled land west of the Mississippi.

Dime novels – short narratives printed on cheap paper and sold for a dime – and land distribution laws contributed mightily to the national fantasy that the West was a wide-open place where no one lived and where anyone could succeed. In cowboy novels, these fantasies gained a protagonist around which they could organize. The cowboy typically lived in solitude but exerted just the right amount of violence mixed with kindness to protect people in surrounding communities. Laws such as the Homestead Act of 1862, which gave 600,000 families roughly 160 acres each to work for five years, capitalized on the image of the cowboy and brought thousands of people west, where they sometimes made the land grow, but just as often died trying. Complementary to these male-oriented

20 See Edwin D. Dickinson, "The Law of Nations as part of the national law of the United States," *The University of Pennsylvania Law Review*, 101 (1952–3): 26; Stewart Jay, "The status of the Law of Nations in early American law," *Vanderbilt Law Review*, 42 (1989), 819.

21 David M. Golove and Daniel J Hulsebosch, "A civilized nation: the early American constitution, the Law of Nations, and the pursuit of international recognition," *New York University Law Review*, 85 (2010), 932.

dime novels, which emphasized independence and adventure, were the Western narratives written by women as early as the 1830s, which revolved around the less glamorous details of domesticating the West and making it a home. For example, Caroline Kirkland's *A New Home – Who'll Follow*, a satirical account of moving to the frontier of Michigan in the 1830s, spared no detail about the mud, extreme temperatures, scarcity of food, and lack of good shelter the pioneer family would encounter. Both strains of Western writing converged toward the end of the century in the first real cowboy novel, *The Virginian*, by Owen Wister, which revolved around a tall, dark, handsome stranger who moves to Wyoming, tames the West, and falls in love all in one fell swoop.

While westward expansion broadened the nation's reach, it also reinforced a lack of cohesiveness that recapitulated the chaos of the country before the declaration of nationhood. As the country grew bigger, it generated more regionally distinctive identities to add to the racial, ethnic, and religious mix, all of which made it more difficult to govern. In addition, there was no established law in the West, although there were many incidents that called for it. Of these, perhaps the most troubling were the clashes between white settlers and Indians, who were either native to the region or, like the Cherokee, Muscogee, Seminole, Chickasaw, and Choctaw nations, forced to relocate by the Indian Removal Act of 1830.[22] These often bloody clashes and the laws that issued from them put pressure on nation formation by turning an internal population into enemies. Before nationhood, the colonists had treated their Indian neighbors as sovereign nations, and while they did not always purchase land legally, their extensive treaty making suggests the extent to which they understood the Indians to be foreign nations that happened to occupy territory inside the United States. By the nineteenth century, however, this approach was being undermined by a pair of Supreme Court cases that distorted American Indian history and redefined the Indians as subjects of a white nation. In *Johnson* v. *MacIntosh* (1823), the Court held that the federal government had title to all Indian lands and that any land sold by the Indians to private parties was null and void. In *Cherokee Nation* v. *Georgia* (1831), the legal status of Indians was completely altered when the Court found that the Indian

[22] The Indian Removal Act, which was signed into law by President Andrew Jackson on May 28, 1830, authorized the president to grant unsettled lands west of the Mississippi in exchange for Indian lands within existing state borders. A few tribes went peacefully, but many resisted the relocation policy. During the fall and winter of 1838/9, the Cherokees were forcibly moved west by the United States government. Approximately 4,000 Cherokees died on this forced march, which became known as the "Trail of Tears."

nations were not like other sovereign nations, but "domestic dependent nations" in a relation with the United States like "that of a ward to his guardian."[23] The only way in which the United States could understand its relationship to foreign nations within its midst, it seemed, was to demote those nations and infantilize their members.

In a classic manifestation of the call-and-response model that shaped the American nation, the Indians made known their dissatisfaction with this national demotion. The writings of many American Indians throughout the nineteenth century demonstrated, to varying degrees, their distinct notions of autonomous nationhood as well as of their place within the nation that became America. While some autobiographies, such as William Apess's A *Son of the Forest* (1829) and George Copway's *The Life, History and Travels of Kah-ge-ga-gah-Bowh* (1847), seemed to acknowledge the dominance of the white version of nationhood, they nevertheless resisted the erasure of the Indians' contribution by insisting on the integration of Indian history into the history of the American nation. It is, for example, impossible to think of Apess, who was born to Indian parents but grew up in white and Indian communities, as anything but supremely American when he relates his experiences as a soldier in the Revolutionary war. More visibly oppositional is the writing of Black Hawk, whose story, *Autobiography of Ma-Ka-Tai-Me-She-Kia-Kiak, or Black Hawk*, gives voice to an indigenous culture that is unmistakably separate from and uninterested in assimilating into white America. While Blackhawk's writing was mediated by a white editor, as was that of Apess and Copway, it is clear that he and he alone envisioned a divided nation with whites and Indians on different sides of a cultural and ideological divide. "If the Great and Good spirit wished us to believe and do as the whites," Black Hawk wrote, "he could easily change our opinions, so that we could see, and think, and act as they do."[24]

Questions about membership within the nation also hung like a shadow over the expansion of America into other parts of the continent, beginning with the Louisiana Purchase from France in 1803, heating up with the annexation of formerly Spanish lands in Florida, and culminating in the Treaty of Guadalupe-Hildalgo in 1848, in which Mexico was forced to cede a great deal of land to the United States. One of the issues in the large annexation of Mexican land was the acquisition of a non-white

[23] *Cherokee Nation* v. *State of Georgia*, 30 U.S. 1 (1831) at 17.

[24] Black Hawk, *Life of Black Hawk, or Ma-ka-tai-me-she-kia-kiak: Dictated by Himself.* Ed. Gerald Kennedy (New York: Penguin Group, 2008), p. 49.

population, which many people saw as a threat to what they thought of as a predominantly white nation. Opponents of the annexation were palliated only by the thought that the areas in question were sparsely populated, but the presence of "foreigners" within the nation posed problems nonetheless. The often unintended consequences of annexing territories and their inhabitants entered into the plots of several novels, none more celebrated than *Ramona*, the 1884 novel by Helen Hunt Jackson, which describes the intersecting lives of Native Americans, Mexican-Americans, and whites in California after Guadalupe-Hildalgo. An interracial love story that tugged on people's heartstrings in much the same way that *Uncle Tom's Cabin* did, *Ramona* influenced the passage of the Dawes Act, which for the first time divided Indian land into individual allotments and granted the Indians private property and with it the protection of American property law. Born in part from a spirit of remediation, the Dawes Act ended by further destabilizing Indian social organization and leading to a series of early twentieth-century laws that gave the United States possession of what was called "excess land" not taken up by individual Indian allotments.

That the Indians were internal nonwhite inhabitants whose presence in America predated that of its white settlers made the struggles over their national status anomalous. Most other non-white inhabitants coming into the United States in the nineteenth century from Ireland, Germany, Italy, and Eastern Europe came from nations outside the borders of the United States and raised questions about how the United States would deal with other, far more powerful nations. For the most part these immigrants came to escape far worse conditions abroad, so it took some time for them and other Americans to wake up to the deplorable conditions they faced in their new home. Brochures and pamphlets in the second half of the nineteenth century exposed these conditions and often spurred protests from the immigrants' countries of origin, involving the United States in domestic and foreign affairs simultaneously.

The story of Chinese immigration to America is a case in point. Although the United States had relied heavily on "coolie" labor to build the transcontinental railroad after the Civil War, it did not want to grant the Chinese or their descendants citizenship after the railroad was completed. Curiously, federal law was relatively silent on the issue of immigration until the end of the nineteenth century, when people started seeking ways to deport the Chinese for cause. Passage of the Chinese Exclusion Act, the first immigration law to ban a people on the basis of their ethnic and national identity, followed in 1882. As with most immigration laws, however, the Chinese Exclusion Act conflicted with other American interests, including those stated in the Burlingame Treaty, which the United States had signed with China in 1868 and which gave China most favored nation status with respect to trade. The Act also had several unintended consequences, among them a boycott of American goods by the Chinese government, which scuttled America's financial interest in using China as a surplus market for excess production. In addition to these multiply determined relationships among immigrants to the United States, the United States government, and foreign countries, the strange intersection of immigration policy and American law found expression in a number of curious resonances in the Reconstruction era. As Edlie Wong points out, the effort to exclude Chinese people seemed to throw what appeared to be the slightly more favorable treatment of former slaves into relief, and at the same time gave the Chinese a touchstone for their own complaints. An influential translation of *Uncle Tom's Cabin* into Chinese in 1901 perpetuated the Chinese boycott of American goods and likened the Chinese to slaves.[25]

The literary and legal projects of nineteenth-century America required imagination and enlisted the special talents of people who cared about articulating and visualizing the nation America was to become. Focused on nation formation above all, the law and literature of nineteenth-century America called and responded to each other, at times sympathetically, at others antagonistically, throughout the century. Its malleable spatial boundaries, temporal ambiguities, speculative market economy, and changing membership made the United States susceptible to the efforts of lawyers and literary artists, who worked in tandem to articulate and test various legal propositions to see if they would meet with approval by the people and endure. So intertwined were law and literature in this period that they often traded generic features and narrative purpose, with the law at times becoming discursively capacious and literature discursively emancipatory. The result was a complex and messy process whose trajectory, if not exactly exceptional, reveals a lot about the mix of law and literature in the making of the American nation.

[25] Harriet Beecher Stowe, *Uncle Tom's Cabin; or, Life among the Lowly* (trans. Lin Shu and Wei Yi) (1901; rpt. Beijing: Shangwu yinshiguan, 1981). For a discussion of the impact of this translation, see Edlie L. Wong, *Racial Reconstruction: Black Inclusion, Chinese Exclusion, and the Fictions of Citizenship* (New York: NYU Press, 2015), pp. 174–6.

CHAPTER 12

Legal Modernism

Rex Ferguson

Introduction

In the past twenty years or so, scholarship in modernist studies has increasingly addressed the disparate incommensurability of various "modernisms." That this is the case is hardly surprising, given that no writer or artist ever defined themselves as modernist: Rather, the term was subsequently imposed upon, among others, the vorticists, imagists, futurists, expressionists, and impressionists of the early twentieth century. But contemporary critical work has also had a constitutive role to play in the creation of such plurality. The stretching of temporal and geographical borders together with the focus upon critically undervalued, popular, and middlebrow writing has led to significant growth in modernist studies – indeed, Douglas Mao and Rebecca Walkowitz write that "were one seeking a single word to sum up transformations in modernist literary scholarship over the past decade or two, one could do worse than light on *expansion*."[1] A key part of this expansion has been the detailed exploration of the conditions which allowed for modernisms and shaped their precise formulation, with one significant example of such being the legal world. Recent work thus lights on the importance of libel, obscenity, and copyright law to the formation of early twentieth-century literary experimentation.[2]

This last term, experimentation, is key, for what continues to unite much of the logic surrounding the concept of modernism is the sense in which it offers a radical commitment to change. Famously, this move was often articulated as a radical break with tradition. Ezra Pound's call to "make it new" is as emblematic here as Virginia Woolf's request for

[1] Douglas Mao and Rebecca L. Walkowitz, "The new modernist studies," *PMLA*, 123(3) (2008), 737.

[2] See Sean Latham, *The Art of Scandal: Modernism, Libel Law, and the Roman à Clef* (Oxford: Oxford University Press, 2015); Rachel Potter, *Obscene Modernism: Literary Censorship and Experiment, 1900–1940* (Oxford: Oxford University Press, 2013); Paul K. Saint-Amour (ed.), *Modernism and Copyright* (Oxford: Oxford University Press, 2011).

"new forms for our new sensations."[3] The palpable sense that many writers had of performing a "break" instigated a view of the literary artist as freed from convention (both literary and social) – not just the isolated genius of Romanticism but the politically significant smasher of codes. This chapter, then, is about how such change is articulated, and how a conceptualization of law both informs and facilitates such articulation. Due to restrictions of space, the chapter will advance this discussion exclusively through thinking about modernist prose writing, though this is not to say that similar phenomena could not be identified in the poetry and drama of the period. It will begin by focusing upon a specific change: namely, the development of prose forms designed to express the problematic relationship between subjective experience and writing. Moving on to examine two modernist short stories – William Faulkner's "Barn Burning" and Franz Kafka's "In the Penal Settlement" – the chapter will conclude by pointing to the way in which modernist prose conceptualized its radicalism as a change in law.

A Formal Subject

That the experimentation seen in prose fiction in the early twentieth century represents a live issue for law and literature studies is a point that is in many ways most effectively made by work not predominantly focused on modernism. Alexander Welsh, Lisa Rodensky, Jan-Melissa Schramm, Jonathan Grossman, Nan Goodman, Wai Chee Dimock, Laura Korobkin, and Nicola Lacey (among others) have all written on the deep connections between law and literature in the nineteenth century and the first three authors in this list, in making cases about the procedures of trials, are especially explicit in concluding at the turn of the twentieth century.[4] The logic here is that while law, and the activity of a trial, both continue to

3 Virginia Woolf, "Hours in a library" in Leonard Woolf (ed.), *Granite and Rainbow: Essays by Virginia Woolf* (London: Hogarth Press, 1958), p. 30.

4 See Alexander Welsh, *Strong Representations: Narrative and Circumstantial Evidence in England* (Baltimore: Johns Hopkins University Press, 1992); Lisa Rodensky, *The Crime in Mind: Criminal Responsibility and the Victorian Novel* (Oxford: Oxford University Press, 2003); Jan-Melissa Schramm, *Testimony and Advocacy in Victorian Law, Literature and Theology* (Cambridge: Cambridge University Press, 2000); Jonathan H. Grossman, *The Art of Alibi: English Law Courts and the Novel* (Baltimore: Johns Hopkins University Press, 2002); Nan Goodman, *Shifting the Blame: Literature, Law, and the Theory of Accidents in Nineteenth-Century America* (Princeton: Princeton University Press, 1998); Wai Chee Dimock, *Residues of Justice: Literature, Law, Philosophy* (Berkeley: University of California Press, 1996); Laura Hanft Korobkin, *Criminal Conversations: Sentimentality and Nineteenth-Century Legal Stories of Adultery* (New York: Columbia University Press, 1998); Nicola Lacey, *Women, Crime, and Character: From Moll Flanders to Tess of the D'Urbervilles* (Oxford: Oxford University Press, 2008).

operate much like a Victorian novel, the novel itself wanders off into strange, experimental territory. It is a logic that is also voiced by Maria Aristodemou, who writes that "legal writers are like writers of realist fiction, trying to maintain the illusion of an omniscient narrator, chronological sequence, plot inevitability, and causal connections between events."[5] Lawyers and realists maintain this form because it serves as the best way to present a narrative in a convincing way – that is, it serves to present a narrative as a veracious account of fact or as pure content. What many modernist writers do is to remove the transparency of the medium and self-reflexively deal with form over content. Or, perhaps to be more accurate (and following the theoretical insight of the Russian Formalists), in modernism, form *becomes* the content.[6]

For Desmond Manderson, this understanding of what modernism is and does has been missing not only from law and literature works which examine modernism, but from law and literature as an enterprise more generally.[7] Manderson characterizes the majority of law and literature studies as being obsessed with content at the expense of form (thus reducing literature to being purely representational) and of presenting a Romantic view of literature as redemptive of the law in some way. But this only captures a certain sense of literature – one which is decidedly of the nineteenth century. To think about the modernist novel, by contrast, would be to recognize the centrality of its form, style, and language; its making (rather than representation) of a world; and its use of multiple voices. Manderson concludes that to think about law through this lens would be to consider legal judgment as a verb rather than a noun, meaning that law becomes something that is continually *being done* rather than existing as an accomplished fact.

There is a critical heritage to Manderson's thesis. His conclusion, for instance, is reminiscent of Robert Cover, who, in Jay Watson's words, "wrote "liberally of law as a bridge, or sometimes simply a 'tension,' lining an actual world with an imagined future. The rules, principles, and precepts we develop in the effort to move from that reality to that future

[5] Maria Aristodemou, *Law and Literature: Journeys from Her to Eternity* (Oxford: Oxford University Press, 2000), p. 25.

[6] See Boris Eichenbaum, "From the theory of the 'formal method'" in Vincent B. Leitch et al (eds.), *The Norton Anthology of Theory and Criticism*, 2nd edn. (New York: W.W. Norton & Company, 2010), pp. 925–50.

[7] Desmond Manderson, "Modernism and the critique of law and literature," *Australian Feminist Law Journal*, 35(1) (2011), 107–25.

are, in the deepest sense, what law is."[8] The critical legal studies school that Cover partly inspired had also already thought about modernism in this sense. David Luban's *Legal Modernism* (1994) thus utilizes the term to designate the critique of the accepted, traditional assumptions of an art through the form of that art itself. Luban argues that, by the 1990s, legal theory (which he identifies as an "art") had become modernist: "modernist legal theory consists in retelling significant legal events in a way that deliberately and conspicuously detaches them from their traditional context. It aims in this way to arouse wonder and to excite our sense of the incongruity of continuing to rely on those traditions."[9] For Luban, then, rather than needing to call on literary modernism in order to animate a different view of law, modernism (as an active questioning of its form) is a concept which describes late twentieth-century legal theory.

The fact that modernist prose exhibits this focus upon form is in many ways attributable to a dissatisfaction with the realism of realism. That is to say, many of the experiments with prose that took place from the very late nineteenth century onwards were motivated by the sense in which the Victorian realist form presented consciousness (if it did at all) as unrealistically rational and complete. Henry James' "point of view," Joseph Conrad's and Ford Madox Ford's "impressionism," Virginia Woolf's "free indirect discourse," and James Joyce's and Dorothy Richardson's "stream of consciousness" all foreground a central consciousness that is not just unreliable but inherently limited. In James' *What Maisie Knew*, for instance, Maisie can only know of her parents' divorce what her limited years allow her to, while in Conrad, consciousness only belatedly decodes what is an initially obscure and meaningless world. In theorizing what both he and Conrad were attempting with their "literary impressionism," Ford wrote of realism's production of a "corrected chronicle" that was too neat and tidy in its packaging of consciousness. Most iconically, in her essay "Modern Fiction," Woolf questioned whether life was anything like the realist novel: "Look within and life, it seems, is very far from being 'like this'. Examine for a moment an ordinary mind on an ordinary day. The mind receives a myriad of impressions – trivial, fantastic, evanescent, or engraved with the sharpness of steel. From all sides they come, an incessant shower of innumerable atoms."[10]

8 Jay Watson, "Dangerous return: the narratives of jurisgenesis in Faulkner's *Requiem for a Nun*," *Modern Fiction Studies*, 60(1) (2014), 109.

9 David Luban, *Legal Modernism* (Ann Arbor: University of Michigan Press, 1994), p. 379.

10 Virginia Woolf, "Modern fiction" in Virginia Woolf (ed.), *The Common Reader* (London: Hogarth Press, 1951), p. 189.

These famous words of Woolf's are addended by a comment that is no less significant in the context of this essay: namely, that "the proper stuff of fiction is a little other than custom would have us believe it."[11]

I will come back to the question of custom and tradition in more detail later, but for the moment I want to emphasize two things about the formal experimentation displayed in modernist prose. First, it is important to recognize that modernist prose leans toward, but does not reach, a point of complete abstraction. Rather, what continually animates the prose forms of modernism are its efforts to render the reality of subjectivity. That this involves mistaken perception, errors in judgment, and misremembered facts is self-evident. What is also entailed, though, is a restless anxiety about what prose, in any form, can capture. This leads to the second point, which is that this anxiety and doubt is predominantly centered upon notions of time. In Woolf's *Jacob's Room*, for instance, Jacob Flanders slips through the nets of definition imposed upon him by others – but the book's power as a narrative of loss is also based upon the impossibility of that narrative itself capturing a Jacob that now only exists in the past. The image of the empty room at the end of the novel is thus an image of the failure of narrative as much as it is an image of the young men who died in World War I. In a similar vein, William Faulkner's *Absalom! Absalom!* writes of an antebellum South that has to be creatively conjured in the mind of Quentin Compson (situated both post-Civil War and in the North) with the suggestion that it can never quite be authentically imagined. That both these examples deal with war is significant, as warfare set a context of loss within which high modernism worked. Even more significantly, though, they see the modern subject as fundamentally traumatized: a figure conditioned by a past that they cannot even quite remember.

Ravit Reichman has written convincingly of the omnipresence of trauma in the period, claiming that the nature of personal injury claims in an increasingly mechanized world pushed the law's ability to define and judge. For Reichman, the law's "attempts at clarity were often undone by the unrepresentable nature of the cases before it, which confounded law's language of visibility and causality."[12] In other words, the law as "realism" was brought into question. It is also the case that many of the developments in psychology which had, in themselves, fueled the turn

[11] Woolf, "Modern fiction," p. 189.

[12] Ravit Reichman, ""New forms for our new sensations": Woolf and the lesson of torts," *Novel*, 36(3) (2003), 399. For a fuller account of trauma, law, and narrative see Reichman's *The Affective Life of Law: Legal Modernism and the Literary Imagination* (Stanford: Stanford University Press, 2009).

to subjectivity in literary modernism also had an influence upon legal thinking. The text which marks the beginning of this development is usually thought to be Hans Gross's *Handbook for Examining Magistrates as a System of Criminalistics*, which was first published in German in 1893 and translated into English in 1911. Gross retained a strong level of Enlightened rationality in that his popular manual, as Lindsay Farmer explains, "explicitly tutored legal professionals on such topics as how to interpret mental states from the outward appearances of witnesses and suspects" – which is to say that an accurate interpretation was possible.[13] The translation of Gross's manual into English was thus timely, as the Criminal Evidence Act (1898) had ended a period of close to a century in which the accused in a criminal trial was not permitted to speak.[14] The criminal trial at the beginning of the twentieth century therefore placed the accused, and their testimony, more centrally than had been the case in the preceding century. Already indicative of a turn toward the subject, the criminal trial was also having to contend with ever more complex notions of responsibility that the work of Gross, and others, prompted and which his rational approach could not fully control. Gross's manual thus indicated a "growing awareness of the complexity, and often opacity, of motives and desires" and was developed by a new "science of testimony"[15] which arose in Continental Europe and was extended through work by Edouard Claparède, Ernst Dupré, Alfred Niceforo, and Hugo Munsterberg – the latter being largely responsible for the spread of these ideas to the United States when he took up a position at Harvard University. While best known for being involved in the development of the polygraph machine, it was in fact the work that Munsterberg and others did on the fallibility of testimony rather than its conscious duplicity that was most significant.

The U.S. context is important here because it was through it that the science of testimony really became part of a legal theory which questioned not just testimony but the form of the legal trial in its entirety. This theory was the "legal realism" of Jerome Frank, first formulated fully in his 1930 work *Law and the Modern Mind*. Completely at odds with any idea of novelistic "realism," Frank's writing is actually much more like the "legal modernism" which Luban identifies in the critical legal studies movement.

13 Lindsay Farmer, "Criminal responsibility and the proof of guilt" in Markus D. Dubber and Lindsay Farmer (eds.), *Modern Histories of Crime and Punishment* (Stanford: Stanford University Press, 2007), p. 53.

14 David Bentley, *English Criminal Justice in the Nineteenth Century* (London: The Hambledon Press, 1998), p. 204.

15 Farmer, "Criminal responsibility and the proof of guilt," p. 53.

Thus, one of Frank's main aims is to critique what the form of the modern trial actually deals in and produces. In a challenge to the commonsense view of legal decisions as rules applied to facts, Frank asserts that, in the trial setting, "facts" are never known in an unproblematic sense. He argues that the courts themselves:

> have observed that testimony is not a mere mechanical repetition or transcription of past events and that testimony often involves fallible inferences; in other words, a witness in testifying to things seen or heard or felt is inevitably making judgments on or inferences from what he has seen, heard or felt. And numerous experiments, made out of court, go to strengthen the conviction that, without any improper motives, witnesses, in forming such inferences, may badly misrepresent the objective facts.[16]

The obvious implication of this fallibility was that "facts" were inevitably distorted once spoken of in court. But Frank wanted to add a further layer to this fallibility by emphasizing the concomitant subjectivity of the trial court. Thus, in his slightly later *Courts on Trial* (1949), he writes that "the trial court's facts are not 'data,' not something that is 'given'; they are not waiting somewhere, ready made, for the court to discover, to 'find'. More accurately, they are processed by the trial court – are, so to speak, 'made' by it, on the basis of its subjective reactions to the witnesses' stories."[17] Frank's ultimate question is to ask how judgments are reached when the form of the trial is recognized in this way. And his answer is that judges and jurors, rather than rationally considering the "facts" in order to reach a valid conclusion, instead begin with vaguely formed conclusions which they subsequently find ways of rationalizing. When thinking about this in the context of literary modernism, it is hard not to be reminded of Ford's ridiculing of the "corrected chronicle" of realism – a form which rationalizes that which was inherently irrational.[18] Indeed, Ford could easily have written Frank's statement that "a man ordinarily starts with . . . a conclusion and afterwards tries to find premises which will substantiate it."[19]

Frank's conclusions about what a court really deals in and produces amount, ultimately, to a drastic undermining of the trial's ability to recover

[16] Jerome Frank, *Law and the Modern Mind* (London: Transaction Publishers, 2009), p. 116.

[17] Jerome Frank, *Courts on Trial: Myth and Reality in American Justice* (Princeton: Princeton University Press, 1950), p. 23.

[18] Ford Madox Ford, "On impressionism" in Martin Stannard (ed.), *The Good Soldier: An Authoritative Text, Textual Appendices, Contemporary Reviews, Literary Impressionism, Biographical and Critical Commentary* (New York: W.W. Norton, 1995), p. 263.

[19] Frank, *Law and the Modern Mind*, p. 108.

the past. Terming the inauguration of court proceedings in Western Europe as an age of the "inquiry," Foucault writes of this as "a new way of extending actuality, of transferring it from one time period to another and of offering it to the gaze, to knowledge, as if it were still present. This integration of the inquiry procedure, reactualizing what had transpired, making it present, tangible, immediate, and true, as if one had witnessed it, constituted a major discovery."[20] That this "reactualization" was becoming questionable is evident not only in the theory of the legal realists but also in the fact that appellate procedures were extended in several jurisdictions in the late nineteenth and early twentieth centuries. In France, for instance, a greater possibility for judicial review was granted to the Cour de Cassation in 1895, while the England and Wales Court of Criminal Appeal was established in 1907. The extension of rights of appeal registers the simple fact that the judgments of courts of first instance were being considered in more doubtful terms. But their remit and processes also point toward the obsession with form that was emblematic of modernist experimentation. For appellate courts do not retry cases – rather, through a careful examination of records, transcripts, and submissions, they determine whether the narrative produced in the original trial was *formally* correct.

From One Law to Another

Despite the congruence between certain acts of legislation and legal theory and a particular thread of modernism that was charted above, it would also be true to say that the law did not, and could not, change either as swiftly or as radically as the novel did. The intransigence of law thus makes it a target for modernist authors. As Kieran Dolin points out, "modernist literature is a space in which traditional boundaries and categories are questioned, and for this reason its representations of the law tend to be deeply critical."[21] What I want to offer are two examples which present something of a counterpoint to this narrative. The first of these is a story by William Faulkner ("Barn Burning") which seems to extol the virtues of the law and place it in a space worthy of ethical choice. The second is Franz Kafka's story "In the Penal Settlement," which, rather than denigrating a static law, uses the example of a justice system in the process of

[20] Michel Foucault, "Truth and juridical forms" in James D. Faubion (ed.), *Power: Essential Works of Foucault 1954–1984* (London: Penguin, 2000), p. 47.

[21] Kieran Dolin, *A Critical Introduction to Law and Literature* (Cambridge: Cambridge University Press, 2007), p. 146.

change in order to explore the dynamics of change – an issue which is prompted by modernist radicalism.

"Barn Burning" (1939) opens in a courthouse. The scene, and the ensuing story, is related by a third-person narrator, but very much through the central consciousness of a young boy. The boy's sharecropper father, it emerges, is accused of burning the barn of his previous employer, and the boy – Colonel Sartoris Snopes, or "Sarty" for short – is asked to testify. In a typically Faulknerian move, some of the most apparently authentic thoughts and emotions of his central character are elicited through italicized prose. On the opening page, the accuser is thus "his father's enemy (*our enemy* he thought in that despair; *ourn! Mine and hisn both! He's my father!*)."[22] In giving evidence, Sarty recognizes that his father "*aims for me to lie,*" which he does.[23] The conflict is therefore immediately set up between the boy's father on the one hand, and the law on the other. While Sarty lies adequately in court, his father has perceived a weakening in his resolve. Later that day, and after the Justice of the Peace has advised Snopes to leave the county, he accuses his son:

> "You were fixing to tell them. You would have told him." He didn't answer. His father struck him with the flat of his hand on the side of the head, hard but without heat, exactly as he had struck the two mules at the store, exactly as he would strike either of them with any stick in order to kill a horse fly, his voice still without heat or anger: "You're getting to be a man. You got to learn. You got to learn to stick to your own blood or you ain't going to have any blood to stick to you. Do you think either of them, any man there this morning, would? Don't you know all they wanted was a chance to get at me because they knew I had them beat? Eh?" Later, twenty years later, he was able to tell himself, "If I had said they wanted only truth, justice, he would have hit me again." But now he said nothing. He was not crying. He just stood there.[24]

Snopes' speech and action here are an exercise in eliciting conformity. He disciplines his son's body as he does his mules,' a brute force exerted "without heat," while with his words he emphasizes his independence from the rule of law. Above all, Snopes extols the virtues of "blood," invoking a sense of kinship and familial bonds but also the authority of genealogy.

Finding a new place to work, on the land of one Major de Spain, Snopes takes his son to the Major's house. The boy reports that "he had never seen a house like this before. *Hit's big as a courthouse* he thought quietly, with a

[22] William Faulkner, "Barn burning" in *Collected Stories of William Faulkner* (New York: Random House, 1950), p. 3.
[23] Faulkner, "Barn burning," p. 4. [24] Faulkner, "Barn burning," p. 8.

surge of peace and joy whose reason he could not have thought into words, being too young for that."[25] From this point onwards, the house and the world of de Spain is associated with the law (which is already engendering feelings of peace and joy). Sarty is described as thinking of the house as safe from "*him*," meaning his father. In a comical turn of events, his father walks horseshit into de Spain's home and ruins a $100 rug. This gives rise to another scene with a new Justice of the Peace who rules that Snopes, unable to recompense the Major for the full cost of the rug, will pay "the amount of ten bushels of corn over and above your contract with him, to be paid to him out of your crop at gathering time" – in other words, $5.[26] This gives rise to a resentful Snopes planning to burn the Major's barn. In a crucial moment in the story and, it is suggested, in the boy's life, he escapes the clutches of his mother and aunt and races to the house to warn the Major, who mounts his horse and rides toward the fire. Shots are later heard, with the inference being that Sarty's father was killed.

That the story ends in the cool early morning following this blazing night and with the boy descending a hill he had ascended the night before with the words "he did not look back" is instructive.[27] Sarty chooses a path when he warns de Spain, and the story suggests that this is the path not just of lawful behaviour but of the law. In one reading of the story, the choice is between that and sheer lawlessness. As with all of Faulkner's fiction, the civil war looms large and it gives rise to a pertinent detail in this regard: namely, that, unbeknownst to his son, Snopes fought in the war only for "booty – it meant nothing and less than nothing to him if it were enemy booty or his own."[28] The text thus positions law as a set of social agreements (communal but not tribal) which are opposed to both mercenary gain and wanton force.

What this reading underestimates, though, is the power of the father *as* Law. In the speech quoted above, Snopes' talk of blood compels his son to accept not just his father's authority, but that of his father's father, and so on. This is to evoke a principle of tradition that can match that of the law's recourse to founding principles and the precedents of case history. And, however illogical it may be, Snopes' conflict with authority, and even his acts of barn-burning, do seem to be based on a certain sense of principle – all of which is to say that, rather than lawlessness, he signifies a certain, perhaps outmoded, form of Law. Significantly, in order to make the leap to the other side, Sarty needs a substitute father figure (de Spain)

[25] Faulkner, "Barn burning," p. 10.
[26] Faulkner, "Barn burning," p. 19.
[27] Faulkner, "Barn burning," p. 25.
[28] Faulkner, "Barn burning," p. 25.

who is connected to his ideas of truth and justice (his house is as big as a courthouse). Even more significantly, the transition from one law to another can only occur through the death of the old father, killed by the new.

In writing about another work, *Requiem for a Nun*, Jay Watson argues that Faulkner's writing is continually expressing a form of jurisgenesis (the creation of legal meaning). Following Robert Cover's insight, Watson argues that courts, rather than being where law is made, are "much more typically places where law is *un*made, where nomos is destroyed. The judges who preside over them "are people of violence" who "do not create law but kill it."[29] Faulkner's writing presents jurisgenesis in this sense but it also practices it. Paradoxically, although he wrote mostly about the past and an old South, the formal innovation of his writing also took part in the creation of a new South, and a shared law to inhabit.

Franz Kafka's "In the Penal Settlement" (1919) can be read as making a similar point to "Barn Burning," though in a strikingly different manner. The story describes the witnessing, by an unnamed "explorer," of the workings of a punitive machine administered by a similarly unnamed "officer" in a colonial settlement somewhere in the "tropics." Indeed, the other two figures in the story – a "condemned man" and a "soldier" – are also unnamed, suggesting at a significant reduction of identities to roles within a system rather than to names within a wider world. The idea of system, and a judicial system at that, is precisely what the machine, or "apparatus," as it is called in the opening sentence of the story, represents. For this apparatus doesn't merely execute the condemned individual; rather, through a complex arrangement of wheels and needles, it also carves the charge and sentence into the prisoner's body. The whole process is designed to take twelve hours and includes a moment of apparent enlightenment at the six-hour point when the prisoner recognizes the sentence passed on him (which to that point he has been ignorant of). In the course of the story, the reader also learns that the officer is the sole judge of penal matters on the island and that the prisoner has been condemned on the basis of an accusation alone. The setting up and working of the apparatus therefore passes judgment on the individual, communicates a verdict, punishes the body, and, finally, executes the sentence. That the act of passing sentence is, at the same time, the act of physical execution is particularly revealing and asserts a point made later in the century by

[29] Watson, "Dangerous return," 112.

Robert Cover: namely, that law *is* violence.[30] In Kafka's story it is specifically through the language in which law asserts its meaning that its violence can be seen.

The judicial system of the colony (both the machine and the system that it designates) is sustained only by the actions of the officer and through an engagement with tradition. In ensuring that the apparatus is maintained and used, the officer is preserving its origins in the designs and wishes of the "old commandant" (the settlement is now governed by a "new commandant" who holds opposing views). Midway through the narrative, the officer betrays a confidence to the explorer to this effect: "This procedure and method of execution, which you are now having the opportunity to admire, has at the moment no longer any open adherents in our colony. I am its sole advocate, and at the same time the sole advocate of the old Commandant's tradition."[31]

Like Faulkner's "Barn Burning," the narrative thus invites a father/son reading. The officer's continued subservience to the "old commandant," which comes with an attendant distrust and even hatred of the "new commandant," is that of an obedient son to his father. Tradition, here, is thus a paternal tradition, a law of the Father. In taking the explorer into his confidence, the officer comments that he knows the "new commandant" wishes to abolish the system and that "he certainly means to use your verdict against me, the verdict of an illustrious foreigner."[32] He then attempts to convince the explorer to side with him and reject the new commandant's claim that the apparatus is inhumane. The explorer refuses but also goes on to claim that his comments to the new commandant would only be as a "private individual" and would carry no judicial weight. Despite this claim, his lack of support is enough: "'So you did not find the procedure convincing,' he [the officer] said to himself and smiled, as an old man smiles at childish nonsense and yet pursues his own meditations behind the smile."[33]

The officer proceeds to serve a written sentence on himself, strip off his clothes, and prostrate himself on the apparatus, serenely confident of the moment of enlightenment to follow. But it never arrives. The broken judicial system (broken because no one now accepts its validity) can only

30 Robert M. Cover, "Violence and the word" in Martha Minow, Michael Ryan, and Austin Sarat (eds.), *Narrative, Violence, and the Law: The Essays of Robert Cover* (Ann Arbor: University of Michigan Press, 1992), pp. 203–38.

31 Franz Kafka, "In the penal settlement" in *Metamorphosis and Other Stories* (trans. Willa Muir and Edwin Muir) (London: Vintage, 1999), p. 183.

32 Kafka, "In the Penal Settlement," p. 185.

33 Kafka, "In the Penal Settlement," p. 191.

be represented by a broken apparatus and, as such, it fails to operate properly. The rods and needles therefore do not spell out the sentence but rather jab at the officer's skin indiscriminately, committing "plain murder" as opposed to "exquisite torture."[34] No longer attaining to a system of justice, the breaking of the apparatus is fundamentally tied to a failure of that system to communicate its sentence and, by extension, to communicate the "justness" of its operation. That this has been prompted by the explorer's inability to be "convinced" by the procedure (to recognize it as just) is matched by the fact that he cannot read the sentences as they are set out on paper. When asked to read the sentence which the officer pronounces on himself, "The explorer bent so close to the paper that the officer feared he might touch it and drew it farther away; the explorer made no remark, yet it was clear that he still could not decipher it. '"Be just!" is what is written there,' said the officer once more. 'Maybe,' said the explorer, 'I am prepared to believe you.'"[35]

In the story, the moment of enlightened understanding experienced by a prisoner is, symbolically, the moment in which the justness and validity of the system, and the individual's place within it, is accepted. But what Kafka refutes is the notion that this can ever be a peaceful act of tacit consent. Rather, law forcibly effects its validity through continuous violence upon subjected bodies. And to break free from this requires not just a movement away from an old order, but a violent burying of it. Thus, the closing pages of the story describe the explorer walking up to the Commandant's "palatial headquarters": "it made on the explorer the impression of a historic tradition of some kind, and he felt the power of past days."[36] Yet in searching for where the old Commandant is buried, he eventually finds an unmarked grave hidden underneath some random tables. Just as in "Barn Burning," a change of law requires a death of the father.

While the killings in "Barn Burning" and "In the Penal Settlement" are literal, what I want to suggest is that radical change is always violent. Modernist experimentation thus entailed nothing less than the death of an old order which was enacted through the creation of new forms of writing while, in the law, such destruction took place through positive acts of interpretation which necessarily misread the past. Not content with undermining the status of "facts" in a courtroom, Jerome Frank had something to say about this also. In the common law system, lawyers and judges are supposed to make use of precedents. Frank asserts that "what the courts

[34] Kafka, "In the Penal Settlement," p. 196. [35] Kafka, "In the Penal Settlement," p. 192.
[36] Kafka, "In the Penal Settlement," p. 197.

in fact do is manipulate the language of former decisions," adding that "somehow or other, there are plenty of precedents to go around."[37] His fellow legal realist, Karl Llewellyn, made a similar point: "there is a distinction between the *ratio decidendi*, the court's own version of the rule of the case, and the true rule of the case, to wit what it will be made to stand for by another later court."[38] The issue is no less one of reading in civil jurisdictions, where the law is to be interpreted, or misinterpreted, from a range of codes and statutes.

Kafka was well aware of this, and the idea finds expression in his most obviously legal work, *The Trial*, a favorite text of law and literature criticism which has often focused upon the "parable of the law," that is told by a priest to Josef K. near the end of the novel. The parable describes a man apparently being barred from entering a doorway which will provide access to the law. The man is told by the doorkeeper that "it is possible" that he may enter, "but not now."[39] The man waits outside the door for many years, until, approaching death, he asks the doorkeeper why, in all those years, no one else has ever attempted to enter the door. The doorkeeper shouts: "No one else could gain admittance here, because this entrance was intended solely for you" and shuts the door.[40] This short section of the novel has given rise to numerous readings,[41] but, rather than going into what these many interpretations say, what I want to register is the way in which Kafka's text engenders such a multiplicity. In fact, *The Trial* even appears to preempt the phenomenon by having K. and the priest immediately dispute the central point of the parable: For K., the man was deceived, for the priest, he failed to listen properly and grasp his opportunity to enter the law. The text, like the law, thus provides the basis on which it may be read logically, yet contradictorily. And such reading, as Hans-Georg Gadamer points out, is a continuous act. A law should not, according to Gadamer, be considered historically, but, like a text, "must be understood at every moment, in every concrete situation, in a new and different way. Understanding here is always application."[42]

37 Frank, *Law and the Modern Mind*, pp. 159, 63.

38 Quoted in Peter Goodrich, *Reading the Law: A Critical Introduction to Legal Method and Techniques* (Oxford: Basil Blackwell, 1986), p. 74.

39 Franz Kafka, *The Trial* (trans. Richard Stokes) (London: Hesperus, 2005), p. 196.

40 Kafka, *The Trial*, p. 197.

41 Some examples include Theodore Ziolkowksi, *The Mirror of Justice: Literary Reflections and Legal Crises* (Princeton: Princeton University Press, 1997); Ian Ward, *Law and Literature: Possibilities and Perspectives* (Cambridge: Cambridge University Press, 2008); Dolin, *A Critical Introduction.*

42 Hans-Georg Gadamer, *Truth and Method*, 2nd edn. (trans. Joel Weinsheimer and Donald G. Marshall) (New York: Continuum, 2004), p. 308.

There have been a number of ways in which twentieth-century literary theory has talked of the multiplicity of interpretation. However, it could also be argued that modernist prose was the first form which self-consciously drew attention to such an idea through formations such as Kafka's, but also through the use of open endings (Woolf), unfinishable projects (Proust, Richardson, Musil), and enough puzzles to keep the professors busy for centuries (Joyce). I began this chapter by writing about modernism as radical change and the idea of performing a break with the past. While this was undoubtedly part of modernist aesthetics, I want to finish by emphasizing what it was a change *to*. For, rather than instituting some kind of artistic anarchism, it is noticeable how so many modernists actually sought to instigate codes and rules for the "new" – often packaged in a form common to the law: that of censure.[43] Thus, Pound famously cites what *imagistes* are *not* to do, Woolf sets out what is no longer valid post-1910, Forster renews a pact with the accepted aspects of the novel, and a dizzying array of manifestos from all over Europe state a set view of artistic endeavor. Both Faulkner's and Kafka's work, as shown in the stories examined above, are part of this change. But as well as instituting formal change in the novel, their writing also contemplates what exactly change is, how it is effected, and how radical it might be – with law providing the apposite form in which to present these matters.

[43] Sascha Bru goes even further, arguing that "the historical avant-garde, as an aesthetic project or process, continues to shape present-day culture and literature. Consensus dictates, therefore, that the laws of literature are very much the laws set out by the avant-garde." See Sascha Bru, *Democracy, Law and the Modernist Avant-Gardes: Writing in the State of Exception* (Edinburgh: Edinburgh University Press, 2009), p. 194.

CHAPTER 13

Representing Lawyers in Contemporary American Literature: The Case of O. J. Simpson

Diana Louis Shahinyan

The New Lawyer in American Culture

The late twentieth and early twenty-first centuries have seen an explosive renewal of interest in the representation of lawyers in popular culture, specifically in film, television, and literature. Moving away from the archetypal white male lawyer-figure either enacting justice (Perry Mason) or revealing injustice (*To Kill a Mockingbird*'s Atticus Finch), more recent incarnations of lawyers in popular culture have focused on either the daily minutiae of the lawyer-figure who must negotiate a particular identity and lifestyle, or legal procedurals, wherein the law is seen as but one apparatus through which state power is exercised. Specific examples of the former include the themes of gender, sexuality, race, and workplace politics which dominate shows like *Ally McBeal*; the latter include self-contained, episodic procedurals such as *Law and Order* and *The Good Wife*. The new lawyer is represented as a figure who cannot simply foreground justice as her noble pursuit; rather, justice competes, and is thus necessarily muddied by, other equally pressing concerns: relationships, politics, personal gain, and ambitions for professional success. In short, we see everyday life and its exigencies, caught in an extant but ever-shifting matrix of political and economic imperatives, intersecting with legal demands, procedures, and rules, in complex, dramatic choreographies.

In contemporary literature, ex-Mississippi lawyer John Grisham, author of *The Firm*, *The Pelican Brief*, and *A Time to Kill*, is known for his exploration of the lawyer-client relationship, while William Gaddis satirizes the banal, knotty, deeply dissatisfying but fundamentally American pastime of civil litigation in *A Frolic of His Own*. The genre of true crime, which hones in on what Mark Seltzer identifies as the paradox of violence and normality,[1] as well as the ways in which specific crimes can tell national

[1] See Mark Seltzer, *True Crime: Observations on Violence and Modernity* (New York: Routledge, 2007).

stories, has also seen a revival. After the popularity of Truman Capote's *In Cold Blood* (1966), Vincent Bugliosi and Curt Gentry's bestselling *Helter Skelter: The True Story of the Manson Murders* (1974), and Ann Rule's *The Stranger Beside Me: Ted Bundy, the Shocking Inside Story* (1980), the 1990s and 2000s saw a renewed interest in law, lawyers, and justice within, and perhaps because of, a shifting media landscape (smartphones, social media, podcasts, and subscription TV such as Netflix), such that celebrity, fanfare, and exposure inflect traditionally held beliefs on crime, criminality, and jurisprudence in startling and original ways. Beginning with the now infamous June 1994 live televised spectacle of the police chase of O. J. Simpson's white Bronco, crawling down the Los Angeles freeway at a dementedly slow pace, and on to the subsequent murder trial in 1995, which was also televised live over 133 days, the tenacity and ubiquity of the O. J. Simpson story – dubbed the "Trial of the Century" – provides a useful case study through which to examine the ways in which lawyers, the law, and the criminal trial are represented in contemporary American literary and visual culture.

Alongside the endless hours of commentary it generated, the O. J. Simpson trial captured the American imaginary, monopolizing televisions around the world. Simpson was accused of the murders of his ex-wife Nicole Brown Simpson and her rumored lover Ronald Goldman, and his trial was noteworthy for the ways in which it repudiated the formal finitude and solemnity of the wood-paneled walls of the courtroom, extending the legal space – the space of accusation, trial, deliberation, and verdict – to an altogether more incommensurable zone: the hyperreal space of the televisual, and, furthermore, the domestic spaces (each living room of each family home) into which its glow irradiated. The trial sparked incessant news coverage, bestselling books, and renewed recent interest in the form of new television documentaries and dramatic reenactments. This chapter will focus on the 2016 FX series *The People v O. J. Simpson: American Crime Story* (henceforth referred to as *American Crime Story*), which, I argue, perfects recent trends in representing both lawyers as complex intersections of identities and values, and the law as a site of civic and political struggle.

The O. J. narrative was one predominantly *about* race in Los Angeles. In the aftermath of the 1991 Rodney King beating which drew the LAPD into scandal, publicizing internationally the ways in which racism was both institutionalized and embedded in the urban geography of Los Angeles, and of the LA riots of 1992, the O. J. Simpson trial quickly turned into a referendum on the wounds inflicted by the LAPD against the black community, with the dazzlingly handsome, rich, and almost incidentally black ex-running back and Hollywood actor at the center of it all. Los Angeles cultural historian Mike Davis writes fluently on the ways in which, in the lead-up to the O. J. case, gang violence, while localized predominantly in the black suburbs of South Central LA, dominated national news cycles, effectively reifying racial divisions within a media ecology marked equally by moral panic and voyeuristic fascination:

> like the Tramp scares of the nineteenth century, and the Red scares of the twentieth, the contemporary Gang scare has become an imaginary class relationship, a terrain of pseudo-knowledge and fantasy projection. But as long as the actual violence was more or less confined to the ghetto, the gang wars were also a voyeuristic titillation to white suburbanites devouring lurid imagery in their newspapers or on television.[2]

The titillation of racialized violence for white viewers, then, was brought to the fore through a lovable and rich celebrity.

During the trial, and immediately afterward, polls showed that approximately three out of four white Americans disagreed with O. J.'s acquittal, just as three out of four black Americans agreed with it.[3] Megan Foley writes: "public commentary imagined an obsessed America split along racial lines. When Simpson's acquittal was announced, images of black triumph and white outrage flooded news outlets."[4] Pundits and journalists alike described the trial as totalizing racial divisions, effectively bifurcating an "American" collective identity and subjectivity along racial lines, creating two distinct, binding gazes. Isabel Wilkerson writes of a "racial fault line between blacks and whites so deep that it seemed the two groups had been watching different movies."[5] Gender also played a part in the reductive framing of the O. J. trial, as, for the prosecution, the apparently clear story of domestic violence was being eclipsed by the brighter race story.

Law and Literature

Recent scholarship in the law and literature movement has seen a crucial movement away from seeing literature in terms of a "salvific belief . . . to

[2] Mike Davis, *City of Quartz: Excavating the Future in Los Angeles* (London and New York: Verso, 1990), p. 270.

[3] Lorraine Adams, "180 degrees separate black, white views of O. J. Simpson case," *Washington Post*, July 30, 1995.

[4] Megan Foley, "Serializing racial subjects: the stagnation and suspense of the O. J. Simpson saga," *Quarterly Journal of Speech*, 96(1) (2010), 74. See also Courtland Milloy, "In white riot, it's smolder, baby, smolder," *Washington Post*, October 8, 1995; and Patricia Edmonds, "The moment," *USA Today*, October 4, 1995.

[5] Isabel Wilkerson, "Whose side to take: women, outrage and the verdict on O. J. Simpson," *The New York Times*, October 8, 1995.

cure law or perfect its justice"[6] – the "romantic fantasy," according to Desmond Manderson, that "art can save the day or complete the law"[7] in its imperfect rigidity and often clunky, or clumsy, application, or that literature's relationship to law is, recalling Lukács, that "Art always says 'And yet!' to life."[8] Rather, moving beyond a mere analysis of the politics and morality of plot, and the hermeneutic-messianic impulse to ascribe meaning to literature, law and literature's interdisciplinary project has embraced the necessity of an aesthetic problematization of the law's interpretative norms. Law and literature uses literature's "form, style, and genre and . . . tapestry of distinct and incommensurable voices" – the fact that it provides "a site of questions not of answers," and "ambiguity not certainty" – in order to better understand law as a system and justice as a pursuit, a "process, an experience, and an opening"[9] critical to an understanding of law's *nomos* and its ethical potential.[10]

Critical to the analysis ahead is the necessity of conceptualizing the nexus of law and literature as a space in which the official legal narrative – insofar as the courtroom operates as a forum where one narrative is championed above all competing narratives and the case is "closed" – meets a plurality of meanings, possibilities, outcomes, and insinuations. In the surreal unfolding of the O. J. Simpson trial narrative in the world imaginary, the initial link between law, literature, and aesthetics – specifically, in this case, the ways in which the law used narrative and, simultaneously, the ways in which this legal narrative was retold, refracted through and into a wider media narrative and event – appears more pervasive than ever before, less an interdisciplinary coupling than several points of intersection resembling a matrix. The O. J. trial, in real time, was already framed and narrativized, encouraging commentary on its framing and narrativization. It is via this hermeneutic that the television series *American Crime Story* – the main example given in this chapter as a dramatization of the O. J. trial – redirects it from the sealed space of memory or nostalgia to a dynamic contemporary setting.

6 Desmond Manderson, "Modernism and the critique of law and literature," *Australian Feminist Law Journal*, 35(2) (2011), 107.

7 Manderson, "Modernism," 108.

8 Georg Lukács, *The Theory of the Novel: A Historico-Philosophical Essay on the Forms of Great Epic Literature* (trans. Anna Bostock) (Cambridge: MIT Press, 1971), p. 72.

9 Manderson, "Modernism," 108.

10 In "Nomos and narrative," *Harvard Law Review*, 97(1) (1983), 9, Robert Cover defines nomos as "a world of law, [which] entails the application of human will to an extant state of affairs as well as toward our visions of alternative futures. A nomos is a present world constituted by a system of tension between reality and vision."

American Crime Story

This chapter seeks to examine *American Crime Story* – a dramatic retelling of the trial and the background story with particular claims to fidelity – in terms of its representation of American lawyers as staging and embodying the very thickets of sex, race, and class defining contemporary American culture in which the "Black Lives Matter"[11] movement appears to be central. By looking back particularly at Los Angeles and O. J. in the 1990s, it affords a specific insight into the present day. The memory of the O. J. trial as "a national soap opera, complete with melodramatic climaxes, transparent characters, and obsessed fans,"[12] which is reconstituted generically as schlock melodrama and serialized in *American Crime Story*, imagines a paratactic contiguity linking the O. J. narrative with contemporary politics of representation, police violence, and intersectional oppression.

Ryan Murphy and Brad Falchuk, creators of *American Crime Story*, are best known for their melodramatic and highly stylized, *camp* worlds. Their cult viewership has emerged around the *American Horror Story* series, as well as *Glee*, *Scream Queens*, and *Nip/Tuck*. *American Crime Story* is based on Jeffrey Toobin's bestselling book, *The People v. O. J. Simpson: The Run of his Life*, in which Simpson's guilt is foregrounded ("their dilemma, then, was the oldest, as well as the most common, quandary of the criminal defence attorney: what to do about a guilty client"[13]), his elitism is continually emphasized, and the tactics of his lawyers are depicted as ruthless and cynical:

> The answer, they decided, was race. Because of the overwhelming evidence of Simpson's guilt, his lawyers could not undertake a defence aimed at proving his innocence – one that sought to establish, say, that somebody

[11] A movement tracing back to the unprovoked fatal shooting of seventeen-year-old black man Trayvon Martin in Sanford, California, by white-passing neighborhood watch volunteer George Zimmerman and Zimmerman's subsequent acquittal on charges of second-degree murder and manslaughter in 2013, and the fatal shooting of unarmed eighteen-year-old black man Michael Brown by white police officer Darren Wilson in Ferguson, Missouri in 2014, with Wilson escaping indictment. Black Lives Matter seeks to call out the institutional racism that pervades American society. Its website contains the following manifesto: "when we say Black Lives Matter, we are broadening the conversation around state violence to include all of the ways in which Black people are intentionally left powerless at the hands of the state." As such, Black Lives Matter as a movement affirms intersections of black oppression: "Black Lives Matter affirms the lives of Black queer and trans folks, disabled folks, black-undocumented folks, folks with records, women, and all Black lives along the gender spectrum. It centers those that have been marginalised within Black liberation movements." For more, see www.blacklivesmatter.com/about/

[12] Foley, "Serialising racial subjects," 77.

[13] Jeffrey Toobin, *The People v. O. J. Simpson: The Run of His Life* (London: Arrow Books, 1997), p. 10.

> else had committed the murders. Instead, in an astonishing act of legal bravado, they sought to create for the client – a man they believed to be a killer – the mantle of victimhood. Almost from the day of Simpson's arrest, his lawyers sought to invent a separate narrative, an alternate reality, for the events of June 12, 1994. This fictional version was both elegant and dramatic. It posited that Simpson was the victim of a wide-ranging conspiracy of racist law enforcement officials who had fabricated and planted evidence in order to frame him for a crime he did not commit. It was also, of course, an obscene parody of an authentic civil rights struggle.[14]

Emphasizing the performance, the larger-than-life personalities, and the dramatic and cynical tactics of Simpson's legal team – "all white, virtually all men, and mostly in their fifties"[15] – and conversely the "arrogance (mostly Marcia Clark's) and ineptitude (largely Christopher Darden's)"[16] of the prosecution, who were "drunk on virtue" and "squandered what little chance they had of victory," Murphy and Falchuk's TV adaptation extends these preoccupations in the direction of camp. Camp as a "sensibility" desires "the unnatural . . . artifice and exaggeration," and is as such well suited, as a mode of representation, to the O. J. Simpson trial, where the lawyers became as famous as the defendant.

The Politics of the Camp Lawyer

Susan Sontag, in "Notes on Camp," foregrounds camp's aestheticism at the expense of political unity: Emphasizing "texture, sensuous surface, and style at the expense of content,"[17] camp, in Sontag's definition, is "disengaged, depoliticised – or at least apolitical."[18] Melodrama, too, often occludes the relationship between "politics and the cyclical theatrics of the media-sphere and other populist narrative engines"[19] such that it is impossible to see beyond its grammar of "sensational characterisations, exaggerated emotion . . . highly complex and involved storylines, characterisations and dialogue" to a cohesive political imagination.

[14] Toobin, *The People v. O. J. Simpson*, p. 11.

[15] Toobin, *The People v. O. J. Simpson*, p. 3. (At this point, Toobin is describing the team before the appointment of Johnnie Cochran.)

[16] Toobin, *The People v. O. J. Simpson*, p. 12.

[17] Susan Sontag, "Notes on camp" in *Against Interpretation and Other Essays* (London: Penguin, 2009), p. 278.

[18] Sontag, "Notes on camp," p. 277.

[19] Monique Rooney, "Voir venir: the future of melodrama?" *Australian Humanities Review*, 54 (2013), 85.

Thus there is initially a clear asymmetry between the camp aesthetic and melodramatic tone of *American Crime Story* and the aggressively political (often didactic) content, especially evident in the form of Johnnie Cochran's diatribes and his manipulation of the media. If *American Crime Story* employs an irreverently apolitical style to engage with such a politically charged history, I argue that it is precisely in order to jolt the viewer and reorient her from the passive position of simple reflection to identification – the active negotiation of textual meaning. It is through the camp stylistics of the show, the ways in which it often seeks to parody current trends in true crime (in TV shows such as *Making a Murderer*, *The Jinx*, and the hugely popular podcast *Serial*) that stress the quality of the forensic recreations, that the political undergoes a displacement from the text proper, and instead becomes a strategy of watching and meaning-making. I argue, then, that it is the totality of these camp representations of lawyers on screen that allows the text to formally enact a critique of political equality under the law. Furthermore, in employing a mode of representation that encourages disobedient, fringe viewing practices, I argue that the use of camp in *American Crime Story* in fact registers a radical, emancipatory impulse, in that the show liberates the law from its own necessary fiction of formalism, thus imagining a scenario in which the law does not collude with the kinds of systemic inequality that *American Crime Story* explores.

American Crime Story tells a story in which the lawyers are the celebrities at the heart of the O. J. trial. The show's exaggerated, camp depictions of, in particular, defense attorneys Robert Shapiro (John Travolta), Johnnie Cochran (Courtney B. Vance), and Robert Kardashian (David Schwimmer), and prosecutor Marcia Clark (Sarah Paulson), foreground the role which identity politics played in both the O. J. trial and in contemporary political rhetoric. Travolta's heavy make-up, Mephistophelean eyebrows, and operatic acting; Cochran's grandiloquent, adjectival rhetoric as a telegenic and calculating civil rights commentator; the fetishization of Marcia Clark's hair, as well as her compulsive cigarette-smoking and emotional investment in the case as hallmarks of her hysterical womanhood; and, of course, the bizarrely unbalanced surfeit of Robert Kardashian's screen time, which echoes the ubiquity of his surname in the present day (evocative of fame *qua* fame, television's cultural capital), figure each character in an explicitly camp register. The lawyers embody antipodes of representational identity in relation to each other – black/white, male/female, and wealthy/middle class – in a provocatively melodramatic form. Drawing on camp and queer tropes, the show structurally reinscribes these seemingly static identities as fluid, overlapping, and interstitial. In borrowing from melodrama and relishing hyperbolic character-types, rather than reducing the narrative to a Manichean landscape of good and evil, the series shows the ways in which melodrama generically shores up "surprising elements and unpredictable effects, doubts or uncertainties that are also an intrinsic part of its mode."[20] Furthermore, the displacement of identity – that the actors themselves are each celebrities actively playing both with and against their familiar personas – creates an affective assonance, and dissonance, from which the viewer is encouraged to consider the allure of celebrity as the driving force in the real O. J. trial, and the manipulative effects it has on the law.

Sarah Paulson's depiction of Marcia Clark brims with pathos. Above and beyond Nicole Brown and Ron Goldman, and the beleaguered O. J. himself, Clark is clearly portrayed as the central victim in the show. Her initial cheerful confidence is depicted in terms of the most delicious hubris, delivering lines such as "I prepped all night . . . I can tell you every single moment of what's going to happen in that court today. I'm ready for anything" and being told by her superior, Gil Garcetti (Bruce Greenwood), to "stop watching so much TV. If you listen to all that noise you're just going to start bringing it into the courtroom. The trial is in there, not out here." In this way the show affectively tortures the viewer who, of course, knows that O. J. is eventually acquitted, for precisely the reason of Clark's *hamartia:* She did not fully appreciate the role the mediasphere would play in the trial.

In this way the depiction of Clark is almost tragic, in that she evokes Aristotelian "pity or fear" because the dramatization of the "change or bad fortune which [she] undergoes is not due to any moral defect or depravity, but to an error of some kind."[21] In fact, Clark's monomaniacal confidence in, and emphasis on, legal positivism and evidentiary rules – and her thoroughgoing investment in the law as a complete system of rules unsullied by politics – is portrayed as naïve and outdated sentimentalism. This is directly contrasted with the defense lawyers' deft utilization of fractious, postmodern jurisprudence based on theoretical constructions of cultural specificity: that is, the ways in which identity, narrative, experience, and contingency spill over into the law, and that law spills back, as it were. Clark has not, as it were, caught up with the times.

Furthermore, the viewer, with full hindsight of the O. J. trial as media event, is acutely attuned to the universe created by the show, picking up on the kitsch, dramatic clues of irony: Deified, the viewer takes her place

[20] Rooney, "Voir venir," 85.

[21] Aristotle, *Poetics* (trans. Malcolm Heath) (London: Penguin, 1996), p. 21.

among the pantheon of "the gods [that] can see everything."[22] Clark's pathos, moreover, sutures tragedy with melodrama's dominant affect, as it is important that she appears "bereft, without divine guidance, and unable to make proper ethical judgments."[23]

In Episode 6 we see, however, that Clark, frequently described as a "bitch" and persecuted for her appearance, is "working a seventy-hour work week and also [taking] care of a family." As a single mother, Clark is consistently, through the use of costume and both diegetic and extradiegetic music, framed as a sympathetic character, and, moreover, an authentically oppressed character. For example, in the opening minutes of Episode 6, she drives home from court listening to Otis Redding's "Chained and Bound." Later, after a news story ridiculing her hair and clothes, and a tender moment with her young son, who embraces her, the song reemerges as extradiegetic music.

This is significant as the now extradiegetic music suggests that the show structurally authenticates her experiences as *Other* and as the subject of persecution, in a way not afforded to O. J., who is cast as a member of the overwhelmingly white, elite Brentwood community. While in *American Crime Story* O. J. is ambiguously raced – reflecting Toni Morrison's description of him as the "race-transcending 'crossover' into the white world"[24] *par excellence* – Marcia Clark's identification with black experience and culture is something *verified* structurally in the series. O. J. – who, as Christopher Darden (Sterling K. Brown) protests, "spends his days playing golf with old white men and his nights sleeping with young white girls," and about whom Dominick Dunne, famed chronicler of the trial for *Vanity Fair*, jibes "c'mon, cops out to get O. J.? O. J. hosted pool parties for them!" – must, in Episode 5, have his stereotypically white *nouveaux riche* home furnishings (photographs in which O. J. poses with nondescript, important old white men, paintings of white women, sports memorabilia) professionally removed and redesigned by Cochran in time for a jury visit to the mansion, so as to appear blacker. With the funk-rap song "Fantastic Voyage" by Coolio playing, we see Cochran purr to himself, "I like me some blackness" while removalists install tribal art and place around the home numerous framed photographs of O. J.'s mother Ruby.

Furthermore, when Clark decides to go to the hairdresser, not only does she, brimming with excitement and naïveté, get Jheri curls, a popular

[22] Aristotle, *Poetics*, p. 25. [23] Rooney, "Voir venir," 84.

[24] Toni Morrison, "The official story: dead man golfing" in Toni Morrison and Claudia Brodsky Lacour (eds.), *Birth of a Nation'Hood: Gaze, Script and Spectacle in the O. J. Simpson Case* (New York: Pantheon Books, 1997), p. xii.

hairstyle among black Americans at the time; in addition, "Kiss from a Rose," a soul song by black icon Seal, plays as a motif alongside her transformation. "Kiss from a Rose" recurs throughout the episode during moments of empowerment and confidence. When *Los Angeles Sentinel* reporter Dennis Schatzman (Leonard Roberts) exclaims "goddamn, who turned her into Rick James?" after a conversation about race ("the police are trying to pull him down and put him in chains like they do with any black man who rises up!"), it is implied that misogyny – as Clark's femininity is the source and cause of her persecution – is inextricably tied to the institutional racism seemingly exploited by the rich white men who comprise the defense team in order to acquit O. J., their peer.

While the rest of Episode 6 deals with the media's savagery regarding Clark's appearance, the use of the Seal song – as well as the Isley Bros' "Who's that Lady?" – further shapes Clark, for the viewer, as a pleasurably tragic character.[25] It is Clark, thus, who represents both sides of persecution in a way denied to O. J.: She is both femininity and blackness; a white woman who internalizes and performs black maleness. In this way, in respect of Clark's literalization of doubleness and liminality, it is important that Sarah Paulson, a frequent collaborator with Murphy and Falchuk, brings her own queer identity to the matrix of intersectional identity and experience her character signifies.

The depiction of Robert Kardashian, and indeed the Kardashian children (who appear, inexplicably, in four out of ten episodes), further draws connections between the trial narrative strategized by O. J.'s defense lawyers; the nature of the televisual – and, specifically, "reality TV"; and the privilege afforded to celebrities in the deeply segregated Los Angeles. Apocryphal scenes provide, perhaps, an originary backstory to the particular fame the Kardashian sisters represent: In Episode 2 they spell out and then loudly chant their name – "Kardashian! Kardashian!" – in a solipsistic and deliberately embarrassing homage to the phenomenon of their current celebrity. In Episode 1, in perhaps the silliest scene of the series, Robert Kardashian, delivers the line, "Juice! . . . Do not kill yourself in Kimmy's bedroom!" with soapy panic, puppy-dog eyes, and a quivering lip, as O. J. holds a gun to his head. In this scene, the hitherto smooth Steadicam shots, which fluidly track in and around interior scenes, begin to simulate a

[25] It is important, then, that numerous reviews of *American Crime Story*, including Rebecca Traister's "Marcia Clark is redeemed" (*New York Magazine*, February 16, 2016), centered on the ways in which Marcia Clark, vilified as a "90s bogeywoman," is "redeemed" by Sarah Paulson.

shaky, handheld camera, in mock-gritty, documentary-style realism, again as if to suture the very name of the Kardashians to the particularly kitsch "reality" mode – the same register employed by the hugely popular reality TV series *Keeping Up with the Kardashians.*

In Episode 1, while mourning at Brown's funeral wearing a grandiose hat resplendent with black lace, mother Kris (Selma Blair), best friend to Nicole Brown, interrupts her conversation with friend Faye Resnick (Connie Britton) to admonish her children, emphatically naming them in what strikes the viewer as a completely superfluous scene: "Khloe! Kourtney! Stop running! Put away that candy!" Finally, when Robert Kardashian arrives at O. J.'s mansion, which is swarming with police and reporters immediately after the news of Nicole's death breaks, he says to a police officer who stops him in his tracks: "O. J.'s expecting me. I'm his friend, Robert Kardashian. I'm sure I'm on the list." The police officer replies, quizzically, "there's no list." Here, the grotesque confusion between a crime scene and the VIP world of glamorous red carpets illustrates the ways in which both celebrity and criminal law borrow from the overblown tropes of melodrama so as to be affectively fed back into – sublated in – Hollywood's particular system of capitalist reproduction.

In the show's particular representation of the ubiquitous Kardashians as a synecdoche for the O. J. trial, we are reminded of the ways in which television and celebrity work to render narrative a key part of law's epistemology; the very inclusion of the *love-to-hate* Kardashians, as a camp aestheticization of legal personas, generates a surfeit of affect (here, *jouissance* as cringe, disgust, humor, irony) in a way that "is not only representative, [but] formative of the pervasive idea that we live in a post-sacred world."[26] In equal parts revered and reviled by the public, and savagely dissected and deified by the media, the particular nature of celebrity-as-*brand* that the Kardashians represent – the powerful affective responses, intensities of feeling, identification, that they provoke – spills into the law as a sphere that is also *post-sacred,* susceptible to the same flows of commodification and manipulation.

In this way, we see deliberately clichéd camerawork in the depictions of Cochran that serve to ironize him as a subject and to encourage subversive explorations of celebrity and law. In Episode 4, while in Judge Lance A. Ito's (Kenneth Choi) chambers, Cochran, accused of "playing the race card," declaims with characteristic pomp:

[26] Monique Rooney, "Voir venir," 82.

> This is the United States of America and we are defending a black man who is fighting to prove his innocence. Now I know I don't have to give anyone here a civics lesson about the historic injustices visited upon black men for no other reason other than they black. We didn't introduce that into this trial . . . it is a plain and simple fact.

And yet, as Cochran is giving this speech, the camera, which pans slowly around his head, behind him, and back again with great fluidity of movement, exaggerates the traditional implication of gravitas associated with this maneuver, thereby simultaneously eliciting its bathetic other. The movement of the camera during this speech, then, invites the viewer to read it as simultaneously authentic and insincere, and to see Cochran as simultaneously an admirable rhetorician and a shallow font of clichés.

It is no coincidence either that, later in the episode, Cochran is in the courthouse building being interviewed about racial prejudice during jury selection while, in a knowingly archaic *mise-en-scène*, receiving a shoeshine from a deferent elderly black man. Even in the leadup to this scene, which follows Cochran striding purposefully down the corridors of the courthouse, the camera is almost on the floor, tilted up at such an angle as to make Cochran appear colossal. Once again, the deliberately clunky, amateurish, and clichéd camerawork invites a resistant response among the viewership. It is precisely in the surplus generated by the coalescence of the camp and the political – the parataxis of frivolity and seriousness – that, in *American Crime Story,* renders the O. J. Simpson story a veritable site for the rearticulation of contemporary intersectional experiences vis-à-vis a particular disenchantment with the law's uneven application to minorities and oppressed groups.

Race, Then and Now

The O. J. trial always had a serialized form in the popular imagination. Beginning with the 1995 trial (and acquittal), which was frequently referred to as a soap opera with daily *episodes*, his subsequent 1997 civil suit, his 2000 road rage trial, his 2004 civil action for cable TV piracy, and most recently his 2008 conviction and jail sentence for the armed robbery of a sports memorabilia store in Las Vegas have also been framed as instalments "subsumed in a chronic pattern"[27] of run-ins with the law. Depictions of O. J. Simpson have, for Megan Foley, always registered on both axes of

[27] Foley, "Serialising racial subjects," 72.

kairos, meaning "a sense of time as occasion," as episodic and contingent, and *chronos*, as "a sense of time as a duration." For Foley, the serial form, which "organises time as chronological progression punctuated by kairotic moments,"[28] undergirds media representations of O. J. Simpson, and thus raises important issues about ways in which race finds expression and containment in legal discursive practices.

While the 1995 trial was the proceeding in which race was depicted as both a context within which O. J. Simpson's crime could phenomenologically be understood (police brutality, institutional racism) and as a defense strategy ("playing the race card"), and where the acquittal reified a "subject-position of 'black America'"[29] distinct from a white American subjectivity, Foley argues that each subsequent iteration of O. J.'s legal woes has worked to recollectivize, or reunify, the American "people" into a singular, shared subjectivity. With each, increasingly bizarre, run-in with the law, O. J.'s guilt in the 1994 murders of Brown and Goldman is reaffirmed; the very serialization of O. J.'s criminal encounters induces the kind of "fatigue that comes from relentless repetition,"[30] this fatigue problematically sublating the black collective subject position back into a white point of view.

If O. J.'s acquittal for the 1994 murders was originally framed as "payback" against the LAPD for their oppressive violence against Los Angeles' black communities, then the unduly heavy sentence for his 2007 sports memorabilia robbery (thirty-three years, with the possibility of parole after nine) complete the narrative, as "payback" against O. J. for his earlier acquittal. There is a sense that law responds according to the exigencies of poetic justice that exist above and beyond each discrete case; in trials of the century, law, it seems, must sacrifice the integrity of its own claims to formalism at the altar of something much bigger – the national imaginary, the way the nation sees itself. Much like another infamous criminal who captured the American imagination – Al Capone, who finally found a place behind bars as a result of tax evasion and not the innumerable murders and assaults he was alleged to have committed – O. J.'s courtroom trials are both elided into and conform structurally to the demands of the media narrative; his trial inevitably takes place in "the court of public opinion."[31]

[28] Foley, "Serialising racial subjects," 71.
[29] Foley, "Serialising racial subjects," 76.
[30] Foley, "Serialising racial subjects," 76.
[31] Steve Friess, "Simpson's past trial looms over court," *New York Times*, September 15, 2008.

Barry Brummett distinguishes "the popular trial" as necessarily "an ideological one."[32] If the 1995 trial both reflected and dramatized a racial faultline, then each subsequent instalment of the O. J. saga seemed, according to Foley, to promote a vision of a reformulated "American racial harmony" undergirded by the insidious implication that "white folks had been right all along."[33] Both the failed prosecution team and the wider mass media initially blamed O. J.'s acquittal on an *emotional* black jury and the manipulative theatrics of Simpson's "dream team" of "defensive linemen"[34] who played the law as a sport. In Clark and Darden's perceived mismanagement of the trial, racial tensions were refueled. Toni Morrison argues that, after his 1995 trial, the portrayal of Simpson shifted such that he was seen as "capable of betraying whites and 'falling' back into blackness."[35] Higginbotham, Francois, and Yeoh describe the aftermath of the verdict colorfully: "the self-righteous teeth-gnashing by many whites and the self-congratulatory chest-thumping by many African Americans" points to a "zero sum game in which any gain by African Americans – real or imagined – is considered to be a loss by whites."[36] The prosecution's perceived culpability in the Simpson debacle, and the machinations of the defense, triggered questions on the role of race in the courtroom.

The camp stylistics and the melodramatic portrayal of each lawyer in *American Crime Story* problematize this reductive narrative of black versus white. If the tide of public opinion has turned emphatically against O. J., who is now universally seen as a kind of serial pest, *American Crime Story* performs a particular revisionism: Rather than reading the aftermath of the O. J. trial as the white American subject-position now encompassing "America as a whole," the very aesthetic engagement which the series demands from the viewer allows her to trace a revised collective subjectivity across intersectional lines of oppression, including working-class, black, queer, and female identities.

In dramatizing the "race card" as something "played" in the series by a ludicrously well-dressed and well-spoken "dream team" of slick lawyers,

32 Barry Brummett, "Mediating the laws: popular trials and the mass media" in Robert Hariman (ed.), *Popular Trials: Rhetoric, Mass Media, and the Law* (Tuscaloosa and London: University of Alabama Press, 1990), p. 179.

33 Foley, "Serialising racial subjects," 76.

34 Joel Achenbach, "O. J. Simpson defensive linemen," *Washington Post*, January 21, 1995.

35 Morrison, "Dead man golfing," p. xii.

36 A. Leon Higginbotham Jr., Aderson Bellegarde Francois and Linda Y. Yueh, "The O. J. Simpson trial: who was improperly 'playing the race card'?" in Toni Morrison and Claudia Brodsky Lacour (eds.), *Birth of a Nation'Hood: Gaze, Script and Spectacle in the O. J. Simpson Case* (New York: Pantheon Books, 1997), p. 33.

American Crime Story does not advocate for race-neutral lawyering. Rather, it allows a plenitude of contradictions to emerge from its camp performances, juxtapositions, and ironies, which force the reader to negotiate competing narratives that overlap, emphasize, and erase one another in multiple ways. Toni Morrison interrogates the ideological valences underpinning the public perception that O. J. Simpson's acquittal was due to the legal system's failure to retain its formal integrity and remain impartial or unbiased:

> There seems to be a universal sorrow that these proceedings were distorted, sullied by race, that its intervention was false, even shrewd; that it should have been . . . race-free – confined wholly to non-raced-inflected evidence, a disinterested legal process in which even to mention race as a major factor rips away the blindfold that Justice wears and forces her to make decisions based on visual bias.[37]

The question *American Crime Story* asks, then, is whether Simpson's case could have been judged without reference to race, and, if so, would it have delivered a better justice? What distinguishes *American Crime Story* from its rival ESPN documentary, *O. J. Simpson: Made in America* – which is, unquestionably, high-quality television – is that its trashy, queered camera, which lovingly and freely dances with the schlocky, over-the-top acting and deliberately sensationalized script, encourages the viewer – from the margins, or from below – to interrogate the very apertures and openings that the law, which claims to be a sealed and self-referential system of knowledge, has, but fails to acknowledge.

Why, for example, should justice be race-neutral when the law (the codes dedicated to enacting justice) is systemically racist? The aforementioned doubleness that characterizes Cochran in the series allows the viewer to see that while a "card" may be "played" by a Machiavellian rhetorician, it is not a perversion of the law (the courtroom, and the jury system, *requires* a coherent, simple and persuasive narrative), and it was remedial for the beleaguered black community: In Episode 2, which centers on the famous Bronco chase, following wide shots of hordes of black men and women reveling with boom boxes and taking to the streets and overpasses to cheer O. J. as he passes, we see in close-up a passerby say decisively: "I'm not cheering for O. J., I'm booing the LAPD." Thus a normative commitment to race-neutrality in the juridical landscape is in fact presented as racist: As Kimberlé Williams Crenshaw writes, "the goal

[37] Morrison, "Dead man golfing," pp. xiv–xv.

of a colour-blind world is one in which race is precluded as a source of identification or analysis,"[38] such that "the moral force of racial equality is mobilised within contemporary settings to stigmatise not only apartheid-era practices but also efforts to identify and challenge manifestations of institutionalised racial power."[39] Ultimately the series critiques and effectively retries the O. J. case, but with the state institutions of the law and the police force as the accused.

Conclusion: Television and History

In "On the Concept of History," Walter Benjamin writes that "articulating the past historically does not mean recognising it 'the way it really was.' It means appropriating a memory as it flashes up in a moment of danger."[40] We see this in the ficto-historical revisionism of *American Crime Story*; perhaps the flash of danger is the erupting image of black oppression, misogyny, and police brutality that now monopolizes the twenty-four-hour news cycle, a twenty-first-century mode of representation that eschews the quaint seriality of nightly news programs and daily newspapers.

As a comment on both the role of the media during the O. J. trial and the stories which dominate news media now vis-à-vis *American Crime Story* as a weekly series, then, we see that the medium of television carries with it a real-time historicization of its content. The televisual framing of the O. J. event in *American Crime Story* demonstrates the ways in which, per George Lipsitz, "the O. J. Simpson case was about an entertainment figure, but it also was entertainment. The reach and scope of media interest in the trial bears a close relation to the financial benefits that media outlets derived from selling the kind of story that fit neatly into their preexisting categories."[41] Lipsitz continues, "the Simpson trial became a story that was easy to sell, in part, because it seemed to replicate so perfectly the world of commercial television and its generic conventions."[42] *American Crime Story*'s

[38] Kimberlé Williams Crenshaw, "Colour-blind dreams and racial nightmares: reconfiguring racism in the post-civil rights era" in Toni Morrison and Claudia Brodsky Lacour (eds.), *Birth of a Nation'Hood: Gaze, Script and Spectacle in the O. J. Simpson Case* (New York: Pantheon Books, 1997), p. 103.

[39] Crenshaw, "Colour-blind dreams," p. 103.

[40] Walter Benjamin. "On the concept of history" in Michael W. Jennings (ed.), *Walter Benjamin: Selected Writings Volume 4, 1938–1940* (Massachusetts: Harvard University Press, 2003), p. 391.

[41] George Lipsitz. "The greatest story ever sold: marketing and the O. J. Simpson Trial" in Toni Morrison and Claudia Brodsky Lacour (eds.), *Birth of a Nation'Hood: Gaze, Script and Spectacle in the O. J. Simpson Case* (New York: Pantheon Books, 1997), p. 7.

[42] Lipsitz, "The greatest story," p. 9.

achievement, then, is in the use of its dazzling all-star cast of actors playing a dazzling all-star cast of lawyers (and, of course, O. J. himself, as a football legend and actor – played by Cuba Gooding, Jr., most renowned for his role as a troubled football star in *Jerry Maguire*) in order to link the ways in which legal narratives in the courtroom must work, with perfect synchronicity, with Los Angeles' primary mode of production: Hollywood, narrative, and celebrity. It is precisely the camp aesthetic of *American Crime Story,* and its retelling of the O. J. Simpson story with particular emphasis on the daily struggles and identities of Clark, Darden, Kardashian, and Cochran, that suggests that the law has too undergone a transformation spawned from its own cultural logic and reach.

CHAPTER 14

Law in Contemporary Anglophone Literature

Eugene McNulty

> We are wasting our time, so many will inform us, if we bother about form when only substance is important. I suppose this might be true if any one could tell us where substance ends and form begins.
>
> Benjamin N. Cardozo[1]

> O body swayed to music, O brightening glance,/How can we know the dancer from the dance?
>
> W. B. Yeats, "Among School Children"[2]

Even the most cursory engagement with contemporary Anglophone culture reveals the extent to which the social imagination is shaped by concerns for the law and its illicit countersigns. To walk into any bookstore with its vertiginous shelves of crime fiction, legal fiction, and true crime narratives or into any multiplex with its self-referential diet of criminal escapades and legal thrillers, or to watch television channels populated with criminal hi-jinks, courtroom dramas, and reality TV judges, is to find oneself in a culturescape fascinated by the law, by breaches to the licit and the imaginative spaces of the illicit.[3] As Kathy Laster puts it, we "seemingly cannot get enough of the political machinations of lawyers, the personal pathos of litigants and the ethical dilemmas embedded in the legal process."[4] In turn, Richard H. Weisberg reads this as symptomatic of the energies shared by the law and man's instinct toward cultural expression. Legal figures, as he reminds us, "both attract and repulse writers"; while often "targets of biting caricature and sarcasm," they also function to metaphorize "the thematic, formal, and even personal concerns of the literary artist who lashes out at

[1] Benjamin N. Cardozo, "Law and literature" (1925) in *Law and Literature, and Other Essays and Addresses* (New York: Harcourt, Brace and Company, 1931), pp. 3–40, 4–5.

[2] W. B. Yeats, "Among school children" in A. Norman Jeffares (ed.), *Yeats's Poems* (London: Gill and Macmillan, 1989), p. 325.

[3] For a fuller discussion of this cultural terrain, see Bran Nicol, Patricia Pulham, and Eugene McNulty (eds.). *Crime Cultures: Figuring Criminality in Fiction and Film* (London: Continuum, 2010).

[4] Kathy Laster, *The Drama of the Courtroom* (Sydney: The Federation Press, 2000), p. 1.

them."[5] After all, the law's search for meaning and explanation, for cause and effect, for motivation and intention, for truth and judgment, speaks quite directly to the concerns of the literary too. More than this, the structural similarity reveals a common source or impulse, with the law and the literary each functioning as "a relativistic *method* of ordering reality through language."[6] This original impulse remains traceable in contemporary culture's sustained exploration of the legal order and the processes through which ruptures to it are detected, defined, explained, contextualized, forgiven, punished. Read for content (substance, as Cardozo might have it), such cultural production traces an ongoing problematization of the "law" – the diachronic marker of real-world legal process – as it shapes and impacts upon the lives of those in its purview. Telescoping out to the level of form, these cultural artefacts also evidence a deep-set and ever-present human need to engage with the "Law" – that synchronic marker of extrahistorical justice and/or judgment, within the contours of which we make and define our sociopolitical ground.

Poetry in the Dock: Words in Action

Flashes of these slippery dialectics appear in the most unlikely places. In a wonderfully tragicomic moment in Richard Ford's novel *Let Me Be Frank With You*, its modern everyman, Frank Bascombe, visits his ex-wife in a nursing home and discovers that when they first met she had lied to him about her age (whether this slip from the truth was repeated on the legal documents pertaining to their marriage is left unclear). Considering the impact this news has had on him, Bascombe muses: "Is any part of my life different because I now know her legal age thirty years after she divorced me? I don't think so. But. *Something*'s different. Possibly only a poet would know what it is and be able to set it prettily out."[7] There is something of the mock epic about this particular moment of later-life crisis, and that suggestion that only the poet would be able to "set it prettily out" is beautifully sardonic. But in this small moment Ford also invites us to consider the ways in which different genres of knowing operate in the world, and the ways in which one plane of discourse may help reveal the full significations of another. In hailing the poet into such service, Ford

[5] Richard H. Weisberg, *The Failure of the Word: The Protagonist as Lawyer in Modern Fiction* (New Haven: Yale University Press, 1984), p. 5.

[6] Weisberg, *The Failure of the Word*, p. xii.

[7] Richard Ford, *Let Me Be Frank with You* (London: Bloomsbury, 2015), p. 132.

subtly points us toward the literary imagination as a necessary ontological supplement to a world of disciplinary knowledge.

The response of most poets to such a call has been understandably multivalent – with most acknowledging the desirability of social engagement while firmly eschewing any sense of instrumental practice. We might take the case of Seamus Heaney as exemplary in this regard. Given that he spent a good deal of his remarkable writing life bearing witness to the political violence of the Northern Irish Troubles, it is unsurprising that he felt impelled to interrogate the relationship between poetry, politics, and social efficacy. The law, moreover, often provided Heaney with a key to examining the imaginative connective tissues that shape our response to such moments of crisis. In a series of lectures examining the role that the poet has played (can play, should play) in confirming (inventing, extending) the very idea of the human as positive agent in the world, for example, he draws on legal imagery to express the literary imagination's power to search out and give voice to our proper obligations. Poets, Heaney tells us, are almost inevitably called to account, "to show how poetry's existence as a form of art relates to our existence as citizens of society – how it is 'of present use'."[8] He presents us here with an image of poetry placed in the dock of public opinion, and of its main advocate, the poet, struggling to present his or her "defences and justifications."[9] Haunting this symbolic courtroom, in Heaney's mind's eye, "stands Plato, calling into question whatever special prerogatives or useful influences poetry would claim for itself within the *polis*."[10] Poetic abstraction, Plato's ghost seems to say, is a distraction, a hindrance, a deception dealing "with the world of appearance, not of reality."[11] It is an idea, of course, that Shelley invoked and pushed back against when declaring that "Poets are the unacknowledged legislators of the world."[12] Heaney too pushes back, and calls on the realm of legal procedure to do so. Rather than banishing the poet from social engagement and "real-world" efficacy, "Plato's world of ideal forms also provides the court of appeal through which poetic imagination seeks to redress whatever is wrong or exacerbating in the prevailing conditions."[13]

The poet, in other words, is able to filter out the white noise of lived reality and detect the contours, and intellectual gravities, of the concepts

[8] Seamus Heaney, *The Redress of Poetry: Oxford Lectures* (London: Faber and Faber, 1995), p. 1.

[9] Heaney, *The Redress*, p. 1. [10] Heaney, *The Redress*, p. 1.

[11] William Chase Greene, "Plato's view of poetry," *Harvard Studies in Classical Philology*, 29 (1918), 1.

[12] Percy Bysshe Shelley, "A defence of poetry" in Duncan Wu (ed.), *Romanticism: An Anthology* (Oxford: Blackwell, 1999), p. 956.

[13] Heaney, *The Redress*, p. 1.

within whose shadows we play out our lived experiences. Something of this haunts the image of final judgment conveyed in "The Stone Verdict": "It will be no justice if the sentence is blabbed out./He will expect more than words in the ultimate court/He relied on through a lifetime's speechlessness."[14] It is also there, with an inverted temporality and a reversal of silence into possible speech, in the image of hope that saturates the most famous lines from *The Cure at Troy* (Heaney's version of *Philoctetes*, 1990): "History says, *Don't hope/On this side of the grave*/But then, once in a lifetime/The longed-for tidal wave/Of justice can rise up/And hope and history rhyme."[15] While the act of poetic transformation may "not intervene in the actual," Heaney argues, it offers "consciousness a chance to recognize its predicaments, foreknow its capacities and rehearse its comebacks in all kinds of venturesome ways." In so doing it constitutes "a beneficent event, for poet and audience alike."[16] We find a similar drive informing Martha Nussbaum's suggestion that literature "expresses, in its structures and its ways of speaking, a sense of life that is incompatible with the vision of the world embodied in the texts of political economy; and engagement with it forms the imagination and the desires in a manner that subverts that science's norm of rationality."[17] While poetry may prove a disappointment to the "political activist" – being in itself not "productive of new events" – its imagery can light up the "field of force" on which such events play out, and can thus retain to itself a form of "political force."[18] More particularly, in terms of the law as an actor in the world of social relations, the poetic imagination's architecture of self-reflexive language can reveal the discursive forcefields that shape our lives *as* discursive forcefields – cultural artefacts that we can examine, unpick, change. In this respect we may see the literary as a site of resistance, acting to force the law into open ground, to reveal its historicity.

In his poem "Punishment" (1975), Heaney grounds such imaginative possibilities in the figure of a "bog body" preserved in the peatlands of Denmark's Jutland and the processes through which this Iron Age sacrificial victim was judged and punished. As the poem unfolds – "like opened

[14] Seamus Heaney, "The stone verdict" in *New Selected Poems 1966–1987* (London: Faber and Faber, 1990), p. 222.

[15] Seamus Heaney, *The Cure at Troy* (Derry: Field Day, 1990), p. 77.

[16] Heaney, *The Redress*, p. 2.

[17] Martha C. Nussbaum, *Poetic Justice: The Literary Imagination and Public Life*. (Boston: Beacon Press, 1995), p. 1.

[18] Heaney, *The Redress*, p. 2. For a critical discussion of the issue of literature's efficacy as agent for political change, see Robin West, *Narrative, Authority and Law* (Ann Arbor: University of Michigan Press, 1993).

ground," as he puts it in another work[19] – Heaney simultaneously moves further into history while standing at one remove from it. In so doing he examines the transhistorical architecture sustaining such concepts as punishment, revenge, retribution, judgment, justice. As he looks on this body – "before they punished you/you were flaxen-haired,/undernourished, and your/tar-black face was beautiful" – for which he imagines a possible crime, "Little adulteress," and which has been processed by an ancient law: "I can feel the tug/of the halter at the nape/of her neck . . . /My poor scapegoat" – he reflects on the punishment meted out to young girls from the nationalist community in contemporary (1970s) Northern Ireland who breached a specific communal taboo by forming relationships with British soldiers: "I who have stood dumb/when your betraying sisters,/ cauled in tar,/wept by the railings."[20] Each in their turn is a horrific image, saturated in their different contexts with the energies of communal revenge. It is this that brings us to the source of the poem's power. History is collapsed, concertinaed in upon itself; the seemingly incommensurate actions of societies separated by centuries and geographical space are held before us for an extraordinarily intimate act of comparison. In placing the two scenes together (on the same small white page), Heaney invites us to consider the forcefields that have shaped them; to consider the impulses that these human communities share and what stands between them – most obviously the history of law and its attempt to contain premodern systems of revenge.[21] "Punishment" invites us to examine the sources of judgment and/or retribution in our contemporary moment and to consider the very idea of legal justice as a cultural and historical artefact. Bearing witness to the terrors of political violence, Heaney knew all too well the fractures in the concept of the law that stand behind this retreat into a particularized form of retribution. The poem builds toward a final guilt-ridden confession as the poet tells us he "would connive/in civilized outrage" but "yet understand the exact/and tribal, intimate revenge."[22] It is Heaney's way of reminding his readers of the forces that lurk behind the very idea of the social, forces that bleed into the realm of public space if the law is discarded (or seen as invalid). Premodern violence not only lies archived just below our feet but lurks within us still, the poem seems to suggest. It is

[19] Seamus Heaney, "Act of Union" in *New Selected Poems 1966–1987*, pp. 74–5.

[20] Seamus Heaney, "Punishment" in *New Selected Poems 1966–1987*, pp. 71–2.

[21] For more on this theme, see Richard A. Posner, "Revenge as legal prototype and literary genre" in *Law and Literature: A Misunderstood Relation*, 3rd edn. (Massachusetts: Harvard University Press, 2009); Susan Jacoby, *Wild Justice: The Evolution of Revenge* (New York: Harper and Row, 1983).

[22] Heaney, "Punishment," p. 72.

easy to see why "Punishment" remains as one of the most controversial poems in Heaney's work, but it remains too as one of his most powerful poetic meditations on the imaginative forces undergirding the prescriptive.

Heaney's fellow Irish writers Eavan Boland and Paul Durcan have likewise explored poetry's potential for drawing into language the proto- and extralegal forces that shape our social and political selfhoods. In Boland's "The Hanging Judge" (1975), for example, the story of a fifteenth-century judge who hanged his son for the murder of a love rival becomes a lens through which to explore not just Ireland's colonial history and the inequalities birthed within it – "In the stare/Which passed slowly between them, a history/Pauses: repression and rebellion, the scaffold/And its songs" – but also the complex intersections of patriarchy and political power in contemporary (late twentieth-century) Irish society. Opening with an exquisitely barbed invitation to the reader, "Come to the country where justice is seen to be done," the first stanza moves toward an image that ironically echoes the Christological narrative as it alludes to the overt and covert injustices disguised within a cultural civility:

> Come to the country where
> Sentence is passed by word of mouth and raw
> Boys are killed for it. Look, here
> We hanged our son. Our only son.
> And hang him still. And still we call it law.[23]

For Boland, the legal conservatism of the Irish state in the 1970s – validated in its 1937 Constitution (*Bunreacht na hÉireann*) – is mirrored, or finds another source of its power, in the internal patriarchies of the family unit. In the final stanza Boland shifts her eye from the story of the fifteenth-century "Hanging Judge" which has haunted her to the image of her father and another kind of haunting: "As you, father, haunt me. The rope trails/From your fingers. Below you the abyss./Your arms balanced as the scales of justice,/You tie the blindfold. Then from your own eyes fall scales."[24] By collapsing the historical narrative into the familial space, the poem speaks to the complexity of the intimate laws which frame our birth as subjects in the world. The poem's power resides in the way its uncanny excavations remind us that our first encounters with the prescriptive, with judgment, with power, are in the intimate places of the home. The juxtaposition of its two central images helps to bring this uncanny

[23] Eavan Boland, "The hanging judge" in *Collected Poems* (Manchester: Carcanet, 1995), p. 31.
[24] Boland, "The hanging judge," p. 31.

knowledge into the light, with the reader encountering anew the private negotiations with intimate laws that haunt our passage through the public spaces of power.

More hopeful in tone, Boland's "The Laws of Love" (1975) is a work addressed to her close friend Mary Robinson, a noted pioneering constitutional lawyer who would be elected Ireland's first female president in 1990 (a role in which she would remain until 1997) and would subsequently take up the post of United Nations High Commissioner for Human Rights (1997–2002). As Jody Allen Randolph notes, the friendship was a formative one for both the poet and the legislator: "Long talks about poetry and the law, and the vital role of the imagination in bringing change led the two young women deeper into friendship."[25] Robinson would later reflect on the impact of these literary-legal dialogues, noting that she and Boland were each attempting to formulate "ways to express [their] uneasiness with society and its attitudes"[26] and, tellingly, that the friendship was particularly important to her because Boland "was the writer I couldn't be ... She was doing it."[27] As part of its attempt to capture this conceptual dynamic, "The Laws of Love" calls the legal into service as a way of tracing the emerging shifts of power in contemporary gender politics – shifts that, in their different ways, Boland and Robinson were both playing their part in bringing about:

At first light the legislator
Who schooled you, creator
Of each force, each element,
Its secret law, its small print
Nature – while dawn, baptismal as waters
Which broke early in dark, began –
First saw the first of your daughters
Become in your arms a citizen.[28]

The central image here is one of a symbolic revolution; a moment, as Kieran Dolin puts it, "in which the struggle over certain words or forms of representation can be traced in both the legal and the literary fields," and the "symbols developed in one migrate to the other."[29] In this instance, conceptual justices born in the realm of the imagination – "the legislator/Who schooled you, creator/Of each force, each element" – finally find

[25] Jody Allen Randolph, *Eavan Boland* (Cork: Cork University Press, 2014), p. 111.

[26] As quoted in Randolph, *Eavan Boland*, p. 111. [27] Randolph, *Eavan Boland*, p. 111.

[28] Eavan Boland, "The laws of love" in *Collected Poems* (Manchester: Carcanet, 1995), pp. 34–5.

[29] Kieran Dolin, *A Critical Introduction to Law and Literature* (Cambridge: Cambridge University Press, 2007), p. 13.

their proper expression in the law – "Become in your arms a citizen." Shadowing this assertion is Robinson's persona as a campaigning lawyer who played a leading role in the reformation of laws designed to constrict women's participation in public life. She campaigned, for example, for the removal in 1973 of the "Marriage Bar," which had disallowed women upon their marriage to continue employment in the civil service and much of the public sector, and subsequently for the removal of the bar on women sitting on juries in 1976 (when the 1927 Juries Act was repealed). The poem's central conceit is that such legal developments are contingent upon an equally necessary revolution in the communal imagination. Law and literature are presented here as working "together in the production of cultural ideals and values."[30] Remembering back to the beginnings of their friendship in the 1960s, and to how the radical young poet and equally radical young lawyer had engaged, as Jody Allen Randolph puts it, in the "easy exchange of disciplines and vocations,"[31] Boland's poem recounts how they traded "Salmond for Shakespeare."[32] While the imagined dialogue between Sir John Salmond, presumably around his definitions of the law in *Jurisprudence: or the Theory of the Law* (1902), and the canonical bard initially left them "none the wiser," a new discursive space begins to open up – "but now I see it focus/Slowly – a miracle, a closing wound" – and the possibility of new vision and speech emerges. The poem concludes with a renewed determination to give full voice to the female citizen while acknowledging that such a voice still struggles to be fully accommodated in the open courthouse of social norms: "with separate speech we find/For them new blood, for them now plead."[33]

In conjuring conceptual dialogues between poetry and the law, Heaney and Boland perform acts of cultural archeology, each, in their different ways, journeys upstream to locate the sources of language and shared imagery from which the law and the literary draw their force as social actors in the world. Paul Durcan, indeed, plays with something of this in the poem "Stellar Manipulator," a work in which he addresses his judicial father's legal ambitions for him – "Judge Durcan, you wanted/Your eldest son to be a lawyer" – and his flight from the law to the world of the imagination: "I became at the age of twenty-five/Stellar Manipulator/At the London Planetarium."[34] Like much else in Durcan, the comedic

[30] Dolin, *A Critical Introduction*, p. 2.
[31] Randolph, *Eavan Boland*, p. 111.
[32] Boland, "The laws of love," p. 34.
[33] Boland, "The laws of love," p. 35.
[34] Paul Durcan, "Stellar manipulator" in *Life is a Dream: 40 Years Reading Poems 1967–2007* (London: Harvill Secker, 2009), pp. 243–4.

overlays a teasing profundity. The judge's wayward son not only refuses the law as a career but also takes up post at the planetarium, a job that requires him to move the heavenly bodies for their human observers. If the law is here a body in motion, the poet, more concerned perhaps with origins and prime motivations, reaches out to the space through which it moves, tracking its effects in much the same way as astronomers search out new planets by looking for the way light bends round them.

Test Cases: Sentences of the Law

If the poetic law-literature dynamic brings us face to face with language as the very building block of literary and legal performance, contemporary fiction has frequently turned to the ways in which the act of narrative can trace the exchanges between the private and public spaces of the law, between legal performance and social consequence, between the law and the Law. While often more oblique, such exchanges sometimes irrupt onto the surface of the text itself: "That will-o'-the-wisp, the law: where shall I begin to speak of it? Is the law the legal rules, or their interpretations by judges, or by juries? Is it the precedent or the present fact? The norm or the practice?"[35]

While John Barth's literary lawyer Todd Andrews may finally dismiss such meditatively theoretical concerns – "I think I'm not interested in what the law is" – their foregrounding in *The Floating Opera* (1956) invites its readers to consider questions central not just to the law as practice (Andrews quickly concedes that he is "curious about things the law can be made to do"), but of legal origins and their regulation of our horizon of expectation.[36] For Robert Cover, in this regard, the prescriptive (law) and narrative "are inseparably related" by their habitation of a normative universe (*nomos*).[37] Thus every "prescription is insistent in its demand to be located in discourse – to be supplied with history and destiny, beginning and end, explanation and purpose. And every narrative is insistent in

[35] John Barth, *The Floating Opera* (New York: Anchor Books, 1988 [1956]), p. 84.

[36] Barth, *The Floating Opera*, p. 84. "Horizon of expectation" is a term closely associated with the reception theory of Hans Robert Jauss. For more see Hans Robert Jauss and Elizabeth Benzinger, "Literary history as a challenge to literary theory," *New Literary History*, 2(1) (1970), 7–37; Hans Robert Jauss, *Towards an Aesthetic of Reception Theory* (Minneapolis: University of Minnesota Press, 1982).

[37] Robert Cover, "Nomos and narrative" in Martha Minow, Michael Ryan, and Austin Sarat (eds.), *Narrative, Violence, and the Law: The Essays of Robert Cover* (Ann Arbor: University of Michigan Press, 1992), p. 95.

its demand for its prescriptive point, its moral."[38] Moreover, while literature cannot escape its "location in a normative universe, nor can prescription, even when embodied in a legal text, escape its origin and its end in experience, in the narratives that are trajectories plotted upon material reality by our imagination."[39] If we look to two recent novels of legal process, Ian McEwan's *The Children Act* and Colm Tóibín's *The Heather Blazing*, we can see the ways in which such dynamics can become the central textual matter.

In the course of *The Children Act*, McEwan's literary judge, Fiona Maye, charts her way through the complexities of a number of cases and the legal-philosophic implications raised by them. In this, McEwan's novel manages to be simultaneously an absorbing piece of realist fiction about the inner workings of legal process and also a metafictional exploration of the intersecting lines connecting the literary imagination and the law. What unfolds is structured around a number of key dynamics: private faith versus public obligation, personal ethic versus legal prescription, sources of the law versus sources of the Law. Haunting all of this is a concern to explore the human impacts of legal pronouncement, to examine the ontological complexities lurking beneath the surface of epistemological demands.

One of the novel's most difficult cases involves a hospital's request to intervene against the wishes of the parents of conjoined twins with the "apostolic names, Matthew and Mark."[40] Without intervention both children will die, but the invasive procedure, while saving Mark, would inevitably kill Matthew (who is only living by sharing his brother's vital organs): "The loving parents, devout Catholics," we are told, "calm in their belief, refused to sanction murder."[41] It is a deeply troubling case for Maye, and its biblical resonances – the New Testament Gospels but also Abraham's test of faith – trigger in her a need to set out the ground upon which she can operate: "This court is a court of law, not of morals, and our task has been to find, and our duty is then to apply, the relevant principles of law to the situation before us – a situation which is unique."[42] Negotiating this ground and its boundaries is complex, and one of the novel's central themes concerns how the literary and its affective knowledges can provide enabling supplements to purely legalistic thinking. Another of the novel's cases, for example, involves the future of two young Jewish girls whose parents – both raised in the orthodox Chareidi tradition – are

38 Cover, "Nomos and narrative," p. 96.
39 Cover, "Nomos and narrative," p. 96.
40 Ian McEwan, *The Children Act* (London: Vintage Books, 2014), p. 25.
41 McEwan, *The Children Act*, p. 26.
42 McEwan, *The Children Act*, pp. 26–27.

divorcing and cannot agree on the girls' education and broader cultural development. The mother wishes to expose the children to a more liberal upbringing, while the father is insistent that they should remain within the contours of an orthodox life. "On the surface," as McEwan puts it, "the dispute concerned Rachel and Nora's schooling. However, at stake was the entire context of the girls' growing up. It was a fight for their souls."[43] The court must choose, Maye comes to realize, between "cultures, identities, states of mind, aspirations, sets of family relations, fundamental definitions, basic loyalties, unknowable futures."[44] The case once again inhabits a challenging interzone, a space in which legal codes provide no ready-made solutions, nor easily discernible signposts. In the end her intellectual guides turn out to be a combination of legal opinion and the literary imagination: Lord Hoffman on value judgements ("These are value judgements on which reasonable people may differ. Since judges are also people, this means some degree of diversity in their application of values is inevitable"[45]); Lord Hailsham on welfare (whom she follows in "allowing the term to be inseparable from well-being and to include all that was relevant to a child's development as a person"[46]); Lord Justice Purchas (echoing the assertion that all religions are deserving of respect provided they were "legally and socially acceptable"); John Donne ("no child is an island"[47]); Shakespeare ("Nor custom stale her infinite variety"[48]); Aristotle ("man is a social animal"[49]). Indeed it is on this final Aristotelian theme that Maye's judgement concludes, filled with "learned references (Adam Smith, John Stuart Mill)" providing, as she sardonically notes, the "kind of civilised reach every good judgement needs."[50] Yet, despite this moment of self-deprecating irony, the intellectual process through which McEwan's literary judge reaches her final judgment (to side with the mother's case) in fact reveals the amenability of the literary imagination as a storehouse of intellectual history as coded in the language of the cultural imaginary. We find traces of this, for example, in a moment in which Maye draws on a synthesis of legal reasoning and literary allusion. In response to the problem of when the courts should intervene against the "religious principles of the parents," Maye "invoked one of her favourites, wise Lord Justice Munby in the Court of Appeal. 'The infinite variety of the human condition precludes arbitrary definition'," and in so doing noted the "admirable

[43] McEwan, *The Children Act*, p. 10.
[44] McEwan, *The Children Act*, pp. 12–13.
[45] McEwan, *The Children Act*, p. 14.
[46] McEwan, *The Children Act*, p. 15.
[47] McEwan, *The Children Act*, p. 10.
[48] McEwan, *The Children Act*, p. 17.
[49] McEwan, *The Children Act*, p. 16.
[50] McEwan, *The Children Act*, p. 16.

Shakespearean touch. *Nor custom stale her infinite variety.*"[51] The concluding reference to *Antony and Cleopatra* here provides a metatextual framework for locating Maye's paralegal struggle. Shakespeare's performance of man's dialectical complexities (and infinite varieties) – reason/emotion, society/family, epistemology/ontology, duty/love (all concretized in the play in the relationship between Rome and Alexandria) – captures much that is at stake in Maye's legal judgment. The Shakespearean allusion draws to it images of infinite futures, of possible selves yet to reveal their proper natures. It is a conceptual reframing that moves Maye away from reading the girls' education in purely instrumental terms and undergirds her legal judgment around their future welfare, allowing her to locate her legal reasoning in its fuller cultural and social contexts: "Welfare, happiness, well-being must embrace the philosophical concept of the good life."[52] "Well-being was social," Maye concludes, "No child an island. Man a social animal, in Aristotle's famous construction."[53]

The crafting of Maye's judgement carries with it echoes of Benjamin Cardozo's eloquent hailing of the literary as a kindred spirit of the law:

> The search is for the just word, the happy phrase, that will give expression to the thought, but somehow the thought itself is transfigured by the phrase when found. There is emancipation in our very bonds. The restraints of rhyme or metre, the exigencies of period or balance, liberate at times the thought which they confine, and in imprisoning release.[54]

Richard Weisberg's assessment of Cardozo's vision of a "judge in the finest tradition of the common law," furthermore, resonates powerfully with McEwan's search for a literary equivalent:

> His judge appreciates every nuance of social meaning discoverable in a difficult set of facts; he or she sets about making the decision by bringing every ethical fibre to bear upon it. But the judge must operate through language; far from stultifying the effort, the requirement of speaking to the world through narrative is liberating, edifying, unifying.[55]

In performing just this act of liberating discursive unification, McEwan's metalegal novel powerfully reminds us (or shows us) that legal reasoning finds its proper fulfilment in conversation with the cultural terrain upon which it operates and from which it draws its legitimacy. It is an example of

[51] McEwan, *The Children Act*, p. 17. [52] McEwan, *The Children Act*, p. 15.
[53] McEwan, *The Children Act*, p. 16.
[54] Benjamin N. Cardozo, *The Growth of the Law* (1925), as quoted in Richard H. Weisberg, "Editor's preface," *Cardozo Studies in Law and Literature*, 1(1) (1989), v.
[55] Weisberg, "Editor's preface," v.

the way in which fiction, as C. R. B. Dunlop puts it, allows us "to get beyond the technical and circumscribed study of legal rules, and to look at law as part of the broader civilisation."[56]

In contradistinction, Colm Tóibín's *The Heather Blazing*, in its charting of the imbrication of the personal and the professional in the life of Irish judge Eamon Redmond, traces the law's retreat from this kind of broader cultural discursive engagement. In its picture of an Irish state still trapped in the contours of a conservative social vision (the novel was written before the rapid liberalization and secularization associated with Ireland's "Celtic Tiger" period of economic growth), *The Heather Blazing* presents us with a judicial protagonist who, as Richard Weisberg might have it, prefers "the safety of wordiness to the risks of spontaneous human interaction," for whom highly "formalised language mediates between [him] and the exigencies of life, protecting but also gradually distancing [him] from the sources of positive and creative action."[57] Tóibín indexes something of this intellectual solipsism in his description of Redmond as he moves between his chambers and the court: "He had learned over the years not to look at anyone as he walked from his rooms to the court, not to offer greetings to a colleague, or nod at a barrister. He kept his eyes fixed on a point in the distance."[58] This sense of judicial isolation is even more marked when we learn how Redmond spends his time in his rural holiday home. His obsessional consumption of the judgments of his colleagues in the Supreme and High Courts – "He became involved in the intricacies of the law, reading as avidly as though the pages were full of easy gossip. He was interested in the workings of his colleagues' minds, their strategies, the words they chose" – is counterpointed with a reflection on his status in the local village – "He was still an outsider who came only in the summer; and he was a judge, and they were careful what they said in his presence."[59] The resultant social remove, and its possible consequences, are captured most pointedly in his admission that he "did not know how they spoke when they were among themselves,"[60] and a later autoconfession that he "was not certain about right and wrong," something he realized "he would have to keep hidden from the court."[61] Tóibín presents his readers with a judge who, among other things, lacks many of the imaginative tools that an

[56] C. R. B. Dunlop, "Literature studies in law schools," *Cardozo Studies in Law and Literature*, 3(1) (1991), 64.

[57] Weisberg, *The Failure of the Word*, p. xi.

[58] Colm Tóibín, *The Heather Blazing* (London: Picador, 2001 [1992]), p. 4.

[59] Tóibín, *Heather Blazing*, pp. 58, 29.

[60] Tóibín, *Heather Blazing*, p. 29.

[61] Tóibín, *Heather Blazing*, p. 90.

engagement with the literary would supply. Redmond thus stands in for Tóibín as representative of a state apparatus that he reads as similarly disconnected from the communal imagination and a society desirous of change, most obviously in the realms of gender and sexual identity equalities. Echoing Richard Posner's reading of E. M. Forster, Tóibín's novel "associates the legal style of thinking with the failure to connect heart and mind."[62]

As with *The Children Act*, in its careful attention to the slow grind of writing legal judgments Tóibín's novel also brings a Cardozo-esque metatextual concern to the interface between the law and its narrativization, between legal substance and form.[63] However, unlike McEwan's central character, Tóibín's literary judge's obsession with form becomes a tactical way of disengaging from substance in its cultural and social dimensions. As Thomas Morawetz puts it, "*The Heather Blazing* is, above all, a study of inhibition and constraint. In his legal judgments, Redmond adheres to what he sees as the strict application of law, uncoloured by empathic or moral concerns."[64] In the course of the novel, the reader observes as Redmond ruminates on the writing of his judgments for two cases, each of which returns the reader to the family as a scene of law. The first involves the care to be offered to a disabled child whose parents wish for him to remain in the care of the hospital, while the medical team feel homecare is now the best solution. We are told how in coming to judgment – to side with the hospital (and thus the state) – Redmond had worked his way through "the implications of articles in the Constitution, the meaning of phrases and the significance which earlier judgments had given to these phrases"; how he had written "it all down, slowly and logically, working each paragraph over and over, erasing, re-checking and re-writing."[65] The real challenge for Redmond, as for all readers and authors of the law, is to somehow contain and give shape to concepts that challenge the very limits of language. For this particular literary judge, however, form and substance stubbornly refuse to meet in unified ideal: "He would find that a single sentence by necessity expanded into a page of careful analysis; then sometimes a page would have to be re-written and its contents would form the basis for several pages, or give rise to further thought, further erasures and consultation."[66] Trapped by form, as it were,

62 Posner, *Law and Literature*, p. 3.

63 "Form is not something added to substance as a mere protuberant adornment, the two are fused in unity." See Cardozo, *Law and Literature*. 5.

64 Thomas Morawetz, *Literature and the Law* (Austin: Wolters Kluwer, 2007), p. 69.

65 Tóibín, *Heather Blazing*, p. 7.

66 Tóibín, *Heather Blazing*, p. 7.

the law only comes into proper view for Redmond when captured in the text he is authoring: "He realised as he wrote the judgment what it meant."[67] Tóibín's rendering of this struggle, and Redmond's sublimated desire for a legal formalism (with its echoes of a "mechanical jurisprudence," perhaps), complexifies the reader's position as an observer who traces the law's gradual retreat from the actual vulnerable body in its purview.

As the novel progresses, Redmond is forced reluctantly to bring his purely legalistic intellectual instincts into dialogue with the forces of social change that shadow the narrative's details. The text's second case concerns a sixteen-year-old girl who, while attending a convent school, had become pregnant, and been expelled as a result. In response, the girl and her mother "sought a court order instructing the school to take her back."[68] The specificities of the case push Redmond into a conceptual space between and behind his usual engagement with the rigors of legal textuality: "Most of the issues raised in the case were moral: the right of an ethos to prevail over the right of an individual. Basically, he was being asked to decide how life should be conducted in a small town. He smiled to himself at the thought and shook his head."[69] His first instinct is one programmed by a form of legal originalism: "He went over to his bookshelves and took down the sacred text: *Bunreacht na hÉireann*, the Irish Constitution," a text that "contained the governing principles to which the law was subject," and which, in terms of the case with which he was faced, "was clear about the Christian nature of the state" with a preamble that "specifically referred to the Holy Trinity."[70] It is an instinct that frames the ideological tensions at the heart of the novel. Redmond now finds himself forced to negotiate between the competing claims of a foundational legal vision and the needs and expectations of a society radically different in nature to the one that birthed that vision. It is a negotiation that leads him toward an extralegal existential crisis. He finds he is "unhappy about the case because he [has] been asked to interpret more than the law" when that is "all he knew: the law, its letter, its traditions, its ambiguities, its codes."[71] The case draws him further into a consideration of the relationship between the constitutional framework and the law as lived reality; a consideration that opens up contingent questions around the law's relationship to history's

[67] Tóibín, *Heather Blazing*, p. 8. [68] Tóibín, *Heather Blazing*, p. 86.

[69] Tóibín, *Heather Blazing*, p. 88.

[70] Tóibín, *Heather Blazing*, p. 89. The opening lines of the preamble to *Bunreacht na hÉireann* (1937) read: "In the name of the Most Holy Trinity, from Whom is all authority and to Whom, as our final end, all actions of both men and States must be referred, We, the people of Éire…"

[71] Tóibín, *Heather Blazing*, pp. 90, 83.

paradigm shifts. As Eoin Daly and Tom Hickey have noted, "constitutions are more than narrow legal instruments concerned with technical institutional functions: they will typically claim to define the political and moral identity of a State, and perhaps that of the people or nation as well."[72] But they are also, as Ian Ward notes, a "product of the imagination," a fact that, for some, "militates against any notion that a constitution is somehow set in stone, that it enjoys some deeper metaphysical legitimacy."[73] Tóibín's novel indeed may be read as a manifesto for just such a position, as an imaginative reinterrogation of the outmoded principles that remain encoded at the heart of Irish law. For Redmond, who will eventually side with the school, the case proves particularly disruptive to his normal way of operating exactly because it requires him to move beyond his usual narrow legal instruments and into the realm not just of moral identity, but of the imagination. While this is a realm that McEwan's literary judge navigates with assurance and nuance – to the enrichment of her judgments, the novel strongly suggests – Redmond struggles to find a new conceptual ground on which to operate and move forward: "he was being asked to decide on something more fundamental [than the purely legal] and now he realized that he had failed and he felt afraid."[74] His failure, like many of our most important failings, is one of the imagination. But then, the unread poets on his bookshelf could have told him that.

[72] Eoin Daly and Tom Hickey, *The Political Theory of the Irish Constitution: Republicanism and the Basic Law* (Manchester: Manchester University Press, 2015), p. 1.

[73] Ian Ward, *Shakespeare and the Legal Imagination* (London: Butterworths, 1999), p. 2.

[74] Tóibín, *Heather Blazing*, p. 83.

CHAPTER 15

Narrative and Legal Plurality in Postcolonial Nations: Chapter and Verse from the East African Court of Appeal

Stephanie Jones

Introduction

Chapter and Verse

This is an idiom of law. As a catechism, "chapter and verse" is to know something verbatim, wholly and without question; it is to memorize and perpetuate; it is to recite an authority. Take these words apart, and they take on different meaning. "Chapter" deflates to a distinguishable part of a story. "Verse" inflates to encompass all sorts of orthodox and unorthodox forms, from the designed to the spontaneous, from doggerel to sonnet, from rhyming text to the text of a song. Etymologically, "verse" carries both "line" and "turning": it may be a demarcation or a veering. Open to rendition, it might recite authority, but it might also re-site authority.

This chapter is keyed around a singular occurrence of verse in a small chapter of British imperial legal history. Offering three readings of the location of song in a judgment, I summarize and exercise concepts in law and literature that are critically postcolonial. Addressing the verses in their juridical situation – staying with rather than outstretching the structure of the court and the acts of quotation and translation – I aim to trace how the songs illuminate and strain the law. While this bears on postcolonial literature and law, it more importantly focuses a postcolonial *approach* to literature in/as law. In this way, it acts as a chapter in this volume's larger story about law and literature. Having introduced my case study, I work it through key debates on evidence, rhetoric, and rights. In the broadest terms and in each part, this is to work the case through a history of ideas

Many thanks to Kieran Dolin for his wise suggestions and careful reading, and to Ann Biersteker, Alex Perullo, and Andrew Eisenberg for their generous responses to my questions about the songs and for directing me to *utenzi*.

that manoeuvre between thoughts of an always future possibility of a critically just law, and thoughts about the law as a critically compromised relation to justice.

Abdullah bin Sheikh bin Yunis on behalf of the Thalatha Thaifa and W. N. MacMillan *v.* (1) The Wakf Commissioners; (2) The Land Officer on behalf of H. M. Government of East Africa [1913] 12 EACA 54

The issue before the East African Court of Appeal (EACA) was the admissibility and value of evidence of "tribal ownership" of 200 acres of Mombasa Island. Bonham-Carter J opens with a description of the disputed estate in relation to harbors and forts, chapels and mosques, wells, a creek, a cemetery, and a city.[1] He identifies what is "ruined," and so infers other places are maintained. He evokes epochs of history in his description of topography, but is alert to the distortions of perspective. In an "archaic" Portuguese map, "nothing is drawn to scale" (Fort Jesus is oversized), and in a nineteenth-century British naval chart, "the country appears from sea to be all bush," although he accepts other evidence indicating cultivation.[2] He has walked the estate under dispute, and had areas cleared in search of evidence of title. It is a surprise when he ends this often subtle geohistorical, ecological, and personal description with the blunt statement that key locations were "abandoned" before 1635.[3]

The next section of the judgment is entitled "History": "Many centuries ago Mombasa was apparently colonised by certain tribes of Asiatic origin who became friendly with the native tribes and lived on the Island." The "corporation" of the *Thalatha Thaifa*, the Three Tribes, is then told as part of a 300-year story of tussling between the Portuguese, the Imam of Oman, and the Sultan of Zanzibar over control of the island.[4] The judge's historiography ends with the Sultan's ascendency, his 1887 concession of the island to the Imperial British East Africa Company, and its 1895 reissue to the British government. The rest of the judgment is given to evidence

[1] *Abdullah bin Sheikh bin Yunis on behalf of the Thalatha Thaifa and W. N. MacMillan* v. *(1) The Wakf Commissioners; (2) The Land Officer on behalf of H. M. Government of East Africa* (1913) 12 EACA 54 at 55.

[2] *Abdullah bin Sheikh* at 55–6. [3] *Abdullah bin Sheikh* at 56.

[4] *Abdullah bin Sheikh* at 57. Mohamed H. Abdulaziz describes the cultural formation and political landscape of the Three Tribes and the Twelve Tribes of Mombasa in his study of an important Swahili poet. See Mohamed H. Abdulaziz, *Muyaka: 19th Century Swahili Popular Poetry* (Nairobi: Kenya Literature Bureau, 1979), pp. 7–37.

tendered in support of the claim that the Three Tribes still own a "remnant" of "tribal land." Evidence includes "Arabic documents," oral testimony of an active shrine to a *mzimli* (a "spirit"), payment received for fishing stakes, permissions to cultivate land, the conveyance of land by alleged delegates of the Sheikh, and three songs.

Bonham-Carter J's predominant tone is magnanimous patience. The documents "have proved very difficult to decipher," and thanks is given for translations that are "as satisfactory as possible" toward the conclusion that they do not evidence title.[5] The *mzimli* is a "pagan survival" that the "stricter Mohamedans" of the Three Tribes consider "not very reputable": and in any case, "No ingenuity can stretch the visiting of a shrine to possession of land."[6] The evidence on fishing and cultivation licenses is too "weak and untrustworthy" to imply "any title to the land resembling a freehold."[7] (The inference might be that a consistent issuing of usufructuary rights could prove such title.) The conveyance of land by occupants related in complex ways to the Three Tribes is deemed "sales of private land privately owned," and not evidence of collective ownership of a larger remaining estate. Oral evidence of conveyancing as proof of previous ownership – and so continuing title over adjacent lands – "is almost the most unconvincing statement I have met even in a long experience in these Courts."[8] The judge concludes that the evidence has been "contradictory and unreliable," and dismisses the appeal with costs. This opinion seems obdurate; proof, if it were lacking, of the involvement of early twentieth-century British imperial courts in the articulation of Kenya from protectorate to colony. But a less implacable reading might emerge from a consideration of the disputants, of the position of the EACA in the imperial courts system, and of Bonham-Carter J, and particularly his understanding of the songs.

The Sheikh of the Three Tribes is not only in dispute with the government Land Officer. The Wakf Commission was, and is, the administrative body for an Islamic charitable trust.[9] On the other side, the Land Officer is not only in dispute with the Sheikh. The interest of W. N. Macmillan is brought into relief when Bonham-Carter J notes that the land, mostly "bare coral," has recently become "valuable for building sites for European residences."[10] That this is a market dispute about seaside real estate,

[5] *Abdullah bin Sheikh* at 59–60. [6] *Abdullah bin Sheikh* at 60–61.

[7] *Abdullah bin Sheikh* at 62. [8] *Abdullah bin Sheikh* at 64.

[9] Wakf Commissioners Act 2012 (1981). See www.kenyalaw.org/lex//actview.xql?actid=CAP.%20109

[10] *Abdullah bin Sheikh* at 57.

bypassing alliances of race and religion, is unsurprising in the context of post-1885/Berlin Conference land grabbing in Africa, and in the context of the consolidation of Kenya as a settler colony in the 1910s. That customary law could, in 1913, yield a freehold title is only surprising against a current context of debates over native title in settler states, and their tight circumscription by principles of nonalienability and collective ownership.

The Three Tribes case of 1913 didn't move to petition to the Judicial Committee of the Privy Council (JCPC), and I have not found it referenced beyond the court record.[11] It is obscure as legal history. But in being obscure, it presents one of many accretive moments in the establishment of a regional legal geography, within a period of energetic creation before and following World War I, and between the arguments over appeal court structures at the Imperial Conferences of 1911 and 1927.[12] This case also occurs – as a muted interruption – between two landmark JCPC cases (of 1901 and 1952) which applied classical and Indian Islamic law to East African situations.[13] Bonham-Carter J's appreciation of local plural relationships between English, local (not imported) Islamic, and customary law instantiates the complex and irregular ways in which appeals through the EACA in relation to petitions to the JCPC partook in a grand narrative

11 The JCPC was variously the highest forum of petition for the dominions and dependencies, protectorates, mandates, and colonies under British administration from its inception in 1833, and in some territories beyond the era of decolonization. See: Bonny Ibhawoh, *Imperial Justice: Africans in Empire's Court* (Oxford: Oxford University Press, 2013). Established in 1902, the EACA soon superseded the High Court of Bombay as a court of appeal for Eastern Africa between local courts and the JCPC, and by 1947 its jurisdiction extended through Uganda, Kenya, Tanganyika, Malawi, Zanzibar, Aden, St Helena, the Seychelles, and Somaliland. See: L. L. Kato, "The Court of Appeal for East Africa: from a colonial court to an international court," *East African Law Journal*, 7(1) (1971), 1–31.

12 Ibhawoh, *Imperial Justice*, p. 25. On the Western Indian Ocean as a legal geography, see: Thomas R. Metcalf, *Imperial Connections: India in the Indian Ocean, 1860–1920* (Oakland: University of California Press, 2008); H. F. Morris, "The reception and rejection of Indian law" in H. F. Morris and James S. Read (eds.), *Indirect Rule and the Search for Justice: Essays in East African Legal History* (Oxford: Clarendon Press, 1972), pp. 109–30. On the involvement of relationships of commerce and debt to the creation of this legal geography, see Fahad Bishara, "Paper routes: inscribing islamic law across the nineteenth-century Western Indian Ocean," *Law and History Review*, 32(4) (2014), 797–820 and "A sea of debt: histories of commerce and obligation in the Indian Ocean, c. 1850–1940," *Enterprise and Society*, 15(4) (2014), 643–54. More broadly, see Ed Simpson and Kai Kresse (eds.). *Struggling with History: Islam and Cosmopolitanism in the Western Indian Ocean* (New York: Columbia University Press, 2008).

13 *The Secretary of State for Foreign Affairs* v. *Charlesworth Pilling and Co.*, AC 373 (1901) at 379; and *Fatuma binti Mohammed bin Bakhshuwen* v. *Mohammed bin Salim Bakhshuwen*, AC 1 (1952). See also Ibhawoh, *Imperial Justice*, p. 121; G. W. Bartholomew and J. A. Iliffe, "Decisions," *International and Comparative Law Journal*, 1(3) (1952), 392, quoted in Ibhawoh, *Imperial Justice*, 170–1.

of imperial justice delivering against the travesties of local colonial and customary rule.[14] Further, Bonham-Carter J's life typifies the movement of career colonial judicial officers, and their significance to the creation of legal territories: He is known for his modification of the Indian penal code for Sudan, where he is said to have "rescued Islamic law courts from decay."[15] Cases like this also deserve scrutiny because "the fact that these Courts [the EACA and the West African Court of Appeal] were more accessible to ordinary Africans than the JCPC made them even more crucial sites of judicial governance."[16] Legal history is not only made by rulings of the highest courts. It is notable that as a critical relation, law and literature is not often exercised through intermediate judgments. While precedent-setting cases, controversial acts, and state constitutions understandably shape the field, this chapter attempts to indicate what might be gained by pausing on less renowned moments of law as a history of encountering literature.

Songs of Two Towers

Verse and Chapter

In his topographic introduction, Bonham-Carter J pays attention to possible proof of a *Mnara Mdogo* (Little Tower) and a *Mnara Mkubwa* (Big Tower). This is because "stress has been laid on the song saying that the Two Towers are our marks."[17] Later in the judgment, this and two other Swahili songs are transcribed. The verse establishing the towers is short:

> Mwanzo wa Kilindini twatemu mwitu
> Minara miwili ni alama yetu
> Sheikh Mohamadi tupe chapa yetu
>
> In the beginning at Kilindini we cleared the bush.
> Two towers are our marks.
> Sheikh Mohamed give us our seal.

While this song is more significant as evidence, Bonham-Carter J gives more attention to a longer song:

[14] Ibhawoh, *Imperial Justice*, 18–19; Y. P. Ghai and J. P. MacAuslan, *Public Law and Political Change in Kenya* (Nairobi: Oxford University Press, 1970), pp. 172.

[15] K. O'C. Hayes, "Carter, Sir Edgar Bonham (1870–1956)" in *Oxford Dictionary of National Biography* (Oxford University Press, 2004), www.oxforddnb.com/view/article/31960.

[16] Ibhawoh, *Imperial Justice*, p. 37.

[17] *Abdullah bin Sheikh* at 55.

Iko Minara Mirefu
Ilyo Wakwa Kadimu
Wakikaa Waongofu
Miji Mitatu Timaam
Na Mtu Akiwashufu
Naye Akamba Naam
Musifanye Usaumu
Ndani Kwenu Shihiri

The judge opines that "the words are not capable of being translated into sense, the best that I can obtain at all literally is":

These tall towers
Which were built in ancient days
And inhabited by an upright folk
Three complete towns.
If a man sees them he will speak with respect
Do not make trouble.
Go home back [*sic*] you Arab scum.

He then explains that he has also had "a free version" supplied to him, which he offers by way of clarification. This translation reads:

Tall minarets of ancient time
Do form the subject of my rhyme.
Three towns there are hard by their place.
The dwelling of an upright race.
When an invader sees their walls
He flies with most respectful squalls.
Hence to your homes, here make no strife,
Go save your Mshihire life.[18]

Bringing his epochal reading and personal walking of the island to an interpretation of the songs, Bonham-Carter J concludes that while there was once a *Mnara Mkubwa* and there is now a *Mnara Mdogo*, they never stood at the same time, and so the towers are incapable of together being a symbol of the identity and customary title to land of the Three Tribes. Ironically, this reading belies the second and preferred translation: for while it might lack sensitivity to the original form and language, it gives rhetorical force to a timeless and symbolic story, not least through maintaining the discipline of rhyme on the last syllable. That the verse's alertness to both a "ruined" and an extant structure might be more rather than less emphatic of an identity with the land is not considered by the judge. So the

[18] *Abdullah bin Sheikh* at 55–7.

further translation is extravagant in not being necessary, it is supplementary in being an over- and under-elaboration of the original, and it is immoderate in introducing a sensibility that the judgment cannot abide. Put another way, the translation makes the law conspicuous as a language that decontextualizes other languages.

Reading One: Evidence

Adverse and Inadvertent

The analysis of works of oral, textual, and visual imagination as a source of law can be distinguished from the acknowledgment of such arts as evidence of law. That song might be source, evidence, testimony, and critique within the same musical movement is emerging as an intriguing approach to the law.[19] This in/distinction might be ingenious or disingenuous, as Bonham-Carter J's opinion demonstrates: By claiming the songs are not a cogent source, he denies that they can be valid evidence, cannot understand them as testimony, and precludes them as critique. Recent work on cultures of translation of Kiswahili verse up to the 1970s indicates subtler interpretative approaches against such legal declinations, but also demonstrates a long history of not attending to the complexities of verse as dialogue, testimony, and coerced speech. This history of translation is critically understood as a "denial of the language of poetry."[20] Now – against histories of limited legal and literary critical interpretation – East African poetry of the late nineteenth and early twentieth centuries is translated and read with attention to authorship, production, and dissemination; intertextual reference; genre and genre breaking; and dialect, repetition, rhyme, metaphor, and symbol. Exemplary scholarship traces and sounds the emergence of voices of resistance, and of nationalist and socialist consciousness, toward understanding Kiswahili literatures as "praxis" in the late nineteenth and early twentieth centuries, and as a precursor to later twentieth and twenty-first-century East African songs.[21] Such modes

[19] See Kieran Dolin, "From Orpheus to Yothu Yindi: music and legal cultures," *Law, Culture and the Humanities*, 12(1) (2016), 29–38.

[20] Ann Biersteker, *Questions of Language and Power in Nineteenth and Twentieth-Century Poetry in Kishwahili* (Ann Arbor: Michigan State University Press, 1996), p. 206.

[21] Biersteker, *Questions of Language*, pp. 23–95; Assibi A. Amidu, "Political poetry among the Swahili: the Kimondo verses from Lamu" in Pat Caplan and Farouk Topan (eds.), *Swahili Modernities: Culture, Politics and Identity on the East African Coast* (Trenton and Asmara: Africa World Press, 2004), pp. 157–72; Andrew J. Eisenberg. *The Resonance of Place: Vocalizing Swahili*

of making literary knowledge have gained paradigm-changing momentum across the world in the postcolonial period, in both literary and legal terms.[22] The juridical positioning of verse is, however, still tightly circumscribed.

Today, "the opposition between state law and local customary or indigenous law is the best-known form of legal pluralism," although these pluralisms are not always drawn as "oppositions," but more commonly framed as negotiation.[23] This is not to argue that procedures of determination are necessarily more delicate or less oppressive than a language of opposition might imply. Rather, it is to appreciate that customary law under British imperial and postcolonial laws was and still is a question of fact.[24] The place of verse within this stipulate continues to be curious. The redaction of the imaginative form to the demand for empirical evidence, as demonstrated in the Three Tribes case, might contrast more supple and sustained readings of verses enacted by native title tribunals and courts today.[25] This is not all, however, that the Three Tribes case yields by way of contrast and continuity between colonial and postcolonial approaches to verse as an expression of customary law.

While Bonham-Carter J does not accept the songs as proof of title, he does not refute them as potential evidence. He rejects the songs on content, not form or duration. This is in line with the rules for distinguishing customary law that the imperial courts were formulating in the first

Ethnicity in Mombasa, Dissertation Abstracts International 70 (2010): 4513. UMI Order Number: AAI3388445; Andrew J. Eisenberg, "Islam, sound and space: acoustemology and Muslim citizenship on the Kenyan coast" in Georgina Bond (ed.), *Music, Sound and Space: Transformations of Public and Private Experience* (Cambridge and New York: Cambridge University Press, 2013), pp. 186–202.

22 For examples from the immediate context, see Alex Perullo, "Conceptions of song: ownership, rights, and African copyright law" in Ruth M. Stone (ed.), *The Garland Handbook of African Music* (New York and London: Routledge, 2015), pp. 44–54; and Alex Perullo and Andrew J. Eisenberg, "Musical property rights regimes in Kenya and Tanzania after TRIPS" in Matthew David and Deborah Halbert (eds.), *The SAGE Handbook of Intellectual Property* (New York: Sage, 2015), pp. 148–65.

23 Franz von Benda-Beckmann and Keebet von Benda-Beckmann, "Places that come and go: a legal anthropological perspective on the temporalities of space in plural legal orders" in Irus Braverman, Nicholas Blomley, David Delaney, and Alexandre Kedar (eds.), *The Expanding Spaces of Law: A Timely Legal Geography* (Stanford: Stanford University Press, 2014), p. 33.

24 For a consideration of customary law as fact under colonial rule and imperial law in East Africa in the early twentieth century, see: James S. Read, "Customary law under colonial rule" in H. F. Morris and James S. Read (eds.), *Indirect Rule and the Search for Justice: Essays in East African Legal History* (Oxford: Clarendon Press, 1972), p. 172; and Brett Shadle, "'Changing traditions to meet current altering conditions': customary law, African courts and the rejection of codification in Kenya, 1930–60," *Journal of African History*, 40 (1999), 411–31.

25 For example, see: Grace Koch, "We have the song, so we have the land: song and ceremony as proof of ownership in Aboriginal and Torres Strait Islander land claims." *AIATSIS Research Discussion Paper No. 33* (Canberra: AIATIS Research Publications, 2013).

decades of the twentieth century, emphasizing notoriety and collective acceptance over longevity and continuance,[26] with a concern to avoid codifying and so stultifying changes in customary law.[27] While this enabled the surreptitious abjection of customary to English law, the framing of song in the Three Tribes case might – without overstating – epitomize an imperial recognition of customary law that troubles the controversial demand for long proofs of continuity that characterize land-rights claims today, and to which song is significant.[28] This reading might be furthered through debates over the "invention of tradition" in Africa: that is, over where, how, why, and whether fluid groupings became "tribes" in response to colonial rule; whether these became hierarchical to meet the dispositions of colonial administration and African elites; and what ideas of authenticity these processes assume and produce.[29]

Bonham-Carter J's suspicion of the land claim is finally expressed in these terms: "The boundaries were in my opinion invented for the purpose of this action to exclude land occupied by Europeans."[30] This seems likely, but may not be proof against title: It may rather tell us that customary law is – like custom, like law – a continual negotiation to meet present circumstances. So the invocation of the two towers and the tall minaret may not consolidate an arcane cultural memory which the judge lacks the acuity or the will to interpret: Rather, the choice of landmarks and boundaries presents a negotiation with a changed landscape and the presence of European title holders that is no less authentic. This reading might be furthered by interpreting "Iko Minara Mirefu" as (possibly) *utenzi*: a form of narrative poem defined by four-line stanzas of eight-syllable lines, traditionally described as "epic,"[31] and deployed in this period and later as a mode of dialogue and political "exchange."[32] Politically resonant because

[26] Ibhawoh, *Imperial Justice*, p. 64.

[27] *Abdullah bin Sheikh bin Yunis* at 71; Shadle, "Changing traditions."

[28] For example, see Lisa Strelein, *Compromised Jurisprudence: Native Title Cases since Mabo* (Canberra: Aboriginal Studies Press, 2009). In this context, the terms of the "Amodu Tijani case," a foundational 1921 JCPC decision recognizing "native title" in Africa but designed for redeployment across the imperium, indicate that the recognition of land rights could have become more difficult to prove in the postcolonial period, even if the opportunity to argue proof is more available. See Ibhawoh, *Imperial Justice*, pp. 3–5. The point is not to suggest that imperial courts were a bastion of equity, but rather to emphasize the iniquitous wariness and circumspection of settler state approaches to land rights today.

[29] Terence Ranger, "The invention of tradition in colonial Africa" in Eric Hobsbawm and Terence Ranger (eds.), *The Invention of Tradition* (Cambridge and Massachusetts: Cambridge University Press, 1983), pp. 211–62. For the tenor of debate in relation to law, see generally Kristin Mann and Richard Roberts (eds.), *Law in Colonial Africa* (Portsmouth: Heinemann, 1991).

[30] *Abdullah bin Sheikh* at 65.

[31] See, for example, Abdulaziz, *Muyaka*, p. 49.

[32] Biersteker, *Questions of Language*, pp. 96–121; 110. Also Abdulaziz, *Muyaka*. 154.

of and despite its form, these verses read as simultaneously consolidating emplacement and identity (in the epic mode) and defiantly negotiating place (in the retooled mode). Under this interpretation, the song does not lack sense. It is pragmatically intelligible as a reinvention of tradition. That the "free translation" lends the verse both an archaic sensibility and a present individual persona ("my rhyme") endorses this reading, even as it also signifies the colonial command for/of traditions and ethnicities that are both longstanding and in comprehensible genres (the first person/the tribe). These Kiswahili songs articulate local agency as temporally and geographically sophisticated – or even tricky, because verse is often a trick, and the songs might be recognized in these terms without falling into stereotypes of wily natives. In other words, to read the verses as natively tricky is to recognize a local capacity, not an essential quality: It is to recognize Swahili modernity.[33] In response, the "free translation" articulates colonial yearning as colonial misrecognition, a distortion that is both a desire and demand. From one perspective, this reads as a mistake, a travesty of translation, and a common moment in histories of imperial and colonial order. Through a broader lens, this reads as a compulsive instance of the law as an act of always failing translation.

Reading Two: Rhetoric

Version and Reversion

Thinking about law as translation has generated different ideas about the possibility of justice. While recognizing that translation is always an approximate activity, identifying law as a similar form of transfiguration in its specialized striving for neutrality, fidelity, and intelligibility provides a hopeful ideal of law as justice.[34] Alternatively, understanding law as an act of translation reveals its constitutive failure to acknowledge the wrong that requires justice,[35] or discloses the law as a dramatic loss of language between people that amounts to a form of violence against them.[36] Such

[33] Caplan and Topan (eds.), *Swahili Modernities*. See also Biersteker, *Questions of Language*, pp. 217–67 for a discussion of answers and parodies as an aspect of Kiswahili poetry of the period.

[34] James Boyd White, *Justice as Translation: An Essay in Cultural and Legal Criticism* (Chicago: University of Chicago Press, 1990).

[35] Jean-Francois Lyotard, *The Differend: Phrases in Dispute* (trans. Georges Van Den Abbeele) (Minneapolis: University of Minnesota Press, 1988).

[36] Jacques Derrida, "What is a relevant translation?" *Critical Inquiry*, 27 (1983), 174–200.

approaches connect to broader debates on the law as rhetoric: on the legal narrative as a sometimes existing and always potential "poethics"[37] or on the legal word – authorized finally and only by the force of the state – as staged, essential, distinctive, ineluctable violence.[38] In these arguments, scenes from prose fiction and fragments of poetry constantly feature, either to make the despair felt in ways that might turn into political thought or action, or to introduce an outside ethic of hope. Commonly, the willful obscurities of the law are retrograde, and the willful ambivalences of literature are radical. Considered more narrowly as a site of literal translation, the law is also often understood as a scene of the critical impossibility of justice, although turns to literary theories and narratives have also framed an understanding of how quasilegal genres – tribunals, truth commissions – enable translation in ways that arguably bypass or underpass such discourses of futility.[39]

In this context, Bonham-Carter J's opinion might present a crude and ready example of the regularly reductive processes of mainstream law as both an act and site of translation. It might instantiate a proclivity of imperial law, or the imprisoning architectures of the language of the colonizer,[40] or a propensity of all law. But focusing on Bonham-Carter J's transcription, translation, and interpretation of the songs, what becomes more intriguing is the unintentional affect of burlesque – of unselfconscious parody – of the failure of the legal word.[41] Read this way, the translations of the verse fade as a marker of the arrogance of imperial law, or the interpellation of the colonial subject, and rather instance the irrepressibility of local plurality and shared knowledge. The verses defy translation, not because they don't make historical geographical sense, as the judge proposes, but because they compact time and space to both celebrate Islamic integration and excoriate Arab incursion. The third line of the poem, "Wakikaa Waongofu,"

[37] Richard H. Weisberg, *Poethics and Other Strategies in Law and Literature* (New York: Columbia University Press, 1992).

[38] Robert M. Cover, "Nomos and narrative," *Harvard Law Review*, 97(4) (1983–4), 4–68.

[39] These include readings of the processes and reports of South Africa's Truth and Reconciliation Commissions, at www.justice.gov.za/trc/report/ – for example, Mark Sanders, *Ambiguities of Witnessing: Law and Literature in the Time of a Truth Commission* (Stanford: Stanford University Press, 2007) – and readings of Australia's *Report of the National Inquiry into the Separation of Aboriginal and Torres Strait Islander Children from Their Families*. See Rosanne Kennedy, "Subversive witnessing: mediating Indigenous testimony in Australian cultural and legal institutions," *Women's Studies Quarterly*, 36(1–2) (2008), 58–75; and Gillian Whitlock, "In the second person: narrative transactions in stolen generations testimony," *Biography*, 24(1) (2001), 197–214.

[40] Ngũgĩ wa Thiong'o, *Decolonising the Mind: The Politics of Language in African Literature* (Portsmouth: Hienemann Educational Publishers, 1986).

[41] Richard Weisberg, *The Failure of the Word* (Yale University Press, 1984).

translated as "upright," holds a meaning of enduring/steadfast/long-resident converts to Islam, against the last line, which may approximate to the reworked "Arab scum," but more accurately carries a specific warning to leave/stay away/keep to themselves. The preferred translation – that felicitous and unfaithful version – retains "Shihiri" as "Mshihiri" (the prefix accentuating the proper noun within the translator's understanding of Kiswahili). A reference to people from the Hadhramaut, the choice not to translate "Shihiri" might be aesthetic (a decision of rhythm or atmosphere), or it might suggest that a specifically hostile term for recent Hadrami migrants did not need translation in the local context.[42] As a moment of legal rhetoric and limit, the versions and reversions of the songs do not capitulate to either a hopeful or hopeless idea of the legal word. Rather, implicitly confounding and asserting ideas of being indigent and migrant, they suspend (if only momentarily) the judgment's reduction of how a right to land can be expressed.

Reading Three: Rights

Obverse and Universe

Today's human rights instruments are often read as irretrievably compromised by their continuity with the sly civilities of the imperial doctrine of repugnancy, a legal term of art allowing the curtailment of customary laws that did not measure up to a minimum standard of "natural morality and humanity" – in the terms of East African legislation of the early twentieth century[43] – or, in more widely circulating parlance, "justice, equity, and good conscience."[44] This joins to broader analyses of the airtight containment of "human rights" to citizens;[45] of rights as sinister tools of subject creation and intimate governance;[46] of "rights talk" as an impoverishment

[42] Many thanks to Ann Biersteker for the translation. [43] Read, "Customary law," p. 175.

[44] J. D. M. Derrit, "Justice, equity and good conscience" in Lauren Benton (ed.), *Law and Colonial Cultures: Legal Regimes in World History, 1400–1900* (Cambridge and New York: Cambridge University Press, 2002); Peter Fitzpatrick, "Terminal legality: imperialism and the (de) composition of law" in Diane Kirkby and Catharine Coleborne (eds.), *Law, History and Colonialism* (Manchester: Manchester University Press, 2001). More generally, see Bonny Ibhawoh, *Imperialism and Human Rights: Colonial Discourses of Rights and Liberties in African History* (Albany: State University of New York Press, 2007).

[45] Hannah Arendt's analysis sets prominent terms of engagement here. For an overview of her various articulations, see Peg Birmingham, *Hannah Arendt and Human Rights: The Predicament of Common Responsibility* (Indianapolis: Indiana University Press, 2004).

[46] For example Wendy Brown, "The most we can hope for...: human rights and the politics of fatalism," *The South Atlantic Quarterly*, 103(2–3) (2004), 451–63.

of political discourse;[47] of rights as an example of capitalism's colonization of "terms of freedom and emancipation";[48] of "the rights industry" as U.S. imperialism;[49] and of humanitarian intervention as a distraction from (not activation of) meaningful social rights.[50]

Alternatively, emphasis might be placed on the "anticolonialist 'capture' of the UN human rights project" in the post-World War II period to posit "human rights" as a qualitatively different mode of universalism: not imperialist reanimation, but true decolonization through attentive and supple cosmopolitanism.[51] This joins to broader discourses of hope that social rights may take on/take back meaning through a politics of staging and occupation,[52] or that a recuperation of rights from liberal discourse can be achieved through an understanding of "reciprocal recognitions" in a community,[53] or that "humanitarianism" can be a form of empathy unbound from the politics of aid.[54]

In the context of indigenous rights, the recuperation from criticism is typically historical and material. For example, in the draft UN Declaration on the Rights of Indigenous Peoples (UNDRIP), "Every paragraph ... is based upon known instances of the violations of the human rights of indigenous peoples. There is nothing theoretical, abstract, or speculative."[55] The gestation and final locutions of the 2007 UNDRIP are salutary, and not only because a "declaration" is a particularly nebulous or ductile form. UNDRIP "exists in an amorphous in-between state of constituting both a 'non-binding,' influential and aspirational statement of soft law" and "an instrument that reflects binding rules of customary

[47] For example Mary Ann Glendon, *Rights Talk: The Impoverishment of Political Discourse* (New York: The Free Press, 1991).

[48] For example Emilios Christodoulidis, "Strategies of rupture," *Law and Critique*, 20(1) (2008), 9.

[49] For example Austin Sarat and Thomas R. Kearns, "The unsettled status of human rights: an introduction" in Austin Sarat and Thomas R. Kearns (eds.), *Human Rights: Concepts, Contests, Contingencies* (Ann Arbor: The University of Michigan Press, 2001), p. 5.

[50] For example Vasuki Nesiah. "The specter of violence that haunts the UDHR: the turn to ethics and expertise," *Maryland Journal of International Law*, 24 (2009), 135–54; Jacques Rancière, "Who is the subject of the Rights of Man?" *South Atlantic Quarterly*, 103(2–3) (2004), 297–310.

[51] Samuel Moyn, *The Last Utopia: Human Rights in History* (Massachusetts: Harvard University Press, 2012), pp. 197; 176–227; 205.

[52] Rancière, "Who is the subject."

[53] Costas Douzinas, *The End of Human Rights: Critical Legal Thought at the End of the Century* (London: Hart, 2000).

[54] Joseph Slaughter, "Humanitarian reading" in Richard Ashby Wilson (ed.), *Humanitarianism and Suffering: The Mobilization of Empathy* (Cambridge and Massachusetts: Cambridge University Press, 2011), pp. 88–107.

[55] Matthew Coone Come (Grand Chief of the Grand Council of the Crees), quoted in Sarah Pritchard and Charlotte Heindow-Doulman. "Indigenous people and international law: a critical overview," *Australian Indigenous Law Reporter*, 3 (1998), 473, 477.

international law."[56] Debate also continues over the extent to which UNDRIP insists upon existing rights in recompense for past wrongs, and the extent to which it generates (or aspires to generate) new rights. Upbeat commentators highlight a tradition of official reference to UNDRIP within national contexts in which it has no official status. Others perceive an impasse between meaningful "self-determination" and state sovereignty, and often concomitantly see intractable theoretical and refractory political trouble between rights located in the individual and rights held by "collectives."[57] Partaking in these discussions, a body of critical work recognizes (and often suspects – even excoriates) a genre of human rights literary fiction that finds moral clarity in the promotion of civil and political rights.[58]

In all these exchanges, indigenous land rights under customary law as a distinct concept, as fundamental to the idea of "peoples," and as essential to "self-determination" are of enormous significance. But articulating these confluences can be a politically and linguistically congested feat, even for the most elegant thinkers: "a people must be presupposed to be self-determinative for them to be legally recognised as a people, but they acquire such legal capacity for self-determination only at the moment that they coalesce as a recognizable people."[59] So the coming together of a right as more than one right, as a lived and local idea and sensibility, might sometimes gather clarity and more robust sense through other means, such as verse:[60]

Shajara lina Wazee
Wanalizuia
Na kwamba nalo ningelitoa
Kulia Mwenye chakwe akikitambua

Your pedigree is kept back by Wazee.
If I had it I would have given it to you.
Then every man would know his own.

[56] Megan Davis, "To bind or not to bind: The United Nations Declaration on the Rights of Indigenous Peoples five years on." *Australian International Law Journal*, 19 (2012), 19.

[57] Davis, "To bind or not to bind," 19. For a review of the literature engaging these different interpretations, see also Antonio Cassese, *Self-Determination of Peoples: A Legal Reappraisal* (Cambridge and Massachusetts: Cambridge University Press, 1995).

[58] See, for example, Sophia A. McClennan and Alexandra Shultheis Moore (eds.), *The Routledge Companion to Literature and Human Rights* (London: Routledge, 2016).

[59] Joseph R. Slaughter, *Human Rights, Inc.: The World Novel, Narrative Form, and International Law* (New York: Fordham University Press, 2007), p. 220.

[60] An approach that is increasingly animating literature and law: for example, Kathleen Birrell, *Indigeneity: Before and Beyond the Law* (Abingdon: Glass House Books, 2016).

In the Three Tribes case, this third song is tendered as evidence of a dispute, forty years previously, over access to the spirit shrine. "Wazee" is not translated, not because it is difficult but because it is a common address to older/senior men; "pedigree" is perhaps better glossed as an appointed or ancestral situation. The song makes sense as the sheikh articulating his will to give his community access to the site. Bonham-Carter J "cannot find anything in this evidencing title to land."[61] This is because the verse is a tautology, as it comes from a desire to gift something that is already a given, and infers ownership by versifying the proclamation of ownership as an inference. Recognizing this might not promote the song as proof of freehold title, even combined with other evidence that the land was initially rented by the Three Tribes to an occupant who refused to leave and blocked access. But that it speaks of a right seems indisputable. On the one hand, the judgment makes the song seem ephemeral; on the other, as a situated legal moment, the verse also becomes a succinct enactment of the insight that "while rights are attributed to individuals . . . they are achieved and won collectively . . . the value of human agency arises from the fact that no one can be liberated by others, although no one can liberate herself or himself *without others*."[62] So tautology in the song does not parallel the hyperbole in which the "character" of human rights law "pretends to legislate for tautological (self-same and sovereign) subjects in the hope of realising such human rights subjects."[63] The tight turns of the verse rather shed a "residue of justice": they articulate something critical to the legal decision and moment, but something "incommensurate" with the court's available terms of recognition and meaning.[64]

Conclusion

Songs of Three Places

Reading literature in search of a critique of law, and reading law as a literature yet-to-come, are both resonant modes of promoting changes in

[61] *Abdullah bin Sheikh* at 63.

[62] Étienne Balibar, "Subjection and subjectivation" in Joan Copjec (ed.), *Supposing the Subject* (New York: Verso, 1994), p. 12.

[63] Slaughter, *Human Rights*, p. 215. Chapter 4 begins with Epeli Hau'ofa's Pacific island storytelling, but primarily offers this insight through a reading of Tsitsi Dangaremba's important novel of the intimate effects of the decolonization of Zimbabwe, *Nervous Conditions* (1988).

[64] Dimock, Wai Chee, *Residues of Justice: Literature, Law, Philosophy* (Oakland: University of California Press, 1996), pp. 1–10, and particularly her chapter on the adequacies and inadequacies of "Rights and reason," pp. 182–223.

postcolonial governance. To understand law as fiction has been to imagine a potential to "bring possibility into normatively determinate existence."[65] This has led to the hope that "the persistence of indigenous claims through law and right may lend further transforming force to the realization of law as fiction, the realization of its constantly created quality."[66] The judgment I have examined does not fortify such a futurity, even if it evidences a history of persistence. The verses – the songs in the place of the judgment – invite a different reading.

Consolidating his thoughts on "human rights" as a holding through repeated/distinct moments of "choice" and "revision," Homi Bhabha turns to Adrienne Rich's verse "Two: movement," from the poetic sequence "Inscriptions."[67] The poem asks the question "When does a life bend toward freedom?" and, in Bhabha's interpretation, it answers by describing "the complex scenario of politics as a transformational process" and through the articulation of a "belated" realization of the self only in the moments of its emergence as a "group subject": the moment of the I/you initially coming into being, as dialogue.[68] The poem leads Bhabha to write about freedom as a project of time, although there are moments in which he also sees it as a "terrain."[69] He doesn't address the next part in Rich's sequence, "Three: origins," which opens:

> Turning points.   We all like to hear about those.   Points
>   on a graph.
> Sudden conversions.   Historical swings.   Some kind of
>   dramatic structure.
> But a life doesn't unfold that way   it moves
> in loops   by switchbacks loosely strung
> around the swelling of one hillside toward another
> one island toward another[70]

In other words, we all like to hear about the law: by no means the least plausible meaning of this verse. Where Rich's "Two" brings space to political time, in "Three," time is secondary to images of place, although this

65 Peter Fitzpatrick, "Juris-fiction: literature and the law of the law," *ARIEL: A Review of International English Literature*, 35(1–2) (2004), 218.

66 Peter Fitzpatrick, "Necessary fictions: Indigenous claims and the humanity of rights," *Journal of Postcolonial Writing*, 46(5) (2010), 454.

67 Homi Bhabha, "Cultural choice and the revision of freedom" in Austin Sarat and Thomas R. Kearns (eds.), *Human Rights: Concepts, Contests, Contingencies* (Ann Arbor: The University of Michigan Press, 2001), pp. 45–62; Adrienne Rich, "Inscriptions" in *Dark Fields of the Republic: Poems 1991–1995* (New York: W.W. Norton and Co., 1995), pp. 59–73.

68 Bhabha, "Cultural choice," pp. 59–60.

69 Bhabha, "Cultural choice," p. 62.

70 Rich, *Dark Fields*, p. 63.

mostly throws into relief the poet's high valuing of words that press together time and space: not points, graphs, structures, but unfolding, bending, looping, swelling. In my readings of the juridical translation and interpretation of the three Kiswahili songs about two towers and Three Tribes, I've also found a compression of history and topography; of geography as expression of distant and recent histories of integration, threat, and occupation. But the verses are quoted as a proof of location, not exactly of an "origin," but of something materially fixed: A beginning is identified, with two towers, one shrine, three places – Three Tribes. A "backswitching" reading of Rich's poem might, then, draw attention away from "movement" and return to the site, the point, the one, two, three, not as that which is transcended, but as that which is established as the condition of movement: within Bhabha's reading, the movement of and for freedom. So it isn't that song can't abide material fixity, or that poetry liberates us from the fixities of the legal word; it isn't that the movements of literature freely flow with ethical corrections to the stultifying language of law. In a lower key, it is that the contingencies – the odd time and space of verse – might help to locate material aspirations for legal plurality in a postcolonial world.

PART III

Applications

CHAPTER 16

Literary Representation and Social Justice in an Age of Civil Rights: Harper Lee's To Kill a Mockingbird

Helle Porsdam

Harper Lee never liked to be in the public eye. Even in death, the author of *To Kill a Mockingbird* and *Go Set a Watchman* seemed "capable of remaining understated."[1] Her funeral was eclipsed by that of Justice Antonin Scalia of the U.S. Supreme Court, whose funeral mass took place on the same day, February 20, 2016. Whereas Washington paused for Justice Scalia's funeral, Lee was memorialized as she had lived: quietly and privately.[2] As one mourner noted on the website of the Johnson Funeral Home, which handled Lee's funeral, "Hey, Boo, you left your mark without a lot of fanfare. The recognition and praise seemed to roll off you like water from a duck's back."[3]

That the nation's leaders gathered for Scalia's funeral mass is not surprising. His funeral was only the second for a sitting justice in more than sixty years, and fierce battles over the seat his death had made vacant erupted within hours after his death was publicly announced. Scalia's tenure spanned almost three decades, and his death gave President Barack Obama the chance to fundamentally change the equilibrium of the Court by replacing a staunch conservative with a more liberal justice.[4]

Scalia was committed to the mode of constitutional interpretation known as "originalism," the theory that judges should hold the Constitution to the "public meaning" it had when it was adopted. Unlike lawyers

[1] Jennifer Crossley Howard, Katherine Webb and Serge F. Kovaleski, "Harper Lee is memorialized as she lived: quietly and privately," *New York Times*, February 20, 2016, www.nytimes.com/2016/02/21/us/harper-lee-is-memorialized-as-she-lived-quietly-and-privately.html.

[2] Peter Baker and Harris Gardiner, "Washington pauses for Justice Antonin Scalia's funeral," *New York Times*, February 20, 2016. www.nytimes.com/2016/02/21/us/politics/justice-antonin-scalias-funeral-lets-washington-pause-in-praise.html.

[3] Quoted in "Harper Lee is memorialized as she lived."

[4] This did not happen, however, as Senate Republicans refused to hold a hearing on the candidate Obama appointed to the Court. According to the U.S. Constitution, it is the president who appoints justices, but these appointments have to be confirmed by the Senate.

who argue that the Constitution is a "living" document that evolves and adapts to new circumstances over time through interpretation, Scalia saw it as a static, unchanging, and enduring document which should only be changed by the voters through the amendment process. The Court is part of the judicial branch of the national government, and Scalia wanted justices to defer to the political branch rather than to use their (interpretive) power to create new laws or policy whenever an issue came before the Court that had a political and not just a legal focus. Judicial restraint, he argued, is the best way to uphold the separation of powers – to prevent the Court from becoming a legislative body, impinging on the power of the legislative branch of the government.

It is judicial review – that is, the ability of a court to decide whether a statute, treaty, or administrative regulation contradicts or violates the provisions of existing law, a state, or the U.S. Constitution – that makes the issue of interpretation ("originalism" versus a "living Constitution") so extremely relevant, and which has turned the Supreme Court into such an important political player in American politics. Judicial review is not mentioned in the Constitution itself; it was asserted by the Supreme Court for the first time in the famous 1803 case *Marbury* v. *Madison*, in which the Court struck down an act of Congress as unconstitutional. That the judicial branch of the government, and especially the Supreme Court, would become so powerful was never envisioned by the Founding Fathers. Indeed, Alexander Hamilton famously called the judicial the "least dangerous branch" of the government in *The Federalist* No. 78.[5] The direction of the Court began to change early on, leading to the perpetual struggle at the intersection of law and politics that has since characterized American culture and society – and that has made the death of a justice and the appointment of his or her successor such headline news.

Harper Lee reacted to the tug-of-war between law and politics in much the same way that Justice Scalia did. She did not like the power of the Supreme Court, a federal legal institution, to decide on issues that are deeply political – and, in her opinion, also very regional. In a scene toward the end of *Go Set a Watchman* (Lee's second novel, which was published in

[5] In The Federalist No. 78, Hamilton wrote that "Whoever attentively considers the different departments of power must perceive, that, in a government in which they are separated from each other, the judiciary, from the nature of its functions, will always be the least dangerous to the political rights of the Constitution; because it will be least in a capacity to annoy or injure them." See Alexander Hamilton. "The Federalist No. 78" (1788), *Constitution Society*, www.constitution.org/fed/federa78.htm. See also Akhil Reed Amar. *America's Constitution: A Biography* (New York: Random House, 2005).

2015 but written before *To Kill a Mockingbird*), both Atticus and Jean Louise (as Scout is called as a grown woman) rather aggressively attack the most famous of all Supreme Court opinions, *Brown* v. *Board of Education of Topeka*. A landmark 1954 Supreme Court decision in which the Court declared state laws establishing separate public schools for black and white students to be unconstitutional, *Brown* has since become a civil rights milestone.[6] What bothers Atticus and Jean Louise about the Supreme Court decision is judicial overreach: the will to make law and fundamental constitutional rights trump politics – especially local, Southern politics.

This scene forms the point of departure for the second section of the present chapter, which concerns the federalism debate, the distribution of power between states and the federal government, and its relation to the issue of race. This section is preceded by one that explores race in/and American law, especially constitutional law. In the trailer to the 2010 documentary marking the fiftieth anniversary of the publication of *To Kill a Mockingbird*, "Hey Boo: Harper Lee and *To Kill a Mockingbird*," Oprah Winfrey calls the novel "our national novel."[7] Winfrey points to the portrayal and discussion of race relations as the primary reason why Lee's novel has come to occupy such an iconic space in the American cultural landscape. The federalism issue, especially when combined with the question of race, constitutes an additional reason, but the most important reason why *To Kill a Mockingbird* is considered one of the most striking literary representations of social justice in an age of civil rights is its preoccupation with the rule of law.

The rule of law and the importance of lawyers and courts is the focus of the third and final section of the chapter. The three issues of race, federalism, and the rule of law overlap with each other in significant ways, and they come together in the depiction of Atticus. Ultimately, this chapter argues, the reason why generations of readers have loved *To Kill a Mockingbird* is that Atticus Finch is presented to us, through the loving and naïve narrative of his daughter Scout, as the personification of that cornerstone of U.S. democracy, the rule of law. Whether or not he is the reactionary Southerner that *Go Set a Watchman* implies he is, what we come away with in the end is the portrayal of Atticus as the quintessential American lawyer.[8]

[6] James T. Patterson, *Brown v. Board of Education: A Civil Rights Milestone and Its Troubled Legacy* (Oxford: Oxford University Press, 2001).

[7] "Hey, Boo: Harper Lee and 'To Kill a Mockingbird': Trailer." *IMDb*, 2010. www.imdb.com/video/imdb/vi402781724l/.

[8] Several authors have engaged with law and literature in the American context. Among these may be mentioned Robert A. Ferguson, *Law and Letters in American Culture* (Massachusetts: Harvard

Race in/and American Law

One of the central plots of *To Kill a Mockingbird* involves Atticus Finch representing a black man accused of raping and beating a white teenager despite very little evidence pointing to the black man's guilt. Scout first hears about this in the schoolyard from one of the other kids. When he teases her by yelling that "Scout Finch's daddy defended niggers," she gets very angry with him and wants to start a fight.[9] This happens at the beginning of chapter 9. For the first eight chapters, we have only heard of life in regional Alabama – for, as Lee has Scout describe the situation: "The Governor was eager to scrape a few barnacles off the ship of state; there were sit-down strikes in Birmingham; bread lines in the cities grew larger, people in the country grew poorer. But these were events remote from the world of Jem and me."[10]

As always, when there is something she does not quite understand, Scout takes the matter up with Atticus. On the day that the issue of his involvement in the defense of Tom Robinson first comes up, she asks him point blank: "Do you defend niggers, Atticus?" When Atticus answers in the affirmative, Scout wants to know whether he thinks he will win this particular case. "No, honey," her father responds, but "if I didn't [defend Tom] I couldn't hold up my head in town, I couldn't represent this county in the legislature . . . Simply by the nature of the work, every lawyer gets at least one case in his lifetime that affects him personally . . . Simply because we were licked a hundred years before we started is no reason for us not to try to win."[11]

For the next few months, Scout and Jem have to endure one insult after another aimed at their father. They can deal with this as long as these insults come from other kids. But when old Mrs. Dubose, an adult, yells at them that their father is "lawing for niggers," Jem gets so angry that he reacts by cutting off all the tops of her camellia bushes. Atticus sends Jem back to apologize to the old lady and then uses the occasion to explain to his daughter that while he knows this is not fair on his children, "this case,

University Press, 1984); David Ray Papke, "Law in American culture: an overview," *Journal of American Culture*, 15(1) (1992), 3–14; Thomas Brook, *Cross Examinations of Law and Literature: Cooper, Hawthorne, Stowe and Melville* (Cambridge: Cambridge University Press, 1987); James Boyd White, *The Legal Imagination: Studies in the Nature of Legal Thought and Expression* (Boston: Little Brown & Co., 1973); Richard Weisberg, *The Failure of the Word: The Protagonist as Lawyer in Modern Fiction* (New Haven: Yale University Press, 2002).

9 Harper Lee, *To Kill a Mockingbird* (New York: Warner Books, 1960), p. 74.

10 Lee, *To Kill*, p. 116.

11 Lee, *To Kill*, pp. 75–6, 104.

Tom Robinson's case, is something that goes to the essence of a man's conscience – Scout, I couldn't go to church and worship God if I didn't try to help that man ... The one thing that doesn't abide by majority rule is a person's conscience."[12] It is his conscience, that is, that drives Atticus to give it his best as Tom Robinson's defense attorney – despite the fact that he well knows this is one case he will not win.

To Kill a Mockingbird was published in 1960, just six short years after the famous U.S. Supreme Court decision in the *Brown* v. *Board of Education of Topeka* case, and thus in the middle of the civil rights era. Most history books refer to the civil rights era as a discrete phase that happened between the 1950s and 1970s, but this mid-twentieth century struggle for racial equality was actually the pinnacle of a struggle that had begun long before that. Some call attention to the era of Reconstruction of the late 1860s and 1870s after the Civil War, but most historians would argue that we have to go all the way back to colonial America, to the beginnings of the new American republic, and to the institution of slavery to get the full picture.

The extent to which *Brown* helped spark the civil rights struggle of what has sometimes been referred to as the Second Reconstruction period has been much discussed by scholars of U.S. history. Some have argued that *Brown* was the culmination of what was essentially or primarily a legal fight for equal rights;[13] others have maintained that politics and social grassroots movements played just as important a role as courts and lawyers in the events that led to civil rights.[14] The answer is probably that it was the combined efforts of all of these groups that made the civil rights movement possible. As we are dealing with a novel one of whose most important plots revolves around a court case and the defense attorney in this case, however, our focus will be on the legal part of the civil rights struggle.

Though the words "slave" and "slavery" do not figure directly in the U.S. Constitution, the document did include three provisions that recognized and protected slavery. These were Article I, Section 2 (known as "the three-fifth clause"), which allowed states to count slaves as three-fifth persons for purposes of taxation and apportionment in Congress; Article I,

[12] Lee, *To Kill*, pp. 101, 104–5.

[13] For example, Michael J. Klarman, *From Jim Crow to Civil Rights: The Supreme Court and the Struggle for Racial Equality* (New York: Oxford University Press, 2006); Mark V. Tushnet, *Making Civil Rights Law: Thurgood Marshall and the Supreme Court, 1936–1961* (New York: Oxford University Press, 1996).

[14] For example Tomiko Brown-Nagin, *Courage to Dissent: Atlanta and the Long History of the Civil Rights Movement* (New York: Oxford University Press, 2012).

section 9, which expressly denied to Congress the power to prohibit importation of new slaves until 1808; and Article IV, Section 2 (known as "the fugitive slave clause"), which prevented free states from enacting laws protecting fugitive slaves.

Without these provisions, Southern delegates to the Constitutional Convention in 1787 would not have voted for the new Constitution. They were, in other words, necessary to achieve the sort of compromise without which the Constitution had no chance of being ratified. Slavery continued to be a divisive issue up through the Civil War period (1861–5). Southern states were afraid that at this point a majority might have developed in Congress in favor of abolishing slavery, and suggested that slavery be extended to new territories and states. *Dred Scott* v. *Sanford* came before the Supreme Court in 1856 and Chief Justice Roger B. Taney, delivering the opinion of the Court in March 1857, declared the 1820 Missouri Compromise (permitting slavery in Missouri, admitting Maine as a slave-free state, and establishing a boundary between free and slave regions across the former Louisiana Territory) unconstitutional, thereby making slavery permissible in all territories.

At the center of this case was Dred Scott, a slave who claimed to have obtained his freedom by living for a while in free territory before moving back to the slave state of Missouri. Using an originalist argument, Chief Justice Taney declared that because Scott was black, he was not a citizen and consequently had no right to bring suit in federal court – indeed, Scott could not be a citizen because, at the time the Constitution was adopted, blacks were considered "as a subordinate and inferior class of beings, who had been subjugated by the dominant race" and were regarded and treated "as an article of property." Furthermore, Taney wrote, "it is not the province of the court to decide upon the justice or injustice, the policy or impolicy, of these laws. The decision of that question belonged to the political or law-making power." If any provision of the Constitution was deemed to be unjust, the Constitution "may be amended; but while it remains unaltered, it must be construed now as it was understood at the time of its adoption."[15]

Abolitionists were enraged – and then decided to take Taney at his word and to work toward amending the Constitution. Before the Civil War ended, they had successfully lobbied Congress to pass the Thirteenth Amendment to the Constitution, which abolished slavery and authorized

[15] *Dred Scott* v. *Sandford*, 60 U.S. 393 (1857) at 404–5, 408, 405, 426. www.law.cornell.edu/supremecourt/text/60/393#writing-USSC_CR_0060_0393_ZO.

Congress to enact "appropriate legislation" implementing the abolition. Proposed and ratified in 1865, the Thirteenth Amendment helped implement the Reconstruction of the South after the Civil War. It was followed in 1868 by the Fourteenth Amendment granting citizenship to all persons "born or naturalized in the United States," including former slaves, and by the Fifteenth Amendment, ratified in 1870, which prohibited states from disenfranchising voters "on account of race, color, or previous condition of servitude." Of special importance for the civil rights era was the Due Process Clause of the Fourteenth Amendment. The Fifth Amendment refers to "due process" as one among several promises of protection that the Bill of Rights gives citizens against the federal government. In the middle of the twentieth century, a series of Supreme Court decisions made most of the important elements of the Bill of Rights applicable also to the fifty states, including "due process." The result was that citizens could now also claim "due process" protection from their state, and not just from the federal government. Together, these three amendments have since become known as the Reconstruction Amendments.

The struggle to fully achieve equality would continue into the twentieth century, with anti-civil rights segregationists putting up a fight every step of the way. One of the most notable fights involved yet another prominent court case: *Plessy* v. *Ferguson*. The case was heard by the Supreme Court in 1896 and upheld the constitutionality of state laws (in this particular case Louisiana state laws) requiring racial segregation in public facilities under the doctrine of "separate but equal." In his majority opinion, Justice Henry Billings Brown argued that "we consider the underlying fallacy of the plaintiff's argument to consist in the assumption that the enforced separation of the two races stamps the colored race with a badge of inferiority." As long as facilities for black schoolchildren were as good as those provided for white children, segregating schoolchildren was just fine; besides, "legislation is powerless to eradicate racial instincts or to abolish distinctions based upon physical differences."[16]

The "separate but equal" doctrine remained the law of the land until it was repudiated by the *Brown* decision in 1954. In a dissent, Justice John Marshall Harlan rebutted the view that federal legislation is powerless to do anything about racism. Stating, famously, that "our Constitution is color-blind, and neither knows nor tolerates classes among citizens," Harlan forcefully argued that state laws, such as the one from Louisiana, "regulating the enjoyment of civil rights upon the basis of race . . . under

[16] *Plessy* v. *Ferguson*, 163 U.S. 537 (1896) at 551. www.law.cornell.edu/supremecourt/text/163/537.

the pretence of recognizing equality of rights, can have no other result than to render permanent peace impossible and to keep alive a conflict of races the continuance of which must do harm to all concerned."[17]

Harlan's famous dissent, exposing the possible (and, in the case of the majority opinion in *Plessy*, also very real) relationship between states' rights and racism, takes us on to the debate concerning the distribution of power between the fifty states and the federal government.

The Federalism Debate

Toward the end of *Go Set a Watchman*, Jean Louise confronts her father about his participation in the Maycomb County Citizens' Council. Attending a meeting of the Council, she hears racist attitudes being voiced of a kind that she never thought Atticus would condone, let alone support. Atticus responds by asking her about her first reaction to "the Supreme Court decision." Considering this "a safe question," Jean Louise immediately answers:

> I was furious ... Well, it seemed that to meet the real needs of a small portion of the population, the Court set up something horrible that could – that could affect the vast majority of folks. Adversely, that is. Atticus, I don't know anything about it – all we have is the Constitution between us and anything some smart fellow wants to start, and there went the Court just breezily canceling one whole amendment, it seemed to me. We have a system of checks and balances and things, but when it comes down to it we don't have much check on the Court.[18]

The Supreme Court decision referred to here is the *Brown* one. Lee wrote *Go Set a Watchman* in 1957. This was three years after the Court handed down its unanimous decision, written by Chief Justice Earl Warren himself, which held that racial segregation of children in public schools violated the Equal Protection Clause of the Fourteenth Amendment, stating that "no state shall make or enforce any law which shall ... deny to any person within its jurisdiction the equal protection of the laws." This clause follows immediately upon the Due Process Clause, and these two clauses had come, by the mid-twentieth century, to be interpreted by the courts as being closely related.[19]

[17] *Plessy* v. *Ferguson* at 559, 560–1.

[18] Harper Lee, *Go Set a Watchman* (New York: Harper Collins, 2015), pp. 238–40.

[19] See entry on 'Due process,' *Legal Information Institute* (Cornell Institute Law Review): "If the courts stretched Fourteenth Amendment 'due process' to apply the Bill of Rights to the states, they

What makes Jean Louise so very angry is the way in which the Court has decided to let the Fourteenth Amendment trump another amendment, the Tenth Amendment: "Well, in trying to satisfy one amendment, it looks like they rubbed out another. The Tenth. It's only a small amendment, only one sentence long, but it seemed to be the one that meant the most, somehow."[20] The Tenth Amendment concerns the rights that are reserved to states or to the American people. Passed in 1789 as the last of the ten amendments forming the Bill of Rights, it evokes themes of popular sovereignty and emphasizes that the national government remains a government of limited and enumerated powers: "The powers not delegated to the United States by the Constitution, nor prohibited by it to the States, are reserved to the States respectively, or to the people."

Jean Louise sees the *Brown* opinion as an exercise of federal power (the Supreme Court heading the judicial branch of the federal government) that exceeds the national government's enumerated powers. As Atticus laughingly points out, she shows herself here as a true "states' rightist": "Sweet, you're such a states' rightist you make me a Roosevelt liberal by comparison."[21] This comes as something of a surprise not only to Jean Louise herself, but also to the reader, as it seems to contradict the character's views on race and her willingness to fight for the rights of African-Americans. The civil rights movement was to a large extent a federal movement and, as law professor Robert Schapiro points out,

> during the Civil Rights era, when Congress and federal courts were taking measures to end racial discrimination, the Tenth Amendment became associated with assertions of "states' rights" to resist claims of civil rights. The Tenth Amendment suffered from the assertion that the powers reserved to the states included the power to enforce racial inequality. Politically, socially, and morally, the Tenth Amendment seemed to speak to the past, not the present or the future.[22]

Shortly before asking his daughter about her reaction to the *Brown* decision, Atticus informs her that there are two reasons for his joining the Maycomb County Citizens' Council: the federal government, and the

stretched Fifth Amendment 'due process' to require the federal government to afford equal protection of the laws." www.law.cornell.edu/wex/due_process.

[20] Lee, *Go Set a Watchman*, p. 239. [21] Lee, *Go Set a Watchman*, p. 240.

[22] Robert Schapiro, "The disappearance and unfortunate revival of the Tenth Amendment," The Interactive Constitution, *National Constitution Center*, 2016. www.constitutioncenter.org/interactive-constitution/amendments/amendment-x/the-disappearance-and-unfortunate-revival-of-the-tenth-amendment-robert-sch/interp/15.

National Association for the Advancement of Colored People (NAACP).[23] Founded in 1909, the NAACP is the oldest, largest, and most widely recognized grassroots-based civil rights organization in the United States. From the very beginning, its leaders decided to pursue legislative and judicial solutions – that is, to work within the system by providing legal representation and aid to members. Its legal arm, the Legal Defense and Educational Fund (LDF), was founded in 1940 under the leadership of Thurgood Marshall, who subsequently became the first African-American U.S. Supreme Court Justice. In its first two decades, the LDF undertook a coordinated legal assault against officially enforced public school segregation. This campaign culminated in the *Brown* decision overturning the "separate but equal" doctrine of *Plessy* v. *Ferguson* from 1896, which, as we saw, legally sanctioned discrimination, widely known as Jim Crow.

Brown v. *Board of Education of Topeka* was a unanimous 9–0 decision – one of the very few in American constitutional history. In his opinion for the Court, Chief Justice Warren wrote that "today, education is perhaps the most important function of state and local government . . . It is the very foundation of good citizenship."[24] The question before the Court was whether the segregation of children in public schools on the basis of race deprived black children of equal educational opportunities, even though the physical facilities of their public schools were as good as those of the schools attended by white children. Warren famously concluded that separating children on the basis of race creates dangerous inferiority complexes that may adversely affect black children's ability to learn, and that "in the field of public education the doctrine of 'separate but equal' has no place. Separate educational facilities are inherently unequal."[25]

The *Brown* decision meant that, at least in the context of public schools, *Plessy* v. *Ferguson* was overruled. In the so-called *Brown II* case decided one year later, the Court ordered the states to integrate their schools "with all deliberate speed." Desegregation proceeded slowly, though, with resistance to *Brown I* and *II* being widespread in the South. With the "Declaration of Constitutional Principles" (known informally as the "Southern Manifesto"), issued and signed by nineteen Southern senators and practically the entire Southern delegation in the House of Representatives and published in the Congressional Record on March 12, 1956, Southern defiance reached a critical point. Senator Strom Thurmond of South Carolina, who had run

[23] Lee, *Go Set a Watchman*, p. 238.
[24] *Brown* v. *Board of Education of Topeka*, 347 U.S. 483 (1954) at 493.
[25] *Brown* v. *Board of Education* at 495.

for president on a states' rights ticket in 1948, was believed to be the mastermind behind the document. Attacking the *Brown* decision and pledging "massive resistance" to integration in the South, the "Southern Manifesto" brought up states' rights as a defense against "judicial usurpation" and urged Southerners to exhaust all "lawful means" in the effort to resist the "chaos and confusion" that would result from school desegregation: "We regard the decision of the Supreme Court in the school cases as clear abuse of judicial power. It climaxes a trend in the federal judiciary undertaking to legislate, in derogation of the authority of Congress, and to encroach upon the reserved rights of the States and the people."[26]

The reaction of many people in the South to *Brown I* and *II* was very similar to the one Atticus and Jean Louise have in *Go Set a Watchman*. "I'd like for my state to be left alone to keep house without advice from the NAACP . . . That organization has stirred up more trouble in the past five years," Atticus says to his daughter toward the end of *Go Set a Watchman*[27] – part of that trouble obviously being the *Brown* decision. To Atticus as to Jean Louise, race relations (and education) are matters for local or state government, not for the federal government – the Tenth Amendment being more important than the Fourteenth.

Many readers have a hard time reconciling the portrayal of Atticus in *To Kill a Mockingbird* with that in *Go Set a Watchman*. Whereas in the former, Atticus comes across as a very positive character, he is shown in the latter to be an upholder of a more traditional racial order who does not think the time has come for equality of the races. Some have argued, though, that the contrast between the Atticus in the two novels is but one of degree – that the Atticus defending an innocent black man accused of rape in *To Kill a Mockingbird* and the Atticus mistrusting civil rights in *Go Set a Watchman,* whose action is set some twenty years later, is essentially the same paternalistic white Southerner who believes he must help a minority that, in his view, cannot yet help itself.[28] In *To Kill a Mockingbird,* as Monroe Freedman had pointed out already in the early 1990s,

[26] "Declaration of Constitutional Principles: The Southern Manifesto (12 March 1956)," Congressional Record, 84th Congress, Second Session, vol. 102, 4459–4460, www.mrphillipshistory.wikispaces.com/file/view/Southern+Manifesto.pdf.

[27] Lee, *Go Set a Watchman*, p. 245.

[28] For example Adam Gopnik, "Sweet home Alabama," *New Yorker*, July 27, 2015, www.newyorker.com/magazine/2015/07/27/sweet-home-alabama); Michiko Kakutani, "Review: Harper Lee's 'Go Set a Watchman' gives Atticus Finch a dark side," *New York Times*, July 10, 2015, www.nytimes.com/2015/07/11/books/review-harper-lees-go-set-a-watchman-gives-atticus-finch-a-dark-side.html?_r=0; Randall Kennedy, "Harper Lee's *Go Set a Watchman*," *New York Times* July 14, 2015, www.nytimes.com/2015/07/14/books/review/harper-lees-go-set-a-watchman.html.

Atticus is appointed by the judge to defend Tom Robinson; he does not volunteer. Also, he never contradicts the obviously racist remarks made by some of his neighbors, just as he challenges neither the obvious racial exclusion of blacks from the jury that wrongly convicts Tom Robinson nor the racial segregation in the courtroom itself, where blacks have to sit on the balcony.[29]

There is an additional way in which the depiction of Atticus in both of Lee's novels is consistent. Cautious and conservative as he may be when it comes to the pace of racial change, Atticus is utterly dedicated to the rule of law. As Adam Gopnik writes in his *New Yorker* review of *Go Set a Watchman*, in both novels, "Atticus's central commitment is to the law, and that commitment is never questioned. We are meant to see Atticus as someone with skewed convictions about Jefferson, but not as someone who would participate in a cross burning or in fire-hosing protesters."[30] It is to Atticus and his commitment to the rule of law that we shall now turn.

The Rule of Law and Its Importance in American Culture and History

"There are some men in this world who were born to do our unpleasant jobs for us," Miss Maudie, a good friend of the Finch family, tells Scout and Jem at some point. "Your father's one of them . . . Atticus Finch won't win, he can't win . . . well, we're making a step – it's just a baby-step, but it's a step."[31] Small as it is, though, Atticus' step very nearly costs him his son's life. Jem is only saved after Bob Ewell's vicious attack by the intervention of the reclusive outsider Boo Radley – the personification of the frail mockingbird, symbolizing hope and innocence that should never be destroyed, alluded to in the title of the novel.

When Miss Maudie talks to Atticus' children about their father helping to make a baby-step, she is thinking of the kind of action that may become a first important – if only symbolic – step in the fight for civil rights. She is referring not to his private life, but to race relations in American history. It is as a lawyer that Atticus makes his baby-step. The courtroom is his stage, and one of his finest moments occurs during the trial of Tom Robinson. Not normally what Scout calls "a thunderer," Atticus takes off his coat and loosens his tie before addressing the jury in a voice that "had lost its aridity, its detachment."[32] In a straightforward manner, Atticus walks the

29 Monroe H. Freedman, "Atticus Finch – right and wrong," *Alabama Law Review*, 45 (1994), 473.
30 Gopnik, "Sweet home Alabama." 31 Lee, *To Kill*, pp. 215–16. 32 Lee, *To Kill*, pp. 204–5.

jury through the facts of the case and the absolute lack of evidence of Tom's guilt, and then ends with this magnificent defense of the rule of law in the United States:

> But there is one way in this country in which all men are created equal – there is one institution that makes a pauper the equal of a Rockefeller, the stupid man the equal of an Einstein, and the ignorant man the equal of any college president. That institution, gentlemen, is a court. It can be the Supreme Court of the United States or the humblest J.P. court in the land, or this honorable court which you serve. Our courts have their faults, as does any human institution, but in this country our courts are the great levelers, and in our courts all men are created equal.[33]

There is admittedly a certain discrepancy between the opinion Atticus voices to Jean Louise about the Supreme Court in *Go Set a Watchman* and his talk here about courts, including the Supreme Court, as "the great levelers." Yet, we are given to understand, it is the human dimension that can make things go wrong. It is the way in which the law is interpreted that makes the system vulnerable. Given the need to relate general rules and principles to particular sets of facts in legal cases, legal personnel may bring their own cultural values into the courtroom, including their racial beliefs and various cultural biases. In *To Kill a Mockingbird*, when Jem is enraged about the verdict of the jury in the Robinson case, Atticus tries to explain to him that "the one place where a man ought to get a square deal is in a courtroom, be he any color of the rainbow, but people have a way of carrying their resentments right into a jury box."[34]

Open as it is to manipulation and prejudice, the legal system is however still perceived to offer the best chance for justice. What we see Atticus voicing is the belief in the rule of law as the project of an American democratic community. In my book *Legally Speaking*, I use the phrase "leap of legal faith" to describe the allegiance to the law as a force for social change and social cohesion to which many Americans – scholars and writers as well as others – seemingly pledge themselves, knowing full well that the law has fabricated its own authority and authenticity. Exposing the rottenness at the core of American democracy by means of showing the sorry state in which the legal system currently finds itself, they still move on to affirm the promise of fundamental legal rights expressed in the Constitution and other legal texts that form the foundation for American nationhood.[35]

[33] Lee, *To Kill*, p. 205. [34] Lee, *To Kill*, p. 220.

[35] Helle Porsdam, *Legally Speaking: Contemporary American Culture and the Law* (Amherst: University of Massachusetts Press, 1999), pp. 248–9.

Law figures prominently in American culture and society. This is reflected in the cultural life of the nation: Countless are the cultural texts – from literary texts to TV series, films, and other manifestations of popular culture – that reflect the way in which the law has become the forum for discussions of issues of importance to Americans.[36] *To Kill a Mockingbird* is one of the most prominent examples, with Atticus at the center as the exemplary attorney fighting for the rights of the oppressed and adhering to legal values, including that of the Fourteenth Amendment, amid a segregationist culture or Jim Crow worldview.

American commitments to the ideal of law are not new. In one of his earliest speeches, Abraham Lincoln spoke about "the political religion" of the United States – a political religion which, he argued, has a lot to do with "reverence for the laws":

> Let reverence for the laws be breathed by every American mother to the lisping babe that prattles on her lap; let it be taught in schools, in seminaries, and in colleges; let it be written in primers, spelling-books, and in almanacs; let it be preached from the pulpit, proclaimed in legislative halls, and enforced in courts of justice. And, in short, let it become the political religion of the nation.[37]

Lincoln's notion of an American "political religion" was anticipated by Alexis de Tocqueville, the young French aristocrat who spent nine months touring the United States in 1831. Originally sent by the French government to study the American prison system, Tocqueville and a partner ended up collecting information on American society in general. *Democracy in America* was published in two volumes, the first in 1835 and the other in 1840, and soon became a classic. Pondering the characteristics of the new, exciting phenomenon of American democracy, Tocqueville argued that it had at its very core the importance of law:

> There is hardly a political question in the United States which does not sooner or later turn into a judicial one. Consequently the language of everyday party-political controversy has to be borrowed from legal phraseology and conceptions. As most public men are or have been lawyers, they apply their legal habits and turn of mind to the conduct of affairs. Juries make all classes familiar with this. So legal language is pretty well adopted into common speech; the spirit of the law ... infiltrates through society

[36] Porsdam, *Legally Speaking*.

[37] Abraham Lincoln, "Address Before the Young Men's Lyceum of Springfield, Illinois," 1838, www.abrahamlincolnonline.org/lincoln/speeches/lyceum.htm.

> right down to the lowest ranks, till finally the whole people have contracted some of the ways and tastes of a magistrate.
>
> In the United States the lawyers constitute a power which is little dreaded and hardly noticed; it has no banner of its own ... but it enwraps the whole of society, penetrating each component class and constantly working in secret upon its unconscious patient, till in the end it has molded it to its desire.[38]

America could best be described, Tocqueville furthermore claimed, as an association of people/immigrants who came from numerous places throughout the world but who held in common certain self-evident truths. Both Lincoln and Tocqueville came close to describing law as a secular, or even a civil, religion.[39]

Referring, in a new book, to Lincoln and his reverence for law, Paul Kahn sums up nicely how the idea of law as a civil religion still resonates: "Lawyers may have a bad reputation, but America remains a country that defines itself by the rule of law. We cannot think of ourselves apart from this commitment to law. Americans are bound together not by a common ethnicity or religion but by the rule of law that begins, but hardly ends, with the Constitution."[40]

Concluding Remarks

In his 1964 Nobel Peace Prize lecture, "The Quest for Peace and Justice," Martin Luther King pointed to three problems which, though appearing to be separate, were inextricably connected: racial injustice, poverty, and war. The only way forward, he argued, was to focus on "the positive affirmation of peace," to work toward a "worldwide fellowship that lifts neighborly concern beyond one's tribe, race, class and nation in a call for an all-embracing and unconditional love for all men," and to make use of that "unique" weapon in history "which cuts without wounding and ennobles the man who wields it" – namely, nonviolence. What should be done, King maintained, was to elevate the concept and "tool" of nonviolence to the level of international affairs – to make it an object of study and serious experimentation in every field of human conflict. He realized that when he spoke of "compassion" and "love" people might think him

[38] Alexis de Tocqueville, *Democracy in America* (New York: Doubleday, 1969), pp. 270.

[39] Helle Porsdam (ed.), *Civil Region, Human Rights, and International Relations: Connecting People Across Cultures and Traditions* (Chatham: Edward Elgar, 2012).

[40] Paul W. Kahn, *Making the Case: The Art of the Judicial Opinion* (New Haven: Yale University Press, 2016), p. 10.

naïve and sentimental, and emphasized that he saw love as the key to that "Hindu-Moslem-Christian-Jewish-Buddhist belief about ultimate reality" which all the great religions have seen as "the supreme unifying principle of life" – an ecumenical rather than a sectional principle.[41]

King's Nobel Lecture reflects the way in which he increasingly saw his fight for civil rights both as a fight that linked civil and political rights to economic rights and as a part of a more global fight for decolonization and human rights.[42] The inspiration on which he drew for the creation of a worldwide fellowship was twofold: his religious views and his belief in human dignity. As a minister, King believed God to be the fundamental source of human worth or dignity, but because of his own encounters with racism he understood early on that the continued practice of racial discrimination marred the sense of human dignity among his fellow African-Americans. Much of his work was consequently devoted to helping to restore – first in his own people and then in people around the world who were also discriminated against – their lost sense of dignity and self-respect.[43]

Forty-four years after King delivered his Nobel Peace Prize lecture, both the overarching leitmotif and one of the six cross-cutting themes chosen to mark the sixtieth anniversary of the Universal Declaration of Human Rights was "dignity and justice for all of us." The idea behind the theme was to reinforce the vision of the Declaration as a commitment to universal dignity and justice, and not something that should be viewed merely as a luxury or an item on a wishlist. No longer explicitly related to religion – which is not mentioned in the description of any of the six cross-cutting themes – the leitmotif of the sixtieth anniversary of the Universal Declaration still recalls King's work toward providing access to justice in practice for all marginalized people around the world.

During the civil rights era, African-Americans fought to be included in the American dream, to gain access to those rights and freedoms outlined in the Constitution that would enable them to lead a life in dignity and self-respect. Many of them, King included, looked to law as a non-violent means by which change could be accomplished. Other minorities followed suit by seeking integration into American society via the courts and by

[41] Martin Luther King Jr. "The quest for peace and justice," Nobel Peace Prize Lecture (1964), www.nobelprize.org/nobel_prizes/peace/laureates/1964/king-lecture.html.

[42] Thomas F. Jackson, *From Civil Rights to Human Rights: Martin Luther King Jr. and the Struggle for Economic Justice* (Philadelphia: University of Pennsylvania Press, 2007).

[43] Rufus Burrow, *God and Human Dignity: The Personalism, Theology, and Ethics of Martin Luther King Jr* (Notre Dame: University of Notre Dame Press, 2006).

using law as an empowering discourse. Some writers have since become disillusioned with the achievements of civil rights litigation. In his 1996 book *Gospel Choirs*, Derrick Bell, who was affiliated with the movement known as Critical Legal Studies, wrote about the civil rights lawyers with whom he had worked in the early 1960s, commenting for example that "in urging the use of law and litigation as the major means to end racial discrimination, we acted in good faith. We failed, however, to recognize that even the most clearly stated protections in law can be undermined when a substantial portion of the population determines to ignore them."[44] To Bell, civil rights judgments were propounded in a social climate that did not accept their legitimacy, and this meant that the growth of real equality was retarded.

To some of Bell's contemporaries, this dismissal of the value of rights talk and civil rights litigation was problematic in that it failed to see how much of a motivational, even semireligious source of hope the prospect of attaining full rights under the law had been for blacks. "'Rights' feels new in the mouths of most black people," Patricia Williams wrote a couple of years earlier. "In discarding rights altogether, one discards a symbol too deeply enmeshed in the psyche of the oppressed to lose without trauma and much resistance."[45] Oddly out of tune, in its insistence on rights rhetoric as an effective and empowering discourse for blacks, with contemporary (and current) intellectual tendencies toward cultural relativism, such a belief reflects a wish to use the law to do good – to see law as the kind of nonviolent instrument toward furthering universal dignity and self-respect that King talked about in his Nobel Lecture. If only at the symbolic level, Williams argued, civil rights worked as a yardstick, an ideal worth striving for as well as a device for securing a fairer society. Today, human rights may be said to work in much the same way, the vision of the authors of the Universal Declaration of Human Rights being to further peace and cooperation in the world.[46]

It is this vision of law as hope for a better future, this willingness to perform a leap of legal faith in spite of being perfectly aware that the legal system is marred by human error and bias, that Atticus Finch personifies, and that makes *To Kill a Mockingbird* exemplary of a broader capacity of

[44] Derrick Bell, *Gospel Choirs: Psalms of Survival for an Alien Land Called Home* (New York: Basic Books, 1996), p. 53.

[45] Patricia Williams, *The Alchemy of Race and Rights: Diary of a Law Professor* (Massachusetts: Harvard University Press, 1991), pp. 164–5.

[46] Helle Porsdam, *From Civil to Human Rights: Dialogues on Law and Humanities in the United States and Europe* (Cheltenham: Edward Elgar, 2011).

literature to represent the struggle for rights.[47] Generations of readers have loved Atticus for at least attempting to provide resolutions to seemingly insolvable problems. Lee managed in her famous novel to show the way in which legal discourse is the type of discourse often used in the American context for addressing issues of importance and for negotiating competing positions.

[47] The same is true for other American cultural manifestations such as reality TV court shows. Helle Porsdam, "Television judge shows" in Michelle Brown (ed.), *Oxford Research Encyclopedia of Crime, Media, and Popular Culture* (New York: Oxford University Press); http://criminology.oxfordre.com/view/10.1093/acrefore/9780190264079.001.0001/acrefore-9780190264079-e-197?rskey=8xxnPr&result=93.

CHAPTER 17

Trauma, Narrative, and Literary or Legal Justice

Golnar Nabizadeh

Introduction

Shoshana Felman suggests that the two world wars and other disastrous events of the twentieth century "brought to the fore the hidden link between trauma and the law," and that this link was "dramatized" for the twenty-first century in the aftermath of the destruction of the World Trade Center's twin towers through the event's widespread transmission on our television screens.[1] Traumatic events such as these shape social, economic, and political contours, and domains of inquiry such as the law come to bear the imprint of those contours in their genealogy. Significantly, the law has increasingly come to recognize victims' claims through the understanding that testimony may be communicated in more complex ways than were previously understood. Within this context, the term "dramatized" reminds us that the ways in which traumatic events are remembered, forgotten, or silenced depends on the stories that accumulate within the breach that instantiates trauma, and how these narratives are focalized.

There are tensions between the law on the one hand, and the recognition of trauma on the other; in many cases, the law traumatizes, grounded in violence as Felman suggests, while in others, evidentiary requirements may occlude some trauma – or traumatized – narratives.[2] Yet this tension can also produce a valuable impulse, so that the recognition of trauma – and those affected by it – propels legal reform. As Steven Winter suggests, one of the "most important aspects of the field of law and humanities is its insight into the constitutive and contingent character of our communicative practices," and as such, trauma and the law continue to abrade

[1] Shoshana Felman, *The Juridical Unconscious* (Cambridge and London: Harvard University Press, 2002), p. 2.

[2] Felman, *The Juridical Unconscious*, p. 270.

against one another, gathering meaning through this process.[3] Felman's focus on the impact of trauma on judicial proceedings – captured most evocatively in her writing on the Eichmann and O. J. Simpson trials, respectively – intersects with the work of literary and legal scholars exploring the possibilities of narrating trauma within the "theatre of justice," to use Yasco Horsman's term, among them Mark Sanders, Michael Rothberg, Cathy Caruth, and Dori Laub. Indeed, in twentieth-century critical literature on trauma there is a remarkable tradition of thinkers who have written on what can be loosely described as trauma theory, such as Sigmund Freud, Walter Benjamin, Paul Ricoeur, Hannah Arendt, and Theodor Adorno, whose respective works have in turn helped shape the field of law and literature.

Derived from the Greek term for "wound," trauma (both psychic and physical) occupied a central role in the analysis of historical and cultural events in the twentieth century and continues to do so in the twenty-first. In *Beyond the Pleasure Principle* (1920), Freud posited that trauma, through the process of introducing an overwhelming shock to the subject, creates a problem whereby the subject struggles to master "the amounts of stimulus which have broken in and of binding them, in the psychical sense, so that they can be disposed of."[4] The excessive stimuli disrupt the subject's conventional relationship to his or her world and must in turn be somehow discharged. In modern parlance, post-traumatic stress disorder (PTSD) was first used to diagnose Vietnam War veterans who experienced "uncontrollable symptoms such as depression, anxiety, nightmares, flashbacks, and insomnia," and its diagnosis continues to be refined in medical and cultural texts, such as the *Diagnostic and Statistical Manual of Mental Disorders* (DSM), currently in its fifth edition.[5] The literary analysis of trauma has often posited the latter as a phenomenon that devastates the lifeworld, and which paves the way for intrusive psychic phenomena to replay the impact of shock within the subject. Taking after Freud, Felman has suggested that "trauma – individual as well as social – is the basic underlying reality of the law," because of the way that individuals are regulated through the operation of the social order from infancy.[6] Given that communal, social, and

[3] Austin Sarat, Matthew Anderson, and Cathrine O. Frank (eds.), *Law and the Humanities: An Introduction* (New York: Cambridge University Press, 2010), p. 21.

[4] Sigmund Freud, *Beyond the Pleasure Principle* (trans. John Reddick) (London and New York: Penguin Books, 2003 [1920]), p. 301.

[5] Jeannie Suk, "Laws of trauma" in Austin Sarat (ed.), *Knowing the Suffering of Others: Legal Perspectives on Pain and Its Meanings* (Tuscaloosa: University of Alabama Press, 2014), p. 213.

[6] Felman, *The Juridical Unconscious*, p. 172.

individual traumata shape cultural frameworks in surprising, productive, and profound ways, it is not surprising that literary narratives, hinged as they are on the art of representation, offer fruitful ways through which we might imagine and formulate what constitutes trauma. How then do literary narratives articulate this deviation, and how does the law grapple with the same?

In response, this chapter will pursue two distinct, yet interrelated avenues of inquiry: first, what is the relationship between trauma and narrative in contemporary legal proceedings; second, how do graphic novels and comics communicate and articulate demands for literary justice when the legal domain fails, in part or altogether, to afford a platform for testimony? The scope of this enquiry is necessarily limited, but will proceed in three steps: first, it explores the relationship between trauma, comics, and visual archives; second, it turns to contemporary analyses of trauma narratives in modern legal proceedings; third and finally, close readings of comics from the twentieth and twenty-first centuries – specifically Safdar Ahmed's "Villawood: Notes from an Immigration Detention Centre" (2015), Winsor McCay's "Little Sammy Sneeze" (1904–6), and Henry Yoshitaka Kiyama's *Four Immigrants Manga* (1931) – demonstrate the narrative strength of the comics medium for illuminating the intersections between trauma narratives and the law.

Trauma and the Law

In *The Juridical Unconscious*, Shoshana Felman suggests that a new jurisprudential dimension arises out of the encounter between the law and trauma, and draws attention to the ways in which law can be a vehicle for injustice through "structural blindness" to issues such as gender and trauma. Specifically, Felman emphasizes her interest in missed encounters between the law and would-be testimony, and the way in which these gaps and silences perform their own narrativity.[7] In a practical sense, interdisciplinarity between legal studies, narrative, and memory studies has recognized the impact of trauma not only on the ability of witnesses, for example, to provide testimony, but also on the complex ways in which memories are encoded. In common law countries, precedent accretes not only through the repetition of principles, but also through their adjustment where the facts and circumstances of a case are considered to properly call for distinction. More radically, there are occasions when the

[7] Felman, *The Juridical Unconscious*, p. 144.

impact of traumatic events is such that the genealogy of the law – what we might consider its structural DNA – must metamorphose to attempt to meet the demands of trauma.

This is one of Felman's central theoretical concerns in *The Juridical Unconscious*, and one that highlights the significance of recognizing narratives that at first may appear muddled, unhelpful, or tangential, but yet which carry within them an important meaning or communication. For Felman, the missed encounter illuminates the limits of the latter as it abuts against silenced narratives to "*reveal* precisely cultural aspects of its traumatic meaning."[8] Taken this way, the cultural interpretation of trauma narratives offers valuable insights into the human condition by taking time to interpret their abstruse and often difficult meanings.[9]

Contemporary approaches to the law demonstrate a keen awareness of how memories may be variably shaped. For example, in its report on uniform evidence law, the Australian Law Reform Commission (ALRC) stated: "There is evidence to suggest that traumatic memory in this sense has its own features distinct from memory for emotional events."[10] In another report, on family violence, the ALRC drew on an earlier report by Professor Robert Chisholm which considered the "victim's dilemma" in proceedings where the complainant seeks orders in respect to family violence. Chisholm suggests that the victim's dilemma may be compounded because "the trauma of family violence may lead the victim to be somewhat unorganised, anxious or depressed, and, for such reasons, an unimpressive witness."[11] Taken together, one can see how the shock of trauma and the potentially ongoing effects of traumatic memories might complicate the ability of a witness (or bystander) to provide testimony – or, in other words, to *narrate* the scene of trauma within the confines of conventional narrative structures, legal or otherwise. Indeed, the legal domain is not alone in its anxiety about the expression of trauma narratives deviating from veracity; as Leigh Gilmore explains, the autobiographical tradition has typically shared this concern:

[8] See note 25 of chapter 4 in Felman, *The Juridical Unconscious*, p. 233. See also Christine Krueger, "Gendered credibility: testimony in fiction and indecent assault" in *Reading for the Law: British Literary History and Gender Advocacy* (Charlottesville: University of Virginia Press, 2010), pp. 157–85.

[9] For further reading on this point see Dori Laub, "Bearing witness or the vicissitudes of listening" in Dori Laub and Shoshana Felman (eds.), *Testimony: Crises of Witnessing in Literature, Psychoanalysis, and History* (New York: Routledge, 1992), pp. 57–73.

[10] *Uniform Evidence Law* (ALRC Report 102), December 2005, 252. On the topic of "trauma and memory" generally, see [8.109]–[8.111].

[11] Richard Chisholm, *Family Courts Violence Review* (2009), pp. 27–8. Cited in *Family Violence – A National Legal Response* (ALRC Report 114), October 2010, p. 834.

> Telling the story of one's life suggests a conversion of trauma's morbid contents into speech, and thereby, the prospect of working through trauma's hold on the subject. Yet, autobiography's impediments to such working through consist of its almost legalistic definition of truth-telling, its anxiety about invention, and its preference for the literal and verifiable, even in the presence of some ambivalence about those criteria.[12]

Gilmore's reference to the "almost legalistic definition of truth-telling" in autobiographical stories demonstrates the broad cultural reach of testimony as a legal construct. The purpose of this chapter, then, is to consider how these conjunctions between law and literature permit, if not demand, us to carefully think through how trauma might be narrated and how we, as listeners and adjudicators, may test the frameworks against which we test the value of that narration.

Shoshana Felman's rereading of Hannah Arendt's description of K-Zetnik (Mr Yehiel Dinoor) in *Eichmann in Jerusalem* provides a striking case in point. K-Zetnik was a writer (or chronicler, to use terminology closer to his own) who fainted while providing testimony at the Eichmann trial, his pseudonym standing for "concentration camp victim."[13] Contrary to Arendt's dismissive approach to K-Zetnik, Felman's reading of the faint suggests that the witness's inability to testify demonstrates the trauma writ large through his body as well as his words, thereby recognizing the significance of his narrative. Moreover, for K-Zetnik, the past is not, as the law would have it, in the past, but rather urgently present. This is evident in his testimony, which shifts from past to present tense as he remembers the ongoing absences left by his fellow inmates at Auschwitz: "They left me, they kept leaving me, left . . . for close to two years they left me and always left me behind . . . I see them, they are watching me, I see them –"[14] At this point, the prosecutor interrupts in an attempt to redirect the witness's evidence, but K-Zetnik continues to affirm the presence of the absent others through his address, before falling into a faint.

In this extract, the phrase "left me" is repeated several times, and with the benefit of hindsight, its hypnotic rhythm seems to provide a linguistic clue that its speaker is about to take leave of the courtroom setting as he

[12] Leigh Gilmore, "Limit-cases: trauma, self-representation, and the jurisdictions of identity," *Biography*, 24(1) (2001), 128–39, here 129. It is worthwhile noting that the category of "life-writing," a term that has gained widespread use, signals a move away from these conventions, as it recognizes the inherent unreliability of the postmodern speaking subject, and the diffusion of the subject rather than a unified whole.

[13] Felman, *The Juridical Unconscious*, p. 135.

[14] Felman, *The Juridical Unconscious*, p. 136. Ellipses in original.

remains entrenched within the scene of the trauma. His faint housed within it a paralytic stroke, and Felman suggests that for K-Zetnik the trial "re-enacts the trauma" of his time in Auschwitz, so much so that when the trial judge urges the witness to "obey – strictly to answer questions and to follow legal rules" in his response, this "impacts the witness *physically* as an invasive call to order by an SS officer."[15] Felman notes that contrary to Arendt's assumptions in *Eichmann in Jerusalem*, K-Zetnik was a reluctant witness, urged by the chief prosecutor to testify before the court as he was one of the few witnesses to have actually met Eichmann at Auschwitz.[16] As the court ordered a recess, the presiding judge Moshe Landau stated "I do not believe we can go on," echoing the witness' own grievous state. In this example, one can discern the limits of the law as it meets trauma, and the ways in which this limit can be productively interpreted (in this case by Felman) to carve out a broader understanding of how narrative can function through multiple layers of signification. Importantly, while K-Zetnik's testimony may at first appear to resist the demands of the law for "useful" testimony, this very resistance speaks to the enormity of the scene he attempts to narrate. And this is where the conjunction of law and literature articulates a verdant field of inquiry.

As legal scholar Thomas Giddens elucidates, "[a]s a broadly aesthetic or humanities-based approach to legal studies, engagement with various forms of art as alternative discourses on legal and jurisprudential issued is a key feature of law and humanities." He adds that "the relationship of the visual to the textual, of the aesthetic to the rational, and of all of these to the 'legal' are central concerns in law and humanities' interdisciplinary blending."[17] Focusing on the work of comics allows us to investigate an alternative discourse on the law, and offers a vitalizing field within which to explore the relationship between law and literature, thanks to the diffusion and interplay of meaning between aesthetics, text, and narrative that comics perform through their particular strategies of representation.

Comics and Narrating Trauma

The confluence between law and visual apprehension is not a new phenomenon. From the early modern figure of Justitia to the use of diagrams

[15] Felman, *The Juridical Unconscious*, p. 146. Emphasis in original.
[16] Felman, *The Juridical Unconscious*, p. 143.
[17] Thomas Giddens, "Comics, law, and aesthetics: towards the use of graphic fictions in legal studies," *Law and Humanities*, 6(1) (2012), 87.

to explain the rules of evidence in law schools, the visual aspects of law (and legal theory) have long been an implicit aspect of its discourse. As Costas Douzinas and Lynda Nead argue, far from being a hermetic and predominantly linguistic domain of meaning, "law has always had a visual policy," and its "force depends partly on the inscription on the soul of a regime of images." They continue that "[t]he power of spiritual, edifying icons is celebrated in every courtroom: in the wigs, robes, and other theatrical paraphernalia of legal performance and in the images of justice that adorn our public buildings."[18] The visual signification of the law – both within material and imaginary regimes – helps to substantiate its jurisdiction, as it were.

To choose another example, Peter Goodrich notes Andrea Alciato's invention in 1531of the "emblem book," whose publisher concluded that the book's didactic messages would be enhanced through the inclusion of woodcut illustrations alongside 97 of the 104 maxims.[19] The co-mixing of words and images provided the reader-viewer of the emblem book ample affective space within which to contemplate the meaning of the illustration, not only in its relation to the text but also as a visual evocation of the law. The etymology of the term "emblem," from the Greek for "to throw in" or "insert," along with its Latin inflection meaning an "inlaid ornamental work," already gesture toward the significance of the artifact as a signifier of iconic and iterative value. In the emblem book, images were used to assist the reader in imagining and understanding the rules or conventions described therein. If we move our gaze to contemporary literary narratives, and specifically graphic novels and comics, we can see that the interdependent valences of image and text are still being utilized to great effect. Here I am not attempting to draw a direct link between the emblem book and comics, but only to observe the ongoing relationship between narrative, affect, and visual representation.

In the West, comics have enjoyed a marked resurgence since the 1970s, particularly in the rich proliferation of autobiographical narratives. Works such as Justin Green's *Binky Brown Meets the Holy Virgin Mary*, as well as Keiji Nakazawa's *Ore Wa Mita* (*I Saw It*), both published in 1972, offered remarkable accounts of trauma of different orders: Green's sets out the vicissitudes of growing up with what came to be diagnosed as obsessive-compulsive disorder, whereas Nakazawa describes the disorienting torment

[18] Costas Dounizas and Lynda Nead (eds.), *Law and the Image: The Authority of Art and the Aesthetics of Law* (Chicago: Chicago University Press, 1999), p. 9.

[19] Peter Goodrich, "Screening the law," *Law & Literature*, 21(1) (2009), 10.

of his first-hand encounter with the atomic bomb dropped on Hiroshima. In turn, Art Spiegelman's Pulitzer Prize-winning *Maus* (1980–91), itself highly influenced by Green's *Binky Brown*, utilized the comics format to visualize and imagine aspects of his father's experiences in Auschwitz, and inspired the creation of many works that have since joined the pantheon of autobiographical comics.[20] Each of these titles explores the laws of cultural convention, from Binky Brown's anguished questioning of his Catholicism through to the implementation of racial profiling in Spiegelman's *Maus*. Beyond the genre of autobiographical comics, traditional superhero comics from DC Comics and Marvel have used disaffection with the law and justice to explore questions about justice, truth, and legality in series such as Superman, Batman, and Justice League of America.[21] In these works and others, readers can see the ways in which their creators use the power of images to undermine, complicate, or reinforce other layers of narrative signification.

In the independent comics genre, works such as Joe Sacco's *Palestine* (1996) and Emmanuel Guibert and Didier Lefèvre's *The Photographer: Into War-Torn Afghanistan with Doctors without Borders* (2006) demonstrate the impact of domestic and international law in relation to humanitarian crises, and the direct consequences of the law in the lives of Palestinian and Afghani people. The co-constitutive relationship between words and images in comics generates a richly layered reading practice that is ideally suited to depicting how ideas about the law, and literary justice, can diverge and converge across different contexts. As Giddens explains, the interaction between words and images "is a key dimension of the [comics] medium, both giving the form a special epistemological orientation and enabling its analysis to engage with important questions in relation to legal theory."[22] Importantly, as these elements work together, they retain their signifying power as discrete bundles of information, generating meaning as they maintain a productive narrative tension.

[20] See Marianne Hirsch, "The generation of postmemory," *Poetics Today*, 29(1) (2008), 103–28 and "Mourning and postmemory" in Michael Chaney (ed.), *Graphic Subjects: Critical Essays on Autobiography and Graphic Novels* (Madison: University of Wisconsin Press, 2011), pp. 17–44.

[21] On the term "autographics," see Gillian Whitlock and Anna Poletti, "Self-regarding art," *Biography*, 31(1) (2008), vxxiii. This term is taken up by, among other scholars, Joseph Darda in "Graphic ethics: theorizing the face in Marjane Satrapi's *Persepolis*," *College Literature: A Journal of Critical Literary Studies*, 40(2) (2013), 31–51; Julia Watson, "Autographic disclosures and genealogies of desire in Alison Bechdel's *Fun Home*," *Biography*, 31(1) (2008), 27–58; Golnar Nabizadeh, "The after-life of images: archives and intergenerational trauma in autographic comics" in Dana Mihăilescu, Roxana Oltean, and Mihaela Precup (eds.), *Mapping Generations of Traumatic Memory in American Narratives* (Newcastle upon Tyne: Cambridge Scholars Publishing, 2014), pp. 171–91.

[22] Giddens, "Comics, law, and aesthetics," 89.

Moreover, this interaction of word and image allows comics creators, and their readers, to encounter spaces in which the lacunae that seemingly mark the rendition of trauma can literally take shape on the page. For example, in Sacco's *Palestine*, the retrospective authorial voice is contained within boxes placed at unusual angles within the page, requiring the reader to pay close attention to the text as it jostles (and is jostled by) the images it accompanies. The reader must constantly adapt his or her eyeline to take in the political realities of living under Occupation, and this reading practice provides a haptic, representational analogue of the complications that mark the lives of many Palestinians.

The "symbolic space" of comics is fashioned out of panels and the spaces in between them (the "gutter") on the page.[23] Perhaps most importantly for the purposes of looking at trauma, the arrangement of the panels allows the artist to play with the representation of time, such that the panels mark time through their physical dimensions and rhythmic properties. For example, a panel with an extended width might be interpreted as incorporating a longer duration in time than a panel of equal height but shorter width. Similarly, a panel without a frame may be regarded as having broken through framing conventions, as a visual representation of the disorienting or dissociative impact of trauma on the individual subject. This device is present through variable aesthetic designs in the work of artists dealing with traumatic events such as *Maus*, Marjane Satrapi's *Persepolis* (2003/4), GB Tran's *Vietnamerica* (2010), or *Stitches* (2009) by David Small. Another element that unites these works is that they are hand-drawn by their creators, and bear these indexical marks within their respective narratives. This is significant not only because of the creativity that the medium generates, but also in the way that these images diversify the visual archive – or create one where other visual records, such as photographs or video, are prohibited. In this way, we can wonder what it means to bear witness through the comics form where other material forms of memorialization are difficult or impossible.

Comics present a productive capacity to shape, process, and materialize trauma narratives because of the medium's ability to hold and represent narrative complexity. One of the practical ways in which comics can resist the limits of the law is by circumnavigating prohibitions against making photographic or audiovisual recordings. Where comics are hand-drawn, they can provide historical and archival value to documenting events where

[23] Yasco Horsman, *Theatres of Justice: Judging, Staging and Working Through in Arendt, Brecht, and Delbo* (Stanford: Stanford University Press, 2011), p. 8.

other modes of record are absent. For example, Art Spiegelman has noted the impact of encountering hand-drawn images by prisoners at Auschwitz and other concentration camps as he conducted research for *Maus*, stating that these images signposted a "return to an earlier function that drawing served before the camera – a kind of commemorating, witnessing, and recording of information."[24] Effectively, these drawings provided some of the few literal insights into camp life, a form of visual record in the absence of others. *Maus* would go on to generate an enormous amount of critical and popular debate about trauma and forms of representation in graphic narratives.

The value of hand-drawn images remains just as urgent in contemporary contexts. For example, in Australia, the judges of the 2015 Walkley Awards awarded Safdar Ahmed, a Sydney-based artist and academic, first prize in the "All Media Artwork" category for his online graphic narrative "Villawood: Notes from an Immigration Detention Centre."[25] In their comments, the judges noted that "[p]hotos are not permitted within Villawood Detention Centre, so Ahmed has conveyed through his graphic novel style the conditions within the Detention Centre" to produce "a moving documentation of [the inmates'] plight, and a damning condemnation of Australia's detention system."[26] Hand-drawn images, then, continue to function as a vital form of expression, particularly where there is a dearth of other points of contact or communication, or indeed where other forms of visual record, such as photographs, are used to promote fear and suspicion.

The use of photographic evidence to establish the occurrence of particular events was, in an Australian context, the subject of a Senate inquiry into "A Certain Maritime Incident," popularly known as the "children overboard" incident, which examined a chain of events in the leadup to a federal election in 2001.[27] Specifically, the inquiry investigated an announcement in October 2001 by the then Minister for Immigration, Mr. Philip Ruddock, that "a number of children had been thrown overboard" from a vessel, SIEV (Suspected Illegal Entry Vessel) 4, as it was

[24] Art Spiegelman, *MetaMaus: A Look Inside a Modern Classic* (London: Penguin Books, 2011), p. 49.

[25] Safdar Ahmed, "Villawood: notes from an immigration detention centre," *The Shipping News*, March 5, 2015, https://medium.com/shipping-news/villawood-9698183e114c#.iv8obia2s.

[26] "GetUp! – The Shipping News, 'Villawood: notes from an immigration detention centre,'" *The Walkley Foundation*, June 29, 2016, www.walkleys.com/walkleys-winners/safdar-ahmed/.

[27] "A Certain Maritime Incident," October 23, 2002, Select Committee on a Certain Maritime Incident, *Commonwealth of Australia*, June 27, 2015, www.aph.gov.au/Parliamentary_Business/Committees/Senate/Former_Committees/maritimeincident/report/index.

intercepted by the Australian Defence Force. A photograph was released that appeared to depict this event, with the implication that refugees on board the SIEV 4 had thrown their children overboard in an attempt to obtain passage to Australia. Among its terms of reference, the Committee examined "Federal Government control of, and use of, information about the incident, including . . . photographs, videotapes and other images," and eventually found that "[p]hotographs released to the media on 10 October as evidence of children thrown overboard on 7 October were actually pictures taken the following day, 8 October, while SIEV 4 was sinking."[28] The manipulation of images is commonplace: as Richard K. Sherwin observes, "[i]mages are routinely produced and broadly disseminated in support of assertions of public necessity, emergency, and patriotism." Here Sherwin refers specifically to then U.S. Secretary of State Colin Powell's "visually assisted performance at the United Nations" proving that Iraq was generating so-called "weapons of mass destruction."[29] Against the would-be evidence of "compelling" and bite-sized images such as those from Iraq and SIEV 4, comics often require readers to slow down their reading, as images are generally read alongside text or other information that complicate their ostensible meanings.

As Teresa Phelps suggests, articulations of life narratives worldwide frequently "reveal human rights abuses that have been carefully hidden by a legal system." She refers to such examples as the storytelling of the Mothers of the Plaza de Mayo in Buenos Aires, the Stolen Generation in Australia, and detainees in Guantanamo. These examples illuminate the animating power of what Phelps calls "transformative storytelling," which is equally apparent in the study of comics and graphic narratives.[30] As "an artistic organization of space," comics create a space of play and innovation as each panel propels the action forward.[31] For example, in "Villawood," Ahmed describes his experiences working as a volunteer for refugees held within Villawood Immigration Detention Centre, and his story

[28] "Executive Summary," October 23, 2002, Select Committee on a Certain Maritime Incident. *Commonwealth of Australia*, June 27, 2015. www.aph.gov.au/Parliamentary_Business/Committees/Senate/Former_Committees/maritimeincident/report/a06.

[29] Richard K. Sherwin, "What screen do you have in mind? contesting the visual context of law and film studies," *Studies in Law, Politics, and Society*, 46 (2009), 11. See also: Richard Sherwin, *When Law Goes Pop: The Vanishing Line Between Law and Popular Culture* (Chicago: University of Chicago Press, 2000).

[30] Teresa Godwin Phelps, "'Reading as if for life': law and literature is more important than ever," *Studies in Law, Politics, and Society: Law and Literature Reconsidered* (Special Issue) 43 (2008), 148–9.

[31] Mieke Bal, *Travelling Concepts in the Humanities: A Rough Guide* (Toronto: University of Toronto Press, 2002), p. 97.

incorporates artwork drawn by refugees from Burma, Sri Lanka, Iran, and Afghanistan. In one passage he quotes an Iranian refugee who describes his plight in seeking asylum as a "legal maze" where "[o]ur stories are doubted at every step by case managers, immigration officials and judges who make it their job to reject us." Below this speech bubble, Ahmed draws an oversized gavel hovering above an individual lying on the sound block. Next to this image, the reader observes a small off-kilter frame that depicts the gavel finding its mark with a terrifying "THWACK" rendered in red. The reader's interpolation within this sequence allows him or her to understand that the individual has symbolically been crushed under the gavel or force of the law. This simple sequence delivers its meaning through both a literal and a metaphorical system of signification, and demonstrates the ability of comics to succinctly convey different orders of meaning.

Another example, an early comic strip by the artist Winsor McCay called *Little Sammy Sneeze* (1904–6), depicts how comics play with narrative and expectations around how stories are framed and focalized. In this strip, the eponymous character's enormous sneeze develops over the course of each episode, its release often wreaking havoc on what is seemingly the main action, usually in the form of a benign social event. In one strip, however, McCay isolates the action of the sneeze, and demonstrates its power not only within the internal logic of the action but also on the framing of the story (Figure 17.1: *Little Sammy Sneeze*).

In this example, we can literally discern the incisive ability of comics to depict the disruption of convention by materializing this deconstruction through a visual metanarrative. Further, this sequence generates meaning through its rhythm; as readers, we absorb the significance of not only each individual panel but also their overall progression, including the increasing size of Sammy's speech bubbles. That is, the final shatter of the frame acquires its particular meaning because we understand that in a conventional sense, comics panels are not meant to be broken. Unlike film, where each frame replaces its predecessor (although viewers may certainly replay, pause, and remember iconic scenes), in comics the frames generally sit adjacent to one another, so that the reader apprehends the contents of the page as a whole (what Molotiu calls "iconostasis"), as well as the individual units of time that constitute each panel.[32]

[32] Andrei Molotiu defines "iconostatis" as "the perception of the layout of a comics page as a unified composition." See "Sequential dynamism and iconostasis in abstract comics and Steve Ditko's *Amazing Spider-Man*" in Matthew J. Smith and Randy Duncan (eds.), *Critical Approaches to Comics: Theories and Methods* (London and New York: Routledge, 2012), p. 91.

Figure 17.1: Winsor McCay, *Little Sammy Sneeze*, *New York Herald*, 24 September 1905

Our understanding of this progression implicitly draws on another critical aspect of comics: the sustained presence of the past on the page. As we focus on the representation of trauma as a structure whereby the past does not remain occluded in time, but breaks forth into the present, we can see how comics artists may choose to play with the visual depiction of trauma by repeating images, or shuttling forth between the present and the past in their respective stories. Indeed, as Crawley and van Rijswijk suggest, "[g]raphic novels can resist law's demands for interpretative and normative finality by drawing our attention to the structural or endemic traumas which constitute legal subjectivity, and the representational practices through which meaning – and justice – become possible."[33]

Indeed, the plasticity of the medium means that it holds open the possibility of visualizing trauma through the perspective of subjects who have experienced its ruptures. Moreover, there is ample evidence that the ways in which communal, cultural, and personal traumas are represented in the comics medium – such as in Sacco's *Palestine*, Art Spiegelman's *In the Shadow of No Towers* (2004), or Phoebe Gloeckner's *A Child's Life*

[33] Karen Crawley and Honni van Rijswijk, "Justice in the gutter: representing everyday trauma in the graphic novels of Art Spiegelman," *Law Text Culture*, 16(1) (2012), 95.

(1998), to mention only a few titles – literally draw attention to the challenges and opportunities of narrating subjectivity through creative and innovative practices.

By deferring normative finalities, to use Crawley and van Rijswijk's phrase, comics allow other narrative possibilities to emerge, possibilities that may illuminate unexpected voices and ideas about justice. If we consider that in comics the past remains materially present, we can wonder whether comics might allow their creators and audiences to remember, and even mourn, traumas that might have been impossible, or illegal, to acknowledge in other forms of record. Michael Rothberg suggests that "[t]o mourn is to move on, but to render justice is to maintain the claims of the past on the present or to maintain the present's interest in the past."[34] Here, Rothberg is referring to the analytical framework of critical melancholia, developed by scholars such as Judith Butler, Ranjana Khanna, and Mark Sanders to think through ideas about justice, and the claims of the past on the present. What might be termed structural melancholy complements Felman's suggestion that, in contradistinction to the "discipline of limits" or law, "[w]e needed art – the language of infinity – to mourn the losses and to face up to what in traumatic memory is not closed and cannot be closed."[35] One can argue that comics precisely incorporate this melancholic condition into their structure, whereby the reader generally remains aware of the presence of the past alongside the present.

Four Immigrants Manga

A little-studied comic from the early twentieth century, *The Four Immigrants Manga: A Japanese Experience in San Francisco, 1904–1924* by Henry Yoshitaka Kiyama, amply demonstrates the ways in which hand-drawn images can supplement historical archives. Described as a "documentary" comic book, this work depicts the (mis)adventures of four young *Issei* (Japanese-Americans) – who adopt the names Henry, Fred, Frank, and Charlie – following their arrival in San Francisco in 1904. Through Kiyama's pen, the episodes provide a unique vantage point on events such as the San Francisco Earthquake of 1906 (and a visit to the city by Dr. Fusakichi Ōmori, a famous seismologist, in the quake's aftermath),

[34] Michael Rothberg, "After apartheid, beyond filiation: witnessing and the work of justice," *Law & Literature*, 21(2) (2009), 277.

[35] Shoshana Felman, "Theatres of justice: Arendt in Jerusalem, the Eichmann trial, and the redefinition of legal meaning in the wake of the Holocaust," *Critical Inquiry*, 27(2) (2001), 202.

the Panama-Pacific International Exposition (1915), and the arrival of Japanese migrants from Hawaii, as well as sociocultural phenomena such as the popularity of so-called "picture brides" and the rise of the Asiatic Exclusion League, which advocated the segregation of all "Asian" children in San Francisco schools. Kiyama himself immigrated to the United States in 1904; the character of Henry appears as the author's avatar and, like Kiyama, studies art at what was at the time the influential Mark Hopkins Institute of Art, before being rebuilt as the San Francisco Institute of Art in the aftermath of the San Francisco Earthquake.

One of the innovations of Kiyama's text is that the original comic was bilingual – written in Japanese and English. This feature allowed Kiyama not only to incorporate the relatively limited English with which the characters speak, but also to convey the mode in which they understand the language as spoken around them (most notably by their employers). Kiyama hand-lettered these "foreign" words in broken English to distinguish them from the Japanese. This technique allowed him to literally draw attention to the other dialects that the characters encounter, such as that of a Chinese character that speaks Japanese hesitantly. I argue that the wavy, attenuated line of Kiyama's lettering depicts the hesitation and the newness of the culture with which Henry and the other characters grapple. Significantly, the names that the main protagonists acquire once in the United States are hand-lettered, and the reader has the impression that these names are being sounded out in ways similar to the characters' testing of their new cultural and physical environments. In these ways, Kiyama depicts the vulnerability of unfamiliarity and the opportunity to test new contours via the indexical form of hand lettering in his comic. This vulnerability is also evident in the spoken dialogue of episode 49, entitled "The Alien Land Act." Here, Charlie and his wife eat dinner with their six children. After bidding the children goodnight, the couple discuss the impact of the Alien Land Act on the right of non-US citizens to own land (Figure 17.2).

After noting that they are lucky because they can transfer title to their US-born children, Charlie notes, "In the twenty years I've been here, there've been laws passed against immigrants from Hawaii, picture brides, and now even our *owning land!*" The final panel on this page depicts his wife responding despondently, "I guess we Japanese immigrants don't have much of a future here, *do we?*"[36] It is unclear why Kiyama left the dates

[36] Italics in original. Henry Yoshitaka Kiyama, *The Four Immigrants Manga: A Japanese Experience in San Francisco, 1904–1924* (trans. Frederik L. Schodt) (California: Stone Bridge Press, 1999), p. 126.

EPISODE 49

The Alien Land Act

Figure 17.2: *Alien Land Act.*

blank here, but the date should presumably read November 1920, when the Californian legislature passed a second set of laws that sought to eliminate loopholes associated with the original Alien Land Act introduced in 1913. In this sequence, the reader is offered an intimate rendering of the Act's potential impact on Charlie's family and the injustice of discrimination, as well as an idea about how he and his wife can retain title. Charlie's observation in the final panel conveys his first-hand experience of the impact of the law in a way that is immediately tangible. His wife appears to face the reader in this scene, and her expression subtly conveys the frustration and hurt of facing discriminatory laws such as the provisions under the Alien Land Act.

One can argue that here Kiyama's text performs the work of cultural witnessing, to use Felman's term – that is, he lays before the reader legal and social challenges, as well as the overt racism endured by Japanese-Americans, in ways that would have been exceedingly rare to encounter in popular forms of record in the early twentieth century. Brian M. Hayashi echoes this sentiment, explaining that the *Four Immigrants Manga* is "a rare first-generation Japanese immigrant literary publication translated into English."[37] As Gains and Cho explain, the Alien Land Act was eventually found to "be an unconstitutional infringement of the right of American citizens (the children born of alien parents in the United States)."[38] Through his rendition of a domestic scene, Kiyama's work allows its readers to visualize not only the Act as a historical document of the law, but also its intimate and tangible impacts on Japanese-American families in the early twentieth century.

Conclusion

The preceding discussion identified only some of the attributes of comics that make them a highly productive medium through which issues of justice, human rights, and trauma are illuminated anew. The way in which the comics bring together multiple and frequently divergent layers of signification allows artists and readers to experiment with how meaning is generated. The burgeoning field of Graphic Justice, which considers issues such as the use of comics to critique the law and the relationship between aesthetics and popular representations of the law, as well as using

[37] Brian M Hayashi, "Not so funny papers," *Pacific Historical Review*, 69(2) (2000), 278.

[38] Brian J. Gaines and Wendy K. Tam Cho, "On California's 1920 Alien Land Law: the psychology and economics of racial discrimination," *State Politics and Policy Quarterly*, 4(3) (2004), 276.

visual devices as a means of providing more clarity on legal processes, for example, is a testament to the important interstices between cultural, visual, and jurisprudential domains of inquiry.

The law and literature project emphasizes the importance of narration, and narrative strategies, to the understanding of the law. The work of witnessing, so central to the experience of trauma, has been recognized as a pivotal repository of meaning, shaped by an oft-precarious relation to language and speech. Within this breach, where the laws of speech may themselves falter, recognizing other attempts at communication becomes even more pressing. The crossmodality of comics, where images and text representing the past, present, and future interact through conscious and unconscious points of contact, offers a single domain in which trauma, representation, narrative, and the law can be explored and imagined. The refusal to close off narrative possibilities characterizes many of the texts that have been considered here, and this resistance speaks of the tenacity and hope that surely mark endeavors to narrate literary and legal forms of justice.

CHAPTER 18

The Regulation of Authorship: Literary Property and the Aesthetics of Resistance

Robin Wharton

> Article 7: Item, It is a dangerous thing, as witnesseth blessed St. Jerome, to translate the text of the holy Scripture out of the tongue into another; for in the translation the same sense is not always easily kept, as the same St. Jerome confesseth, that although he were inspired, yet oftentimes in this he erred; we therefore do decree and ordain, that no man, hereafter, by his own authority translate any text of the Scripture into English or any other tongue, by way of a book, libel or treatise . . . in part or in whole, privily or apertly, upon pain of greater excommunication, until the said translation be allowed by the ordinary of the place, or if the case so require by the council provincial. He that shall do contrary to this, shall likewise be punished as a favourer of error and heresy.[1]

Arundel's *Constitutions* were published in England in 1409 in an attempt to regulate preaching and vernacular biblical translation, among other things. The *Constitutions* are just one example in a long history of legal interventions designed to control authors and ensure the ideological purity of the fruits of their labors. This essay addresses modern intellectual property law, rather than censorship, as its primary subject matter. At the outset, however, I want to make clear that the roots of literary property, in both common and statutory law and in literary practice itself, predate copyright by centuries. To provide a definitive history of the origins and evolution of the concepts of author, authorship, and literary property in just the Anglo-American legal and literary traditions would require far more than the space I have been allotted here. Instead, I am using this chapter in a volume on law and literature to begin answering some questions related to how copyright law functions as an area of applied humanities. Copyright law is

[1] Article VII of Arundel's *Constitutions* in Nicholas Watson, "Censorship and cultural change in late-medieval England: vernacular theology, the Oxford translation debate, and Arundel's *Constitutions* of 1409," *Speculum*, 70(4) (1995), 828–9. Note 25, citing John Foxe, *The Acts and Monuments of John Foxe*. Ed. George Townshend (New York, AMS Press, 1965), vol. 3, p. 245.

a site where literary concepts determine legal outcomes, and consequently exert significant influence on the economy and human behavior. First, I want to consider the aesthetics of literary property as they have emerged in American copyright law and try to understand literary property as an object of interdisciplinary study and discourse. Second, I will elucidate some of the significant regulatory consequences of the current understanding of literary property for authors, artists, teachers, and scholars. Finally, in a more speculative mode, to the extent that copyright law requires judges and juries to apply concepts drawn from literary studies when making determinations about what constitutes literary property and whether that property has been infringed, I ask whether we can imagine an aesthetics or narrative poetics of resistance that would serve the interests of individuals, free speech, the public domain, and artistic expression, rather than corporations and cultural monopolies.

A number of scholars have studied the connection between censorship and copyright.[2] The two might at first appear to be at odds with one another. Censorship laws seek to limit the circulation of works containing certain ideologically dangerous or illicit content, while copyright is ostensibly content-neutral legislation aimed at promoting the free circulation of ideas and a robust public domain. Nevertheless, both bodies of law provide a mechanism through which the judicial system manages and controls cultural production. By encouraging authors to take ownership of their texts, copyright law arguably clarifies the targets of censorship, libel, and obscenity laws. Further, even though copyright may not explicitly regulate content, it nevertheless has the effect of encouraging some modes of cultural production while discouraging others.[3] Some acts of authorship are rewarded, while others – such as copying – are punished. Finally, as I will explain in more detail below, some of the aesthetic and ideological judgments about which texts are worth reading and making, and which are not, that are or have been previously embodied in censorship, libel, and obscenity laws inform the judicial concept of literary property, which is that species of intangible *intellectual* property that copyright protects.

[2] See, for example, Jody Greene, *The Trouble with Ownership : Literary Property and Authorial Liability in England, 1660–1730* (Philadelphia: University of Pennsylvania Press, 2005); Richard Dutton, *Licensing, Censorship, and Authorship in Early Modern England: Buggeswords* (London: Palgrave MacMillan, 2000).

[3] Derek Lowe, "'Poems so materially different': eighteenth-century literary property and Wordsworth's mechanisms of proprietary authorship in the 1800 Lyrical Ballads," *Studies in Romanticism*, 55(1) (2016), 12–14. In this recent study, Lowe examines how the evolving legal concept of literary property influenced both Wordsworth's poetry and the composition of the second edition of *Lyrical Ballads*.

By manipulating the shape and contours of literary property as it is defined in statutes and judicial opinions, lawmakers and judges not only regulate the production and circulation of tangible commodities in which that property is embodied, but also directly and indirectly regulate relationships among and the behavior of authors and users. By examining how copyright jurisprudence has constructed literary property from a hodgepodge of the common law of real and moveable property and literary aesthetics, we can learn something about where the law relies most heavily on extralegal ideas about authors, poetics, "Literature," and artistic creation, and where it may therefore be most vulnerable to productive reinterpretation.

Authors and the Things They Make

A copyright is distinct from the literary property it covers, similar to how a deed or title is distinct from the plot of land or moveable chattel over which it conveys ownership. Copyright is a legal construct, but literary property is a strange hybrid, part law, part applied literary scholarship. A copyright has an owner. Literary property has an author, which is itself yet another legal/literary hybrid. As an object of study and regulation, literary property yokes, or sutures, or interpenetrates two discursive communities – law on the one hand, and literary studies on the other. For example, if I simply copy a large chunk of text from one of the most recent articles about my current subject matter from a prestigious journal, I infringe the journal's copyright – that is, the exclusive license to publish that the journal has been given by the author – but I plagiarize the author. Similarly, a work in the public domain is no longer subject to copyright of any sort, but I would nonetheless still be plagiarizing if I passed that work off as my own. When I ask whether we can read an aesthetics of literary property from copyright law, I am looking to identify the features of an object of scrutiny that is shared between legal and literary study, and to understand how that object functions as a kind of discursive conduit through which these two modes of cultural production inform one another.[4]

[4] My methodology presumes the literary property with which these two related but distinct discourses are concerned is a singular object, rather than two different things that share a name. This presumption is grounded in the identity of literary property as a commodity, and is supported by recent work in literary and cultural studies. See, for example, Michael Wreen, "The ontology of intellectual property," *The Monist*, 93(3) (2010), 433–49; Chad Luck, *The Body of Property: Antebellum American Fiction and the Phenomenology of Possession* (New York: Fordham University Press, 2014); José María Durán, "Artistic labor and the production of value: an attempt at a Marxist interpretation," *Rethinking Marxism*, 28(2) (2016), 220–37.

One of the most fundamental characteristics of literary property is that it comes into being through the labor of an author.[5] As Foucault observes in "What Is an Author?":

> The author's name manifests the appearance of a certain discursive set and indicates the status of this discourse within a society and a culture. It has no legal status, nor is it located in the fiction of the work; rather, it is located in the break that founds a certain discursive construct and its very particular mode of being. As a result, we could say that in a civilization like our own there are a certain number of discourses endowed with the "author function" while others are deprived of it. A private letter may well have a signer – it does not have an author; a contract may well have a guarantor – it does not have an author. An anonymous text posted on a wall probably has an editor – but not an author.[6]

Here Foucault is thinking through how authors function as discursive or epistemological identifiers. In delineating the characteristics of those "discursive sets" endowed with the "author function," as opposed to those like the "anonymous text posted on a wall" which "probably has an editor – but not an author," Foucault reveals an implicit aesthetics that distinguishes literary property – those discursive sets associated with an author – from everything else. Thus for Foucault, literary property is arguably intended for public consumption (perhaps because it becomes a "discourse" through public circulation); private letters do not have authors. Literary property is more than utilitarian legal boilerplate; contracts do not have authors. Advertisements, graffiti, notices, and billboards, while they are public, are not literary property because, being anonymous, they are by definition authorless.

Copyright law preserves this connection between authorial labor and literary property:

(a) Copyright protection subsists, in accordance with this title, in original works of authorship fixed in any tangible medium of expression, now known or later developed, from which they can be perceived, reproduced, or otherwise communicated, either directly or with the aid of a machine or device. Works of authorship include the following categories:
 (1) literary works;
 (2) musical works, including any accompanying words;
 (3) dramatic works, including any accompanying music;

[5] Durán, "Artistic labor," 221.

[6] Michel Foucault, "What is an author?" in James D. Faubion (ed.), *Essential Works of Michel Foucault: Aesthetics, Method, and Epistemology* (New York: The New York Press, 1998), vol. 2, p. 211.

(4) pantomimes and choreographic works;
(5) pictorial, graphic, and sculptural works;
(6) motion pictures and other audiovisual works;
(7) sound recordings; and
(8) architectural works.[7]

As described in Title 17 of the United States Code, section 102 "Subject matter of copyright: In general," the literary property covered by U.S. copyright law includes any "work of authorship fixed in any tangible medium of expression." Absent from the legal definition, however, are any of the aesthetic or formal limitations Foucault suggests. Works of authorship can be published or unpublished. They include everything from doodles on a cocktail napkin to massive architectural works. Literally anyone can be an author, and copyright arises automatically, as soon as a work of authorship comes into being. At the same time, copyright law in its expansive definition suggests additional aesthetic characteristics of literary property. It is multimodal; that is, it can be visual, spatial, gestural, linguistic, or aural.[8] Further, it must be *embodied.* Literary property does not exist until it is fixed in a "tangible medium of expression," which could be anything from which it "can be perceived, reproduced, or otherwise communicated, either directly or with the aid of a machine or device."

Comparing these two descriptions of literary property, we might say that literary property as defined by Foucault is a subset of the broader category of literary property covered by copyright. To put it another way, we might argue that, in attempting to identify literary property as an object of regulation, copyright law to some extent sidesteps the thorny questions – "What is poetry?" "What is art?" "What is the difference between a novel and an autobiography?" and so on – that often preoccupy humanities scholars. In the nearly fifty years since Foucault delivered his lecture, however, copyright law and literary studies have evolved in ways which suggest that the relationship between these two discourses is far more complicated. To begin with, English and modern language departments – where the work of literary studies has traditionally been done – have expanded the scope of their inquiry to include film, television, folklore, internet memes, technical documentation, and even computer code. Thus literary property as an object of inquiry for the humanities has acquired some of the multimodal and generically heterogeneous character of its

[7] 17 U.S. Code, § 102.

[8] The New London Group, "A pedagogy of multiliteracies: designing social futures," *Harvard Educational Review*, 66(1) (1996), www.sfu.ca/~decaste/newlondon.htm.

counterpart in law. At the same time, legal decisions suggest that in spite of the statute's egalitarian language, aesthetic categories borrowed from literary studies continue to inform judicial interpretation through legal doctrines such as the idea/expression dichotomy, "thick" vs. "thin" copyright, and fair use. An interdisciplinary law-and-literature approach to literary property provides an opportunity to tease apart the discursive tangle, and follow how the thread of literary property binds them together.

The Aesthetics of Authorial Labor

I have previously argued that literary aesthetics inform copyright law via both the idea/expression dichotomy and the fair use doctrine.[9] As outlined in section 102 of the law, in the United States, "copyright protection for an original work of authorship" may never "extend to any idea, procedure, process, system, method of operation, concept, principle, or discovery." This provision of the Copyright Act codifies the common law distinction between ideas and expression that originated in the early case of *Baker* v. *Selden*:

> The underlying action [in that case] arose from Baker's publication and use of accounting ledgers predicated on a system Charles Selden had invented and described in a prior publication. The evidence clearly demonstrated the words, charts, and forms Baker employed were similar to but still distinct from those Selden used, but Selden's widow, the plaintiff in the original action, argued Selden's copyright covered the ideas expressed in the work as well as the expression used to convey them. The Supreme Court, arguing from a set of hypothetical situations involving technical manuals on subjects such as medicine, perspective drawing, and mathematics, held expression is the purview of copyright and ideas are the purview of patent law ... Only copying of expression gives rise to copyright infringement; use of the ideas does not.[10]

The Court went on to hold that the forms at issue were not copyrightable because the ideas and expression were "merged," and copyright protection could not be extended to the expression without removing the ideas from the public domain. The Court's opinion relies heavily upon legal line drawing predicated upon aesthetic distinctions between "useful" and "technical" works on the one hand, and "lines of the poet" and "pictorial illustrations addressed to the taste" on the other.[11]

[9] Robin Wharton, "Digital humanities, copyright law, and the literary," *Digital Humanities Quarterly*, 7(1) (2013), www.digitalhumanities.org/dhq/vol/7/1/000147/000147.html.

[10] Wharton, "Digital humanities." [11] Wharton, "Digital humanities."

These same aesthetic categories have been codified in section 107 of the U.S. copyright law,[12] and in judicial cases in which the fair use doctrine has been interpreted and applied:

> The first factor [of the four factors to be used in determining whether a use is fair], regarding the "purpose and character" of the allegedly infringing use, is supposed to cull thieves of creative expression from the herd of those who are simply borrowing facts, figures, and ideas, or who are treating creative expression like "facts" to be displayed, dissected, and discussed, i.e., critiqued. The second factor, concerning the "nature of the copyrighted work," is designed to separate works that are really cobbled together out of facts, figures, and history – i.e., works where the copyright is "thin" – from those high literary works that comprise mostly creative expression and thus get "thicker" protection. Under the law as it has been interpreted and applied, creative, artistic works get a high level of copyright protection in the fair use analysis. They are also less likely to be viewed as fair uses.[13]

The preference for creative, expressive forms of literary property over utilitarian works is deeply embedded in copyright law and is in all likelihood a direct result of the influence which authors – e.g., Pope, Whitman, Dickens, Joyce – themselves exerted over extensions of copyright in England and the United States throughout the nineteenth and into the twentieth centuries.[14] Nonetheless, in spite of this preference, the question of whether the workaday "sweat of the brow" labor – that is, the labor involved in recording, compiling, and preparing facts or information

[12] "U.S. Copyright Act of 1991 – Title 17," section 107:

> Notwithstanding the provisions of sections 106 and 106A, the fair use of a copyrighted work, including such use by reproduction in copies or phonorecords or by any other means specified by that section, for purposes such as criticism, comment, news reporting, teaching (including multiple copies for classroom use), scholarship, or research, is not an infringement of copyright. In determining whether the use made of a work in any particular case is a fair use the factors to be considered shall include —
>
> the purpose and character of the use, including whether such use is of a commercial nature or is for nonprofit educational purposes;
>
> the nature of the copyrighted work;
>
> the amount and substantiality of the portion used in relation to the copyrighted work as a whole; and
>
> the effect of the use upon the potential market for or value of the copyrighted work.
>
> The fact that a work is unpublished shall not itself bar a finding of fair use if such finding is made upon consideration of all the above factors.

[13] Wharton, "Digital humanities."

[14] A number of scholars have explored how authorial self-fashioning influenced the evolution of Anglo-American copyright law. See, for example: Lowe, "Poems so materially different"; Paul K. Saint-Amour, *The Copywrights: Intellectual Property and the Literary Imagination* (New York: Cornell University Press, 2011); Joseph Loewenstein, *The Author's Due: Printing and the Prehistory of Copyright* (Chicago: University of Chicago Press, 2010).

so that they are aggregated into a useful composite – involved in creating a purely utilitarian text was entitled to any copyright protection at all, however thin, remained open until 1991 and the Supreme Court's decision in *Feist Publications, Inc.* v. *Rural Telephone Service Company.*[15]

Feist Publications involved a telephone service provider, Rural Telephone Service Company, that, as a condition of its monopoly franchise, was required to publish a telephone directory, including white pages listings of all telephone service subscribers and their numbers in alphabetical order, and yellow pages comprising paid advertisements and listings of local businesses organized alphabetically within categories. With regard to the white pages, which were the only thing at issue in the case, the Supreme Court stated the facts as follows: "As the sole provider of telephone service in its service area, Rural obtains subscriber information quite easily. Persons desiring telephone service must apply to Rural and provide their names and addresses; Rural then assigns them a telephone number." Feist Publications published regional phone directories that aggregated white pages listings from across a large geographic area. To obtain this information, Feist Publications approached the local service providers in the area and requested a license to use their white pages data; "[o]f the 11 telephone companies, only Rural refused to license its listings to Feist."[16] Faced with the prospect of leaving "a gaping hole in its area-wide directory, rendering it less attractive to potential yellow pages advertisers," Feist Publications copied approximately 5,000 white pages listings from Rural's directory, supplementing Rural's data with additional information gathered while verifying Rural's listings.[17] Although the district court below subsequently concluded that Rural's refusal to license its white pages "was motivated by an unlawful purpose 'to extend its monopoly in telephone service to a monopoly in yellow pages advertising,'" it found in favor of Rural on the copyright infringement claims, "explaining that '[c]ourts have consistently held that telephone directories are copyrightable' and citing a string of lower court decisions."[18]

The Supreme Court reversed, putting to rest a lingering question regarding "sweat of the brow" copyright protection:

> Without a doubt, the "sweat of the brow" doctrine flouted basic copyright principles. Throughout history, copyright law has "recognize[d] a greater need to disseminate factual works than works of fiction or fantasy."

[15] *Feist Pubs., Inc.* v. *Rural Tel. Svc. Co., Inc. 499 U.S. 340* (1991). Supreme Court of the United States.

[16] *Feist Pubs., Inc.* at 342–3. [17] *Feist Pubs., Inc.* at 343–4. [18] *Feist Pubs., Inc.* at 343–4.

> *Harper & Row*, 471 U.S. at 471 U.S. 563. *Accord,* Gorman, Fact or Fancy: The Implications for Copyright, 29 J.Copyright Soc. 560, 563 (1982). But "sweat of the brow" courts took a contrary view; they handed out proprietary interests in facts and declared that authors are absolutely precluded from saving time and effort by relying upon the facts contained in prior works. In truth, "[i]t is just such wasted effort that the proscription against the copyright of ideas and facts . . . [is] designed to prevent." *Rosemont Enterprises, Inc. v. Random House, Inc.*, 366 F.2d 303, 310 (CA2 1966), *cert. denied* 385 U.S. 1009 (1967).[19]

While the facts of *Feist* are dry, and its holding at first blush appears unremarkable, when read closely the decision offers a fascinating example of how the economic logic that supposedly motivates U.S. copyright law in the first instance breaks down in the face of literary aesthetics. The U.S. Constitution proclaims that copyright is necessary to "promote the Progress of Science and useful Arts, by securing for limited Times to Authors and Inventors the exclusive Right to their respective Writings and Discoveries." Further, in the *Feist* opinion, even as it strips away protection from utilitarian texts, the Court cites "a greater need to disseminate factual works than works of fiction or fantasy" in justification of its holding.[20] Yet literary property, the carrot extended to authors in order to encourage them to create and publish their work, is at its thinnest and least valuable when works are arguably the most useful, the most laden with facts laboriously collected and assembled by the sweat of the author's brow.

Copyright law incentivizes creativity and originality at the expense of other forms of authorial labor. Because the law has expanded to include unlicensed derivative works – remixes, adaptations, translations, etc. – in addition to unlicensed copies as actionable infringement, the law makes it more difficult to accomplish the work of disseminating and making use of the utilitarian knowledge contained in copyrightable works. At the same time, the law offers very little, if any, incentive to undertake the difficult labor of collecting, curating, and archiving useful knowledge in the public domain. To understand the real import of *Feist* and the aesthetics of originality in literary property, we have to look past its bad facts. In *Feist*, Rural was a bad actor, profiting from data that came into its possession not through laborious research and thousands of cold calls or door-to-door canvassing, but in the course of its monopoly franchise: "We note in passing that the selection featured in Rural's white pages may also fail

[19] *Feist Pubs., Inc.* at 354. [20] *Feist Pubs., Inc.* at 354.

the originality requirement for another reason. Feist points out that Rural did not truly 'select' to publish the names and telephone numbers of its subscribers; rather, it was required to do so by the Kansas Corporation Commission as part of its monopoly franchise."[21] In Rural's place, let us presume instead an individual or even a collective that painstakingly assembles an enormously useful and comprehensive data set from historical records, presented in the simplest and most straightforward manner they can devise. As a regulatory measure, copyright law as interpreted in *Feist* would not reward any of the labor involved in such a project. The very comprehensiveness of the dataset – because it requires no creativity in selection – and the usability of the presentation – because it lacks originality in its coordination and arrangement – weigh against a conclusion that the fruits of such labor would be copyrightable. The maker(s) of such a data set might be unable to invoke U.S. copyright law to prevent even wholesale direct copying of their work.[22]

As a regulatory construct designed to promote the progress of science and the useful arts by encouraging the making and circulation of literary commodities in which useful knowledge is embodied, literary property is a failure. Whatever small economic incentive copyright law may provide to the authors of utilitarian works, in the realities of today's marketplace, that incentive is largely realized by a diminishing set of increasingly gigantic publishing conglomerates. Given the hurdles scholars, journalists, biographers, and authors of educational resources often encounter when trying to reuse previously published material, one might even say the work of promoting the progress of science and the useful arts is just as often done in spite of, rather than because of, copyright law and the protections it affords original, creative literary property. Mary L. Dudziak has recently described "the way law makes an indelible mark, or acts as a legitimizing force, affecting what historical actors imagine to be possible" in the field of international relations.[23] Within the humanities, the aesthetics of authorial labor embedded within the Copyright Act so circumscribes our thinking that it creates a closed feedback loop between law and narrative. Legal

[21] *Feist Pubs., Inc.* at 363.

[22] To the extent that such a work were embodied in a digital medium, the creators might be able to make use of an end user license agreement to market and extract value from it. In such a case, the data set would derive its commercial value from its status as an ordinary commodity made available under a contract of sale, rather than as a piece of literary property covered by copyright.

[23] Mary L. Dudziak, "Legal history as foreign relations history" in Michael J. Hogan, Thomas G. Patterson, and Frank Costigliola (eds.), *Explaining the History of American Foreign Relations*, 3rd edn. (Cambridge and Massachusetts: Cambridge University Press, 2016), p. 135.

decision-making is hamstrung by an aesthetics of literary property that demands that, in order to be rewarded, an author's labor must be "original," not simply in the sense that an author has created a new text through whatever means that never existed before, but in the narrower sense of intellectually "inventive." In order to reaffirm those aesthetics of originality, the Supreme Court in *Feist* ignored or overlooked potential alternative grounds for finding against Rural and in favor of Feist Publications that might actually have set legal precedent for more robust defenses predicated on the equitable doctrine of copyright misuse, the fair use exception, and even the First Amendment in future cases. At the same time, within literary studies and the humanities more broadly, we continue to reify a similarly unproductive distinction between "creative" authorship narrowly defined and "non-creative" authorship, e.g., all of the other authorial labor that accounts for the lion's share of cultural production. As Cydney Alexis observes in a recent essay:

> One sphere of writing is marked off as "creative" while others are devalued.
>
> People who write everything except poetry and fiction – those who contribute the vast majority of writing to the world, in the form of lists, essays, emails, blog posts, texts, instruction manuals and so on – see their work as less creative and important.
>
> This mass of unrecognized writing and labor is virtually unrepresented in popular culture, and academics and other workplace writers are not part of the cultural narrative around creativity (save for some exceptional examples, such as the way writing is represented in the TV show *The West Wing*, often a powerful meditation on the importance of collaboration and revision in workplace writing, and in *Her*, a movie that celebrates the ghostwriting of love letters, not generally a celebrated writing genre).[24]

This continued investment of humanities scholars in an aesthetics that obscures so much of the real and necessary work of cultural production is problematic in and of itself, and it deprives us of a potentially powerful argument for legal reform.

Before moving on to an exploration of how we might evolve a more productive aesthetics of literary property by recognizing and encouraging resistant poetics, I want to highlight for a moment the important legal distinction between the subject matter of copyright – that is, the literary property that can be legally regulated pursuant to authority granted

[24] Cydney Alexis, "Let's banish the phrase 'creative writing,'" *Inside Higher Ed*, January 3, 2017, www.insidehighered.com/views/2017/01/03/we-should-stop-distinguishing-between-creative-and-other-forms-writing-essay.

Congress in the Copyright Clause – and the bundle of rights comprised within, as well as the duration of copyright. Affording sweat-of-the-brow authorship *some* protection under the Copyright Act by including it within the broader category of literary property would not necessarily require affording it the full panoply of copyright protections. The Copyright Act itself, and the regulations promulgated under it by the Library of Congress, can be an important source of limiting authority. For example, the compulsory license provision of 17 USC section 117 already significantly limits copyrights in musical compositions. Copyright is a creature of legislative as well as judicial legal decision-making. Courts since *Baker* v. *Selden*, up to and including the Supreme Court in *Feist*, have justified court-imposed aesthetic limitations on the subject matter of copyright as necessary to promote free speech, industrial and epistemological progress, and the public domain. Such limitations, however, are arguably only necessary because Congress has abrogated entirely its constitutional obligation to promote the public good, and instead has created a regulatory scheme that – without judicial intervention – would reward only private commercial interests. Thus, I offer this close reading of the tortured logic of *Feist* as an argument *against* the ever-expanding bundle of copyright protections and copyright's seemingly infinitely extendable term. At the same time, I contend that adopting a broader definition of literary property in both law and literature would better "promote the Progress of Science and useful Arts."

An Aesthetics of Resistance

If aesthetics are the standards by which literary property is judged, poetics might be understood to describe the processes through which it comes into being and makes meaning within a given context. As a medievalist turned digital rhetoric and composition scholar, I tend to take a long view of intellectual history in which the material and cultural forms of print are but a phase, and a relatively short one at that, in the long evolution of literary property. The poetics from which the current aesthetics of literary property emerged are adapted to print publication, the medial affordances and constraints of the book, Romantic ideas about creative genius, the genres of lyric and *Bildungsroman*, solo authorship, relatively passive consumption of textual commodities, developed nation-states that deploy censorship as a tool of ideological control, and a cultural obsession with authenticity and originality. We can use literary property as a lever to pry apart the constraints copyright law currently places upon our work as artists and scholars,[25] but only if we are willing to embrace an expanded poetics that includes collaborative, social authoring and reading practices, and to move beyond an aesthetics primarily designed to sort "art" or "literature" from everything else.

An aesthetics of resistance might begin by first calling into question the unequal values that humanities scholars, judges, and legislators alike place upon the many different kinds of labor that go into making literary property. I remember reading for the first time the following passage from Martha Woodmansee's pioneering study "The Genius and the Copyright":

> [T]o the author of the entry "Book" in the *Allegemeines Oeconomisches Lexicon* of 1753 ... where the book is still perceived as a "convenient instrument for conveying the truth," none of the many craftsmen involved in its production is privileged. Listed in the order of their appearance in the production, "the scholar and the writer, the paper maker, the type founder, the typesetter and the printer, the proofreader, the publisher, the book binder, ..." are all presented as deserving equal credit for the finished product and as having an equal claim to the profits it brings: "Thus many mouths are fed by this branch of manufacture." This definition of the book ... makes tangible just how much had to change before consensus could build around [a] bold assertion of the priority of the writer as peculiarly responsible – and therefore uniquely deserving of credit – for the finished product, "Book," which he helped to make.[26]

My reaction at the time was exactly what one might expect from a copyright lawyer recently turned neophyte literary studies scholar. I saw the "change" Woodmansee describes, and the "bold assertion of the priority of the writer," as an inevitable recognition of the inherent and special value of authorial labor. Now, though, I read this passage with a better understanding of the craftsmanship involved in medieval and early modern bookmaking. I read it with an awareness of the role that labor proscribed by the Copyright Act – unauthorized copying and translation, piracy, hacking, etc. – played in the medieval recovery and transmission of classical knowledge, and the formation of protohumanist political theory.[27] I also read it as an editor and a builder of a digital archive, and as teaching faculty working at a large research institution where teaching is valued, but still less than other forms of creative intellectual labor. Today, as I reread

[25] I offer an expanded discussion of some of these constraints, particularly as they relate to academic work in the digital humanities, in a previous essay. See Wharton, "Digital humanities."

[26] Martha Woodmansee, "The genius and the copyright: economic and legal conditions of the emergence of the 'author'," *Eighteenth-Century Studies*, 17(4) (1984), 425–48.

[27] Kathleen E. Kennedy, *Medieval Hackers* (New York and Toronto: Punctum Books, 2015).

Woodmansee's words, I am also an academic writing in an age of ubiquitous surveillance, living in a country where free speech protections for faculty and students are under attack and the new president has threatened reprisal against independent journalists and his political opponents.

In the weeks since the forty-fifth President of the United States took office, I have observed first-hand the social, political, cultural, and even commercial value of what current legal and literary aesthetics categorize as "non-creative" labor. Thousands of women knitted hundreds of thousands of pink "pussy hats," contributing anonymous labor to the creation of a powerful visual statement of protest documented in perhaps millions of copyrightable images of the demonstrations that took place in the United States and across the world in the days following the inauguration.[28] The craft and skill that went into making those hats (and perhaps even the simple act of wearing them) was as essential to the process from which the images emerged and acquired meaning as the photographers' talents. As scientific regulatory agencies such as NASA, the National Parks Service, and the Environmental Protection Administration have been muzzled by the new administration, hackers have worked to copy and archive decades of data and research.[29] Individual internet users have responded to calls to preserve the traces of disappeared governmental web pages related to previously established but now suddenly debatable and controversial subjects such as climate change and the rights of persons with disabilities to public education.[30] Faced with a White House that disseminates lies and falsehoods, and repeatedly disavows its own previous and contradictory assertions on matters of urgent national interest, unearthing and recirculating verbatim items from the public record has become a social media pastime.[31] Faculty are organizing public readings of George Orwell's *1984* and other dissident works, an act of resistance that might also be characterized as unlicensed public performance, e.g., copyright infringement.

Copying, collaboration, anonymity, archiving, public performance, translation, remix, reuse, reinterpretation, and adaptation: these were activities of dissent, reform, and revolution in England in the late fourteenth and early

[28] "About," *Pussyhat Project*, www.pussyhatproject.com/; Adrienne LaFrance, "Calling out a presidential lie," *The Atlantic*, January 27, 2017, www.theatlantic.com/technology/archive/2017/01/calling-out-a-presidential-lie/514568/.

[29] Laura Parker and Craig Welch, "3 things you need to know about the science rebellion against Trump," *National Geographic News*, January 27, 2017, http://news.nationalgeographic.com/2017/01/scientists-march-on-washington-national-parks-twitter-war-climate-science-donald-trump/.

[30] Dana Varinsky, "A new browser extension lets you see what government websites looked like before the Trump administration," www.businessinsider.com/internet-archive-browser-extension-2017-1.

[31] LaFrance, "Calling out a presidential lie."

fifteenth centuries when Arundel's *Constitutions* were enacted, and they continue to be so in the United States today. We might begin constructing an "aesthetics of resistance" by examining the role such work plays, alongside rhetorical and artistic invention, within contemporary poetics. For the most part, this labor does not give rise to literary property in either a legal or a literary sense, and providing legal protection to literary property makes practicing a poetics of resistance more difficult. What purpose, whose interests does literary property serve? The entangled genealogies of copyright and censorship have taught us that narratives, histories, and texts that can be owned can be controlled. By privileging and rewarding some of the labor that goes into producing narratives, histories, and texts and not the rest, copyright law concentrates ownership – and with it control – of literary property in the hands of a relative few.

Within U.S. copyright jurisprudence, courts have used an aesthetically narrow, extrajudicial definition of literary property to limit copyright's encroachment into the public domain and create breathing room for what the law has defined largely as "derivative" cultural production that by definition makes use of, reproduces, explains, or critiques "original" literary property. Such derivative activities include news reporting, scholarship, archiving, and teaching, which often constitute fair uses, as well as other activities that are usually only legal if licensed, such as translation, editing, remix, and adaptation. In doing so, judges have propped up a regulatory framework that might otherwise have been dismantled by unresolvable tensions between the aims of the Copyright Clause, the First Amendment, and the increasingly broad and long-lived rights granted to authors under the Copyright Act. Literary property, though, as a hybrid discursive form, is not entirely within the control of judges and legislators writing opinions and laws. A large body of scholarship has been written about the relationship between copyright law and modern artistic and cultural production. Read together with judicial interpretations of the Copyright Act, that work demonstrates fairly conclusively that humanities scholars, visual artists, musicians, choreographers, and, yes, poets and novelists have had just as much influence over the shifting meaning within the law of "author" and "literary property" as have legislators, lawyers, judges, and juries. These concepts, and others such as "fair use," "transformative use," "commentary," and "criticism," have a profound impact on how the law is applied and the shape copyright legislation takes.

Within the arts and humanities, we have contributed to an aesthetics of literary property in which some kinds of labor – and thus some forms of cultural production – are marked off as distinctive and worthy of particular recognition because they are defined as "intellectual" and "creative" and "original." The almost inevitable consequence is, of course, that other kinds of labor – and forms of cultural production that might otherwise be classified as literary property – are obscured, disregarded, and devalued. I am not arguing that rhetorical and artistic innovation are insignificant forms of cultural production or should not be valued. We must question, though, whether the elevation, within humanist aesthetics and poetics, of intellectual invention above the other kinds of arguably skilled (and unskilled), intellectual (and manual), *essential* labor of cultural production is grounded in racism, classism, cultural imperialism, sexism, ableism, etc.

To the extent that our aesthetics perpetuate damaging hierarchies and inequality, we must be prepared to remake them. Our aesthetics – how we evaluate, judge, and reward the labor of cultural production – within the academy obscures our poetics – the shared processes through which we create and disseminate knowledge. Like it or not, humanist aesthetics that govern judgments about who can claim the mantle of an author, and what works count as "literary" property, and what authorial labor is "creative" or even just worth doing – as such aesthetics are currently configured – are propping up a prestige economy and an intellectual property regime that many of us would readily admit are irreparably broken. In a sense, I am arguing that, as Dudziak suggests, we should take our cue from the Copyright Act itself and imagine a humanist aesthetics that gathers all "original works of authorship fixed in any tangible medium of expression, now known or later developed, from which they can be perceived, reproduced, or otherwise communicated, either directly or with the aid of a machine or device" under the umbrella of literary property. If within the humanities we adopt an aesthetics that attends to and values the many different kinds of labor involved in cultural production, the narrower aesthetics currently embalmed in copyright law jurisprudence would lose some of its anchoring discursive authority.

When we acknowledge and encourage the poetics of resistance, and build our disciplines, our scholarship, and our classrooms around the many ways in which individuals and collectives become authors and generate literary property, we call into question the hierarchies of originality and labor reified in the law. Literary property might become literally ungovernable, at least within the current regulatory framework. The more active we are in demonstrating through our own work as artists, teachers, and scholars that the aesthetics informing the application of copyright law are no longer normative, if they ever were, and no longer accurately reflect the poetics of cultural production, if they ever did, the more friction we create between the world as it is reflected in the stories told in statutes and legal decisions, and the world as we experience it. I am not arguing that we have to scrap it all and start over from the beginning, but we do need to pay more attention to how the work we do influences the regulatory apparatus. We also need to think more deeply and broadly about whether a literary aesthetics informed by and to some extent perpetuating racism, imperialism, and Western and Northern cultural and economic privilege should continue to influence our scholarship and guide the regulatory structures we create to govern our institutions and our work.

CHAPTER 19

Cases as Cultural Events: Privacy, the Hossack Trial and Susan Glaspell's "A Jury of Her Peers"

Marco Wan

On the night of December 2, 1900, someone murdered John Hossack in cold blood by striking two blows to his head. The killer's first blow was made with a sharp instrument; it opened a gash more than five inches wide in the victim's head from which "brain substance oozed."[1] The second blow was made with a blunt instrument, most likely the handle of the weapon, and crushed his skull. John Hossack's wife, who was sleeping in the same bed that night and claimed not to have awoken until after the attack took place, was named a suspect in the murder and arrested almost as soon as her husband was buried.[2] Margaret Hossack was convicted of murder in the first degree in the Warren County District Court in 1901. Her appeal led to a second trial in the Iowa Supreme Court the following year that ended with a hung jury. The state did not pursue a third trial.

Though interest in the case had largely waned by the time of the proceedings in the state Supreme Court, the first Hossack murder trial in 1901 was a sensational event. As the state's largest newspaper, the *Des Moines Daily News,* noted, it drew such a "promiscuous multitude" that "the seating capacity of the court room proved inadequate to the demand, and scores of people crowded into the aisles and stood packed in about the railing" between the spectators' stand and the bar.[3] More importantly, the trial resonates beyond its immediate historical moment. As is well known, the case forms the basis of Susan Glaspell's short story "A Jury of Her Peers," an integral part of the law and literature canon. Glaspell was a legislative reporter for the *Des Moines Daily News* and covered the case for the newspaper. She quit journalism not long after the trial ended, but the

I would like to thank Elaine Ho and Andrew Counter for their comments on this chapter.

[1] *State* v. *Hossack* 89 N.W. 1077 (1902).

[2] Patricia L. Bryan, "Stories in fiction and in fact: Susan Glaspell's 'A Jury of Her Peers' and the 1901 murder trials of Margaret Hossack,' *Stanford Law Review* 49(6) (1997): 1327.

[3] "Hossack begged wife to aid him," *Des Moines Daily News*, April 3, 1901.

experience stayed with her: She wrote a play entitled *Trifles* based on the facts of the case, and later reworked it into the short story. "A Jury of Her Peers" was in turn adapted into a film by Sally Heckel in 1980.[4]

From Margaret Hossack's trial in 1901, to the Charles Lindbergh Jr. kidnapping case in 1935, to O. J. Simpson's trial for the murder of his wife in 1994–5, the twentieth century seems to be marked by an intense interest in sensational criminal trials. What accounts for the curious fascination in these gruesome cases? Does it simply attest to modern society's morbid fascination with the grisly details of criminal narratives, or is more at stake? Various critics have attempted to address the interest in sensational trials. Richard Sherwin has argued that the media arouses and sustains interest in legal events by turning them into spectacle, thereby blurring the crucial line between law and popular culture.[5] Writing from a psychoanalytic standpoint, Shoshana Felman has posited that twentieth-century "trials of the century" can be interpreted as public, juridical forums for attempting to adjudicate and make sense of historical traumas: She argues that each trial encapsulated "a crisis of legitimacy and a crisis of truth that organized themselves around a *central traumatic content* that, like a magnet, polarized the cultural, the political, the moral, and the epistemological crises of their generations."[6]

By using the Hossack trial and "A Jury of Her Peers" as a case study, I argue that some criminal cases become culturally significant beyond their immediate historical contexts because they prompt literary and other cultural discourses to interrogate the relationship between law and justice. The outcomes of these trials often make one wonder whether justice has indeed been done, and the gap between law and justice which they reveal prompts writers, artists, and filmmakers to reimagine the justice system through their work. I argue that the 1901 Hossack trial reveals deep-seated problems in the legal construction of privacy, and that Glaspell's short story and the film that it inspired constitute cultural discourses that interrogated the ways in which the law defines private space for women. Literature and film can function as discursive critiques of law, and their interrogation of the relationship between law and justice underpins the cultural afterlives of these criminal cases.

4 *A Jury of Her Peers* (dir.) Sally Heckel. New York: Women Make Movies, 1980. Glaspell's story was also adapted for television by Robert Florey in 1961.

5 Richard Sherwin, *When Law Goes Pop: The Vanishing Line between Law and Popular Culture* (Chicago: Chicago University Press, 2000).

6 Shoshana Felman, *The Juridical Unconscious: Trials and Traumas in the Twenty-First Century* (Massachusetts: Harvard University Press, 2002), pp. 4–5.

Privacy and the 1901 Hossack Murder Case

The modern American law of privacy can be said to be premised on the sanctity of the home: The law does not interfere with a person's action within the four walls of his or her house, and it does not intrude into intimate spaces such as the bedroom. Feminist legal scholars point out that despite its seeming gender neutrality, this legal construction of space is in fact deeply harmful to women: By placing the home, and in particular the bedroom, beyond the reach of the law, the doctrine of privacy leaves women at the mercy of their husbands and hence places them at risk of domestic abuse. Catharine MacKinnon argues that "when women are segregated in private, separated from each other one at a time, a right *to* that privacy isolates women at once from each other and from public discourse."[7] She concludes that the law of privacy erects an "epistemic and material division that keeps the private in male hands, beyond public redress, and depoliticizes women's subjection within it." In a similar vein, Elisabeth Schneider notes that the vulnerability which the legal demarcation of space imposes on married women constitutes "the dark and violent side of privacy."[8] Reva Siegel lends historical specificity to the feminist critique by arguing that the law of privacy arose as a way for the courts to turn a blind eye to domestic violence following the abolition of a husband's formal legal prerogative to chastise his wife in the nineteenth century. She traces the shift from the eighteenth-century notion of marriage as gendered hierarchy to the more modern conception of marriage as companionate relationship, and demonstrates that the courts' purported reluctance to be embroiled in disputes in the family home constituted a way of placing propertied men outside legal regulation. The demise of one legal doctrine – marital chastisement – and the rise of another – privacy – meant that "judges no longer insisted that a husband had the legal prerogative to beat this wife; instead, they often asserted that the legal system should not interfere in cases of wife beating, in order to protect the privacy of the marriage relationship and to promote domestic harmony."[9] Even though the language of the law changed, with "tropes of interiority" gradually replacing an earlier "trope of hierarchy," the subordination and

[7] Catharine MacKinnon, *Toward a Feminist Theory of the State* (Massachusetts: Harvard University Press, 1989), pp. 194.

[8] Elisabeth M. Schneider, "The violence of privacy," *Connecticut Law Review*, 23 (1991), 974.

[9] Reva B. Siegel, "'The rule of love': wife-beating as prerogative and privacy," *Yale Law Journal*, 105 (1996), 2120.

vulnerability of married women remained largely unchanged.[10] As such, "privacy talk was deployed in the domestic violence context to enforce and preserve authority relations between man and wife."[11] More recently, Jeannie Suk has examined the rhetoric of legal opinions on privacy to show that the doctrine remains inextricably intertwined with various figures of femininity in our own time, including figures such as the lady of the house, the battered woman, and the absent woman.[12]

As the idea that acts and relations between a married couple within the personal space of the family home should not be exposed or intruded upon gained traction, not only did the law courts become reluctant to intervene in spousal disputes and domestic violence, but society as a whole came to regard these matters as out of bounds. A case in point is the neighbors' willful blindness toward the signs of abuse in the Hossacks' marriage. There was ample evidence that the marriage between John and Margaret Hossack was not a happy one. John did not simply have a bad temper; he caused his wife to fear for her life and her children's. There were frequent quarrels, and Margaret once said that "it would be a Godsend if Mr. Hossack was gone."[13] She tried multiple times to seek help from the people living nearby after particularly turbulent disagreements with her husband, but to no avail. On one occasion, Margaret ran to a neighbor's house and asked to be taken away, only to be told by several men to return home.[14] Patricia L. Bryan observes that even though the neighbors were troubled by Margaret's account of the disputes, they were "always reluctant to listen to her stories of what they viewed as private family matters. Clearly, they wanted to ignore the situation as much as possible."[15] Their reluctance to come to her aid despite clear evidence of spousal abuse was based on deeply entrenched attitudes about the inviolability of the home. Bryan concludes that "the men on the jury were likely to have felt, as had the neighbors, that John Hossack's treatment of his family should not have been a matter of public concern." Moreover, she underscores the gendered implications of the legal and cultural conceptions of privacy by demonstrating that Margaret's recourse to the neighbors was regarded not only as inappropriate, but more specifically as unwomanly: By going public with her private grievances about her husband, she acted "in a way that was uncharacteristic of a good wife and mother."

[10] Siegel, "The rule of love," 2168. [11] Siegel, "The rule of love," 2158.

[12] Jeannie Suk, *At Home in the Law: How the Domestic Violence Revolution Is Transforming Privacy* (New Haven: Yale University Press, 2009), pp. 106–32.

[13] "Hossack begged wife to aid him," 1901. [14] Bryan, "Stories in fiction," 1322.

[15] Bryan, "Stories in fiction," 1337.

One neighbor, Mrs. Haines, testified that Margaret once asked the Haines and some other neighbors to intervene in a domestic quarrel because she was afraid John Hossack "would kill the family before morning."[16] Yet, once again, the norms of privacy of the time meant that such recourse to people outside of one's immediate family was seen as a breach of the divide between the public and the private, to the extent that, as Bryan notes, the prosecution could depict Margaret's calls for help as nothing more than attempts to "humiliate and disgrace her husband behind his back."[17] The societal attitude of the time deemed it inappropriate for either officers of the law or the neighbors to encroach upon the private realm of the home, and wrong of Margaret Hossack to invite them to do so.

While the neighbors had been reluctant to step in when approached by Margaret Hossack, they faithfully recounted what they knew about the Hossack family quarrels when crossexamined in the courtroom. As Marina Angel points out, at the time, evidence of violence perpetrated by a husband against his wife would have been interpreted as evidence of, rather than as a defense for, the murder of one's husband. The logic seemed to be that evidence of domestic violence furnished the woman's motive for the crime.[18] It is therefore unsurprising that, as Glaspell observes in her coverage of the trial, the jury became "more and more set and stern" as they listened to the multiple witness testimonies of Margaret's previous pleas for intervention, for they became increasingly convinced that she had concrete reasons for wanting to rid herself of her husband.[19] Inside the courtroom, the neighbors talked a lot about Margaret's turn to them for help. Outside the courtroom, however, they did little to offer the help that she needed, for fear of breaching the legally and culturally constructed divide between the public and the private. The seemingly gender-neutral law of privacy and the cultural norms to which it gave rise created a divide which left women such as Margaret vulnerable. It is precisely this divide that "A Jury of Her Peers" interrogates though the story of Minnie Foster.

"A Jury of Her Peers" as Literary Critique of Privacy

Glaspell's short story, like her play *Trifles*, is clearly premised on the facts of the Hossack case, yet there are a number of differences between the

[16] "Hossack begged wife to aid him," 1901. [17] Bryan, "Stories in fiction," 1337.

[18] Marina Angel, "Criminal law and women: giving the abused woman who kills a jury of her peers who appreciate trifles," *American Criminal Law Review*, 33 (1996), 243.

[19] "Looks bad for Mrs Hossack," *Des Moines Daily News*, April 5, 1901.

narrative and the trial that are worth noting at the outset. First, while Minnie Wright murders her husband in his sleep, Glaspell changes the method of killing in the story so that instead of two blows to the head, John Wright is killed by a rope around his neck. This change in narrative detail creates a sense of poetic justice by underscoring that Minnie's action was a direct reaction to her husband's cruelty: Just as he killed her beloved canary by wringing its neck, so she took his life by throttling him. Second, there is a change in perspective: Glaspell's story is told from the viewpoint of two women, Martha Hale (whose husband was the first person to alert the officers of the law to John's death) and Mrs. Peters (the wife of the sheriff). The presentation of the investigation from the women's perspective places the need to reevaluate the female experience of marriage and privacy at the forefront of the story. Third, unlike the Hossacks, the Wrights have no children. By sidestepping the question of the children's perspective, Glaspell's narrative again signals that it is women's experience that takes center stage. Finally, Glaspell's narrative does not depict actual scenes of domestic abuse but only hints at them, and also underscores Minnie's loneliness. It therefore signals that the problems with the division of space brought about by the law of privacy extend beyond female vulnerability to legally cognizable forms of physical abuse, but encompass feelings of isolation, helplessness, and depression that are no less harmful to women.

"A Jury of Her Peers" is organized around the spatial division between the residence of the Wrights and the community: Minnie's house constitutes a private space that separates her from the outside world. However, far from being a shelter or a place of comfort to her, the narrative makes clear that the space to which she is confined becomes a trap, cutting her off from her friends and leaving her with no one but her husband. To the community, John Wright presents the public face of a respectable man: "he didn't drink, and kept his word as well as most ... and paid his debts."[20] Within the private space of the home, however, his wife knows him as "a hard man." The narrative unequivocally identifies John Wright as the reason for the misery associated with this private space. Mrs. Hale shivers at the thought of spending the day alone in the house with John, describing the experience as "like a raw wind that gets to the bone." When Mrs. Hale observes that the house "never seemed a very cheerful place," the sheriff assumes she means that Minnie lacked "the home-making

[20] Susan Glaspell, "A jury of her peers" in *Lifted Masks and Other Works*. Ed. Eric S. Rabkin (Ann Arbor: University of Michigan Press, 1993), p. 299.

instinct" to make the house welcoming.[21] However, Mrs. Hale immediately corrects him, starkly stating: "I don't think a place would be any the cheerfuller for John Wright's bein' in it."[22] Mrs. Peters sums up the pernicious effect of marital privacy on women's psychological wellbeing when she makes the heartfelt comment that after years of confinement to the marital space with a husband like John, "a person gets discouraged – and loses heart."[23]

The separation between the public and the private is further underscored by Mrs. Hale's sense that "she could not cross that threshold" between the outside world and Minnie's house the first time she tries to enter the Wright residence in the story.[24] So central is that divide between the exterior space of the community and the interior space of the building that for a moment Mrs. Hale can only stand on the porch with her hand on the doorknob. Minnie's house is repeatedly described as "lonesome": as Mrs. Hale travels toward it, she notes that "it had always been a lonesome-looking place," surrounded by "lonesome-looking trees," and that "it looked very lonesome this cold March morning." As she reflects upon her friendship with Minnie, she remembers that "it's more than a year" since she had last paid a visit to the house, suggesting that Minnie had few visitors.[25] Mr. Hale also comments that the house is located on a "lonesome stretch of road."[26] Even Mrs. Peters, who, as the sheriff's wife, is supposed to adopt the perspective of the law officers, cannot help but observe that "it would have been lonesome" for her to visit the house without Mrs. Hale.[27] The repetition of the word "lonesome" underscores Minnie's isolation and suggests that the privacy surrounding marriage which a wife supposedly enjoys in fact relegates her to "years and years of – nothing."[28]

The effect of such prolonged seclusion, vulnerability to abuse, and general disillusionment associated with an unhappy marital home is further underscored by the narrative's emphasis on Minnie's two names: Minnie Wright, the wife of John Wright, and Minnie Foster, the lively and cheerful girl that she used to be before marriage. The distinction is underscored early in the story, when the reader is told that Martha Hale "still thought of her as Minnie Foster, though for twenty years she had been Mrs. Wright."[29] She "used to wear pretty clothes and be lively – when she was Minnie Foster, one of the town girls, singing in the choir."[30]

[21] Glaspell, "A jury," p. 288.
[22] Glaspell, "A jury," p. 289.
[23] Glaspell, "A jury," p. 294.
[24] Glaspell, "A jury," p. 280.
[25] Glaspell, "A jury," p. 288.
[26] Glaspell, "A jury," p. 283.
[27] Glaspell, "A jury," p. 298.
[28] Glaspell, "A jury," p. 302.
[29] Glaspell, "A jury," p. 281.
[30] Glaspell, "A jury," p. 291.

By the time of the crime, however, little of her original spirit is left: Mr. Hale enters the house to find her sitting silently on a "dingy red" rocker with a chair that "sagged to the side."[31] Mrs. Hale immediately remarks that the woman in the rocker "didn't look in the least like Minnie Foster – the Minnie Foster of twenty years before." She remembers that "Minnie used to sing," but knew that John "killed that too."[32] It was the twenty years of marital life with John that drove the girl who "wore a white dress with blue ribbons, and stood up there in the choir and sang" to become a murderess.[33] Privacy was less a form of legal protection than a kind of legally sanctioned cultural imprisonment imposed on women.

"A Jury of Her Peers" and the Opening of Private Space

Glaspell's short story demonstrates the urgent need to open up the confined space created by the law of privacy to which women had been relegated, so as to establish a sense of female solidarity and a new idea of community. In other words, reconfiguring the strict division between the interior or private world of marriage and the exterior or public world can provide married women greater protection against loneliness, depression, and abuse. The spatial and conceptual borders that the marital home erects cut women off from each other, so that, as Mrs. Hale observes, even though they "live close together," they also "live far apart." The experiential insight of Mrs. Hale and Mrs. Peters leads them to realize that Minnie was deeply unhappy, and it is from the insight that "We all go through the same things – it's all just a different kind of the same thing!" that the two women eventually reconstruct not only the events but also the thought processes that led to the murder. The narrative suggests that allowing other women in the community into the previously exclusive private space of the marital household can help bring those who are "far apart" closer together.

As Mrs. Hale and Mrs. Peters piece together the objects in the kitchen that eventually lead them to the canary, the narrative emphasizes that their interpretation of these seemingly unconnected items is enabled by their shared experience of being married women in a small farming community in early twentieth-century America. Mrs. Hale is first alerted to the fact that Minnie had been provoked by her husband through her attention to a bucket of sugar in the kitchen: The cover has been taken off the bucket, and beside the bucket is a half-full bag of sugar. She immediately understands that Minnie had been interrupted in her task of filling the bucket

[31] Glaspell, "A jury," p. 283. [32] Glaspell, "A jury," p. 302. [33] Glaspell, "A jury," p. 303.

with sugar: "What had interrupted Minnie Foster? Why had that work been left half done?"[34] Her interpretative lens here is the experience of being interrupted in her own kitchen in order to assist in the investigation of the murder: "She thought of the flour in her kitchen at home – half sifted, half not sifted. She had been interrupted, and had left things half done." As she surveys Minnie's kitchen, she sees a half-wiped dining table and a similar realization dawns on her: "Her eye was caught by a dish-towel in the middle of the kitchen table. Slowly she moved toward the table. One half of it was wiped clean, the other half messy ... Things begun – and not finished."[35]

The realization that these objects are clues or indications of an interrupted task that could shed light on the crime also contrasts with the men's lack of comprehension and their ready dismissal of "kitchen things" as trifles.[36] The different reactions to Minnie's jar of preserves which the county attorney finds in the kitchen underscore this difference. As he reaches inside the cupboard, his hand touches the jar, which had burst in the night. He does not understand what it is that he has touched, and describes the jam as no more than "a nice mess." The women, however, not only understand that the jar contained jam, but immediately understand that Minnie had been worried about the jar bursting in the cold of the night. The different, gendered reactions to the burst jar point to the isolation that women feel when they are cut off from the community of other women: Mrs. Hale and Mrs. Peters have a "sympathetic understanding" of Minnie's worries, whereas to the men her concerns are no more than trifles or "a nice mess."

The sense of female solidarity enabled by the new organization of space which the narrative proposes is further underscored by the repeated meeting of eyes between Mrs. Hale and Mrs. Peters as they continue to decipher the clues provided by the various "kitchen things" in the house. When they examine the irregular pattern in the quilt, the narrator notes that "their eyes met – something flashed to life, passed between them."[37] Both women are able to understand the significance of the interruption to an otherwise even pattern: Something had made Minnie Wright nervous. When they examine the door to the canary's cage that John had forcibly pulled apart, a similar moment of shared comprehension arises. "Looks as if some one must have been – rough with it," Mrs. Hale observes, and "again their eyes met – startled, questioning, apprehensive."[38] Finally,

[34] Glaspell, "A jury," p. 290.
[35] Glaspell, "A jury," p. 293.
[36] Glaspell, "A jury," p. 287.
[37] Glaspell, "A jury," p. 295.
[38] Glaspell, "A jury," pp. 297–8.

when they find the dead canary, "the eyes of the two women met – this time clung together in a look of dawning comprehension, of growing horror."[39] As they hear the men return to the kitchen from the bedroom above, they look at each other "in a covert way" and then quickly look away to avoid arousing suspicion.[40] Right before making the simultaneous decision to hide the canary from their husbands, they "held each other in a steady, burning look in which there was no evasion or flinching" in a moment of solidarity not only with each other, but also with Minnie, "that woman who was not there and yet who had been there with them all through that hour." The story suggests that it is only when existing notions of privacy are opened up that the shared experience and mutual support so sorely needed among married women can be found.

Film and the Construction of Private Space

Glaspell's writings do not constitute the entire cultural afterlife of the Hossack trial. Sally Heckel's 1980 film adaptation of "A Jury of Her Peers" was screened in America, Britain, Australia, New Zealand and Germany, and received an Academy Award Nomination for Best Dramatic Live Action Short Film that year. Apart from the change of name from John and Minnie Wright to John and Minnie Burke, it remains largely faithful to Glaspell's short story. Heckel's late-twentieth-century film furthers the cultural engagement with problems of gender, privacy, and space that the case and Glaspell's narrative initiated in the opening decades of the century. The remainder of this chapter examines the ways in which the film adaptation engages with these problems through its cinematography.

Heckel's film opens with shots of various aspects of the Burke household: a water pump, some wood for the fire, dirty dishes in the sink, fading kitchen wallpaper, a pin cushion by the window, a blackened wall, and a bad stove. The series of single shots seems to suggest that these objects constitute the entirety of Minnie's lonely existence; they are literally the scenes of her life. The music also adds to the sense of isolation: The film opens with the first verse of the Christmas carol *In the Bleak Midwinter*, based on the poem of the same name by Christina Rossetti, and that is also the song which Minnie hums at the beginning of the film. The lines "In the bleak midwinter/Frosty wind made moan/Earth stood hard as iron/Water like a stone" allude here to both the physical and the psychological hardship that Minnie Burke had to endure, and the repetition of "snow on

[39] Glaspell, "A jury," p. 300. [40] Glaspell, "A jury," p. 304.

snow" suggests that her former happy self is now snuffed out by the cold reality. As the film progresses, we understand that the murder has recently taken place, and that she is sitting alone in the house waiting for someone to discover the body.

The way in which Minnie is introduced in the film is significant. As the film opens, we hear a woman's voice humming the song, but we do not see her face. The camera then cuts to her hands, yet we still do not know who this person is. The camera continues to focus on the hands even as she responds to Mr. Hale's greeting. It is not until Minnie speaks about John's death that we catch a glimpse of her face. The cinematographic delay in showing her face and the focus on her hands both underscore the inferior position of women in the community: Farmers' wives are valued more for their hard work (their hands) than as individuals (their faces). As Mr. Hale says in the opening scene, "I don't know whether what his wife wanted ever made much of a difference to John Burke." Mr. Hale invites his son Harry into Minnie's house without asking her, and they proceed to the bedroom to look at John's body without seeking her permission.

Heckel adds a telling detail to the story in the film. As Mrs. Hale looks through the front room, she comes across a book of Bible songs belonging to Minnie. Hidden inside the book is a black-and-white photo of Minnie as a girl, and in the film it is the photo that prompts Mrs. Hale to talk about Minnie's former days in the choir. The location of the photo suggests that there is no space for the lively young girl in the marriage: whatever is left of her is buried in a book, an object within an object that nobody sees or remembers.

The film places emphasis on two objects of particular significance in the story through the use of camera. The first is the birdcage. When Mrs. Peters first finds it in the corner of the kitchen, the camera highlights its thematic significance as a metaphor for Minnie's entrapment in the marital home by zooming in as Mrs. Peters slowly lifts it onto the table. The birdcage remains mostly visible on the screen through the various shots and countershots as they continue their conversation. The second object is the sewing basket in which the box with the canary is hidden. The county attorney wants to inspect the basket because it contains some of Minnie's personal belongings which the two women will bring to her in prison. There is a moment of tension as he comes dangerously close to discovering the box with the canary that lies underneath the pieces of fabric. In Glaspell's narrative, this tension is created through a description of Mrs. Hale's anxious state of mind: "He picked up one of the quilt blocks which she had piled on to cover the box. Her eyes felt like fire.

She had a feeling that if he took up the basket she would snatch it from him."[41] In the film, the tension is created through the cinema's focus on the county attorney's action. The camera zooms in on his hand as he examines the quilt patches, and the dramatic tension is heightened as we see him flip them back one by one. With each patch set aside, he gets closer to the motive of the crime. As he looks through the quilt blocks, Mrs. Hale is shown to be nervously biting her lip, eyes darting about her, while Mrs. Peters stands petrified by the window.

The camera's emphasis on the birdcage and the sewing basket returns us to the question of space. The focus on the birdcage underscores its representation of the private marital space as a form of confinement for women. Moreover, the film gives the audience a progressive narrowing of spaces: From the initial shots of the house, the camera then focuses on the smaller space of the kitchen, where much of the action takes place. The focus then shifts to the even smaller space of the basket, in which the quilt pieces are kept. Finally, the camera zooms in on the box inside the sewing basket. As the men move around the house, the film creates the impression that the space allowed to women becomes increasingly limited: The men enter the house where John Burke was killed, then rummage around in the kitchen – the only space where the two women can speak frankly to each other, then the county attorney threatens to pry into all the contents of the basket. By the end of the film, all that is left of the space that is not yet intruded upon by the men is the box with the canary, and even that tiny space is, as we saw, briefly under threat. The shrinking of private space for women in a patriarchal society which the film portrays – from the house, to the kitchen, to the basket, to the box, and finally to nothing but a two-dimensional photographic surface buried within a book of Bible songs – underscores the urgency of exposing the silent suffering that some women were subjected to within those spaces, so that they can find mutual support and solidarity.

Conclusion

Toward the end of Glaspell's narrative, Martha reproaches herself for not having been more attuned to Minnie's unhappiness, and for having neglected their friendship: "'Oh, I wish I'd come over here once in a while!' she cried. 'That was a crime! Who's going to punish that?'"[42] Martha's self-reproach brings us back to the neighbors to whom Margaret Hossack

[41] Glaspell, "A jury," p. 305. [42] Glaspell, "A jury," p. 303.

turned in her time of need. Just like Margaret's neighbors, Martha Hale did not intrude into the affairs of the marital home and did not appreciate the extent of her friend's desperation. However, perhaps the true "crime" in this situation is not that Martha did not visit her friend, or that she failed to appreciate the marital tensions within the Wright residence, but rather that law and society constructed a form of privacy which taught married women's friends and neighbors to actively refrain from caring about their wellbeing because to do so would be tantamount to an intrusion upon their private life. It is this problem of the organization of space enacted by notions of privacy in the Hossack trial that Glaspell's text and Heckel's film probe, interrogate, and challenge. Both the short story and the film suggest that dispensing with the idea that marriage and the marital home necessarily constitute a private space whose contours cannot be breached can potentially enable other forms of valuable shared experience to enter into women's lives, creating a sense of solidarity and community that would reduce women's vulnerability to isolation and abuse. In this context, fiction and film can be interpreted as critiques of the law, and it is therefore no surprise that "A Jury of Her Peers" has in turn become a staple of another discursive domain, that of feminist legal scholarship. For instance, Robin West argues that Glaspell's story exposes the "process of legitimation" whereby certain forms of harm to women are made unrecognizable – and hence invisible – by the law.[43] According to West, Minnie Wright's experience reveals that legal constructs can be complicit with patriarchy because the "absence of emotional nourishment" that many married women have to endure often becomes "entirely unnoticed, unrecognized, and uncompensated by the law."[44] The Israeli scholar Orit Kamir draws on her own experience as a teacher who has taught *A Jury of Her Peers* "several times in three law schools in two different parts of the world" to argue that the short story should be included in the twenty-first-century law school curriculum because its insights are "as relevant today as they were at the turn of the twentieth century, and need to be presented to law students today as then."[45] In a recent article, Marilyn Taylor reads "A Jury of Her Peers" in light of questions of jury nullification and psychological harm to women to posit that literature provides a vision not only of what the law is but of what the law can be, thereby acting as "an agent for change"

[43] Robin West, *Caring for Justice* (New York: New York University Press, 1997), p. 220.

[44] West, *Caring for Justice*, p. 244.

[45] Orit Kamir, "To kill a songbird: a community of women, feminist jurisprudence, conscientious objection and revolution in 'A Jury of Her Peers' and contemporary film," *Law and Literature*, 19(3) (2007), 370.

as well as "a voice for social consciousness."[46] Over a century has passed since Margaret Hossack was brought to the dock, and feminist scholars continue to find inspiration in "A Jury of Her Peers" as they address problems of domestic violence and gender inequality in our own time. Literature and film's imaginative engagement with the Hossack trial serves as a powerful reminder that the law is far from perfect, and by exposing its flaws they contribute to bringing it one step closer to that elusive ideal of a just system.

[46] Marilyn R. Tayler, "Legal and moral justification for homicide in Susan Glaspell's 'A Jury of Her Peers.'" *Law, Culture and the Humanities* (2015), 17. DOI: 1743872115575205.

CHAPTER 20

Creativity and Censorship Laws: Lessons from the 1920s

Nancy L. Paxton

> Art should be, must be, and is creative and original. In order to bloom with these qualities, it must be unhampered. Any artist who works with the tapeworm of censorship gnawing in his vitals, knowing that some blue-law committee is to sit in judgment on his work, would be stultified from the onset.
>
> Sinclair Lewis[1]

In his intriguing essay "Before the Law," Jacques Derrida asserts that "literature has the power to make the law, beginning with its own."[2] While he recognizes that a literary text is "protected by its guardians (author, publisher, critics, academics, archivists, librarians, lawyers and so on)" and that it "cannot establish law unless a more powerful system of laws ... guarantees it," he focuses on the "laws" that define a literary text and shows how Kafka's fable "Before the Law" challenges them. While Derrida's essay explores the relationship between literature and law in a philosophical framework, I will, in the essay that follows, explore how and why some literary texts failed to "make the law" in the most literal sense.[3] I have chosen three representative novels written in the 1920s that literally failed to "make the law" and were legally suppressed in the nation where they were written. However, I will also show that these texts nonetheless illustrate how the threat of censorship prompted some writers to develop their most daring creative experiments in order to take advantage of new conditions of authorship; as a consequence, these novels were able to travel and "make the law" in other national contexts because they addressed readers in the larger, more globalized literary marketplace of the 1920s.

1 Sinclair Lewis, "Letter," *New York World*, August 20, 1922. As cited by Mark Schorer, *Sinclair Lewis: An American Life* (New York: McGraw-Hill, 1961), p. 341.

2 Jacques Derrida, *Acts of Literature*. Ed. Derek Attridge (London and New York: Routledge, 1992), p. 214.

3 Derrida, *Acts of Literature*, p. 214.

In her important book *British Modernism and Censorship*, Celia Marshik analyzes print censorship in Great Britain between 1885 and 1939 and shows that the "censorship dynamic" was "repressive" and "productive" as well as profoundly gendered.[4] Marshik focuses on the British antiprostitution movement, which promoted state censorship well into the twentieth century, and shows how authors used an "enlivening and politicized irony" in order to resist it. My research on banned novels of the modernist period confirms Marshik's argument that censorship produced both repressive and productive effects. In this chapter, I will consider three novels published in the 1920s that are notorious for their lack of irony. Two are well known – D. H. Lawrence's *Lady Chatterley's Lover* (1928) and Radclyffe Hall's *The Well of Loneliness* (1928) – in part because they prompted multiple censorship hearings in London and New York, making them two of the most famous *causes célèbres* of the twentieth century. While most studies of censorship in recent years have focused on a single national context, I invite readers to see beyond this critical horizon by considering a third novel, *The Butcher Shop*, written by Jean Devanny.[5] Born in New Zealand, Devanny wrote about life on a sheep station on the North Island in this novel, but she arranged for it to be published in London in 1926. When the first shipment of *The Butcher Shop* arrived in Wellington, it was confiscated and banned in New Zealand, even though it continued to circulate unchallenged in England. Considered together, these three novels highlight some of the creative strategies that authors developed in the 1920s to expand their readership and to escape national borders that were policed to enforce particular censorship regimes.

I offer two justifications for considering these banned novels in a more global context. First, the Great War prompted the development of more complex censorship bureaucracies and new surveillance systems in Great Britain, and these techniques were soon adopted, with local variations, in the United States, New Zealand, Australia, and elsewhere.[6] Book censorship increased in the 1920s in Great Britain during Sir William Joynson-Hicks' tenure as Home Secretary; however, governmental censors were

[4] Celia Marshik, *British Modernism and Censorship* (Cambridge and New York: Cambridge University Press, 2006), pp. 4, 11.

[5] Jean Devanny, *The Butcher Shop*. Ed. Heather Roberts (Auckland: Auckland University Press, 1981). I refer to this edition throughout.

[6] See Peter Bruitenhaus, *The Great War of Words: British, American, and Canadian Propaganda and Fiction 1914–1933* (Vancouver: University of British Columbia Press, 1987); Mark Wollaeger, *Modernism, Media, and Propaganda: British Narrative from 1900 to 1945* (Princeton: Princeton University Press, 2006).

responsive not only to the purity campaigns against prostitution that Marshik analyzes, but to a wide range of other social and political issues as well. As Paul Boyer shows, there was a parallel "explosion" of book censorship in the United States following the Red Scare of 1919 and the repeal of the Sedition Act in 1920, though legal challenges were often initiated by local vice societies and enforced by surveillance of the mail by the U.S. Postmaster General, as authorized by the Comstock Act.[7] Legal censorship and the government bureaucracies that enforced it developed later in New Zealand and Australia, but they incorporated many British and American legal concepts and practices.[8]

At the same time, new developments in the book trade in the 1920s encouraged publishers and authors to redefine their audience in ways that countered nation-based censorship.[9] The presses that emerged in the 1920s in New York, including the firms that accepted Lawrence's, Hall's, and Devanny's novels, found new ways to capitalize on the social and political controversies that prompted calls for censorship. Their advertising practices and segmented marketing plans allowed them to sell to larger, more varied, and more international Anglophone audiences.[10] Indeed, as I will show, Hall's and Devanny's creative experiments in *The Well of Loneliness* and *The Butcher Shop* ultimately allowed their novels to escape banning in the United States.

In her recent study *The Affective Life of Law: Legal Modernism and the Literary Imagination*, Ravit Reichman argues that World War I altered "legal justice, social justice, and the narrative spaces between them."[11] She shows that the staggering number of soldiers killed in the Great War

[7] Paul Boyer, *Purity in Print: The Vice Society Movement and Book Censorship in America* (New York: Scribner, 1968); Geoffrey Stone, *Perilous Times: Free Speech in Wartime, from the Sedition Act of 1798 to the War on Terrorism* (New York: Norton, 2004).

[8] Nicole Moore's *The Censor's Library: Uncovering the Lost History of Australia's Banned Books* (St. Lucia: University of Queensland Press, 2012) and Stevan Eldred-Grigg's *Pleasures of the Flesh: Sex and Drugs in Colonial New Zealand, 1840–1915* (Wellington: Reed, 1984) demonstrate some of these parallels.

[9] Paul Delany in *Literature, Money and the Market: From Trollope to Amis* (Houndmills: Palgrave, 2002) and Catherine Turner in *Marketing Modernism: Between the Two World Wars* (Amherst: University of Massachusetts Press, 2003) provide excellent overviews of British and American publishing in the 1920s. Joyce Piell Wexler, in *Who Paid for Modernism: Art, Money, and the Fiction of Conrad, Joyce, and Lawrence* (Fayetteville: University of Arkansas Press, 1997), describes the changing literary marketplace and demonstrates the importance of literary agents in the 1920s.

[10] See David Carter, "The mystery of the missing middlebrow, or the c(o)urse of good taste" in Judith Ryan and Chris Wallace-Crabbe (eds.), *Imagining Australia: Literature and Culture in the New New World* (Cambridge: Harvard University Press, 2004), pp. 174–99.

[11] Ravit Reichman, *The Affective Life of Law: Legal Modernism and the Literary Imagination* (Stanford: Stanford Law Books, 2009), p. 1.

produced unprecedented challenges in the application of laws concerning injury, inheritance, and property in England after the war. Reichman's analysis of *Jacob's Room* (1922), *Mrs. Dalloway* (1924), and *To the Lighthouse* (1927) demonstrates Woolf's turn away from the "advocacy" techniques that Victorian writers used to diagnose what is wrong with society; she represents, instead, "how to live" in a world transformed by the massive losses of war. While I agree that Woolf abandoned Victorian techniques of "advocacy,"[12] I will show that Lawrence, Hall, and Devanny explored some of the same themes that Reichman identifies as "legal modernism," but retained narrative techniques that were essential to their advocacy of the causes close to their hearts. The novels I consider in this essay, thus, illustrate in poignant ways how the "sense of justice and responsibility" changed in the "wake of war, that 'hardest place' where our firmest convictions falter and our sense of what we ought to do – indeed of what we can do – erodes."[13] They became targets of state censorship precisely because they did not employ the formal experimental features and pervasive irony that Woolf and other modernists developed.

Virginia Woolf's novels are central to many recent studies of British censorship in the 1920s, and critics often cite her famous description of herself as "the only woman in England free to write what I like" or her comment that it was "the greatest mercy to be able to do what one likes – no editors, or publishers."[14] Marshik persuasively argues, however, that since *Jacob's Room* (1922) and all the novels that followed it were published by Hogarth Press, a firm that Virginia and Leonard Woolf owned, Woolf's creative freedom was constrained by the Obscene Publications Act of 1857, which made publishers and printers "liable for financial penalties and losses should a work be convicted of obscene libel."[15] Although Woolf escaped the supervision of editors by publishing her own work, this freedom "made her own sense of discretion all the more crucial: she, Leonard, and the Hogarth Press would suffer from an obscenity prosecution."[16]

Woolf no doubt invited state censorship when she displayed an unseemly knowledge about "public" women by including female prostitutes in *The Voyage Out* and *Jacob's Room*, but these novels were not banned. Woolf's

[12] I borrow this term from Christine Krueger's *Reading for the Law: British Literary History and Gender Advocacy* (Charlottesville: University of Virginia Press, 2010).

[13] Reichman, *Affective Life of Law*, p. 1.

[14] Virginia Woolf, *The Diary of Virginia Woolf.* Ed. Anne Olivier Bell, 5 vols. (New York: Harcourt Brace Jovanovich, 1977–1984), pp. 3, 43.

[15] Marshik, *British Modernism and Censorship*, p. 92.

[16] Marshik, *British Modernism and Censorship*, p. 92.

Orlando (1928), on the other hand, came closer to becoming the target of state censorship than she or her public – then and now – have realized. In her review of newly released documents in Great Britain's National Archives, Marshik discovered that the Home Office was alerted to *Orlando*'s "flirtation with obscenity" on October 16, 1928, and officials considered taking action to suppress it. The file on *Orlando* has been lost so it is not possible to know exactly what objections triggered this initiative, but Marshik argues that it was Orlando's visit with some prostitutes in eighteenth-century London that caused readers to complain.[17]

Orlando includes other themes that could have prompted complaints from prudish reformers or evangelical bureaucrats in the Home Office. Woolf challenges readers' heteronormative assumptions, for example, when Orlando decides to cross-dress in a "black velvet suit richly trimmed with Venetian lace," but the text demonstrates that this costume was perfectly appropriate when Orlando was "a young man of fashion," before her fantastical transformation from man to woman.[18] Numerous episodes in Woolf's genre-bending novel illustrate, as Pamela Caughie observes, that "sexual categories were in flux in the modernist era," showing how concepts like "homosexuality, inversion, intersexuality, and bisexuality" coexisted uneasily with sexologists' "taxonomic efforts" to distinguish the categories of "transvestite" and "transsexual."[19] Woolf playfully deconstructs not only sexual categories but also gender norms by representing Orlando's life through three centuries, showing that gender is "an historically specific cultural process, a matter of literary forms and legal institutions, psychology and medicine, fashion and social customs."[20] Throughout the novel, Woolf artfully shows how Orlando escapes such scientific straitjackets.

Finally, *Orlando*, like the earlier novels that Reichman analyzes, is preoccupied with the crisis of property and inheritance, and it demonstrates that both hinged on English marriage laws. After her nineteenth-century marriage and pregnancy, Orlando asks herself, "If one's husband was always sailing round Cape Horn, was it marriage? If one liked him, was it marriage? If one liked other people, was it marriage? And finally, if one still wished . . . to write poetry, was it marriage? She had her doubts."[21]

[17] Marshik, *British Modernism and Censorship*, p. 118.

[18] Virginia Woolf, *Orlando*. Ed. Mark Hussey (New York: Harcourt, 2006). 157. I cite from this text throughout.

[19] Pamela L. Caughie, "The temporality of modernist life writing in the era of transsexualism: Virginia Woolf's *Orlando* and Einar Wegener's *Man into Woman*," *Modern Fiction Studies*, 59(3) (2013), 504.

[20] Caughie, "Temporality," p. 518.

[21] Woolf, *Orlando*, p. 195.

One of the basic ironies of the novel is that the "iron countenance of the law" fails to recognize these uncertainties.[22] Shortly before her marriage, the lawsuits that have shaped her life for over a century are settled, and Orlando's "sex" is "pronounced indisputably, and beyond the shadow of a doubt" to be "female."[23] While Woolf's narrator mocks the literalmindedness of the law here, and elsewhere in the text, the novel shows that Orlando's life as a woman is disciplined and limited by laws that do not apply to the male Orlando. As a fantasy, *Orlando* refuses to privilege the literal over the figurative, but it also displays the power of censorship laws which compelled Woolf to write in this playfully ironic way about a protagonist who is "neither wrongly sexed nor tragically gendered."[24]

Virginia Woolf was able to avoid the interference of editors by publishing with Hogarth Press, but D. H. Lawrence did not have this option. He had a long history of resisting editorial intervention even before he felt the disciplining power of state censorship, and the surveillance that accompanied it, when *The Rainbow* was legally banned in 1915. Lawrence's English publisher, Methuen, did not inform him about the Bow Street hearing on *The Rainbow* or its legal suppression, and Lawrence was so embittered by his experiences during the war that he left England permanently as soon as he could. As Mark Kinkead-Weekes observes, "it is impossible to exaggerate the effect" of *The Rainbow*'s suppression on Lawrence: "He had been made to feel a contemptible alien in his homeland."[25] In 1919, Lawrence began the restless world travel that transformed his fiction and his relationship with his Anglophone audiences around the world.

In November 1927, Lawrence developed his most daring creative strategy to evade what he later called his "moron censors" by contracting with Pino Orioli to print *Lady Chatterley's Lover*. Nine months earlier, he had told his literary agent, Nancy Pearn, that the second draft of the novel was so "improper" that he hesitated to turn it over to an editor or even a typist.[26] Lawrence's decision to publish *Lady Chatterley's Lover* privately, as Joyce Wexler points out, allowed him to "establish an intimate connection with a select group of readers and still earn money from his writing."[27]

22 Woolf, *Orlando*, p. 124. 23 Woolf, *Orlando*, p. 187.

24 Caughie, "Temporality," 518. In this essay, Caughie cites Judith Halberstam's definition of the "tragic queer." See *In a Queer Time and Place: Transgender Bodies, Subcultural Lives* (New York: New York University Press, 2005), p. 87.

25 Mark Kinkead-Weekes, *D. H. Lawrence: Triumph to Exile, 1912–1922* (Cambridge: Cambridge University Press, 1996), vol. 2, p. 282.

26 James T. Boulton and Margaret Boulton (eds.), *The Letters of D. H. Lawrence* (Cambridge: Cambridge University Press, 1991), vol. 6, p. 29.

27 Wexler, *Who Paid for Modernism*, p. 117.

It also allowed him to market his novel directly to readers in the United Kingdom, the United States, Australia, and elsewhere. While private publication freed Lawrence from editorial interference, it was not without financial risk, since *Lady Chatterley's Lover* had no copyright protection and, as Pearn warned, private publication could jeopardize her ability to place his short fiction with reputable magazines, since pornography was usually also published privately.

No longer constrained by editors' or publishers' concerns that his readers might find his novel unpatriotic or too explicit about sex, in the final version of *Lady Chatterley's Lover* Lawrence presents a franker narrative about the literal and metaphorical crisis of inheritance in England as a result of the massive deaths and injuries of the Great War. He describes, for example, how the war affected men at all levels of British society, from titled landowners to working-class men such as Oliver Mellors. Sir Clifford is a victim of one of the unpredictable traumatic injuries of mechanized warfare when he is wounded and paralyzed from the hips down. He remains confined to a "bath-chair with a motor attachment," which vividly symbolizes his spiritual injuries as well as his physical limitations.[28] Clifford's first response to the Great War is to see his father, the government, the army, and the war itself as "ridiculous," but he later volunteers and serves on the Western Front.[29] After his older brother is killed, he dutifully marries, as his father advises, in order to produce an heir for the family estate.

Oliver Mellors is more sophisticated and more separate from his working-class roots than is Oliver Parkin in the earlier versions of the novel. Mellors's war service is specifically described: He enlists in 1915 and serves in Egypt and India under a commander he "loves";[30] when his supervisor dies of pneumonia and Mellors himself suffers an illness that permanently damages his health, he leaves the army and returns to Tevershall; after his return, he is alienated from his working-class wife and displays a violent bitterness that is evident, for instance, when he diagnoses Bertha's sexual failures and "lesbian" inclinations.[31]

Like Woolf, Lawrence demonstrates how the Great War transformed the "narrative space" of the postwar world as well as the landscape and society. As Connie Chatterley observes, "All the great words ... were

[28] D. H. Lawrence, *Lady Chatterley's Lover*. Ed. Michael Squires (New York: Penguin, 1994 [1928]), p. 16. I cite from this edition throughout.

[29] Lawrence, *Lady Chatterley*, p. 10.

[30] Lawrence, *Lady Chatterley*, p. 141.

[31] Lawrence, *Lady Chatterley*, p. 213.

cancelled for her generation: love, joy, happiness, home, mother, father, husband, all these great dynamic words were half-dead now and dying from day to day."[32] Connie does not experience the war directly, but confirms Reichman's analysis because her "encounter with death" is "mediated by property." Sir Clifford and Connie struggle to solve new dilemmas posed by property and inheritance when they search for an acceptable way to produce a legitimate heir for Wragby Hall, someone who, as Sir Clifford puts it, "will be able to rule his portion" after his death.[33] Lawrence's novel displays modernist irony when Connie, rather than her husband, decides how his property will be transmitted. Sir Clifford tells Connie, pragmatically, "If we had the child to rear, it would be our own," but she overturns his assumptions that she will choose a "gentleman" as her partner and rejects his claim that her unborn child is his property.[34]

While Woolf shows her creativity in *Orlando* by playfully transforming the conventions of the *roman à clef*, in *Lady Chatterley's Lover* Lawrence challenges the genre "laws" that define the pastoral. Connie's encounters with the gamekeeper in the "greenwood" undo the traditional hierarchical gender roles of the pastoral, and Lawrence exposes the class arrangements it consolidates by including Mellors's blunt working-class dialect. Lawrence likewise pushes against the boundaries of literary decorum in his explicit descriptions of the lovers' naked bodies and joyful sex that prompted such outrage from his censors. In detailing the tender, if scandalous, pagan ritual that the lovers create to celebrate the union of John Thomas and Lady Jane, when Mellors threads flowers in Connie's maidenhair and winds creeping-jenny around his penis, Lawrence contrasts the wistful beauty of this private ceremony with the sterility of upper-class English marriage practices and the laws that supported them.

Lawrence does not leave his lovers in the pastoral greenwood; instead, he returns them to a world in ruins – a world defaced by war, arid commercialism, and the General Strike of 1926 – and this ending shows the limits of modernist irony and individualist solutions. Connie's trip to Venice demonstrates the emptiness of the distractions offered by modern mechanized travel and tourism. Bowing to family pressure, she agrees to join her father and sister on a holiday, but when Connie meets her sister after her infamous "night of shame" with the gamekeeper, Hilda directs her to put on a "motoring helmet," a pair of "disfiguring goggles," and a

32 Lawrence, *Lady Chatterley*, p. 62.
33 Lawrence, *Lady Chatterley*, p. 183.
34 Lawrence, *Lady Chatterley*, p. 43.

long "motoring coat," a costume which signals her reluctant return to modernity.[35] Transformed by love and by her sensual experiences with Mellors, Connie later sees the fashionable pedestrians in London as "people who seemed so spectral and blank. They had no alive happiness, no matter how brisk and good-looking they were."[36] Likewise, in Venice she finds only a sort of "drugged enjoyment" that repels her.[37] When Connie realizes she is pregnant and cannot bear to return to her marriage with Sir Clifford, she and Mellors are forced to confront the realities of English marriage and divorce laws. Connie's decision to seek a divorce frustrates Sir Clifford's plans for an heir and implicitly criticizes the property arrangements of English upper-class marriages; yet the novel ends with an affirmation of legal marriage as a means to recognize the sacredness of Connie and Mellors's physical union even as it insures that his patriarchal power is legally protected.[38]

In *The Well of Loneliness* (1928), Radclyffe Hall chose a different, though arguably no less creative, approach by writing, after a long period of self-censorship, about Stephen Gordon, a protagonist that Pamela Caughie characterizes as "tragically" gendered.[39] In her earlier poetry Hall wrote openly about "Sapphic love," but she, like Woolf, felt compelled to exercise self-censorship when she began to write novels, as *The Unlit Lamp* (1924) demonstrates. When she was unable to find a firm willing to publish this novel, Hall hired Audrey Heath, her skillful and loyal literary agent, who encouraged her to write the *romans à clef The Forge* (1924) and *The Saturday Life* (1925). This literary form allowed Hall to entertain an outsider audience while at the same time addressing insiders who could decode the autobiographical references and representations of same-sex desire in these works.[40] When *Adam's Breed* (1926) won two prestigious literary prizes, Hall decided that she had acquired enough cultural capital to risk censorship by writing more openly in defense of lesbians such as Stephen Gordon.

[35] Lawrence, *Lady Chatterley*, pp. 251–2. [36] Lawrence, *Lady Chatterley*, p. 254.

[37] Lawrence, *Lady Chatterley*, p. 259.

[38] In "A propos of *Lady Chatterley's Lover*," included in Squires' edition of *Lady Chatterley's Lover*, Lawrence argues that marriage must be "phallic" (p. 324).

[39] I echo Caughie's language (in "Temporality," 518) here. Casey Charles, in *Critical Queer Studies: Law, Film, and Fiction in Contemporary American Culture* (Surrey: Ashgate, 2012), analyzes the work of several other queer theorists who use this term and illustrates how the conventions of tragedy also apply to recent films about queer subjects.

[40] See Richard Dellamora, *Radclyffe Hall: A Life in the Writing* (Philadelphia: University of Pennsylvania Press, 2011), pp. 115–63; Sean Latham, *The Art of Scandal: Modernism, Libel Law and the Roman à Clef* (New York: Oxford University Press, 2009); Sashi Nair, *Secrecy and Sapphic Modernism: Reading Romans à Clef between the Wars* (London: Palgrave, 2012).

One creative strategy which Hall used in *The Well of Loneliness* that has been overlooked by most of her critics is her deliberate address of the novel to American as well as British readers. The narrator of *The Well of Loneliness* consistently describes Stephen Gordon as a congenital "female invert," much to the chagrin of later feminist readers, but Hall selected this term – popularized by Havelock Ellis – not only to lend scientific authority to Stephen's experiences of gender dysphoria and same-sex attraction, but also to include American readers, who were more likely to know Ellis' work than studies by the German sexologists.[41] Moreover, by detailing the traumatic rejections that Stephen experiences as a child and young adult, Hall also opened her novel to sophisticated readers on both sides of the Atlantic who were familiar with Freud's emerging analysis of childhood sexuality.[42]

Hall transforms the usual British narratives about the war by dramatizing Stephen Gordon's strength, bravery, and heroism as an ambulance driver on the Western Front, showing a feminist advocacy by demonstrating that machines like the automobile made it possible for women to perform some of the same battlefield tasks as males. To be sure, the narrator insists that Stephen's heroism and physical daring come naturally to her because "bombs do not trouble the nerves of the invert,"[43] but she also characterizes the women in the Breakspeare unit as coming from different classes, regions, gender identities, and sexual orientations. By dramatizing their courage, skill, and devotion, the text shows how dramatically the Great War transformed Victorian gender norms and shifted the borders between the public and the private. Mary Llewellyn also exposes the "confused zone" in sexologists' taxonomies by displaying more feminine physical and emotional characteristics than "female inverts" like Stephen even as she asserts and acts out her lesbian desires.[44] Mary demonstrates her youthful "ardent, courageous, impulsive nature,"[45] her modest skills as a mechanic, and her competence in driving on the battlefield;

41 Siobhan Somerville, *Queering the Color Line: Race and the Invention of Homosexuality in American Culture* (Durham: Duke University Press, 2000), pp. 18–21.

42 See, for example, Heather Love, *Feeling Backward: Loss and the Politics of Queer History* (Cambridge: Harvard University Press, 2007), pp. 100–28. In *Women, Writing and Fetishism, 1890–1950: Female Cross-Gendering* (Oxford: Clarendon Press, 2003), Clare Taylor provides a more general discussion of Hall's knowledge of Freudian psychology in the 1920s.

43 Radclyffe Hall, *The Well of Loneliness* (New York: Doubleday, 1990), p. 217. I cite from this edition throughout.

44 Margot Gayle Backus, "Sexual orientation in the (post) imperial nation: Celticism and inversion theory in Radclyffe Hall's *Well of Loneliness*," *Tulsa Studies in Women's Literature*, 15(2) (1996), 253–66.

45 Hall, *Well of Loneliness*, p. 285.

she also shows her moral courage in avowing her lesbian desire when she declares her love for Stephen and dares to live openly with her after the war.

Like Woolf and Lawrence, Hall creatively experiments with genres in this text, blending the *roman à clef* with the *kuntslerroman* to show how Stephen Gordon gradually frees herself to accept her sex/gender identity and redefine her writing voice. By remaining in Paris after the war rather than returning to her family's provincial estate in England, Stephen avoids the social sanctions directed at lesbians who openly show what Judith Halberstam calls "female masculinity," as well as British laws that discipline homosexual men like Jonathan Brockett.[46] Because she is an "outlaw" who is "law-abiding at heart,"[47] Stephen chooses to remain in France, where homosexuality had not been prohibited by civil law since 1804 and where more social tolerance was extended to male and female "inverts" than Stephen had experienced in England. However, even though she realizes that she will be "the last of the Gordons," Stephen longs to offer Mary Llewellyn the respectability and social acceptance that a legal same-sex marriage could provide. When she sees that she cannot offer Mary this "protection," she takes it upon herself to sacrifice her own happiness and "give" Mary to Martin Hallam.[48]

Moreover, Stephen's life in postwar Paris dramatizes what Scott Herring calls her "coming out into gay society."[49] Stephen's transformation begins when she follows Brockett's advice and attends Valerie Seymour's Paris salon, but this group reinforces her upper-class identity, with its privileges of wealth and leisure. When Stephen creates a social circle of her own after the war, she includes Jamie and Barbara, who, like Mary Llewellyn, are less privileged, middle-class outcasts from the Celtic fringe of the empire; she also invites Wanda, who is a refugee from Poland, a struggling painter who loved "wildly" and turned to Catholicism for solace.[50] Compelled by a desire to describe "a responsible vision of how the modern citizen could and should rebuild a just social world,"[51] Stephen ultimately commits herself to writing on behalf of the male and female "inverts" who, even in Paris, remain among the most marginalized of its citizens. While Hall's narrative charts Stephen's development as a writer, it does not describe the novels she writes after her decision to sacrifice her own personal happiness

[46] Judith Halberstam, *Female Masculinity* (Durham: Duke University Press, 1998).
[47] Hall, *Well of Loneliness*, p. 394. [48] Dellamora, *Radclyffe Hall*, pp. 198–203.
[49] Scott Herring, *Queering the Underworld: Slumming Literature and the Undoing of Lesbian and Gay History* (Chicago: University of Chicago Press, 2007), pp. 168–69.
[50] Hall, *Well of Loneliness*, p. 356. [51] Reichman, *Affective Life of Law*, p. 1.

in order to write on behalf of the queer subjects that she has accepted as her kin, as represented in the final melodramatic scene of the novel.

In her reading of Virginia Woolf's early novels, Ravit Reichman demonstrates how modernist texts helped to make possible changes in the law that recognize the traumas of World War I, arguing that "modernist experimentation did not shape legal concepts or procedures . . . But literary modernism, I submit, necessarily preceded these changes in law. Literature had to change before law did – simply because it could."[52] If Reichman had included novels like *The Well of Loneliness* in her study, she might have drawn different conclusions. Even though Hall resisted many of the experimental features of modernist prose and employed a more traditional realistic narrative style, she also advocated more directly for changes in British laws that punished homosexual acts and prohibited same-sex marriage.

Although *The Well of Loneliness* failed to "make the law" in England, where it was banned from 1928 until 1949, and in Australia, where it was banned from 1928 until 1954, it survived legal challenges in the United States and has circulated widely from 1929 up to the present day. Hall's novel has been the target of countless feminist critiques, but was one of only a few Anglophone novels about lesbian life that was able to "make the law" in the interwar years. It was republished frequently in the United States and attracted many other readers in Europe and elsewhere in translation. Its direct appeal for sympathy and tolerance for lesbians, gay men, and queer subjects helped to make possible the decriminalization of homosexual acts and the legalization of same-sex marriage in England and the United States, reforms Hall fervently supported.

Jean Devanny's *The Butcher Shop* also illustrates the effects of the gendered censorship dynamic that Marshik posits, but it demonstrates at the same time the additional difficulties faced by writers who, like Devanny, lived far from the commercial centers of the book trade in London and New York. Devanny did not seek a publisher for her first novel in Wellington, where she was living at the time; rather, she sent her manuscript to London, as most of her contemporaries typically did. Devanny did not have the benefit of a professional literary agent in placing her first work, but, by a lucky coincidence, the editor who received it passed it on to Gerald Duckworth. Though Duckworth rejected Devanny's first work, he invited her to submit another, and when she sent him *The Butcher Shop*, he accepted and published it in 1926. Duckworth subsequently published

[52] Reichman, *Affective Life of Law*, p. 99.

five more novels by Devanny set in New Zealand and three representing life in Australia. While Duckworth's list included modernist works such as Lawrence's *The Trespasser* (1912) and *Sons and Lovers* (1913) and Woolf's *The Voyage Out* (1915) and *Night and Day* (1918), it also included numerous "exotic romances" like Devanny's. Duckworth anticipated that his politically more liberal readers would appreciate her blunt critiques of British imperialism and regard her novels as examples of "modernist primitivism," in contrast to the consumers of the imperial romances marketed by other English presses at the time. *The Butcher Shop* sold relatively well in England; it was reprinted twice in 1926 and reached its fourth edition by 1928.[53]

When the first edition of *The Butcher Shop* arrived in New Zealand in 1926, however, it was seized by customs officials in response to a cable from the office of the New Zealand High Commissioner in London which warned that it included depictions of life on a New Zealand sheep station that were "disgusting indecent communistic."[54] On April 26, 1926, New Zealand's Board of Censorship officially banned *The Butcher Shop*, but Devanny was not informed, and would have had no legal basis to appeal. As one customs official later explained, the censorship process in New Zealand avoided the "undesirable publicity" of a hearing; as a result, "hardly anyone knows of the existence" of books that were banned.[55] The travels of Devanny's first novel thus shows how English censorship practices were exported and reproduced in New Zealand and in Australia, where it was banned in 1929. At the same time, *The Butcher Shop* remained in circulation in Great Britain and the United States after its publication by Macauley's in 1926; shortly afterwards, it was challenged by a vice society in Boston, but it escaped legal suppression.[56]

The Butcher Shop describes the production of one of New Zealand's main exports – lamb – and, like Upton Sinclair's *The Jungle* (1909), it describes the demanding – and sometimes revolting – work that laborers performed as they castrated, sheared, and later slaughtered the sheep destined to serve this large export market. It dramatizes the theme of inheritance, since the protagonist of the novel, Barry Messenger, acquires "twenty thousand acres" on the North Island of New Zealand and manages large herds of sheep and cattle after his English father's untimely

[53] Carole Ferrier, *Jean Devanny: Romantic Revolutionary* (Melbourne: Melbourne University Press, 1998), pp. 34–6.
[54] Robert Pearson, "The banning of *The Butcher Shop*" in *The Butcher Shop*, p. 226.
[55] Pearson, "Banning," p. 225. [56] Boyer, *Purity in Print*, p. 183.

death. Unlike the novels of Woolf, Lawrence, and Hall, however, inheritance is not the central problem in this text. Instead, Devanny's novel challenges the racial and sexual politics that were typically confirmed in British-authored imperial romances and other popular novels of the 1920s. Barry Messenger is designed to appeal to more left-leaning English, American, and Commonwealth readers; he works long hours outdoors, side by side with the white and Maori laborers on his staff. His closest friend is Jimmy Tutaki, a handsome, intelligent, well-educated Maori man that he met at school.

Devanny also openly advocates for postsuffrage feminist causes by critiquing the class and gender hierarchies that are usually confirmed by marriages in British imperial romances. Her heroine, Margaret, is a young, attractive, athletic, and intelligent woman, from a middle-class family whose fortunes are in decline. After she is hired as a maid in Messenger's home, she promptly falls in love with her handsome employer, and they soon decide to marry. On the day before her marriage, in a reversal of Connie Chatterley's story, Margaret invites her fiancé to have sex with her outdoors, saying, "This is our wedding-day. Make me your wife today."[57] After their marriage they live contentedly together for several years, and Margaret gives birth to two daughters and a son, ensuring that Messenger will have a male heir for his property. The crisis in this narrative comes instead when her husband is away and Margaret falls passionately in love with his new station manager, Angus Glengarry. Margaret initiates an affair with him, and after they have sex for the first time she tells him, "I did not know what it was to love."[58] The novel ends melodramatically when Barry Messenger commits suicide after learning of his wife's adultery, and Margaret, in a moment of regret and deranged passion, kills her lover, declaring, "'Never again shall man claim property rights over me.'"[59]

Devanny's text clearly does not show the skillful control of irony evident in Woolf's novels or in other modernist fiction, but it advocates much more directly for greater rights for modern women and for working-class people. It dramatizes the social and political consequences of New Zealand's Labour Party shedding "its original socialist programme in favour of a reactionary, opportunist policy" that favored landowners like Messenger.[60] The novel also ingeniously transforms British postwar narratives about the trauma suffered by survivors of the Great War by including an injured Englishman, Ian Longstairs, who immigrates to Messenger's

[57] Devanny, *Butcher Shop*, p. 58. [58] Devanny, *Butcher Shop*, p. 129.
[59] Devanny, *Butcher Shop*, p. 313. [60] Devanny, *Butcher Shop*, p. 193.

station when he can no longer find work in England – but he is disabled as a result of an accident in his workplace rather than on the battlefield. Longstairs regards himself and his wife as members of the "most advanced school of socialists" in England, but the novel repeatedly shows that his outdated politics do not apply to the material realities of postwar New Zealand. He compensates for being a victim of English capitalism by lording it over his French wife, Miette, who later retaliates by enticing Jimmy Tutaki into a passionate affair that she hides from her husband by appealing to his racist "English ideas about coloured people."[61] In other words, Devanny demonstrates what is wrong with the social and political arrangements in New Zealand in the 1920s and invites her readers to look beyond the borders of the British Empire to consider solutions offered, for instance, by the Bolshevik Revolution in Russia. Devanny's novels suggest how she and other politically engaged writers of the 1920s found new ways to identify and connect with networks of readers around the world who shared her revolutionary politics.

Like Lawrence and Hall, Devanny was not silenced by the banning of *The Butcher Shop*, and her later career shows her creativity and extraordinary resilience as a writer of genre fiction. As Nicole Moore observes, Devanny wrote about the "major feminist dilemmas of the 1920s and 1930s" and the modern women in her fiction face the challenges of "sex, maternity, marriage, birth control and abortion."[62] Her next novel, *Lenore Divine* (1926), exposed the racist assumptions of British imperial culture through her white heroine happily marrying a distinguished Maori landholder. While this novel circulated unchallenged in Great Britain and New Zealand, it was not published in the United States, probably because it challenged the racist miscegenation laws in force in many states. Devanny and her family moved to Australia in 1929, but she remained a productive and controversial fiction writer; when her tenth novel, *The Virtuous Courtesan* (1935), was banned in Australia, she turned from genre fiction to create her most famous, innovative, and critically respected novel, *Sugar Heaven* (1936).

In short, Lawrence's, Hall's, and Devanny's careers dispute Sinclair Lewis' claim that a writer cannot be creative with the "tapeworm of censorship gnawing in his vitals." Instead, like other authors of challenged books, all three subsequently found productive and creative ways to evade state-sponsored censorship. Nearly one hundred years after these novels were banned, literary scholars can still learn new lessons about

[61] Devanny, *Butcher Shop*, p. 185. [62] Moore, *The Censor's Library*, p. 161.

the complex, ever changing relationships between literature and law. Moreover, as we begin to recognize how electronic self-publishing, instant global communication, unmediated social networking, and related innovations have created a paradigm shift in literary production and censorship practices, we must also recognize that these changes have transformed the laws and the roles of the "guardians" of the text that Jacques Derrida identified in "Before the Law." Scholars interested in understanding the complex relationships between law and the literature written in the twenty-first century will need to consider how the roles of the "author, publisher, critics, academics, archivists, librarians, lawyers and so on" have been transformed by new technologies in order to determine where, how, and why a literary text fails or succeeds in "making the law."[63]

[63] Derrida, *Acts of Literature*, p. 214.

Bibliography

Abdulaziz, Mohamed H. Muyaka. *19th Century Swahili Popular Poetry* (Nairobi: Kenya Literature Bureau, 1979).

Abdullah bin Sheikh bin Yunis on behalf of the Thalatha Thaifa and W.N. MacMillan v. *(1) The Wakf Commissioners; (2) The Land Officer on behalf of H. M. Government of East Africa*, 12 EACA (1913).

"About."*Pussyhat Project.* March 18, 2017. Web. www.pussyhatproject.com/.

"About the Black Lives Matter Network." *Black Lives Matter.* December 5, 2016. Web. www.blacklivesmatter.com/about/.

"A Certain Maritime Incident." Select Committee on a Certain Maritime Incident. *Commonwealth of Australia.* October 23, 2002. Web. www.aph.gov.au/Parliamentary_Business/Committees/Senate/Former_Committees/maritimeincident/report/index.

Achenbach, Joel. "O. J. Simpson defensive linemen," *Washington Post*, January 21, 1995.

Adams, Charles Warren. *The Notting Hill Mystery* (1862–3) (London: British Library, 2012).

Adams, Hazard (ed.). *Critical Theory since Plato* (New York: Harcourt Brace Jovanovich, 1971).

Adams, Lorraine. "180 degrees separate black, white views of O. J. Simpson case," *Washington Post*, July 30, 1995.

Agamben, Giorgio. *Homo Sacer: Sovereign Power and Bare Life* (trans. Daniel Heller-Roazen) (Stanford: Stanford University Press, 1998).

The Use of Bodies (trans. Adam Kotsko) (Stanford: Stanford University Press, 2015).

Ahmed, Safdar. "Villawood: notes from an immigration detention centre," *The Shipping News*, March 5, 2015. Web. https://medium.com/shipping-news/villawood-9698183e114c#.iv80bia2s.

A Jury of Her Peers. Film. Dir. Sally Heckel. New York: Women Make Movies, 1980.

Alexis, Cydney. "Let's banish the phrase 'creative writing.'" *Inside High Ed*, January 3, 2017. Web. www.insidehighered.com/views/2017/01/03/we-should-stop-distinguishing-between-creative-and-other-forms-writing-essay.

Allo, Awol (ed.). *The Courtroom as a Space of Resistance: Reflections on the Legacy of the Rivonia Trial* (Burlington: Ashgate Publishing, 2015).

Amar, Akhil Reed. *America's Constitution: A Biography* (New York: Random House, 2005).

Ames, William. *Conscience with the Power and Cases Thereof* (Amsterdam: Walter J. Johnson Inc., 1975).

Amidu, Assibi A. "Political poetry among the Swahili: the Kimondo verses from Lamu" in Pat Caplan and Farouk Topan (eds.), *Swahili Modernities: Culture, Politics and Identity on the East African Coast* (Trenton and Asmara: Africa World Press, 2004), pp. 157–72.

Anderson, Benedict. *Imagined Communities: Reflections on the Origin and Spread of Nationalism* (London: Verso, 2006).

Angel, Marina. "Criminal law and women: giving the abused woman who kills a jury of her peers who appreciate trifles," *American Criminal Law Review*, 33 (1996), 229–349.

Annear, Robyn. *The Man Who Lost Himself: The Unbelievable Story of the Tichborne Claimant* (London: Robinson, 2003).

Apostolakis, Kostas. "Pitiable dramas on the podium of the Athenian law courts" in Sophia Papaioannou, Andreas Serafim, and Beatrice de Vela (eds.), *The Theatre of Justice: Aspects of Performance in Greco-Roman Oratory and Rhetoric* (Leiden: Brill, 2017), pp. 133–56.

Aristodemou, Maria. *Law and Literature: Journeys from Her to Eternity* (Oxford: Oxford University Press, 2000).

Aristotle. *The Ethics of Aristotle* (trans. J. A. K. Thomson) (Harmondsworth: Penguin, 1955).

Poetics (trans. Malcolm Heath) (London: Penguin, 1996).

Armitage, David. *The Declaration of Independence: A Global History* (Cambridge: Harvard University Press, 2007).

Armstrong, John A. "Nationalism: five roads to modernity," *History and Theory*, 33(1) (1994), 79–95.

Armstrong, Nancy K. *Desire and Domestic Fiction: A Political History of the Novel* (Oxford: Oxford University Press, 1987).

Arnold, Matthew. *Culture and Anarchy* (New Haven: Yale University Press, [1869] 1994).

Attorney-General v. *St. Cross Hospital* (1853) 51 English Reports, 1114.

Bachmann-Medick, Doris. *Cultural Turns: Neuorientierungen in den Kulturwissenschaften* (Hamburg: Rowohlt, 2006).

Cultural Turns: New Orientations in the Study of Culture (Berlin and Boston: De Gruyter, 2016).

Backus, Margot Gayle. "Sexual orientation in the (post) imperial nation: Celticism and inversion theory in Radclyffe Hall's *The Well of Loneliness*," *Tulsa Studies in Women's Literature*, 15(2) (1996), 253–66.

Baker, John H. *An Introduction to English Legal History*, 1st ed. (London: Butterworths, 1971).

An Introduction to English Legal History, 4th ed. (London: Butterworths, 2002).

An Introduction to English Legal History (Oxford: Oxford University Press, 2005).

Why the History of English Law Has Not Been Finished (Cambridge: Cambridge University Press, 1999).

Baker, Peter and Gardiner, Harris. "Washington pauses for Justice Antonin Scalia's funeral," *New York Times*, February 20, 2016. Web. www.nytimes.com/2016/02/21/us/politics/justice-antonin-scalias-funeral-lets-washington-pause-in-praise.html

Bal, Mieke. *Travelling Concepts in the Humanities: A Rough Guide* (Toronto: University of Toronto Press, 2002).

Balibar, Étienne. "Subjection and subjectivation" in Joan Copjec (ed.), *Supposing the Subject* (London: Verso, 1994), pp. 1–15.

Balkin, Jack M. "Deconstructive practice and legal theory," *Yale Law Journal*, 96 (1987), 1–48.

"Tradition, betrayal and the politics of deconstruction," *Cardozo Law Review*, 11 (1990), 1–18.

Bannet, Eve T. *The Domestic Revolution: Enlightenment Feminisms and the Novel* (Baltimore: Johns Hopkins University Press, 2000).

Barnes, Julian. *Arthur & George* (London: Jonathan Cape, 2005).

"Interview by Xesús Fraga, 10 July 2006" in V. Guignery and R. Roberts (eds.), *Conversations with Julian Barnes* (Jackson: University of Mississippi Press, 2009), pp. 134–147.

Barth, John. *The Floating Opera and The End of the Road* (New York: Anchor Books, 1988).

Barthes, Roland. *S/Z* (trans. Richard Miller) (London: Cape, 1974).

The Pleasure of the Text (trans. Richard Miller) (New York: Hill and Wang, 1975).

Bartholomew, G. W. and Iliffe, J. A. "Decisions," *International and Comparative Law Journal*, 1(3) (1952), 392–402.

Beattie, John. *Crime and the Courts in England, 1660–1800* (Princeton: Princeton University Press, 1986).

Bell, Derrick. *Gospel Choirs: Psalms of Survival for an Alien Land Called Home* (New York: Basic Books, 1996).

Ben-Yishai, Avelet. *Common Precedents: The Presentness of the Past in Victorian Law and Fiction* (Oxford: Oxford University Press, 2013).

Bender, John. *Imagining the Penitentiary: Fiction and the Architecture of Mind in Eighteenth-Century England* (Chicago: University of Chicago Press, 1987).

Bender, Thomas. *A Nation among Nations: America's Place in World History* (Boston: Hill and Wang, 2006).

Benjamin, Walter. "On the Concept of History" in Michael W. Jennings (ed.), *Walter Benjamin: Selected Writings Volume 4, 1938–1940* (Massachusetts: Harvard University Press, 2003), pp. 389–400.

Bentham, Jeremy. *Bentham: A Fragment on Government*. Ed. J. H. Burns and H. L. A. Hart (Cambridge: Cambridge University Press, 1988).

Bentley, David. *English Criminal Justice in the Nineteenth Century* (London: The Hambledon Press, 1998).

Berlant, Lauren. "On the case," *Critical Inquiry*, 33(4) (2007), 663–72.

Bertens, Hans. *Literary Theory: The Basics* (London and New York: Taylor and Francis, 2008).

Bevington, David. "Equity in *Measure for Measure*" in Bradin Cormack, Martha C. Nussbaum, and Richard Strier (eds.), *Shakespeare and the Law: A Conversation among Disciplines and Professions* (Chicago: University of Chicago Press, 2013), pp. 164–73.

Bhabha, Homi. "Cultural choice and the revision of freedom" in Austin Sarat and Thomas R. Kearns (eds.), *Human Rights: Concepts, Contests, Contingencies* (Ann Arbor: The University of Michigan Press, 2001), pp. 45–62.

The Location of Culture (London and New York: Routledge, 1994).

Bierstecker, Ann. *Questions of Language and Power in Nineteenth and Twentieth-Century Poetry in Kishwahili* (East Lansing: Michigan State University Press, 1996).

Binder, Guyora and Robert Weisberg (eds.). *Literary Criticisms of Law* (Princeton: Princeton University Press, 2000).

Birmingham, Peg. *Hannah Arendt and Human Rights: The Predicament of Common Responsibility* (Indianapolis: Indiana University Press, 2004).

Birrell, Kathleen. *Indigeneity: Before and Beyond the Law* (Abingdon: Glass House Books, 2016).

Bishara, Fahad. "Paper routes: inscribing Islamic law across the nineteenth-century Western Indian Ocean," *Law and History Review*, 32(4) (2014), 797–820.

"A sea of debt: histories of commerce and obligation in the Indian Ocean, c. 1850–1940," *Enterprise and Society*, 15(4) (2014), 643–54.

Black Hawk. *Life of Black Hawk, or Ma-ka-tai-me-she-kia-kiak: Dictated by Himself*. Ed. Gerald Kennedy (New York: Penguin Group, 2008).

Blackstone, William. *Commentaries on the Laws of England*, vol. 1 (Oxford: Clarendon Press, 1765).

Commentaries on the Laws of England: In Four Books (New York: J.B. Lippincott, 1859).

Blake, William. "London" in William Blake: *The Complete Illuminated Books* (London: Thames & Hudson, 2000), p. 88.

Blom-Cooper, Louis. *The Law as Literature* (London: Bodley Head, 1961).

Boland, Eavan. *Collected Poems* (Manchester: Carcanet, 1995).

Boulton, James and Margaret Boulton (eds.). *The Letters of D. H. Lawrence*, vol. 6 (Cambridge: Cambridge University Press, 1991).

Boyer, Paul. *Purity in Print: The Vice Society Movement and Book Censorship in America* (New York: Scribner, 1968).

Brantlinger, Patrick. *The Spirit of Reform: British Literature and Politics, 1832–1867* (Cambridge: Harvard University Press, 1977).

Bricker, Andrew. "Is narrative essential to the law? Precedent, case law, and judicial emplotment," *Law, Culture, and the Humanities* (2015), 1–13. DOI: 10.1177/1743872115627413.

Bringing Them Home: Report of the National Inquiry into the Separation of Aboriginal and Torres Strait Islander Children from Their Families. Human Rights and Equal Opportunity Commission, Commonwealth of Australia. May 1997.

Brombert, Victor H. *The Romantic Prison: The French Tradition* (Princeton: Princeton University Press, 1978).

Brooks, Peter. "Narrative transactions: does the law need a narratology?" *Yale Journal of Law and Humanities*, 18(1) (2006), 1–28.

Brown v. *Board of Education of Topeka*, 347 U.S. 483 (1954).

Brown-Nagin, Tomiko. *Courage to Dissent: Atlanta and the Long History of the Civil Rights Movement* (New York: Oxford University Press, 2012).

Brown, Charles Brockden. *Ormond, Or, The Secret Witness: With Related Texts. 1799*. Eds. Philip Barnard and Stephen Shapiro (Indianapolis: Hackett Publishing, 2009).

Brown, Wendy. *Edgework: Critical Essays on Knowledge and Politics* (Princeton: Princeton University Press, 2005).

"The most we can hope for...: human rights and the politics of fatalism," *The South Atlantic Quarterly*, 103(2–3) (2004), 451–63.

Browning, Robert. "Red-Cotton Night-Cap Country" in John Pettigrew (ed.), *Robert Browning: The Poems II* (Harmondsworth: Penguin, 1981), pp. 75–184.

Bru, Sascha. *Democracy, Law and the Modernist Avant-Gardes: Writing in the State of Exception* (Edinburgh: Edinburgh University Press, 2009).

Bruitenhaus, Peter. *The Great War of Words: British, American, and Canadian Propaganda and Fiction 1914–1933* (Vancouver: University of British Columbia Press, 1987).

Brummett, Barry. "Mediating the laws: popular trials and the mass media" in Robert Hariman (ed.), *Popular Trials: Rhetoric, Mass Media, and the Law* (Tuscaloosa and London: University of Alabama Press, 1990), pp. 179–93.

Bryan, Patricia L. "Stories in fiction and in fact: Susan Glaspell's 'A Jury of Her Peers' and the 1901 murder trial of Margaret Hossack," *Stanford Law Review*, 49(6) (1997), 1293–1363.

Burke, Edmund. *Reflections on the Revolution in France*. Ed. Leslie George Mitchell (Oxford: Oxford University Press, 1999).

Burney, Frances. *Evelina* (Oxford: Oxford University Press, 2002).

Burrow, Rufus. *God and Human Dignity: The Personalism, Theology, and Ethics of Martin Luther King Jr.* (Notre Dame: University of Notre Dame Press, 2006).

Calabresi, Guido. "Some thoughts on risk distribution and the law of torts," *Yale Law Journal*, 70(4) (1961), 499–553.

Calvin, Jean. *A Harmonie upon the Three Evangelists, Matthew Mark and Luke* (London, 1584).

Cardozo, Benjamin N. *The Growth of the Law* (New Haven: Yale University Press, 1925).

Law and Literature, and Other Essays and Addresses (New York: Harcourt, Brace and Company, 1931).

Carter, David. "The mystery of the missing middlebrow, or the c(o)urse of good taste" in Judith Ryan and Chris Wallace-Crabbe (eds.), *Imagining Australia: Literature and Culture in the New New World* (Cambridge: Harvard University Press, 2004), pp. 174–99.

Cassese, Antonio. *Self-Determination of Peoples: A Legal Reappraisal* (Cambridge: Cambridge University Press, 1995).

Caughie, Pamela L. "The temporality of modernist life writing in the era of transsexualism: Virginia Woolf's *Orlando* and Einar Wegener's *Man into Woman*," *Modern Fiction Studies*, 59(3) (2013), 501–25.

Cerniglia, David. "Constellation" in Michael Ryan (ed.), *The Encyclopedia of Literary and Cultural Theory* (Maldon: Wiley-Blackwell, 2011).

Chambers, Robert. *History of the English Language and Literature* (Edinburgh: William and Robert Chambers and London: Orr and Smith, 1836).

Chandler, James K. *England in 1819: The Politics of Literary Culture and the Case of Romantic Historicism* (Chicago: University of Chicago Press, 1998).

"On the face of the case: Conrad, Lord Jim, and the sentimental novel," *Critical Inquiry*, 33 (2007), 837–64.

Chaplin, Susan. *The Gothic and the Rule of the Law, 1764–1820* (London: Palgrave Macmillan, 2007).

Law, Sensibility, and the Sublime in Eighteenth-Century Women's Fiction: Speaking of Dread (Burlington: Ashgate, 2004).

Charles, Casey. *Critical Queer Studies: Law, Film, and Fiction in Contemporary American Culture* (Farnham: Ashgate, 2012).

Cherokee Nation v. *State of Georgia*, 30 U.S. 1 (1831).

Chisholm, Richard. *Family Courts Violence Review*. November 2009. Web. http://apo.org.au/node/20315

Christodoulidis, Emilios. "Strategies of rupture," *Law and Critique* 20(1) (2008), 3–26.

Claybaugh, Amanda. *The Novel of Purpose: Literature and Social Reform in the Anglo-American World* (Ithaca: Cornell University Press, 2007).

Clover, Carol J. "Law and the order of popular culture" in Austin Sarat and Thomas R. Kearns (eds.), *Law in the Domains of Culture* (Ann Arbor: University of Michigan Press, 1998), pp. 97–19.

Coase, Ronald. "The problem of social cost," *Journal of Law and Economics*, 3 (1960), 1–44.

Cohen, Stephen. "From mistress to master: political transition and formal conflict in *Measure for Measure*," *Criticism*, 41(4) (1999), 431–64.

Coleridge, Samuel Taylor. "Coleridge: a letter to Wordsworth" (1810) in John O. Hayden (ed.), *Walter Scott: The Critical Heritage* (London and New York: Routledge, 1970), pp. 56–61.

Collins, Wilkie. *The Woman in White* (London: Penguin, 1985 [1860]).

Comyns, John. *A Digest of the Laws of England: By the Right Honourable Sir John Comyns . . . The Fourth Edition, corrected, and continued to the present time, by Samuel Rose*, 2nd edn. (London: Strahan, 1800).

"Conan Doyle solves a new Dreyfus case," *New York Times*, February 2, 1907.
Cooper, Craig. "Demosthenes, actor on the political and forensic stage" in Christopher Mackie (ed.), *Oral Performance and Its Context* (Leiden: Brill, 2004), pp. 145–61.
"Hyperides and the trial of Phryne," *Phoenix*, 49 (1995), 303–18.
Cooter, Robert and Ulen, Thomas. *Law and Economics*, 6th edn. (Boston: Pearson Education, 2012).
Corcos, Christine A. *An International Guide to Law and Literature Studies* (Buffalo and New York: William S. Hein & Co., 2000).
Cornell, Drucilla. "Violence of the masquerade: law dressed up as justice" in Jonathan Culler (ed.), *Deconstruction: Critical Concepts in Literary and Cultural Studies*, vol. 2 (London and New York: Routledge, 2003), pp. 194–210.
Cornish, William. "The sources of the law" in William Cornish et al (ed.), *The Oxford History of English Law*, vol. XI (Oxford: Oxford University Press, 2003), pp. 41–71.
Corrigan, Brian J. *Playhouse Law in Shakespeare's World* (Madison: Fairleigh Dickinson University Press, 2004).
Cover, Robert. "Nomos and narrative," *Harvard Law Review*, 97(1) (1983), 4–68.
"Nomos and narrative" in Martha Minow, Michael Ryan, and Austin Sarat (eds.), *Narrative, Violence and the Law: The Essays of Robert Cover* (Ann Arbor: Michigan University Press, 1993) pp. 95–172.
"Violence and the word," *Yale Law Journal*, 95 (1986), 1601–29.
Craig, Randall. *Promising Language: Betrothal in Victorian Law and Fiction* (Albany: State University of New York Press, 2010).
Crane, Gregg D. *Race, Citizenship, and Law in American Literature* (Cambridge: University of Cambridge Press, 2002).
Crawley, Karen and Honni van Rijswijk. "Justice in the gutter: representing everyday trauma in the graphic novels of Art Spiegelman," *Law Text Culture*, 16(1) (2012), 93–118.
Crenshaw, Kimberlé Williams. "Colour-blind dreams and racial nightmares: reconfiguring racism in the post-civil rights era" in Toni Morrison and Claudia Brodsky Lacour (eds.), *Birth of a Nation'Hood: Gaze, Script and Spectacle in the O. J. Simpson Case* (New York: Pantheon Books, 1997), pp. 97–168.
"Race, form and retrenchment: transformation and legitimation in antidiscrimination law," *Harvard Law Review*, 101(7) (1988), 1331–87.
Croft, Clyde. "Lord Hardwicke's use of precedent in equity" in Thomas G. Watkin (ed.), *Legal Record and Historical Reality: Proceedings of the Eighth British Legal History Conference* (London: Hambledon Press, 1989), pp. 121–56.
Culler, Jonathan. "Deconstruction and the law" in Jonathon Culler (ed.), *Deconstruction: Critical Concepts in Literary and Cultural Studies*, vol. 2 (London and New York: Routledge, 2003).

Cunningham, Ian (trans.). *Herodas: Mimes* (Cambridge: Harvard University Press, 2003).

Dalton, Clare. "An essay in the deconstruction of contract doctrine" in Sanford Levinson and Steven Mailloux (eds.), *Interpreting Law and Literature: A Hermeneutic Reader* (Evanston: Northwestern University Press, 1988), pp. 285–318.

Daly, Eoin and Hickey, Tom. *The Political Theory of the Irish Constitution: Republicanism and the Basic Law* (Manchester: Manchester University Press, 2015).

Dangaremba, Tsitsi. *Nervous Conditions* (London: Women's Press, 1988).

Darda, Joseph. "Graphic ethics: theorizing the face in Marjane Satrapi's *Persepolis*," *College Literature: A Journal of Critical Literary Studies*, 40(2) (2013), 31–51.

Davies, Malcolm. *Epicorum Graecorum Fragmenta* (Göttingen: Vandenhoeck & Ruprecht, 1988).

Poetarum Melicorum Fragmenta I: Alcman, Stesichorus, Ibycus (Oxford: Oxford University Press, 1991).

Davis, Megan. "To bind or not to bind: The United Nations Declaration on the Rights of Indigenous Peoples five years on," *Australian International Law Journal*, 19 (2012), 17–48.

Davis, Mike. *City of Quartz: Excavating the Future in Los Angeles* (London and New York: Verso, 1990).

de Crevecoeur, J. Hector St. John. *Letters from an American Farmer and Sketches of Eighteenth-Century America*. Ed. Albert Stone (New York: Penguin Group, 1981).

de Tocqueville, Alexis. *Democracy in America* (New York: Doubleday, 1969).

Deans, R. Storry. *Notable Trials: Romances of the Law* (London: Cassell, 1906).

"Declaration of Constitutional Principles: The Southern Manifesto (March 12, 1956)," Congressional Record, 84th Congress, Second Session, vol. 102, 4459–4460. Web. http://mrphillipshistory.wikispaces.com/file/view/Southern+Manifesto.pdf.

Delany, Paul. *Literature, Money and the Market: From Trollope to Amis* (Basingstoke: Palgrave, 2002).

Delgado, Richard. "Storytelling for oppositionists and others: a plea for narrative," *Michigan Law Review*, 87 (1989), 2411–41.

Dellamora, Richard. *Radclyffe Hall: A Life in the Writing* (Philadelphia: University of Pennsylvania Press, 2011).

DeLombard, Jeannine Marie. *Slavery on Trial: Law Abolitionism, and Print Culture* (Chapel Hill: University of North Carolina Press, 2007).

Derrida, Jacques. *Acts of Literature*. Ed. Derek Attridge (London and New York: Routledge, 1992).

"Force of law: the 'mystical foundation of authority'" in Drucilla Cornell, Michel Rosenfeld, and David G. Carlson (eds.), *Deconstruction and the Possibility of Justice* (London and New York: Routledge, 1992), pp. 3–67.

"What is a relevant translation?" *Critical Inquiry*, 27 (1983), 174–200.

Derrit, J. D. M. "Justice, equity and good conscience" in Lauren Benton (ed.), *Law and Colonial Cultures: Legal Regimes in World History, 1400–1900* (Cambridge and New York: Cambridge University Press, 2002).

Devanny, Jean. *The Butcher Shop*. Ed. Heather Roberts (Auckland: Auckland University Press, 1981 [1926]).

Dicey, A. V. *Lectures on the Relation between Law and Public Opinion in England*, 2nd edn. (London: Macmillan, 1962).

Dickinson, Edwin D. "The Law of Nations as part of the national law of the United States," *The University of Pennsylvania Law Review*, 101 (1952–3): 26–56.

Dimock, Wai Chee. *Residues of Justice: Literature, Law, Philosophy* (Berkeley: University of California Press, 1996).

Through Other Continents: American Literature across Deep Time (Princeton: Princeton University Press, 2008).

Dolin, Kieran. *A Critical Introduction to Law and Literature* (Cambridge: Cambridge University Press, 2007).

"From Orpheus to Yothu Yindi: music and legal cultures," *Law, Culture and the Humanities*, 12(1) (2016), 29–38.

Dolin, Tim. *Mistress of the House: Women of Property in the Victorian Novel* (Aldershot: Ashgate, 1997).

Douglass, Frederick. "The Dred Scott Decision: speech delivered before American Anti-Slavery Society, New York, May 14, 1857" in Philip S. Foner (ed.), *Frederick Douglass: Selected Speeches and Writings* (Chicago: Lawrence Hill Books, 1999), pp. 344–58.

Douzinas, Costas. *The End of Human Rights: Critical Legal Thought at the End of the Century* (London: Hart, 2000).

Douzinas, Costas and Lynda Nead. *Law and the Image: The Authority of Art and the Aesthetics of Law* (Chicago: Chicago University Press, 1999).

Doyle, Arthur Conan. "The strange case of George Edalji," *New York Times*, February 2, 1907.

"The strange case of George Edalji," *New York Times*, February 3, 1907.

Dred Scott v. *John F.A. Sanford*, 60 U.S. 393 (1857).

Dudziak, Mary L. "Legal history as foreign relations history" in Michael J. Hogan, Thomas G. Patterson, and Frank Costigliola (eds.), *Explaining the History of American Foreign Relations*, 3rd edn. (Cambridge and Massachusetts: Cambridge University Press, 2016), pp. 135–50.

"Due process." Legal Information Institute, Cornell University Law School. Web. www.law.cornell.edu/wex/due_process.

Dunlop, C. R. B. "Literature studies in law schools," *Cardozo Studies in Law and Literature*, 3(1) (1991), 63–110.

Dunseath, D. K. *Spenser's Allegory of Justice in Book V of The Fairie Queene* (Princeton: Princeton University Press, 1968).

Durán, José María. "Artistic labor and the production of value: an attempt at a Marxist interpretation," *Rethinking Marxism*, 28(2) (2016), 220–37.

Durant, David. "Ann Radcliffe and the conservative Gothic," *Studies in English Literature, 1500–1900*, 22 (1982), 519–30.

Durcan, Paul. *Life Is a Dream: 40 Years Reading Poems 1967–2007* (London: Harvill Secker, 2009).

Dutton, Richard. *Licensing, Censorship, and Authorship in Early Modern England: Buggeswords* (London: Palgrave MacMillan, 2000).

Dworkin, Ronald. "Law as interpretation," *Texas Law Review*, 60 (1982), 495–505.

Eden, Kathy. *Poetic and Legal Fiction in the Aristotelian Tradition* (Princeton: Princeton University Press, 2014).

Edmonds, Patricia. "The moment," *USA Today*, October 4, 1995.

Eichenbaum, Boris. "From the theory of the 'formal method'" in Vincent B. Leitch et al (eds.), *The Norton Anthology of Theory and Criticism*, 2nd edn. (New York: W.W. Norton & Company, 2010), pp. 925–50.

Eidinow, Esther. *Envy, Poison, and Death: Women on Trial in Classical Athens* (Oxford: Oxford University Press, 2016).

Eisenberg, Andrew J. "Islam, sound and space: acoustemology and Muslim citizenship on the Kenyan coast" in Georgina Born (ed.), *Music, Sound and Space: Transformations of Public and Private Experience* (Cambridge: Cambridge University Press, 2013), pp. 186–202.

The Resonance of Place: Vocalizing Swahili Ethnicity in Mombasa. Dissertation Abstracts International 70 (2010), 4513. UMI Order Number: AAI3388445.

Eldred-Grigg, Stevan. *Pleasures of the Flesh: Sex and Drugs in Colonial New Zealand, 1840–1915* (Wellington: Reed, 1984).

Eliot, George. *Adam Bede* (Oxford: Oxford University Press, 1996 [1859]).

Emerson, Ralph Waldo. "The American scholar" in *The Essential Writings of Ralph Waldo Emerson* (New York: Random House, 2000), pp. 43–62.

Erickson, Amy L. *Women and Property in Early Modern England* (London: Routledge, 1993).

"Executive Summary." October 23, 2002. Select Committee on a Certain Maritime Incident. *Commonwealth of Australia*. Web. June 27, 2015. www.aph.gov.au/Parliamentary_Business/Committees/Senate/Former_Committees/maritimeincident/report/a06.

Family Violence – A National Legal Response (ALRC Report 114). Australian Government: Australian Law Reform Commission. October 2010.

Fanon, F. *Black Skins, White Masks* (New York: Grove Press, 1967).

The Wretched of the Earth (New York: Grove Press, 2004).

Farmer, Lindsay. "Criminal responsibility and the proof of guilt" in Markus D. Dubber and Lindsay Farmer (eds.), *Modern Histories of Crime and Punishment* (Stanford: Stanford University Press, 2007), pp. 42–65.

Farrar, John H. "Reasoning by analogy in the law," *Bond Law Review*, 9 (1997), 149–76.

Fatuma binti Mohammed bin Bakhshuwen v. *Mohammed bin Salim Bakhshuwen*, AC 1 (1952).

Faulkner, William. "Barn burning" in *Collected Stories of William Faulkner* (New York: Random House, 1950), pp. 3–25.

Feist Pubs., Inc. v. *Rural Tel. Svc. Co., Inc. 499.* U.S. 340 (1991). Supreme Court of the United States.

Felman, Shoshana. "Theatres of justice: Arendt in Jerusalem, the Eichmann trial, and the redefinition of legal meaning in the wake of the Holocaust," *Critical Inquiry*, 27(2) (2001), 201–38.

The Juridical Unconscious: Trials and Traumas in the Twentieth Century (Cambridge, Harvard University Press, 2002).

Felman, Shoshana and Dori Laub. *Testimony: Crises of Witnessing in Literature, Psychoanalysis and History* (London: Taylor and Francis, 1992).

Ferguson, Robert A. *Law and Letters in American Culture* (Cambridge: Harvard University Press, 1984).

"Untold stories in the law" in Peter Brooks and Paul Gewirtz (eds.), *Law's Stories: Narrative and Rhetoric in the Law* (New Haven and London: Yale University Press, 1996), pp. 84–98.

Ferrier, Carole. *Jean Devanny: Romantic Revolutionary* (Melbourne: Melbourne University Press, 1998).

Fishman, James J. "Charity scandals as a catalyst of legal change and literary inspiration," *Michigan State Law Review* (2005), 369–416.

Fiss, Owen. "The challenge ahead," *Yale Journal of Law and the Humanities*, 2 (1988–9), iii–vi.

"The death of the law?" *Cornell Law Review*, 72(1) (1986), 1–16.

"Objectivity and interpretation" in Sanford Levinson and Steven Mailloux (eds.), *Interpreting Law and Literature: A Hermeneutic Reader.* Evanston: Northwestern University Press, 1988), pp. 229–49.

Fitzpatrick, Peter. "Juris-fiction: literature and the law of the law," *ARIEL: A Review of International English Literature*, 35, 1–2 (2004), 215–29.

The Mythology of Modern Law (London: Routledge, 1992).

"Necessary fictions: Indigenous claims and the humanity of rights," *Journal of Postcolonial Writing*, 46(5) (2010), 446–56.

"Terminal legality: imperialism and the (de) composition of law" in Diane Kirkby and Catharine Coleborne (eds.), *Law, History and Colonialism* (Manchester: Manchester University Press, 2001), pp. 9–25.

Foley, Megan. "Serializing racial subjects: the stagnation and suspense of the O. J. Simpson saga," *Quarterly Journal of Speech*, 96(1) (2010), 69–88.

Ford, Ford Madox. 'On impressionism' in Martin Stannard (ed.), *The Good Soldier: An Authoritative Text, Textual Appendices, Contemporary Reviews, Literary Impressionism, Biographical and Critical Commentary* (New York: W.W. Norton, 1995), pp. 257–74.

Ford, Richard. *Let Me Be Frank with You* (London: Bloomsbury, 2015).

Fortier, Mark. *The Culture of Equity in Early Modern England* (Aldershot: Ashgate, 2005).

Foucault, Michel. "The eye of power" in Colin Gordon (ed.), *Power/Knowledge: Selected Interviews and Other Writings, 1972–1977* (New York: Pantheon Books, 1980), pp. 146–65.

"Truth and juridical forms" in James D. Faubion (ed.), *Power: Essential Works of Foucault 1954–1984* (London: Penguin, 2000), pp. 1–89.

"What is an author?" in James D. Faubion (ed.) *Essential Works of Michel Foucault: Aesthetics, Method, and Epistemology*, vol. 2 (New York: The New York Press, 1998), pp. 205–22.

Foxe, John. *Acts and Monuments*, vol. 3 (New York: AMS Press, 1965).

Frank, Jerome. *Courts on Trial: Myth and Reality in American Justice* (Princeton: Princeton University Press, 1950).

Law and the Modern Mind (London: Transaction Publishers, 2009).

Fraser, Hilary, Judith Johnston, and Stephanie Green. *Gender and the Victorian Periodical* (Cambridge: Cambridge University Press, 2008).

Freedman, Monroe H. "Atticus Finch – right and wrong," *Alabama Law Review*, 45 (1994), 473–82.

Freeman, Michael and Andrew D. Lewis (eds.). *Law and Literature: Current Legal Issues*, vol. 2 (Oxford: Oxford University Press, 1999).

Freud, Sigmund. *Beyond the Pleasure Principle* (trans. John Reddick) (London and New York: Penguin Books, 2003).

Fried, Charles. "Opinion of Fried, J., concurring in the judgment" in Bradin Cormack, Martha C. Nussbaum, and Richard Strier (eds.), *Shakespeare and the Law: A Conversation among Disciplines and Professions* (Chicago: University of Chicago Press, 2013), pp. 156–63.

Friedman, Lawrence M. *A History of American Law*, 3rd edn. (New York: Simon & Schuster, 2005).

Friess, Steve. "Simpson's past trial looms over court," *New York Times*, September 15, 2008.

Frye, Northrop. "Literature and the law," *Law Society of Upper Canada Gazette*, 4 (1970), 70–7.

"Full text of the Peonage cases." Web. www.archive.org/stream/jstor-1109963/1109963_djvu.txt.

Gaakeer, Jeanne. "Close encounters of the 'third' kind" in Daniela Carpi and Klaus Stierstorfer (eds.), *Diaspora, Law and Literature* (Berlin and Boston: De Gruyter, 2016), pp. 41–68.

Hope Springs Eternal: An Introduction to the Work of James Boyd White (Amsterdam: Amsterdam University Press, 1998).

Gadamer, Hans-Georg. *Truth and Method* (trans. Joel Weinsheimer and Donald G. Marshall), 2nd edn. (New York: Continuum, 2004).

Gagarin, Michael. "Rhetoric and law in ancient Greece" in Michael MacDonald (ed.), *The Oxford Handbook of Rhetorical Studies. Oxford Handbooks Online* (Oxford: Oxford University Press, 2014), www.oxfordhandbooks.com/view/10.1093/oxfordhb/9780199731596.001.0001/oxfordhb-9780199731596-e-002

Gaines, Brian J. and Cho, Wendy K. Tam. "On California's 1920 Alien Land Law: the psychology and economics of racial discrimination," *State Politics and Policy Quarterly*, 4(3) (2004), 271–93.

Garside, Peter, Raven, James, and Schöwerling, Rainer (eds.). *The English Novel, 1770–1829: A Bibliographical Survey of Prose Fiction Published in the British Isles*, vol. 1 (Oxford: Oxford University Press, 2004).

Gebhardt, Ulricht. *Sermo Iuris: Rechtssprache und Recht in der augusteischen Dichtung* (Leiden: Brill, 2009).

Gelter, Martin and Grechenig, Kristoffel. "History of law and economics," *Reprints of the Max Planck Institute for Research on Collective Goods* (2014–15), pp. 1–10.

"GetUp! – The Shipping News, 'Villawood: Notes from an Immigration Detention Centre'." *The Walkley Foundation*, June 29, 2016. Web. www.walkleys.com/walkleys-winners/safdar-ahmed/.

Gewirtz, Paul. "Narrative and rhetoric in the law" in Peter Brooks and Paul Gewirtz (eds.), *Law's Stories: Narrative and Rhetoric in the Law* (Yale: Yale University Press, 1996), pp. 2–13.

Ghai, Y. P. and MacAuslan, J. P. *Public Law and Political Change in Kenya* (Nairobi: Oxford University Press, 1970).

Giddens, Thomas. "Comics, law, and aesthetics: towards the use of graphic fictions in legal studies," *Law and Humanities*, 6(1) (2012), 85–109.

Gilbert, Nora. *Better Left Unsaid: Victorian Novels, the Hays Code and the Benefits of Censorship* (Stanford: Stanford University Press, 2013).

Gillet, Charles. *Burned Books: Neglected Chapters in British History and Literature* (New York: Columbia University Press, 1932).

Gilmore, Leigh. "Limit-cases: trauma, self-representation, and the jurisdictions of identity," *Biography*, 24(1) (2001), 128–39.

Gladfelder, Hal. *Criminality and Narrative in Eighteenth-Century England: Beyond the Law* (Baltimore: Johns Hopkins University Press, 2001).

Glashan, Roy. "The case of Mr. George Edalji,"*Project Gutenberg Australia*, July 2012. Web. http://gutenberg.net.au/ebooks12/1202671h.html

Glaspell, Susan. "A jury of her peers" in *Susan Glaspell, Lifted Masks and Other Works*. Ed. Eric S. Rabkin (Ann Arbor: University of Michigan Press, 1993), pp. 279–307.

Glendon, Mary Ann. *Rights Talk: The Impoverishment of Political Discourse* (New York: The Free Press, 1991).

Godobo-Madikizela, Pumla. *A Human Being Died That Night: A South African Story of Forgiveness* (Boston: Mariner Books, 2003).

Godwin, William. *Caleb Williams*. Ed. Gary Handwerk and A. A. Markley (Peterborough: Broadview Press, 2000).

Goldberg, David Theo, Musheno, Michael, and Bowers, Lisa C. (eds.) *Between Law and Culture: Relocating Legal Studies* (Minneapolis: University of Minnesota Press, 2001).

Golove, David M. and Hulsebosch, Daniel J. "A civilized nation: the early American Constitution, the Law of Nations, and the pursuit of international recognition," *New York University Law Review*, 85(4) (2010), 932–1066.

Goodman, Nan. *Shifting the Blame: Literature, Law, and the Theory of Accidents in Nineteenth-Century America* (Princeton: Princeton University Press, 1998).

Goodrich, Peter. *Law in the Courts of Love: Literature and Other Minor Jurisprudences* (London and New York: Routledge, 1996).

Oedipus Lex: Psychoanalysis, History, Law (Berkeley: University of California Press, 1995).

Reading the Law: A Critical Introduction to Legal Method and Techniques (Oxford: Basil Blackwell, 1986).

"Screening the law," *Law & Literature*, 21(1) (2009), 1–23.

Gopnik, Adam. "Sweet home Alabama," *New Yorker*, July 27, 2015. Web. www.newyorker.com/magazine/2015/07/27/sweet-home-alabama

Greene, Jody. *The Trouble with Ownership : Literary Property and Authorial Liability in England, 1660–1730* (Philadelphia: University of Pennsylvania Press, 2005).

Greene, William Chase. "Plato's view of poetry," *Harvard Studies in Classical Philology*, 29 (1918), 1–75.

Greenfeld, Liah. *Nationalism: Five Roads to Modernity* (Cambridge: Harvard University Press, 1992).

Greenfield, Susan. *Mothering Daughters: Novels and the Politics of Family Romance, Frances Burney to Jane Austen* (Detroit: Wayne State University Press, 2002).

Greiner, Rae. 'The art of knowing your own nothingness.' *English Literary History*, 77 (2010), 893–914.

Grimm, Jakob. "Von der Poesie im Recht," *Zietschrift für die geschichtliche Rechtswissenschaft*, 2(1) (1816), 25–99.

Grossi, Renata and Neoh, Joshua (eds.). *Law and Love: Law in Context* (Special Issue) 34(1) (2016).

Grossman, Jonathan H. *The Art of Alibi: English Law Courts and the Novel* (Baltimore: Johns Hopkins University Press, 2002).

Guy, J. A. (ed.). *Christopher St German on Statute and Chancery* (London: Selden Society, 1985).

Guy, Josephine M. *The Victorian Social Problem Novel* (Houndmills: Macmillan, 1996).

Haas, Guenther H. *The Concept of Equity in Calvin's Ethics* (Ontario: Wilfrid Laurier University Press, 1997).

Habermas, Jürgen. *The Structural Transformation of the Public Sphere: An Inquiry into a Category of Bourgeois Society* (Cambridge: MIT Press, 1991).

Hadfield, Andrew. *Edmund Spenser's Irish Experience: Wilde Fruit and Salvage Soyl* (Oxford: Oxford University Press, 1997).

Hager, Kelly. *Dickens and the Rise of Divorce: The Failed-Marriage Plot and the Novel Tradition* (Farnham: Ashgate, 2010).

Hake, Edward. *Epieikeia: A Dialogue on Equity in Three Parts* (New Haven: Yale University Press, 1953).

Halberstam, Judith. *Female Masculinity* (Durham: Duke University Press, 1998).

In a Queer Time and Place: Transgender Bodies, Subcultural Lives (New York: New York University Press, 2005).

Hall, Edith. *The Theatrical Cast of Athens: Interactions between Ancient Greek Drama and Society* (Oxford: Oxford University Press, 2006), pp. 353–92.

Hall, Joseph. *Characters of Vertues and Vices* (London, 1608).

Hall, Radclyffe. *The Well of Loneliness* (New York: Doubleday, 1990 [1928]).

Halley, Janet. "What is family law? A genealogy, part I," *Yale Journal of Law & the Humanities*, 23(1) (2011), 1–109.

Hamilton, A. C. *Sir Philip Sidney: A Study of His Life and Works* (Cambridge: Cambridge University Press, 1977).

Hamilton, Alexander. "The Federalist No. 78" (1788). Constitution Society.

Hardy, Thomas. "Candour in English fiction" in Harold Orel (ed.), *Thomas Hardy: Personal Writings* (London: Macmillan, 1967), pp. 125–33.

Harris, Edward. "How to 'act' in an Athenian court: emotions and forensic performance" in Sophia Papaioannou, Andreas Serafim, and Beatrice de Vela (eds.), *The Theatre of Justice: Aspects of Performance in Creco-Roman Oratory and Rhetoric* (Leiden: Brill, 2017), pp. 223–42.

Hartman, Saidiya V. *Scenes of Subjection: Terror, Slavery, and Self-Making in Nineteenth-Century America* (New York: Oxford University Press, 1997).

Haverkamp, Anselm and Vismann, Cornelia. "*Habeas corpus*: the law's desire to have the body" in Hent De Vries and Samuel Weber (eds.), *Violence, Identity, and Self-Determination* (Stanford: Stanford University Press, 1997), pp. 223–35.

Hayashi, Brian M. "Not so funny papers," *Pacific Historical Review*, 69(2) (2000), 217–78.

Hayes, K. O'C. "Carter, Sir Edgar Bonham (1870–1956)" in *Oxford Dictionary of National Biography* (Oxford University Press, 2004). Web. www.oxforddnb .com/view/article/31960

Hayman, Robert L., Levit, Nancy, and Delgado, Richard (eds.). *Jurisprudence Classical and Contemporary: From Natural Law to Postmodernism* (Minnesota: West Group, 2002).

Haywood, Eliza. *The Rash Resolve, Or, The Untimely Discovery* (London: D. Browne and S. Chapman, 1724).

Heaney, Seamus. *The Cure at Troy* (Derry: Field Day, 1990).

New Selected Poems 1966–1987 (London: Faber and Faber, 1990).

The Redress of Poetry: Oxford Lectures (London: Faber and Faber, 1995).

Heilbrun, Carolyn and Resnik, Judith. "Convergences: law, literature and feminism," *Yale Law Journal*, 99 (1990), 1913–56.

Heinzelman, Susan S. *Riding the Black Ram: Law, Literature, and Gender* (Stanford: Stanford University Press, 2010).

Heinzelman, Susan Sage and Wiseman, Zipporah (eds.). *Representing Women: Law, Literature and Feminism* (Durham: Duke University Press, 1994).

Henderson, Jeffrey (trans.). *Aristophanes. Birds. Lysistrata. Women at the Thesmophoria* (Massachusetts: Harvard University Press, 2000).

Herring, Scott. *Queering the Underworld: Slumming Literature and the Undoing of Lesbian and Gay History* (Chicago: University of Chicago Press, 2007).

Hewitt, Regina. "Utopianism and Joanna Baillie: a preface to converging revolutions," *Romantic Circles*. Web. www.rc.umd.edu/praxis/utopia/hewitt_preface/hewitt_preface.html.

"Hey, Boo: Harper Lee and 'To Kill a Mockingbird': Trailer," *IMDb*, 2010. Web. www.imdb.com/video/imdb/vi4027817241/.

Higginbotham, A. Leon, François, Aderson Bellegard, and Yueh, Linda Y. "The O. J. Simpson trial: who was improperly 'playing the race card'?" in Toni Morrison and Claudia Brodsky Lacour (eds.), *Birth of a Nation'Hood: Gaze, Script and Spectacle in the O. J. Simpson Case* (New York: Pantheon Books, 1997), pp. 31–56.

Hines, Stephen and Womack, Steven. *The True Crime Files of Sir Arthur Conan Doyle* (New York: Berkeley Prime Crime, 2001).

Hirsch, Marianne. "The generation of postmemory," *Poetics Today*, 29(1) (2008), 103–28.

"Mourning and postmemory" in Michael Chaney (ed.), *Graphic Subjects: Critical Essays on Autobiography and Graphic Novels* (Madison: University of Wisconsin Press, 2011), pp. 17–44.

Hoeveler, Diane Long. "Anti-Catholicism and the Gothic imaginary: the historical and literary contexts" in Brett C. McInelly (ed.), *Religion in the Age of Enlightenment*, vol. 3 (Brooklyn: AMS Press, 2012), pp. 1–31.

Hoeveler, Diane Long, and Jenkins, James D. "Where the evidence leads: Gothic narratives and legal technologies," *European Romantic Review*, 18(3) (2007), 317–37.

Holdsworth, William. *A History of English Laws*, vol. 12 (London: Methuen, 1971 [1903]).

Horsman, Yasco. *Theatres of Justice: Judging, Staging and Working Through in Arendt, Brecht, and Delbo* (Stanford: Stanford University Press, 2011).

Horwitz, Henry. *Chancery Equity Record and Proceedings, 1600–1800* (Kew: Public Records Office Publications, 1998).

"Hossack begged wife to aid him," *Des Moines Daily News*, April 3, 1901.

House of Commons Debate, Great Britain, June 10, 1907. vol. 175. cc 1079–80.

House of Commons Debate, Great Britain, July 18, 1907. vol. 178. cc 994–1017.

Howard, Jennifer, Crossley, Katherine Webb, and Kovaleski, Serge F. "Harper Lee is memorialized as she lived: quietly and privately," *New York Times*, February 20, 2016.

Ibhawoh, Bonny. *Imperial Justice: Africans in Empire's Court* (Oxford: Oxford University Press, 2013).

Imperialism and Human Rights: Colonial Discourses of Rights and Liberties in African History (Albany: State University of New York Press, 2007).

Irving, Washington. "Rip Van Winkle" in *The Legend of Sleepy Hollow and Other Stories from the Sketchbook* (New York: Signet, 2006).

Jackson, Thomas F. *From Civil Rights to Human Rights: Martin Luther King, Jr. and the Struggle for Economic Justice* (Philadelphia: University of Pennsylvania Press, 2007).

Jacobson, Arthur J. "The idolatry of rules: writing law according to Moses, with reference to other jurisprudences" in Drucilla Cornell, Michel Rosenfeld, and David G. Carlson (eds.), *Deconstruction and the Possibility of Justice* (London and New York: Routledge, 1992), pp. 95–151.

Jacoby, Susan. *Wild Justice: The Evolution of Revenge* (New York: Harper and Row, 1983).

James I. *Workes* (London, 1616).

Jauss, Hans Robert, and Benzinger, Elizabeth. "Literary history as a challenge to literary theory," *New Literary History*, 2(1) (1970), 7–37.

Jauss, Hans Robert. *Towards an Aesthetic of Reception Theory* (Minneapolis: University of Minnesota Press, 1982).

Jay, Stewart. "The status of the Law of Nations in early American law," *Vanderbilt Law Review*, 42 (1989), 819–49.

Johnson, Barbara. *Persons and Things* (Massachusetts: Harvard University Press, 2008).

Jones, Vivian (ed.). *Introduction to Women and Literature in Britain, 1700–1800* (Cambridge: Cambridge University Press, 2000).

Jonson, Ben. *Works*, vol. 5. Eds. C. H. Herford and Percy Simpson (Oxford: Clarendon Press, 1937).

Jordan, Constance. *Renaissance Feminism: Literary Texts and Political Models* (Ithaca: Cornell University Press, 1990).

Joyce, Simon. *Capital Offences: Geographies of Class and Crime in Victorian London* (Charlottesville: University of Virginia Press, 2003).

Justice, George. *The Manufacturers of Literature: Writing and the Literary Marketplace in Eighteenth-Century England* (Newark: University of Delaware Press, 2002).

Kafka, Franz. "In the Penal Settlement" in *Metamorphosis and Other Stories* (trans. Willa Muir and Edwin Muir) (London: Vintage, 1999), pp. 167–99.

The Trial (trans. Richard Stokes) (London: Hesperus, 2005).

Kahil, Lilly. "Hélène," *Lexicon Iconographicum Mythologiae Classicae*, 4 (1988), 538–50.

Kahn, Paul W. *Law and Love: The Trials of King Lear* (New Haven: Yale University Press, 2000).

Making the Case: The Art of the Judicial Opinion (New Haven: Yale University Press, 2016).

Kakutani, Michiko. "Review: Harper Lee's 'Go Set a Watchman' gives Atticus Finch a dark side," *New York Times*, July 10, 2015.

Kamir, Orit. "To kill a songbird: a community of women, feminist jurisprudence, conscientious objection and revolution in *A Jury of Her Peers* and contemporary film," *Law & Literature*, 19(3) (2007), 357–77.

Kane, Sean. *Spenser's Moral Allegory* (Toronto: University of Toronto Press, 1989).

Kato, L. L. "The Court of Appeal for East Africa: from a colonial court to an international court," *East African Law Journal*, 7(1) (1971), 1–31.

Kennedy, Duncan. *The Arts of Love: Five Studies in the Discourse of Roman Love Elegy* (Cambridge: Cambridge University Press, 1993).

Kennedy, Kathleen E. *Medieval Hackers* (New York and Toronto: Punctum Books, 2015).

Kennedy, Randall. "Harper Lee's 'Go Set a Watchman'," *New York Times*, July 14, 2015.

Kennedy, Rosanne. "Subversive witnessing: mediating Indigenous testimony in Australian cultural and legal institutions," *Women's Studies Quarterly*, 36(1–2) (2008), 58–75.

Kenney, Edward. "Ovid and the law," *Yale Classical Studies*, 21 (1969), 241–63.

King, Martin Luther (Jr). "The Quest for Peace and Justice," Nobel Peace Prize Lecture (1964). Nobelprize.org. *Nobel Media*, 2014. Web. www.nobelprize.org/nobel_prizes/peace/laureates/1964/king-lecture.html

Kinkead-Weekes, Mark. *D. H. Lawrence: Triumph to Exile, 1912–1922*, vol. 2 (Cambridge: Cambridge University Press, 1996).

Kiyama, Henry Yoshitaka. *The Four Immigrants Manga: A Japanese Experience in San Francisco, 1904–1924* (trans. Frederik L. Schodt) (Berkeley: Stone Bridge Press, 1999).

Klarman, Michael J. *From Jim Crow to Civil Rights: The Supreme Court and the Struggle for Racial Equality* (New York: Oxford University Press, 2006).

Koch, Grace. "We have the song, so we have the land: song and ceremony as proof of ownership in Aboriginal and Torres Strait Islander land claims," *AIATSIS Research Discussion Paper.* No. 33, Canberra. AIATIS Research Publications, 2013.

Kornstein, Daniel J. *Kill All the Lawyers? Shakespeare's Legal Appeal* (Princeton: Princeton University Press, 1994).

Korobkin, Laura Hanft. *Criminal Conversations: Sentimentality and Nineteenth-Century Legal Stories of Adultery* (New York: Columbia University Press, 1998).

Kovacs, David (trans.). *Euripides: Children of Heracles. Hippolytus. Andromache. Hecuba Euripides* (Massachusetts: Harvard University Press, 1995).

(trans.). *Euripides, Trojan Women. Iphigenia among the Taurians. Ion* (Massachusetts: Harvard University Press, 1999).

Kronman, Anthony. *The Lost Lawyer: Failing Ideals of the Legal Profession* (Massachusetts: Belknap Press, 1993).

Krueger, Christine. *Reading for the Law: British Literary History and Gender Advocacy* (Charlottesville: University of Virginia Press, 2010).

Kuller Shuger, Deborah. *Political Theologies in Shakespeare's England: The Sacred and the State in Measure for Measure* (Basingstoke: Palgrave, 2001).

L'Estrange, Roger. *L'Estrange His Apology* (London, 1660).

La Capra, Dominick. *History and Memory after Auschwitz* (Ithaca: Cornell University Press, 1998).

Lacey, Nicola. "The resurgence of character: responsibility in the context of criminalization" in R. A. Duff and Stuart Green (eds.), *Philosophical Foundations of Criminal Law* (Oxford: Oxford University Press, 2011), pp. 151–78.

Women, Crime, and Character: From Moll Flanders to Tess of the D'Urbervilles (Oxford: Oxford University Press, 2008).

LaCroix, Alison L. and Nussbaum, Martha C. (eds.). *Subversion and Sympathy: Gender, Law, and the British Novel* (Oxford: Oxford University Press, 2013).

LaFrance, Adrienne. "Calling out a presidential lie," *The Atlantic*, January 27, 2017.

Lambarde, William. *Archeion or, a Discourse upon the High Courts of Justice in England* (Massachusetts: Harvard University Press, 1957).

Laster, Kathy. *The Drama of the Courtroom* (Sydney: The Federation Press, 2000).

Latham, Sean. *The Art of Scandal: Modernism, Libel Law, and the Roman à Clef* (Oxford: Oxford University Press, 2015).

Lattimore, Richmond (trans.). *The Iliad of Homer* (Chicago: Programmed Classics, 1951).

Laub, Dori. "Bearing witness or the vicissitudes of listening" in Dori Laub and Shoshana Felman (eds.), *Testimony: Crises of Witnessing in Literature, Psychoanalysis, and History* (New York: Routledge, 1992), pp. 57–73.

Lawrence, D. H. *Lady Chatterley's Lover*. Ed. Michael Squires (New York: Penguin, 1994).

Leckie, Barbara. *Culture and Adultery: The Novel, the Newspaper and the Law, 1857–1914* (Philadelphia: University of Pennsylvania Press, 1999).

Lee, Harper. *Go Set a Watchman* (New York: Harper Collins, 2015).

To Kill a Mockingbird (New York: Warner Books, 1960).

Levin, Joel. "The measure of law and equity: tolerance in Shakespeare's Vienna" in Bruce L. Rockwood (ed.), *Law and Literature Perspectives* (New York: Peter Lang, 1996), pp. 193–207.

Levinson, Sanford and Mailloux, Steven. "Preface" in Sanford Levinson and Steven Mailloux (eds.), *Interpreting Law and Literature: A Hermeneutic Reader* (Illinois: Northwestern University Press, 1988), pp. ix–xiii.

Levinson, Sanford. "Law as literature" in Sanford Levinson and Steven Mailloux (eds.), *Interpreting Law and Literature: A Hermeneutic Reader* (Evanston: Northwestern University Press, 1988), pp. 155–74.

Lewis, Matthew Gregory. *The Monk* (Peterborough: Broadview Press, 2003).

Lewis, Sinclair. "Letter," *New York World*, August 20, 1922.

Lincoln, Abraham. "Address before the Young Men's Lyceum of Springfield, Illinois," 1838. *Abraham Lincoln Online*. Web. www.abrahamlincolnonline.org/lincoln/speeches/lyceum.htm

Lindheim, Nancy. *The Structures of Sidney's Arcadia* (Toronto: University of Toronto Press, 1982).

Lipsitz, George. "The greatest story ever sold: marketing and the O. J. Simpson Trial" in Toni Morrison and Claudia Brodsky Lacour (eds.), *Birth of a Nation'Hood: Gaze, Script and Spectacle in the O. J. Simpson Case* (New York: Pantheon Books, 1997), pp. 3–30.

"literature, n." *OED Online, Oxford University Press*. September 2016.

Lockridge, Laurence S. *The Ethics of Romanticism* (Cambridge: Cambridge University Press, 1989).

Loewenstein, Joseph. *The Author's Due: Printing and the Prehistory of Copyright* (Chicago: University of Chicago Press, 2010).

"Looks bad for Mrs Hossack,"*Des Moines Daily News*, April 5, 1901.
Love, Heather. *Feeling Backward: Loss and the Politics of Queer History* (Cambridge: Harvard University Press, 2007).
Lowe, Derek. "'Poems so materially different': eighteenth-century literary property and Wordsworth's mechanisms of proprietary authorship in the 1800 Lyrical Ballads,"*Studies in Romanticism*, 55(1) (2016), 3–28.
Luban, David. *Legal Modernism* (Ann Arbor: University of Michigan Press, 1994).
Luck, Chad. *The Body of Property: Antebellum American Fiction and the Phenomenology of Possession* (New York: Fordham University Press, 2014).
Lukács, Georg. *The Theory of the Novel: A Historico-Philosophical Essay on the Forms of Great Epic Literature* (trans. Anna Bostock) (Cambridge: MIT Press, 1971).
Lyotard, Jean-Francois. *The Differend: Phrases in Dispute* (trans. Georges Van Den Abbeele) (Minneapolis: University of Minnesota Press, 1988).
MacKinnon, Catharine. "Points against postmodernism," *Chicago-Kent Law Review*, 75(3) (2000), 687–712.
Toward a Feminist Theory of the State (Cambridge: Harvard University Press, 1989).
Majeske, Andrew. "Equity in Book V of Spenser's *The Faerie Queene*," *Law & Literature*, 18(1) (2006), 69–99.
Mallette, Richard. "Book V of The Fairie Queene: An Elizabethan Apocalypse," *Spenser Studies*, XI (1994), 129–59.
Manderson, Desmond. "Klimt's *Jurisprudence*: sovereign violence and the rule of law," *Oxford Journal of Legal Studies*, 35 (2015), 515–42.
"Modernism and the critique of law and literature," *Australian Feminist Law Journal*, 35(1) (2011), 107–25.
Mann, Kristin and Richard Roberts (eds.). *Law in Colonial Africa* (Portsmouth: Heinemann, 1991).
Mao, Douglas and Walkowitz, Rebecca L. "The new modernist studies," *PMLA*, 123(3) (2008), 737–48.
Marsh, Joss. *Word Crimes: Blasphemy, Culture and Literature in Nineteenth-Century England* (Chicago: University of Chicago Press, 1998).
Marshik, Celia. *British Modernism and Censorship* (Cambridge: Cambridge University Press, 2006).
Martel, James. *The One and Only Law: Walter Benjamin and the Second Commandment* (Ann Arbor: University of Michigan Press, 2014).
Matsuda, Mari. "Public response to racist speech: considering the victim's story," *Michigan Law Review*, 87 (1989): 2320–81.
McClennan, Sophia and Moore, Alexandra Shultheis (eds.). *The Routledge Companion to Literature and Human Rights* (London: Routledge, 2016).
McEwan, Ian. *The Children Act* (London: Vintage Books, 2014).
McKeon, Michael. *The Origins of the English Novel 1600–1740* (Baltimore: Johns Hopkins University Press, 1987).
McKeown, James. *Ovid: Amores. Volume III: A Commentary on Book Two* (Leeds: Francis Cairns, 1998).

McMaster, R. D. *Trollope and the Law* (London: Macmillan, 1986).

McWilliam, Rohan. "Radicalism and popular culture: the Tichborne case and politics of 'fair play,' 1867–86" in Eugenio F. Biagini and Alastair J. Reid (eds.), *Currents of Radicalism: Popular Radicalism, Organised Labour and Party Politics in Britain 1850–1914* (Cambridge: Cambridge University Press, 1991), pp. 44–64.

Medrano, Juan Diez. "Nationalism: five roads to modernity," *American Journal of Sociology*, 99(4) (1994), 1443–5.

Melville, Herman. "Bartleby the scrivener" in *Billy Budd, Bartleby, and Other Stories* (New York: Penguin Random House, 2016), pp. 17–54.

Metcalf, Thomas R. *Imperial Connections: India in the Indian Ocean, 1860–1920* (Oakland: University of California Press, 2008).

Miles, Robert. "Ann Radcliffe and Matthew Lewis" in David Punter (ed.), *A New Companion to The Gothic* (Chichester: Wiley-Blackwell, 2012), pp. 93–109.

Miller, Paul. *Subjecting Verses: Latin Love Elegy and the Emergence of the Real* (Princeton: Princeton University Press, 2004).

Milloy, Courtland. "In white riot, it's smolder, baby, smolder," *Washington Post*, October 8, 1995.

Milton, John. *Complete Poems and Major Prose* (Indianapolis: Odyssey Press, 1957).

Complete Prose Works, vol. 2 (New Haven: Yale University Press, 1959).

Minda, Gary. "The law and economics and critical legal studies movements in American law" in Nicholas Mercuro (ed.), *Law and Economics* (Dordrecht: Springer Netherlands, 1989), pp. 87–122.

Minow, Martha (ed.). *Between Vengeance and Forgiveness: Facing History after Genocide and Mass Violence* (Boston: Beacon Press, 1998).

Minow, Martha. *Breaking the Cycles of Hatred: Memory, Law and Repair* (Princeton: Princeton University Press, 2002).

"Law turning outward," *Telos*, 73 (1987), 79–100.

Molotiu, Andrei. "Sequential dynamism and iconostasis in abstract comics and Steve Ditko's *Amazing Spider-Man*" in Matthew J. Smith and Randy Duncan (eds.), *Critical Approaches to Comics: Theories and Methods* (London and New York: Routledge, 2012), pp. 84–100.

Monateri, Pier Giuseppe. "Diaspora, the West and the law" in Daniela Carpi and Klaus Stierstorfer (eds.), *Diaspora, Law and Literature* (Berlin and Boston: De Gruyter, 2016), pp. 7–22.

Moon, Claire. *Narrating Political Reconciliation: South Africa's Truth and Reconciliation Commission* (Lanham and London: Lexington Books, 2008).

Moore, Nicole. *The Censor's Library: Uncovering the Lost History of Australia's Banned Books* (St. Lucia: University of Queensland Press, 2012).

Moran, Leslie J. "Gothic law,"*Griffith Law Review*, 10(2) (2001), 75–100.

Morawetz, Thomas. *Literature and the Law* (Austin: Wolters Kluwer, 2007).

Morgan, Patrick. "The reading habits of the Tichborne claimant," *Margins* (November 2003). Web. www.thefreelibrary.com/The+fiction+reading+habits+of+the+Tichborne+claimant.-a0111856221

Morris, H. F. "The reception and rejection of Indian law" in H. F. Morris and James S. Read (eds.), *Indirect Rule and the Search for Justice: Essays in East African Legal History* (Oxford: Clarendon Press, 1972), pp. 109–30.

Morrison, Toni. "The official story: dead man golfing" in Toni Morrison and Claudia Brodsky Lacour (eds.), *Birth of a Nation'Hood: Gaze, Script and Spectacle in the O. J. Simpson Case* (New York: Pantheon Books, 1997), pp. vii–xxviii.

Moyn, Samuel. *The Last Utopia: Human Rights in History* (Massachusetts: Harvard University Press, 2012).

Mukherji, Subha. "'Understood relations': law and literature in early modern studies," *Literature Compass*, 6(3) (2009), 706–25.

Nabizadeh, Golnar. "The after-life of images: archives and intergenerational trauma in autographic comics" in Dana Mihăilescu, Roxana Oltean, and Mihaela Precup (eds.), *Mapping Generations of Traumatic Memory in American Narratives* (Newcastle upon Tyne: Cambridge Scholars Publishing, 2014), pp. 171–91.

Nair, Sashi. *Secrecy and Sapphic Modernism: Reading Romans à Clef between the Wars* (London: Palgrave, 2012).

Nairn, John Arbuthnot. *The Mimes of Herodas* (Oxford: Oxford University Press, 1904).

Nancy, Jean-Luc. *A Finite Thinking*. Ed. Simon Sparks (Stanford: Stanford University Press, 2003).

"National Endowment for the Humanities (NEH) Funding Levels." *Humanities Indicators: A Project of the American Academy of Arts and Sciences.* Web. October 8, 2016. www.humanitiesindicators.org.

Nesiah, Vesuki. "The specter of violence that haunts the UDHR: the turn to ethics and expertise," *Maryland Journal of International Law*, 24 (2009), 135–54.

Ngũgĩ wa Thiong'o. *Decolonising the Mind: The Politics of Language in African Literature* (Portsmouth: Hienemann Educational Publishers, 1986).

Nicol, Bran, Pulham, Patricia, and McNulty, Eugene (eds.). *Crime Cultures: Figuring Criminality in Fiction and Film* (London: Continuum, 2010).

Nixon, Cheryl. *The Orphan in Eighteenth-Century Law and Literature: Estate, Blood, and Body* (Burlington: Ashgate, 2011).

Norhnberg, James. *The Analogy of The Fairie Queene* (Princeton: Princeton University Press, 1989).

Nussbaum, Martha C. *Poetic Justice: The Literary Imagination and Public Life* (Boston: Beacon Press, 1995).

O'Donnell, Bernard. *Cavalcade of Justice* (New York: MacMillan, 1952).

Olson, Douglas (trans.). *Athenaeus, The Learned Banqueters*, vol. VI (Cambridge: Harvard University Press, 2010).

Olson, Greta. "De-Americanizing law-and-literature narratives: opening up the story," *Law & Literature*, 22(2) (2010), 338–64.

Ovid. *Metamorphoses*. Trans. Frank Justus Miller. Rev. ed. G. P. Gooch (Cambridge: Harvard University Press, 1977).

Papke, David Ray. "Law in American culture: an overview," *Journal of American Culture*, 15(1) (1992), 3–14.

Parisi, Francesco and Rowley, Charles K. (eds.). *The Origins of Law and Economics: Essays by the Founding Fathers, The Locke Institute Series* (Northampton: Edward Elgar Publishing, 2005).

Parker, Laura and Welch, Craig. "3 things you need to know about the science rebellion against Trump," *National Geographic News*, January 27, 2017.

Patterson, Annabel. *Censorship and Interpretation: The Conditions of Writing and Reading in Early Modern England* (Madison: University of Wisconsin Press, 1984).

Patterson, James T. *Brown v. Board of Education: A Civil Rights Milestone and Its Troubled Legacy* (Oxford: Oxford University Press, 2001).

Patterson, Lyman Ray. *Copyright in Historical Perspective* (Nashville: Vanderbilt University Press, 1968).

Pearson, Raymond. "Nationalism: five roads to modernity," *The Journal of Modern History*, 67(4) (1995), 903–4.

Pearson, Robert. "The banning of The Butcher Shop" in Jean Devanny, *The Butcher Shop*. Ed. Heather Roberts (Auckland: Auckland University Press, 1981), pp. 225–34.

Pease, Donald. "Rethinking American studies after US exceptionalism,"*American Literary History*, 21(1) (2009), 19–27.

Perkins, William. *William Perkins, 1558–1602, English Puritanist* (Nieuwkoop: B. De Graaf, 1966).

Perry, Ruth. *Novel Relations: The Transformation of Kinship in English Literature and Culture* (London: Cambridge University Press, 2004).

Perullo, Alex. "Conceptions of song: ownership, rights, and African copyright law" in Ruth M. Stone (ed.), *The Garland Handbook of African Music* (New York and London: Routledge, 2015), pp. 44–54.

Perullo, Alex and Eisenberg, Andrew J. "Musical property rights regimes in Kenya and Tanzania after TRIPS" in Matthew David and Deborah Halbert (eds.), *The SAGE Handbook of Intellectual Property* (New York: Sage, 2015), pp. 148–65.

Peters, Julie Stone. "Law, literature and the vanishing real: on the future of an interdisciplinary illusion" in Austin Sarat, Cathrine O. Frank, and Matthew Anderson (eds.), *Teaching Law and Literature* (New York: Modern Languages Association, 2011), pp. 71–85.

"Literature," the "Rights of Man," and narratives of atrocity: historical backgrounds to the culture of testimony," *Yale Journal of Law and the Humanities*, 17(2) (2003), 253–83.

Pettitt, Clare. *Patent Inventions: Intellectual Property and the Victorian Novel* (Oxford: Oxford University Press, 2004).

Phelps, Teresa Godwin. "'Reading as if for life': law and literature is more important than ever," *Studies in Law, Politics, and Society: Law and Literature Reconsidered* (Special Issue) 43 (2008), 133–52.

Pinkerton, Allan, *The Molly Maguires and the Detectives* (New York: G.W. Carleton and Co., 1876).

Plessy v. *Ferguson, 163*, U.S. 537 (1896). 551.

Plutarch. Lives of the Ten Orators *in Moralia*, vol. X. Trans. H. N. Fowler (Cambridge: Harvard University Press, 1936), pp. 344–457.

Porsdam, Helle (ed.). *Civil Religion, Human Rights, and International Relations: Connecting People across Cultures and Traditions* (Cheltenham: Edward Elgar, 2012).

Porsdam, Helle. *From Civil to Human Rights: Dialogues on Law and Humanities in the United States and Europe* (Cheltenham: Edward Elgar, 2011).

Legally Speaking: Contemporary American Culture and the Law (Amherst: University of Massachusetts Press, 1999).

"Television judge shows: Nordic and US perspectives" in Michelle Brown (ed.), *Oxford Encyclopedia of Crime, Media, and Popular Culture* (New York: Oxford University Press, in press).

Posner, Richard A. "From Billy Budd to Buchenwald (Reviewing Weisberg, Richard H., *The Failure of the Word: The Protagonist as Lawyer in Modern Fiction* (1984))," *Yale Law Journal*, 96 (1987), 1173–89.

Economic Analysis of the Law, 9th edn. (New York: Walters Kluwer Law and Business, 2014).

"Foreword" in Michael Faure and Roger van den Bergh (eds.), *Essays in Law and Economics: Corporations, Accident Prevention and Compensation for Losses* (Antwerpen: MAKLU, 1989), pp. 5–6.

"Law and commerce in *The Merchant of Venice*" in Bradin Cormack, Martha C. Nussbaum, and Richard Strier (eds.), *Shakespeare and the Law: A Conversation among Disciplines and Professions* (Chicago: University of Chicago Press, 2013), pp. 147–55.

Law and Literature, 3rd edn. (Cambridge and London: Harvard University Press, 2009 [1988]).

Law and Literature: A Misunderstood Relation (Cambridge and London: Harvard University Press, 1998).

"Law and literature: a relation reargued," *Virginia Law Review*, 72 (1986), 1351–92.

Potter, Rachel. *Obscene Modernism: Literary Censorship and Experiment, 1900–1940* (Oxford: Oxford University Press, 2013).

Price, Leah. *The Anthology and the Rise of the Novel from Richardson to George Eliot* (Cambridge: Cambridge University Press, 2000).

Pritchard, Sarah and Charlotte Heindow-Doulman. "Indigenous people and international law: a critical overview," *Australian Indigenous Law Reporter*, 3 (1998), 473–509.

Pue, W. Wesley. "Book review: *The Law of Evidence in Victorian England* by Christopher Allen," *Victorian Studies*, 43(2) (2001), 335–8.

Punter, David. *Gothic Pathologies: The Text, the Body and the Law* (London: Palgrave Macmillan, 1998).

Quitslund, Jon A. *Spenser's Supreme Fiction: Platonic Natural Philosophy and The Fairie Queene* (Toronto: University of Toronto Press, 2001).

Radcliffe, Ann. *The Italian, or the Confessional of the Black Penitents: A Romance*. Ed. Frederick Garber (Oxford: Oxford University Press, 1986).

The Romance of the Forest. Ed. Chloe Chard (Oxford: Oxford University Press, 1986).
Radzinowicz, Leon. *History of English Criminal Law and Its Administration from 1750*, 3 vols. (London: Macmillan, 1948–1968).
Ram, James. *A Treatise on Facts as Subjects of Inquiry by a Jury* (London, 1861).
The Science of Legal Judgment (London, 1834).
Rancière, Jacques. "Who is the subject of the Rights of Man?" *South Atlantic Quarterly*, 103(2–3) (2004), 297–310.
Randolph, Jody Allen. *Eavan Boland* (Cork: Cork University Press, 2014).
Ranger, Terence. "The invention of tradition in colonial Africa" in Eric Hobsbawm and Terence Ranger (eds.), *The Invention of Tradition* (Cambridge and Massachusetts: Cambridge University Press, 1983), pp. 211–62.
Rappaport, Mike. *1848: The Year of Revolution* (New York: Basic Books, 2009).
Raven, James. "The book trades" in Isabel Rivers (ed.), *Books and Their Readers in Eighteenth-Century England: New Essays* (London and New York: Continuum, 2001), pp. 1–34.
British Fiction, 1750–1770: A Chronological Check-List of Prose Fiction Printed in Britain and Ireland (Newark: University of Delaware Press, 1987).
Read, James S. "Customary Law under Colonial Rule" in H. F. Morris and James S. Read (eds.), *Indirect Rule and the Search for Justice: Essays in East African Legal History* (Oxford: Clarendon Press, 1972), pp. 167–212.
Reeve, Clara. *The Old English Baron*. Ed. James Trainer and James Watt (Oxford: Oxford University Press, 2003).
Reichman, Ravit. *The Affective Life of Law: Legal Modernism and the Literary Imagination* (Stanford: Stanford Law Books, 2009).
"'New forms for our new sensations': Woolf and the lesson of torts," *Novel*, 36(3) (2003), 398–422.
Resnik, Judith. "Singular and aggregate voices: audiences and authority in law & literature and in law & feminism" in Michael Freeman and Andrew Lewis (eds.), *Literature and Law: Current Legal Issues*, vol. 2 (Oxford: Oxford University Press, 1999), pp. 687–727.
Rich, Adrienne. *Dark Fields of the Republic: Poems 1991–1995* (New York: W.W. Norton and Co., 1995).
Risinger, Michael. "Boxes in boxes: Julian Barnes, Conan Doyle, Sherlock Holmes and the Edalji case,"*International Commentary on Evidence*, 4(2) (2006), 1–90.
Rodensky, Lisa. *The Crime in Mind: Criminal Responsibility and the Victorian Novel* (New York: Oxford University Press, 2003).
Rolph, C. H. (ed.). *The Trial of Lady Chatterley* (Harmondsworth: Penguin, 1961).
Rooney, Monique. "Voir venir: The future of melodrama?" *Australian Humanities Review*, 54 (2013), 81–102.
Rose, Mark. *Authors and Owners: The Invention of Copyright* (Massachusetts: Harvard University Press, 1993).
Rosenfeld, Michel. "Deconstruction and legal interpretation: conflict, indeterminacy and the temptations of the new legal formalism" in Drucilla Cornell,

Michel Rosenfeld and David G. Carlson (eds.), *Deconstruction and the Possibility of Justice* (London and New York: Routledge, 1992), pp. 152–210.

Rostenberg, Leona. *The Minority Press and the English Crown: A Study in Repression, 1558–1625* (Nieuwkoop: B. De Graaf, 1971).

Rothberg, Michael. "After apartheid, beyond filiation: witnessing and the work of justice," *Law & Literature*, 21(2) (2009), 275–90.

Röther, Klaus. *Die Germanistenverbände und ihre Tagungen. Eine Beitrag zur germanistischen Organisations-und Wissenschaftsgeschitchte* (Koln: Pahl-Ruggenstein, 1980).

Said, E. *Orientalism* (New York: Pantheon, 1978).

Saint German, Christopher. *The Doctor and Student* (Cincinnati: Robert Clarke & Co., 1874).

Saint-Amour, Paul K. *The Copywrights : Intellectual Property and the Literary Imagination* (New York: Cornell University Press, 2011).

(ed.). *Modernism and Copyright* (Oxford: Oxford University Press, 2011).

Sanders, Mark. *Ambiguities of Witnessing: Law and Literature in the Time of a Truth Commission* (Stanford: Stanford University Press, 2007).

Sarat, Austin and Kearns, Thomas R. "The unsettled status of human rights: an introduction" in Austin Sarat and Thomas R. Kearns (eds.), *Human Rights: Concepts, Contests, Contingencies* (Ann Arbor: The University of Michigan Press, 2001), pp. 1–24.

Sarat, Austin, Anderson, Matthew, and Frank, Cathrine O. (eds.). *Law and the Humanities: An Introduction* (New York: Cambridge University Press, 2010).

Sarat, Austin, Frank, Cathrine O. and Anderson, Matthew (eds.). *Teaching Law and Literature* (New York: MLA, 2011).

Schapiro, Robert. "The disappearance and unfortunate revival of the Tenth Amendment," *The Interactive Constitution, National Constitution Center*, 2016. Web. https://constitutioncenter.org/interactive-constitution/amendments/amendment-x/the-disappearance-and-unfortunate-revival-of-the-tenth-amendment-robert-sch/interp/15

Scheppele, Kim L. "Foreword: telling stories," *Michigan Law Review* 87 (1989), 2073–98.

Schneider, Elisabeth M. "The violence of privacy," *Connecticut Law Review*, 23 (1991), 973–99.

Schorer, Mark. *Sinclair Lewis: An American Life* (New York: McGraw-Hill, 1961).

Schramm, Jan-Melissa. *Atonement and Self-Sacrifice in Nineteenth-Century Narrative* (Cambridge: Cambridge University Press, 2012).

Testimony and Advocacy in Victorian Law, Literature and Theology (Cambridge: Cambridge University Press, 2000).

Scott, Sarah. *Millenium Hall.* Ed. Gary Kelly (Peterborough: Broadview Press, 1999).

Scrivener, Michael. "Trials in Romantic-era writing: modernity, guilt, and the scene of justice," *The Wordsworth Circle*, 25 (2004), 128–33.

Selden, John. *The Table Talk of John Selden* (London: Quaritch, 1927).

Seltzer, Mark. *True Crime: Observations on Violence and Modernity* (New York: Routledge, 2007).

Semenov, Anatol. "Hepereides und Phryne," *Klio*, 28 (1935), 271–9.

Shadle, Brett. "'Changing traditions to meet current altering conditions': customary law, African courts and the rejection of codification in Kenya, 1930–60," *Journal of African History*, 40 (1999), 411–31.

Shakespeare, William. *The Riverside Shakespeare*. Ed. Gwynne Blakemore Evans (Boston: Houghton Mifflin, 1974).

Shapiro, Barbara. *"Beyond Reasonable Doubt" and "Probable Cause": Historical Perspectives on the Anglo-American Law of Evidence* (Berkeley: University of California Press, 1991).

Shelley, Percy Bysshe. *The Cenci: A Tragedy in Five Acts* (New York: Phaeton Press, 1970).

"A defence of poetry" in Duncan Wu (ed.), *Romanticism: An Anthology* (Oxford: Blackwell, 1999), pp. 944–56.

Sherwin, Richard K. "What screen do you have in mind? Contesting the visual context of law and film studies," *Studies in Law, Politics, and Society*, 46 (2009), 3–31.

When Law Goes Pop: The Vanishing Line between Law and Popular Culture (Chicago: University of Chicago Press, 2000).

Showerman, Grant (trans.). *Ovid, Heroides, Amores* (Massachusetts: Harvard University Press, 1914).

Sidney, Philip. *The Countess of Pembroke's Arcadia* (Middlesex: Penguin, 1977).

Siebert, F. S. *Freedom of the Press in England, 1476–1776* (Urbana: University of Illinois Press, 1952).

Siegel, Reva B. "'The rule of love': wife-beating as prerogative and privacy," *Yale Law Journal*, 105 (1996), 2117–208.

Simpson, A. W. Brian. *Leading Cases in the Common Law* (Oxford: Clarendon Press, 1995).

Simpson, Ed and Kresse, Kai (eds.). *Struggling with History: Islam and Cosmopolitanism in the Western Indian Ocean* (New York: Columbia University Press, 2008).

Simpson, James. *Reform and Cultural Revolution. The Oxford English Literary History, Vol. 2: 1350–1547* (Oxford: Oxford University Press, 2002).

Sinclair, Upton. *The Jungle* (New York: Dover Thrift Editions, 2001).

Slaughter, Joseph. "Humanitarian reading" in Richard Ashby Wilson (ed.), *Humanitarianism and Suffering: The Mobilization of Empathy* (Cambridge: Cambridge University Press, 2011), pp. 88–107.

Human Rights, Inc.: The World Novel, Narrative Form, and International Law (New York: Fordham University Press, 2007).

Smith, Charlotte. *The Old Manor House*. Ed. Anne Henry Ehrenpreis (Oxford: Oxford University Press, 1989).

Sokol, B. J. and Sokol, Mary. *Shakespeare, Law, and Marriage* (Cambridge: Cambridge University Press, 2003).

Somerville, Siobhan. *Queering the Color Line: Race and the Invention of Homosexuality in American Culture* (Durham: Duke University Press, 2000).

Sommerstein, Alan (trans.). *Aeschylus, Oresteia: Agamemnon, Libation-Bearers, Eumenides, Aeschylus* (Massachusetts: Harvard University Press, 2009).

Sontag, Susan. "Notes on 'camp'" in *Against Interpretation and Other Essays* (London: Penguin, 2009), pp. 275–92.

Spengemann, William C. *A New World of Words: Redefining Early American Literature* (New Haven: Yale University Press, 1994).

Spenser, Edmund. *Poetical Works* (London: Oxford University Press, 1970).

Spiegelman, Art. *MetaMaus: A Look Inside a Modern Classic, Maus* (London: Penguin Books, 2011).

Sprecher, Thomas. *Literature und Recht: Eine Bibliographie für Leser* (Frankfurt: Vittorio Klostermann, 2011).

Spring, Eileen. *Law, Land, and Family: Aristocratic Inheritance in England, 1300 to 1800* (Chapel Hill: University of North Carolina Press, 1993).

St. Clair, William. *The Reading Nation in the Romantic Period* (Cambridge: Cambridge University Press, 2004).

State v. *Hossack, 89 N.W.* 1077 (1902).

Staves, Susan. *Married Women's Separate Property in England, 1660–1833* (Cambridge: Harvard University Press, 1990).

Stierstorfer, Klaus. "Law and (which?) literature: New directions in post-theory?" *Law and Humanities*, 5(1) (2011), 41–51.

Stone, Geoffrey. *Perilous Times: Free Speech in Wartime, From the Sedition Act of 1798 to the War on Terrorism* (New York: Norton, 2004).

Stone, Lawrence. *Road to Divorce: England 1530–1987* (Oxford: Oxford University Press, 1992).

Strelein, L. *Compromised Jurisprudence: Native Title Cases since Mabo* (Canberra: Aboriginal Studies Press, 2009).

Suk, Jeannie. *At Home in the Law: How the Domestic Violence Revolution Is Transforming Privacy* (New Haven: Yale University Press, 2009).

"Laws of trauma" in Austin Sarat (ed.), *Knowing the Suffering of Others: Legal Perspectives on Pain and Its Meanings* (Tuscaloosa: University of Alabama Press, 2014), pp. 212–35.

Suretsky, Harold. "Search for a theory: An annotated bibliography of writings in the relation of law to literature and the humanities," *Rutgers Law Review* 32 (1979), 727–39.

Surridge, Lisa. *Bleak Houses: Marital Violence in Victorian Fiction* (Athens: Ohio University Press, 2005).

Swetnam, the Woman-Hater, Arraigned by Women (New York: AMS Press, 1970).

Tayler, Marilyn R. "Legal and Moral Justification for Homicide in Susan Glaspell's A Jury of Her Peers," *Law, Culture and the Humanities* (2015), 1–18. Web. DOI: 1743872115575205.

Taylor, Clare. *Women, Writing and Fetishism, 1890–1950: Female Cross-Gendering* (Oxford: Clarendon Press, 2003).

Tessone, Natasha. *Disputed Titles: Ireland, Scotland, and the Novel of Inheritance, 1798–1832* (Lewisburg and Pennsylvania: Bucknell University Press, 2015).

The Earl of Oxford's Case, The Third Part of Reports of Cases Taken and Adjudged in the Court of Chancery. London, 1716.

"The Great Wyrley outrages," *Mercury (Litchfield)*, October 23, 1903.

"The Great Wyrley outrages," *Mercury (Litchfield)*, October 30, 1903.

The King's Order and Decree in Chancery, Reports or Causes in Chancery (London, 1650).

The New London Group. "A pedagogy of multiliteracies: designing social futures," *Harvard Educational Review*, 66(1) (1996). Web. www.sfu.ca/~decaste/newlondon.htm.

The Secretary of State for Foreign Affairs v Charlesworth Pilling and Co., AC 373 (1901).

"The TRC Report." *Truth and Reconciliation Commission*, South Africa. Web. www.justice.gov.za/trc/report/.

Thomas, Brook. *Civic Myths: A Law-and-Literature Approach to Citizenship* (Chapel Hill: University of North Carolina Press, 2007).

Cross Examinations of Law and Literature: Cooper, Hawthorne, Stowe and Melville (Cambridge: Cambridge University Press, 1987).

Cross-Examinations of Law and Literature (Cambridge: Cambridge University Press, 1987).

"Reflections on the law and literature revival," *Critical Inquiry* 17(3) (1991), 510–39.

Thomas, David Wayne. *Cultivating Victorians: Liberal Culture and the Aesthetic* (Philadelphia: University of Pennsylvania Press, 2004).

Thomas, Donald. *A Long Time Burning: The History of Literary Censorship in England* (New York: Praeger Publishers, 1969).

Thompson, Helen. *Ingenious Subjection: Compliance and Power in the Eighteenth-Century Domestic Novel* (Philadelphia: University of Pennsylvania Press, 2005).

Tóibín, Colm. *The Heather Blazing* (London: Picador, 2001).

Toobin, Jeffrey. *The People v. O. J. Simpson: The Run of His Life* (London: Arrow Books, 1997).

Traister, Rebecca. "Marcia Clark Is redeemed," *New York Magazine*, February 16, 2016.

Trilling, Lionel. "Preface," *The Liberal Imagination: Essays on Literature and Society* (New York: New York Review of Books, 1950).

Trollope, Anthony. *The Warden* (Oxford: Oxford University Press, 1998).

Turner, Catherine. *Marketing Modernism: Between the Two World Wars* (Amherst: University of Massachusetts Press, 2003).

Tushnet, Mark V. *Making Civil Rights Law: Thurgood Marshall and the Supreme Court, 1936–1961* (New York: Oxford University Press, 1996).

Unger, Roberto. *The Critical Legal Studies Movement* (Massachusetts: Harvard University Press, 1986.

Uniform Evidence Law (ALRC Report 102). Australian Government: Australian Law Reform Commission. December 2005.

"U.S. Copyright Act of 1991 – Title 17." *United States Copyright Office.*

Varinsky, Dana. "A new browser extension lets you see what government websites looked like before the Trump administration," *Business Insider Australia.* January 28, 2017.

Viner, Charles. *A General Abridgment of Law and Equity*, vol. 7 (Aldershot: The Author, 1741–58).

von Benda-Beckmann, Franz and Keebet von Benda-Beckmann. "Places that come and go: a legal anthropological perspective on the temporalities of space in plural legal orders" in Irus Braverman, Nicholas Blomley, David Delaney, and Alexandre Kedar (eds.), *The Expanding Spaces of Law: A Timely Legal Geography* (Stanford: Stanford University Press, 2014), pp. 30–52.

Wakf Commissioners Act 2012 (1981). The Republic of Kenya. Web. www.kenya law.org.

Walpole, Horace. *The Castle of Otranto and The Mysterious Mother.* Ed. Frederick S. Frank. (Peterborough: Broadview Press, 2003).

Wan, Marco. "*Stare decisis*, binding precedent and Anthony Trollope's *The Eustace Diamonds*" in Marco Wan (ed.), *Reading the Legal Case: Cross-Currents between Law and the Humanities* (Abingdon: Routledge, 2012), pp. 205–16.

Ward, Ian. *Law and Literature: Possibilities and Perspectives* (Cambridge: Cambridge University Press, 2008).

Shakespeare and the Legal Imagination (London: Butterworths, 1999).

Warr, John. *A Spark in the Ashes: The Pamphlets of John Warr* (London: Verso, 1992).

Watson, Jay. "Dangerous return: The narratives of jurisgenesis in Faulkner's *Requiem for a Nun*," *Modern Fiction Studies*, 60(1) (2014), 108–37.

Watson, Julia. "Autographic disclosures and genealogies of desire in Alison Bechdel's *Fun Home*,"*Biography*, 31(1) (2008), 27–58.

Watson, Nicholas. "Censorship and cultural change in late-medieval england: vernacular theology, the Oxford Translation Debate, and Arundel's *Constitutions* of 1409," *Speculum*, 70(4) (1995), 822–64.

Watt, Gary. *Equity Stirring* (Oxford: Hart Publishing, 2009).

Watt, Ian. *The Rise of the Novel* (London: Chatto and Windus, 1957).

The Rise of the Novel: Studies in Defoe, Richardson and Fielding (Berkeley: University of California Press, 1957).

Weaver, Gordon. *Conan Doyle and the Parson's Son* (Cambridge: Vanguard Press, 2006).

Weisberg, Richard H. "Editor's preface," *Cardozo Studies in Law and Literature*, 1(1) (1989), v–x.

The Failure of the Word: The Protagonist as Lawyer in Modern Fiction (New Haven: Yale University Press, 1984).

"Family feud: a response to Robert Weisberg on law and literature," *Yale Journal of Law and the Humanities*, 1 (1988–9): 69–77.

"Literature's twenty-year crossing into the domain of law: continuing trespass or right by adverse possession?" in Michael Freeman and Andrew Lewis (eds.), *Literature and Law: Current Legal Issues*, vol. 2 (Oxford: Oxford University Press, 1999), pp. 48–61.

Vichy Law and the Holocaust in France (London and New York: Routledge, 1996).

Weisberg, Richard H. and Jean-Pierre Barricelli. "Literature and law" in Joseph Gibaldi and Jean-Pierre Barricelli (eds.), *Interrelations of Literature* (New York: Modern Languages Association, 1982), pp. 150–75.

Weisberg, Robert. "The law-literature enterprise," *Yale Journal of Law and the Humanities*, 1 (1988–9), 1–67.

Wells, Robin Headlam. *Spenser's Fairie Queene and the Cult of Elizabeth* (London: Croom Helm, 1983).

Welsh, Alexander. "Burke and Bentham on the narrative potential of circumstantial evidence," *New Literary History*, 21 (1989–90), 607–27.

Strong Representations: Narrative and Circumstantial Evidence in England (Baltimore: Johns Hopkins University Press, 1992).

Wendell Holmes, Oliver. *The Common Law* (Massachusetts: Belknap Press, 2009 [1881]).

West, Robin. "Adjudication is not interpretation: some reservations about the law-as-literature movement," *Tennessee Law Review*, 54 (1987), 203–69.

Caring for Justice (New York: New York University Press, 1997).

"Communities, texts and law: reflections on the law and literature movement," *Yale Journal of Law and the Humanities*, 1 (1988–9), 129–56.

Narrative, Authority and Law (Ann Arbor: University of Michigan Press, 1993).

Wexler, Joyce Piell. *Who Paid for Modernism: Art, Money, and the Fiction of Conrad, Joyce, and Lawrence* (Fayetteville: University of Arkansas Press. 1997).

Wharton, Robin. "Digital humanities, copyright law, and the literary," *Digital Humanities Quarterly*, 7(1) (2013). Web. www.digitalhumanities.org/dhq/vol/7/1/000147/000147.html.

Wharton, Robin and Miller, Derek. "New directions in law and narrative," *Law, Culture, and the Humanities* (2016), 1–11. Web. DOI: 10.1177/1743872116652865.

Whetstone, George. *The Right Excellent and Famous Historye, of Promos and Cassandra* (New York: AMS Press, 1970), C1r.

White, James Boyd. *Justice as Translation: An Essay in Cultural and Legal Criticism* (Chicago: University of Chicago Press, 1990).

The Legal Imagination: Abridged Edition (Chicago: University of Chicago Press, 1984 [1973]).

The Legal Imagination: Studies in the Nature of Legal Thought and Expression (Boston: Little Brown & Co., 1973).

When Words Lose Their Meaning (Chicago: University of Chicago Press, 1984).

Whitlock, Gillian. "In the second person: narrative transactions in stolen generations testimony," *Biography*, 24(1) (2001), 197–214.

Whitlock, Gillian and Anna Poletti. "Self-regarding art," *Biography*, 31(1) (2008), v–xxiii.

Wilkerson, Isabel. "Whose side to take: women, outrage and the verdict on O. J. Simpson," *The New York Times*, October 8, 1995.

Williams, Patricia. *The Alchemy of Race and Rights: Diary of a Law Professor* (Massachusetts: Harvard University Press, 1991).

Williams, Patricia J. "Alchemical notes: reconstructing ideals from deconstructed rights" in Robert L. Hayman, Nancy Levit, and Richard Delgado (eds.), *Jurisprudence Classical and Contemporary: From Natural Law to Postmodernism* (Minnesota: West Group, 2002), pp. 417–21.

"The obliging shell: an informal essay on formal equal opportunity," *Michigan Law Review*, 87(8) (1989), 2128–51.

Wilson, Arthur, Wharton, John Lloyd, and de Rutzen, Albert. "Papers relating to the case of George Edalji" in *House of Commons Papers*, Great Britain, Parliament. vol. 67. Cd. 3503 (1907). (London: Eyre and Spottiswoode, 1907).

Wilson, David. *Pain and Retribution: A Short History of British Prisons 1066 to the Present* (London: Reaktion Books, 2014).

Wollaeger, Mark. *Modernism, Media, and Propaganda: British Narrative from 1900 to 1945* (Princeton: Princeton University Press, 2006).

Wollstonecraft, Mary. *Maria*. Ed. Janet Todd (London: Penguin, 1992).

"Vindication of the rights of men" (1790) in Janet Todd (ed.), *A Vindication of the Rights of Men; A Vindication of the Rights of Woman; An Historical and Moral View of the French Revolution* (Oxford: Oxford University Press, 1999), pp. 1–62.

Wong, Edlie. *Racial Reconstruction: Black Inclusion, Chinese Exclusion, and the Fictions of Citizenship* (New York: NYU Press, 2015).

Woodmansee, Martha. "The genius and the copyright: economic and legal conditions of the emergence of the 'author,'" *Eighteenth-Century Studies*, 17(4) (1984), 425–48.

'The Romantic Author' in Isabella Alexander and H. Tomás Gómez-Arostegui (eds.), *Research Handbook on the History of Copyright Law* (London: Edward Elgar, 2016), pp. 53–76.

Woolf, Virginia. *The Diary of Virginia Woolf.* Ed. Anne Olivier Bell. 5 vols. (New York: Harcourt Brace Jovanovich, 1977–1984).

"Hours in a library" in Leonard Woolf (ed.), *Granite and Rainbow: Essays by Virginia Woolf* (London: Hogarth Press, 1958), pp. 24–31.

"Modern fiction" in Virginia Woolf (ed.), *The Common Reader* (London: Hogarth Press, 1951).

Orlando. Ed. Mark Hussey (New York: Harcourt, 2006).

Worman, Nancy. "The body as argument: Helen in four Greek texts," *Classical Antiquity*, 16 (1997), 151–203.

Wreen, Michael. "The ontology of intellectual property," *The Monist*, 93(3) (2010), 433–49.

Wyke, Maria. *The Roman Mistress* (Oxford: Oxford University Press, 2002).

Yeats, W. B. "Among school children" in A. Norman Jeffares (ed.), *Yeats's Poems* (London: Gill and Macmillan, 1989), pp. 323–5.

Young, G. M. *Victorian England: Portrait of an Age* (Oxford: Oxford University Press, 1936).

Ziolkowksi, Theodore. *The Mirror of Justice: Literary Reflections and Legal Crises* (Princeton: Princeton University Press, 1997).

Zomchick, John. *Family and the Law in Eighteenth-Century Fiction: The Public Conscience in the Private Sphere* (Cambridge: Cambridge University Press, 1993).

Index